Some Versions of Empson

Some Versions of Empson

Edited by

Matthew Bevis

CLARENDON PRESS · OXFORD

OXFORD
UNIVERSITY PRESS

Great Clarendon Street, Oxford OX2 6DP

Oxford University Press is a department of the University of Oxford.
It furthers the University's objective of excellence in research, scholarship,
and education by publishing worldwide in

Oxford New York

Auckland Cape Town Dar es Salaam Hong Kong Karachi
Kuala Lumpur Madrid Melbourne Mexico City Nairobi
New Delhi Shanghai Taipei Toronto

With offices in

Argentina Austria Brazil Chile Czech Republic France Greece
Guatemala Hungary Italy Japan Poland Portugal Singapore
South Korea Switzerland Thailand Turkey Ukraine Vietnam

Oxford is a registered trade mark of Oxford University Press
in the UK and in certain other countries

Published in the United States
by Oxford University Press Inc., New York

First published 2007

British Library Cataloguing in Publication Data

Data available

Library of Congress Cataloging in Publication Data

Data available

Typeset by Laserwords Private Limited, Chennai, India
Printed in Great Britain
on acid-free paper by
Biddles Ltd., King's Lynn, Norfolk

ISBN 978–0–19–928636–2

3 5 7 9 10 8 6 4 2

ACKNOWLEDGEMENTS

Two essays in this volume contain some work published previously: Peter Robinson's 'C. Hatakeyama and W.E.' adapts passages from his article, 'C. Hatakeyama [trans. W.E.]', in *PN Review*, 31: 2 (Nov.–Dec. 2004), 55–60; Susan Wolfson's 'Empson's Pregnancy' uses material from an article of the same name in *Literary Imagination*, 6: 2 (Spring 2004), 282–305. I thank the publishers for permission to reprint.

Many of the ideas and arguments in this collection were first presented and discussed at a conference on Empson held at the University of Sheffield in July 2003. Funding for that event was provided by the Department of English Literature at Sheffield and by the British Academy, and I am grateful for their support. I also greatly appreciate the input of all those who attended the conference, and all the staff and students at Sheffield who helped to make it run smoothly.

I would like to thank Andrew McNeillie, Pat Lawrence, and the two anonymous readers at the Press, who provided suggestions and enthusiasm in equal measure. The volume has also benefited hugely from the scrupulous eye of Claire Lockwood, who helped with the editing process in the final stages. I am especially thankful to Matthew Campbell, Hugh Haughton, Freya Johnston, Brigid Lowe, and Christopher Ricks for their advice, criticism, and encouragement. Finally, I owe a great debt of gratitude to John Haffenden for his guidance and his support over the years. This book could not have come into being without his dedication to Empson, and the volume is dedicated to him.

M.B.

For John Haffenden

CONTENTS

ABBREVIATIONS

Unless stated otherwise, all works below are by William Empson.

A	*Argufying: Essays on Literature and Culture*, ed. John Haffenden (London: Chatto & Windus, 1987)
CP	*Complete Poems of William Empson*, ed. John Haffenden (London: Allen Lane, 2000)
CV	*Coleridge's Verse: A Selection*, ed. William Empson and David B. Pirie (London: Faber and Faber, 1972)
EG	*Empson in Granta* (Tunbridge Wells: Foundling Press, 1993)
ERL1	*Essays on Renaissance Literature*, i. *Donne and the New Philosophy*, ed. John Haffenden (Cambridge: Cambridge University Press, 1993)
ERL2	*Essays on Renaissance Literature*, ii. *The Drama*, ed. John Haffenden (Cambridge: Cambridge University Press, 1994)
ES	*Essays on Shakespeare*, ed. David B. Pirie (Cambridge: Cambridge University Press, 1986)
FC	*Faustus and the Censor: The English Faust-book and Marlowe's 'Doctor Faustus'*, ed. John Henry Jones (Oxford: Blackwell, 1987)
MG	*Milton's God*, rev. edn. (Cambridge: Cambridge University Press, 1981)
RB	*The Royal Beasts and Other Works*, ed. John Haffenden (London: Chatto & Windus, 1986)
SCW	*The Structure of Complex Words*, 3rd edn. (1977; repr. London: Penguin, 1995)
SL	*Selected Letters of William Empson*, ed. John Haffenden (Oxford: Oxford University Press, 2006)
SSS	*The Strengths of Shakespeare's Shrew: Essays, Memoirs and Reviews*, ed. John Haffenden (Sheffield: Sheffield Academic Press, 1996)
STA	*Seven Types of Ambiguity*, 3rd edn. (1953; repr. London: Penguin, 1995)
SVP	*Some Versions of Pastoral* (1935; repr. London: Penguin, 1995)
UB	*Using Biography* (London: Chatto & Windus, 1984)

WE1	John Haffenden, *William Empson*, i. *Among the Mandarins* (Oxford: Oxford University Press, 2005)
WE2	John Haffenden, *William Empson*, ii. *Against the Christians* (Oxford: Oxford University Press, 2006)

NOTES ON THE CONTRIBUTORS

Matthew Bevis is a lecturer in English Literature at the University of York. He is the author of *Lives of Victorian Literary Figures: Tennyson* (Pickering & Chatto, 2003) and *The Art of Eloquence: Byron, Dickens, Tennyson, Joyce* (Oxford University Press, 2007). He is currently working on *The Cambridge Edition of the Novels of Thomas Love Peacock*, co-edited with Freya Johnston, 3 vols. (Cambridge University Press, 2012).

Deborah Bowman is a Fellow and Director of Studies in English at Gonville and Caius College, Cambridge, where she teaches English and Comparative Literature. She is currently researching a monograph on Empson.

Matthew Creasy is a lecturer at Glasgow University. He was educated at Cambridge and Oxford, and has taught at the University of Sheffield. His primary research interests lie in Irish literature in English and the writings of James Joyce, and he is currently completing a monograph entitled *'Ulysses' and Misquotation.*

Paul H. Fry is the William Lampson Professor of English and former Master of Ezra Stiles College at Yale University. He is the author of *The Poet's Calling in the English Ode* (1980), *The Reach of Criticism: Method and Perception in Literary Criticism* (1984), *William Empson: Prophet Against Sacrifice* (1991), *A Defense of Poetry: Reflections on the Occasion of Writing* (1995), and has edited *'The Rime of the Ancient Mariner'* (1999). *Wordsworth and the Anthropology of Lyric* is forthcoming.

Eric Griffiths teaches English at Trinity College, Cambridge. He is the author of *The Printed Voice of Victorian Poetry* (Oxford University Press, 1989) and co-editor of *Dante in English* (Penguin, 2005).

John Haffenden is Professor of English Literature at the University of Sheffield. His books include a critically acclaimed two-volume biography of William Empson, as well as *The Life of John Berryman; W. H. Auden: The Critical Heritage; Viewpoints: Poets in Conversation*; and *Novelists in Interview*. He has edited *Berryman's Shakespeare* and several collections of works by Empson including *Complete Poems* and *Selected Letters*. He is a Fellow of the Royal Society of Literature and has been a British Academy Research Reader.

Jason Harding is a lecturer in English at the University of Durham. He is the author of *'The Criterion': Cultural Politics and Periodical Networks in Interwar Britain* (Oxford University Press, 2002) and a co-editor (with Giovanni Cianci) of *T. S. Eliot and the Concept of Tradition* (Cambridge University Press, 2007). He has contributed articles and reviews to a variety of periodicals including the *Times Literary Supplement, London Review of Books*, and *The Cambridge Quarterly*.

Hugh Haughton teaches English at the University of York. He has recently completed *Derek Mahon and Modern Irish Poetry* (Oxford University Press, 2007). He is the editor of *The Chatto Book of Nonsense Poetry* (1985), *John Clare in Context* (with Adam Phillips, Cambridge University Press, 1994), *Alice in Wonderland and Through the Looking-Glass* (Penguin, 1998), Sigmund Freud, *The Uncanny* (New Penguin Freud, 2003), and *Second World War Poems* (Faber and Faber, 2004). He is currently co-editing (with Valerie Eliot) *T. S. Eliot, The Letters*, vols. i–iii (Faber and Faber).

Christopher Norris is Distinguished Research Professor in Philosophy at Cardiff University, where he has taught since 1978. He has published many books on aspects of philosophy and critical theory, among them—most recently—*Language, Logic and Epistemology* (2004), *Philosophy of Language and the Challenge to Scientific Realism* (2004), *On Truth and Meaning* (2006), and *Platonism, Music and the Listener's Share* (2006). He has also written extensively on Empson's work, often in the hope of persuading philosophers to recognize its relevance to issues in philosophical semantics and cognitive psychology.

Seamus Perry is a Fellow of Balliol College, where he is Tutor in English Literature, and a lecturer in the English Faculty, University of Oxford. He is author of *Coleridge and the Uses of Division* (1999) and *Tennyson* (2005), and an editor of the Oxford journal *Essays in Criticism*.

Adam Piette is Professor in Modern English Literature at the University of Sheffield. He has previously worked at the Universities of Paris XIII, Geneva, Lausanne, and Glasgow. He is the author of *Remembering and the Sound of Words* (1996) and *Imagination at War* (1995), and is currently working on a book about Cold War writing.

Katy Price is lecturer in English at Anglia Ruskin University in Cambridge and an Affiliated Research Scholar in the Department of History and Philosophy of Science at the University of Cambridge. She is Communications Officer for

History of Science at the BA Science Festival. Her essay on Empson's 'Letter I', 'Flame far too hot: William Empson's non-Euclidean predicament', was published in *Interdisciplinary Science Reviews*, 30: 4 (Dec. 2005).

Peter Robinson has published many books of poetry, literary criticism, and translations, including most recently: *Selected Poems* (Carcanet Press, 2003), *Twentieth-Century Poetry: Selves and Situations* (Oxford University Press, 2005), *The Greener Meadow: Selected Poems of Luciano Erba* (Princeton University Press, 2006), and, with Marcus Perryman, *Selected Poetry and Prose of Vittorio Sereni* (Chicago University Press, 2006). After teaching English literature for many years in Japan, he has recently taken up a professorial post at the University of Reading.

David Wilson has taught English linguistics at universities in Britain, Norway, and Finland. He has published mainly in the area of linguistics, but also articles on John Donne, e. e. cummings, and I. A. Richards. He has also co-edited an anthology, *Henceforth the Anglo-Saxon is the Brother of the Finn! Poems about Finland 1634–2000* (2003).

Susan J. Wolfson is Professor of English at Princeton University, and author of *Borderlines: The Shiftings of Gender in British Romanticism* (2006), and *Formal Charges: The Shaping of Poetry in British Romanticism* (1998). Her innovative *Keats: A Longman Cultural Edition* has just been published.

1

Introduction: Empson in the Round

Matthew Bevis

Empson was not one for straightforward introductions. 'I have noticed that, when you give a party, the best thing is not to rush at everybody and try to force them to talk to each other; in a party that goes unexpectedly well (in the way of making disparate groups talk to each other) you often notice that the host has been stuck away in the corner most of the time, talking to some expert about a technical point he is really interested in' (*A* 109). One can imagine parties that might not go particularly well if the host adopted this method (is he merely 'stuck away' in the corner, or has he stuck the expert there, cornering him on a point of detail? And meanwhile, although those 'disparate groups' should perhaps not be 'forced' to talk, they may need to be coaxed if they are to feel a little less disparate.) Still, Empson has a point, and his noticing in some ways hints at the shape of his own career and critical influence: playing the not-quite-genial host to different groups and interests, encouraging the openness of 'talk' yet defending the need to get 'technical'. Indeed, his comment is part of a discussion about 'the co-operative work of critics': 'As to co-operation, I hope I don't refuse it, but I have noticed that, when you give a party . . . '

An invitation to the Empson party is an invitation to the unexpected. Guests should be ready for combat as well as for courtship. He may be a party-giver and goer, but he is not a signed-up member of any particular party. His debut, *Seven Types of Ambiguity*, established him as the closest of close readers. That impression remains dominant, as Stefan Collini has recently noted: 'In textbook surveys, Empson still tends to figure as the star performer of the whizz-bang school of criticism, the verbal fireworks of what, after I. A. Richards, was termed "Practical Criticism" in Britain, with the "New Criticism" as its close American relative.'[1] Yet relations between close relatives can be fraught affairs, and Empson would soon direct his fire against New Critical orthodoxies. He wanted criticism to be practical, and was wary of the potential slide from minute to exclusive verbal analysis. Hence his fury at the anti-intentionalists: 'To say that you won't be bothered with anything but the words on the page . . . strikes me as petulant, like saying "of course I won't visit him unless he has first-class plumbing." If you cared enough you would' (*A* 125). In Empson's work, discussion about well-wrought urns and verbal icons also involved consideration of other, messier matters.

A willingness to talk about poetry and plumbing in the same breath is also evident in his observation that 'A profound enough criticism could extract an entire cultural history from a simple lyric' (*A* 107). This is a criticism that plumbs the depths of things, and his next book—*Some Versions of Pastoral*—made it clear that 'literature is a social process, and also an attempt to reconcile the conflicts of an individual in whom those of society will be mirrored' (*SVP* 22). Kenneth Burke was right to discern a 'profoundly Marxist analysis of literature'[2] in the book, but—lest we think that Empson might be co-opted as an '-ist' of some sort—we might note the statement that immediately follows his sentence about literature as a 'social process': 'The belief that a man's ideas are wholly the product of his economic setting is of course as fatuous as the belief that they are wholly independent of it' (22). For Empson, the reasonable desire to 'extract' a political, cultural, economic, or any other kind of history from a text would need to take account of the various ways that the 'words on the page' may resist what was happening in and around the margins of that page. Summing up his next book, *The Structure of Complex Words*, he again pointed to his interest in the practical element of Practical Criticism: 'the moral is that a developing society decides practical questions more by the way it interprets words it thinks obvious and traditional than by its official statements of current dogma' (*SCW*, p. xiv). Needless to say, Empson felt that most of the authors he chose to study in the book confronted readers with something more than 'official statements'.

[1] Stefan Collini, 'Smack Up: Argufying and Illumination in the Letters of William Empson', *Times Literary Supplement* (7 July 2006), 3–5 (p. 5).

[2] Kenneth Burke, 'Exceptional Improvisation', *Poetry*, 49: 6 (Mar. 1937), 347–50 (p. 350).

The fight against 'current dogma' would become increasingly prominent (and belligerent) after *Complex Words*, as Empson's battle against Christianity and what he termed the 'neo-Christian' school of criticism shaped much of his later work. *Milton's God*, and his subsequent writings on Donne, Marlowe, Coleridge, and Joyce, saw many writers enlisted in the cause (some more successfully than others), as he shifted from the whizz-bang to the big-bang school of criticism. Barbara Everett observed 'a passionate—almost religious—hatred of Christian theology'[3] in his work, and rightly drew attention to the oversights that could accompany Empson's passionate hatreds. As Adam Phillips has recently put it: 'The extremity of his rejection of Christianity—he wrote as though to value any of it was to value all of it—needs the kind of explanation he was inclined to give when dogma was uncontested in a writer.'[4]

Empson frequently refuses to co-operate: left-wing yet posing serious obstacles for 'any Marxist appropriation of his work';[5] a keen reader of Freud and of unconscious intentions but wary of psychoanalytic criticism; a precursor of certain forms of deconstruction, yet at odds with what he perceived to be a negative and suspicious hermeneutics;[6] theoretically inclined yet opposed to some aspects of the rise of Theory.[7] It is hard to place him, but then, 'It is not human to feel safely placed' (*CP* 85), and the longevity of his criticism owes much to the fact that he rarely plumped for the safe option. He continues to exercise claims on many schools of critical thought precisely because he cannot be easily adopted by any one of them, and developments in recent years provide an opportunity for a reassessment of what these claims might be.

Towards the end of his life Empson wrote to John Haffenden: 'If you show that my work takes a coherent position, and is not just a series of pointless cooked-up shocks, you will be doing me a great service' (*SL* 672). Haffenden has rendered this service magnificently, and recent volumes—*The Complete Poems*, the *Selected Letters*, and the two-volume biography—provide strong foundations for further critical study. This is the first volume of essays on

3 Barbara Everett, 'Reviews', *Modern Language Review*, 57: 3 (July 1962), 415–17 (p. 415).

4 Adam Phillips, 'No Reason For Not Asking', *LRB* (3 Aug. 2006), 26–7 (p. 26).

5 Terry Eagleton, *Against The Grain: Essays 1975–1985* (London: Verso, 1986), 165.

6 See Paul de Man, *Blindness and Insight: Essays in the Logic of Contemporary Criticism*, 2nd edn. (Minneapolis: University of Minnesota Press, 1983), 234–41; Christopher Norris, 'Some Versions of Rhetoric: Empson and de Man', *Genre*, 17: 1–2 (Spring and Summer 1984), 191–214.

7 The last collection of essays to appear on Empson explored this tension: see Christopher Norris and Nigel Mapp (eds.), *William Empson: The Critical Achievement* (Cambridge: Cambridge University Press, 1993).

Empson to appear in over a decade, and it aims to build on these foundations. Collini's comment that 'In textbook surveys, Empson still tends to figure as the star performer of the whizz-bang school of criticism' suggests the need for a broader, more detailed sense of where Empson is coming from, and of where he might lead us. Happily, the most recent textbook survey has refused to straitjacket him into any clearly definable 'school', and has emphasized the range of his interests and achievement.[8] This volume shares that emphasis, and seeks to evaluate the 'coherent' alongside the 'cooked-up' aspects of his work.

The last collection of essays to appear on Empson focused, as its title suggested, on his *critical* achievement. But rather than see him solely as a literary critic, most contributors to this volume examine his poetry alongside his criticism. As Hilary Corke once suggested, Empson's 'poems are as much criticisms of his criticism as his criticisms are in another sense poems about his poems' (*WE1* 373). By focusing on two sides of his work, this volume engages not only with Empson's critical arguments and agendas, but also with the characteristic pitches and uses of style in his writing, suggesting ways in which style allows him to conduct a debate with himself as well as with others. *Some Versions of Empson*, then, aims to see its subject in the round. By way of introduction to some of these versions, a tour round some of the tricks of his critical and poetic trade may be appropriate.

I

John Gross once rang Empson to ask a favour: 'When I took over at the *Times Literary Supplement* I was anxious to secure his services as a contributor, and he was one of the first people I called. "Oh, it's you," came his strange sing-song voice over the phone. "Are you in the chair already?" "Yes." A long pause. "*Does it swivel?*" '[9] Empson's imagination and wit were frequently drawn to figures of turning, and to a language that orbited around images of roundness. George Herbert is admired for 'his power to see all round' his subject (*SSS* 123), the strength of Milton's writing is founded on his ability to 'see all round

[8] David Fuller, 'William Empson: From Verbal Analysis to Cultural Criticism', in Patricia Waugh (ed.), *Literary Theory and Criticism: An Oxford Guide* (Oxford: Oxford University Press, 2006), 152–65.

[9] John Gross, *A Double Thread: Growing Up English and Jewish in London* (Chicago: Ivan Dee, 2002), 188.

the issues' (*MG* 153), and the achievement of *Tom Jones* is related to Fielding's sympathy, which 'is so broad that he can see the question all round' (*UB* 148). The phrasing also pops up when Empson is offering advice. Writing to Francis Berry about the duties incumbent upon those 'in the chair', he reminds him that 'it is very important for you to be an *all-round* Prof. of Eng. Lit.' (*SL* 455).

The endeavour to be 'all-round' recalls one of Empson's fictional heroes, Leopold Bloom, a man whom Joyce felt to be 'all-round . . . a complete man . . . a good man'.[10] In *Ulysses* Bloom thinks to himself, 'Roundness you think good', and so endeavours to 'Look at it the other way round'.[11] Perhaps this is one reason why, when reviewing E. M. Forster's *Aspects of the Novel* in 1927, Empson should employ a language of 'turning' in order to take issue with Forster's antipathy to Joyce's novel. We see Forster 'turning merely in horror from *Ulysses*', before Empson swoops: 'An attempt, successful or not, to include all possible attitudes, to turn upon a given situation every tool, however irrelevant or disconnected, of the contemporary mind, would be far too strenuous and metaphysical an exertion' (*EG* 21–2). Empson's other early reviews suggest that this model of artistic and critical conduct ('turning *upon*' rather than '*from*') was in his thoughts from the beginning; he praises another author for showing his subject 'from enough points of view to make one feel something in the real world is being considered' (*EG* 90), and his own writing often contains asides that show a readiness to consider those other points of view. When worrying over how 'theory' can lead the critic astray, he quickly rounds upon himself: 'All the same, there clearly is a need for such theories; for one thing, without a tolerable supply of handy generalizations you can't stretch your mind to see all round a particular case' (*A* 104).

For Empson, literary writing tacitly encourages such stretches of mind and imagination. He enjoys A. C. Bradley's work because Bradley 'always sees a human situation in the round, thus becoming a uniquely good critic of Shakespeare, who does the same' (*SL* 550). All good plays embody and inspire such modes of seeing: 'Any "solid" play, which can give the individual a rich satisfaction at one time, and therefore different satisfactions at different times from different "points of view," is likely to be a play that can satisfy different individuals; it can face an audience' (*SVP* 58). Even when he is not discussing

[10] Joyce, cited in Frank Budgen, *James Joyce and the Making of 'Ulysses' and Other Writings*, introd. Clive Hart (Oxford: Oxford University Press, 1972), 18.

[11] James Joyce, *Ulysses*, ed. Hans Walter Gabler (London: Bodley Head, 2002), 8. 860, 13. 1219. References are to episode and line number.

the theatre, Empson has recourse to similar language: 'solid' is one of his favourite terms of endearment (from *solidus*, a gold coin)—a microcosmic, two-dimensional Globe, then, and an apposite shape for a critic who habitually imagines things in the round. His titles sometimes contain a similar kind of buried treasure: *Some Versions of Pastoral* ('Versions' from *vertere*, 'to turn'; *OED*, sense 3.a 'A turning about') and *The Structure of Complex Words* ('Complex' from *complexus*, meaning 'encircling'). Indeed, the last sentence of *Complex Words* (the book he considered his masterpiece) returns us to circular motion: 'All I should claim for this chapter is that it gives a sort of final canter round the field' (*SCW* 413). 'Sort of final' (like the phrase 'Some Versions') eschews conclusiveness; but then, circles have no end.

Some Versions of Empson considers his work from a variety of angles: aesthetic, philosophical, psychological, linguistic, scientific, socio-political, religious, and sexual points of view shed new light on the peculiar solidity of his achievement. Moreover, like his critical works, Empson's poems are drawn to circular imaginings and motions; G. W. Stonier once remarked that 'His poetry is so self-enclosed, so perfectly and primly circular, that for most readers it will probably always remain inaccessible.'[12] Yet a sense of the 'inaccessible' is not always a marker of the 'self-enclosed' in Empson's work; it is often accompanied by a feeling of hesitant connection. As the speaker of 'To an Old Lady' acknowledges when considering the distance between himself and his mother: 'Strange that she too should be inaccessible | Who shares my sun' (*CP* 24).

The poems are full of planets, suns, orbits, spherical objects, and spinning axes. The old lady 'reads a compass certain of her pole . . . finds no confines on her sphere', and the poem contains both a respect for distance and a hushed longing for closer contact. Empson's poems sometimes intimate—as he suggested in his work on Donne—that 'the separate planet' stands for a kind of 'freedom' (*ERL1* 76), and his love poetry resonates with the feeling that 'living on another planet is an extremely powerful symbol for the claim of the lovers to have independent rights' (*ERL1* 21). Yet Empson's fascination with these spaces, and with space-travel, fills his poems with a concern about vicious as well as beneficent circles. 'The World's End' begins with a call to 'Fly with me then to all's and the world's end | And plumb for safety down the gaps of stars | . . . What tyrant there our variance debars?' (*CP* 13), but this break for the border meets with a new sense of confinement, for Empson's Donne-like

[12] G. W. Stonier, 'Complexity', *New Statesman and Nation*, 10: 243 (19 Oct. 1935), 568–70 (p. 568).

battle-cry is haunted by a new science. The poem was originally published as 'Relativity', and Empson noted that 'The finite but unbounded universe, popularized by Eddington . . . makes flight seem useless for the lovers' (*CP* 162). This universe—brought into being by theories about the curvature of space—brings with it the answering voice of the second stanza: 'Alas, how hope for freedom, no bars bind; | Space is like earth, rounded, a padded cell' (*CP* 13). As Eddington would later write: 'the curvature actually leads to a complete bending round and closing up of space, so that it becomes a domain of finite extent.'[13] This version of Empson's need to see things in the round brings him back down to earth with a bump.

A true commitment to seeing things in the round will also need to give that very commitment a sceptical side glance from time to time. As Empson once noted of this ideal: 'most men don't feel free to look all round a question, unless their position is comfortable enough' (*UB* 156). This is a salutary reminder that looking 'all round' may be something of a luxury when other kinds of seeing and uncomfortable circumstances exert their own demands and pressures. The same form of double vision is applied to Empson's enthusiasm for 'interplanetary spaces' and the freedom they might betoken; he also acknowledged that such spaces 'are inherently lonely and ill-provided' (*ERL1* 84), and he would later suggest that 'The most impressive poems by Donne using lovers on planets' carried a 'marooned' feeling and had less 'bounce' in them (*ERL1* 223). Accordingly, his own poems often feature turnings and returnings that indicate something other than bounce: 'Two songs from a libretto' admits that 'Simply we do not know what are the turnings | Expound our poising of obscure desires' (*CP* 9), and in 'Invitation to Juno' we turn to Ixion who 'rides upon a single wheel' (*CP* 12). In the former poem, the speaker acknowledges that 'She may on her return return', and this is the kind of movement that Empson's criticism makes over and over again.

Christopher Ricks has singled out Empson's reading of Gray's *Elegy* in *Some Versions of Pastoral* as a central example of this movement. After drawing out the potential complacency of the politics of the poem (chiefly of the 'flower' that 'is born to blush unseen | And waste its sweetness on the desert air'), Empson notes:

> And yet what is said is one of the permanent truths; it is only in degree that any improvement of society could prevent wastage of human powers; the waste even in

[13] Arthur Eddington, *The Expanding Universe* (London: Harmondsworth, 1940), 39.

a fortunate life, the isolation even of a life rich in intimacy, cannot but be felt deeply, and is the central feeling of tragedy . . . A statement of this is certainly non-political because it is true in any society, and yet nearly all the great poetic statements of it are in a way 'bourgeois', like this one; they suggest to many readers, though they do not say, that for the poor man things cannot be improved even in degree. (*SVP* 12)

Ricks observes: 'if politics has its needed rights and claims, so too does a tragic sense of life. . . . The movement ("And yet . . . ") is one of the great returns of the mind on itself, and is itself followed with a further return ("and yet").'[14] These returnings are part of the way Empson thinks, even when defending his central values. Mulling over ambiguity, for example, he asks: 'is all good poetry supposed to be ambiguous? I think that it is' (*STA* 16). And yet, ambiguity 'is not to be respected in so far as it is due to weakness or thinness of thought . . . so that it is merely an opportunism in the handling of the material' (*STA* 190). Or, as he put it later when considering his relish for what poets could do with complex words: 'Someone objected that Pope was "profiteering from the looseness of a word's meaning rather than profiting from its complexity", and I agree that a critic needs to judge whether this has happened' (*SCW*, pp. xxx–xxxi).

Empson's freewheeling criticism often draws attention to the process of its own voyages of discovery. This volume accordingly revolves for consideration *how* Empson argues—the peculiar rhythms of his yets and ifs and buts. Before he launches into his analysis of a Shakespeare sonnet, for example, he gathers his breath with 'one must pause before shadowing with irony this noble compound of eulogy and apology. But . . . ' (*STA* 161). Likewise, after quoting lines by Hood, he steadies himself by beginning with the gambit: 'Such virtuosity cannot be despised; I have warmed to admiration in copying it out. But . . . ' (*STA* 135). These double-takes extend right across his career. Thinking about the significance of Oliver Twist's ability to speak Queen's English despite being brought up in an orphanage, for instance, he begins one paragraph with another version of 'And yet' ('However') and suggests that a political moral of Oliver's refined speech might boil down to this: 'All you need do, really, is go through these workhouses and pick out the little gentlemen, because all the other little boys are just pigs . . . . if he [Dickens] had been warned of this misreading he would (obviously, I think), have struggled to find a way of

[14] Christopher Ricks, *Essays in Appreciation* (Oxford: Oxford University Press, 1998), 344.

getting round it' (*A* 488). This 'however' is met by a later addition in the form of a footnote, as Empson 'gets round' his earlier point by seeing things in the round: 'I was so confident of this that I did not check it as I should have done; Dickens is an author we are prone to re-write in our minds. Since then I have found that he *did* "take precautions", chiefly by using reported speech for all the charity boys, the hero included' (*A* 489).

Such moments are testament to a more general trend in Empson's work. John Haffenden has observed how reading him gives one 'the feeling that he is thinking on the hoof', yet also that 'he has the honesty to go back and pick a bone with himself' (*WE1* 392). The writing goes back in order to go forward, and is frequently marked by a willingness to listen to itself think. While teasing out the multiple insinuations of words and phrases in *Seven Types of Ambiguity*, Empson concedes that 'I have myself usually said "either . . . or" when meaning "both . . . and" ' (*STA* 104), and when discussing *Volpone* he begins one paragraph with the admission that 'You may have noticed that my last paragraph set out to shoo away the feeling of tragedy but ended by yielding to it' (*ERL2* 80). Much like his circlings round Gray's elegy, in fact, where the feeling of tragedy was by turns questioned and acknowledged.

'Indeed, come to think of it' (*SSS* 31). Such a phrase captures the delinquent, delightful energy of Empson's prose, and signals its aspiration towards speech—full of second thoughts that review first impressions, and of alternately risky and inspired pot-shots that search out a more rounded view of the situation. Indeed, come to think of it, knowledge of a style 'can sometimes feel so like a knowledge of the spoken voice that we seem to pick up the intonation directly'. (*SCW* 63). This is perhaps why Empson so often displays a sure feel for the sounds within the words he reads: one of Donne's Valedictions contains 'broken pieces of grammar which may be fitted together in so many ways . . . lost phrases jerked out whilst sobbing' (*STA* 170); *Paradise Lost* is permeated by 'the Virgilian moan at the sorrow inherent in the whole story' (*SCW* 102); the voice of Marvell's housekeeper in her deposition 'sounds very plain and true . . . I can hear her panting' (*UB* 44).

Like that Elizabethan audience in which he takes such pleasure, this critic is all ears. Listening to Falstaff's boast about how he's in cahoots with the King, Empson notes: 'the terrible sentence "the laws of England are at my commandment, . . . and woe to my Lord Chief Justice" meant something so practical to the audience that they may actually have stopped cracking nuts to hear what happened next' (*ES* 68). Such wry briskness has its own practical designs on an audience, as George Fraser appreciated:

I had noticed in Empson's writing several pleasant little tricks, of the sort that keep a reader wakeful: a way of saying 'of course', when drawing some conclusion that seemed likely to jar and startle; a habit of alluding to rather out-of-the-way quotations as 'these famous lines'. In conversation, Empson had similar ways of jogging one: a trick of saying 'To be sure, to be sure', for instance, before taking hold of some vague and inept remark of one's own and handing it back twisted by irony or perception into some new and intriguing shape.[15]

That this shape-changing occurs in Empson's criticism as well as in his conversation implies that he sees the two activities as closely related, and that he treats his own remarks as fair game for these twistings and turnings, shadowing with irony his own compounds of eulogy and apology. Indeed, as he once observed, 'an irony has no point unless it is true, in some degree, in both senses . . . The fundamental impulse of irony is to score off both the arguments that have been puzzling you, both sets of sympathies in your mind, both sorts of fool who will hear you, a plague on both their houses' (*SVP* 51, 56).

The shift from the caress of 'sympathies' to the snipe of 'a plague on both their houses' alerts us to the bite within Empson's affability, and some of his work (the later work especially) is more inclined to settle scores than to 'score off both the arguments', more willing to shout 'fool' than to extend friendship. Still, while he can be 'difficult' (both obstinate and hard to understand), his prose often tries to make conversation, and to be conversable. As Lisa Rodensky has observed when comparing the style of his work with that of some recent literary-critical writing: 'I'm not claiming that I understand every word of the book [*Seven Types*], but I know that it wants me to. It's always rooting for me.'[16] In this sense, Empson's writing tries to emulate what it admires in others; he is frequently alert to what he calls 'careless ease'—a form of writing that can root for an audience whilst also offering challenges. When thinking about how the end of the *Beggar's Opera* invites the audience to clap (and so 'confess that they were half on the side of the rebels'), he notes that 'It was a display

[15] G. S. Fraser, *A Stranger and Afraid: The Autobiography of an Intellectual* (Manchester: Carcanet New Press, 1983), 181.

[16] Lisa Rodensky, 'Empson's Seven Types of Ambiguity', *Essays in Criticism*, 53: 1 (2003), 54–67 (p. 65).

of careless ease, but the call for applause was bound to have a certain fighting political point' (*ERL2* 80). Similarly, when considering Dryden's 'grand style', he observes that it carries with it 'the careless ease of a gentleman' yet is 'arranged with labour' (*UB* 101; the socio-political inflection of 'labour' carries its own 'fighting political point').

Annoyed by critics who 'talk as if they were androids from Andromeda' (*ERL2* 72; note 'talk', not 'write'), Empson warms to the critic-as-earthling, especially one drawn to the seventh type of ambiguity, and to the fact that 'human life is so much a matter of juggling with contradictory impulses' (*STA* 230). By admitting and exploring such tensions in a style that embodies yet also somehow ennobles them, the writer 'claims the sympathy of his audience in that "we can none of us say more than this," and gains dignity in that even from the poor material of human ignorance he can distil grace of style' (230). This is one reason why his gregarious yet compacted style matters so much to Empson; it is a form of coping as well as of communicating, and itself a version of pastoral ('putting the complex into the simple' (*SVP* 25)). To Rosemund Tuve he writes, with his characteristic mixture of grace and gruffness, 'I rewrite everything I print about twelve times, mainly in the interests of intelligibility, and I think you had much better do that too . . . if you tried to write more clearly you would find your own ideas are a great deal more muddled than you suppose' (*SL* 196).

Rewriting twelve times—composing around the clock, as it were—is a way of seeing your own work in the round even as you plan the best mode of attack for your fighting talk. Though Empson notes that 'some reviewers thought *Pastoral* was just dashed off, merely because I had taken so much pains to make it easy to read' (*WE2* 132), he describes himself as 'comforted by an adverse review' that said his style was 'slack, like a fireside chat . . . I had spent so many years trying to make the style natural' (*SL*, p. xlv). George Watson recalls a chat with Empson about this style: ' "I still have to put in the careless ease," he once remarked . . . when I reproached him gently for not collecting his essays. "The careless ease always goes in last." '[17] Taking these pains last is a little like the process described in the final stanzas of Empson's poem 'This Last Pain'—'build an edifice of form . . . And learn a style from a despair' (*CP* 53). Or, as he puts it in his letters—where he often felt 'The duty of sounding

[17] George Watson, *Never Ones for Theory? England and the War of Ideas* (Cambridge: Lutterworth, 2000), 70.

cheerful in prose' (*SL*, p. xvii)—'putting in the careless ease often amounts to discovering what the point of the whole thing was and rewriting it completely' (*SL* 469–70). He observed on another occasion, 'Really it is only the art of writing that makes me think at all' (*WE1* 469). The 'art' here refers to his own writing as well as that to which he responds. Style is, for Empson, something to think *with*, as well as *through* or *about*; his 'careless ease' is an enabling catalyst as well as an ornamental flourish, at once a refuge and a resource.

And yet, whilst writing notes for the second edition of *Milton's God*, Empson confessed: 'pretending careless ease drives me to drink' (*SL* 368). His endeavour to forge a style that allowed him to see in the round often led him to another round. Writing up *Complex Words*, he found himself 'drinking rather solemnly to see if that makes me think of broad points left out. Not drinking cuts one off very much' (*WE2* 273). Drink was a way of loosening his prose's tongue. All the same, that could never be the whole story. He also wrote that 'my experience has been that getting a thing started requires drink and finishing it sobriety' (*WE2* 32). The process of reading Empson is akin to that of indulging in a tipple, quickly followed by a strong coffee. Paragraphs move from the exhilaration of the chase to a sense of the chastened ('You may have noticed that my last paragraph set out to shoo away the feeling of tragedy but ended by yielding to it'). Or to take a less tragic, but no less delightful example:

> Some readers of this chapter, I should like to believe, will have shared the excitement with which it was written, will have felt that it casts a new light on the very nature of language, and must either be all nonsense or very startling and new. A glance at an annotated edition of Shakespeare, however, will be enough to dispel this generous illusion; most of what I find to say about Shakespeare has been copied out of the Arden text. (*STA* 104)

'Copied out'? The phrase winningly sells its author short, even as it responsibly checks the exuberant satisfaction of the preceding sentence. Empson's books display similar impulses, as starry- and clear-eyed claims frequently take the measure of one another. His prodigious debut, for example, opens with a mischievous suggestion that 'ambiguity . . . may be stretched absurdly far' (*STA* 19). It ends, however, with a sobering tone that 'seems a sufficient apology for many niggling pages' (294). This deft ending is itself ambiguous, stationed between pride and humility. An 'apology', after all, is a defence and a vindication, as well as a way of making excuses and expressing regret.

John Henry Jones observed at first hand how such niggling pages were put together:

> he would deliberately make himself 'tipsy' before sitting at the typewriter and dashing out the first few pages . . . he wanted to establish a flow, to get a 'gut reaction'. Then he would sleep until sober and retype from the beginning, expanding the material but striving not to disturb the line he had set up. More drink was required for each continuation, each new draft being corrected and reworked in sobriety.[18]

These rhythms are part of the life of Empson's writing, and they find their way into what he considered his 'best poem' (*CP* 295), 'Bacchus', a hymn to drink that inspired perhaps his most famous remark: 'life involves maintaining oneself between contradictions that can't be solved by analysis' (*CP* 290). Drink is taken as 'typical of this power [maintaining oneself between contradictions] because it makes you more outgoing and unself-critical, able to do it more heartily' (*CP* 290). In addition, 'the claim of the drink is that it really does excite both new ideas and new sympathies, though at a cost . . . The human mind cannot be prevented from working like this, is what it [the poem] is celebrating—though with regret, so to speak' (*CP* 293, 295). The human mind's imaginings are compared to and fuelled by rounds of drink, and by a sense of how seeing in the round might be both valuable and risky: drink makes the world go round—allows for high spirits, as it were—but it sets the room spinning; it may help people to get round one another, but it may also encourage them to round *on* each other, and to drive each other round the bend.

'Bacchus' is emboldened and haunted by these variations on the theme. Indeed, the word 'round' does the rounds of the poem: from 'the round goblet' that opens proceedings in the first stanza ('the roundest ones crack least'), to 'Ixion at the wheel' who 'Still makes go round the whirled fooled clouded wheal', and on to the 'Round steel behind the lights of the god's car' and the 'wheel of fire' in the closing stanza (*CP* 64–6). We also find it in Empson's copious notes for the poem:

> Having to be round it [the flask] is the same shape as a sky-map or world-map . . . *whirled*—'world' . . . The same kind of control is needed inside your head, a place also round . . . thus making the world go round, like a drunk's head . . . Ixion

[18] John Henry Jones, 'Empson Soup: A Personal Memory of William Empson', *The CEA Forum*, 18: 2–4 (1988), 7.

on the wheel of torture in hell is at the tiller-wheel of the turning earth . . . After this look-round of the subject I try to present a person feeling tragic exultation in it . . . King Lear says he is bound upon a wheel of fire. (*CP* 290–2)

This 'look-round' the roundness of the poem includes an affirmative picture of Prometheus, 'the idealist revolutionary . . . willing to start a new world' (*CP* 294–5), but also the tortured circular motions of Ixion and Lear. Though alcohol may oil the wheels of sociability and progress, the poem also takes into account 'the quarrelsome stage of drink', its 'neurotic effects', and 'increasingly bad hangovers' (*CP* 291–3). The dramas housed within this vertiginous poem are like those in the toings and froings of Empson's criticism: quick to sense fellow feeling in unlikely places, yet also prone to tetchiness and quarrelling; drawn to praise the value of seeing double, yet aware of how this balance needs to be watched lest it veer into deadlock; keen to display a relish for the apparently nonsensical or 'tipsy' interpretation, yet eager to cultivate a sobering, no-nonsense kind of approach to literary criticism. Such contradictions are not always solved by Empson's analyses; rather, they are held in solution by them, maintained in and through a style that resists distillation. Indeed, he seems to enjoy argufying like the way he enjoys his drinks: mixed.

In Empson's wonderland, a disagreement is a sort of compliment—and, on occasion, a form of complicity. Satan is viewed with fear in *Paradise Lost* because, the critic suggests, we sense he may be telling some monstrous truth: 'a passionate denial of his arguments is a way of taking them seriously' (*MG* 312). To argue with the devil, then, might be a way of playing devil's advocate. As Empson explains in another context: 'if you attack a view in any detail that proves you to have some sympathy with it; there is already a conflict in you which mirrors the conflict in which you take part; that is why you understand it sufficiently to take part in it' (*A* 83). Rounding on an opponent can thus provide you with an opportunity to see yourself (and the object of your disagreement) in the round, for 'the act of knowing is itself an act of sympathizing' (*SSS* 68). Knowing your enemy may render them less an enemy, as though argufying were the sharing of a dilemma. 'Controversy demands imagination; you must try to understand your opponent's position, so that you can select the things worth talking about; so that you can find the root of his errors, or of your disagreement with him' (*SL* 30). To be sure, Empson's unbending practice does not always live up to the roundness of this general principle; he does not always do justice to his opponent's position, and he can be fiercely and stubbornly doctrinal—more concerned to play God's prosecutor than devil's advocate. Still, it is the 'or' (not 'and') here that is distinctly Empsonian—a pivot that allows a turn from fault-finding to a sense that disagreement need not necessarily imply 'error' on either side.

Hence Empson's enjoyment of a quarrel that wears its sympathy on its sleeve: 'I was delighted to see Mr Sparrow attacking Mr Richards in *Farrago*; much was to be expected from so fundamental a quarrel. But some degree of imaginative sympathy is necessary if criticism is to be profitable' (*SL* 21). His own reviews often try to take this tone: 'Probably the best way to review this good book is to quarrel with it on points of detail; that is often the best way of showing that a thing is interesting' (*A* 206). Likewise in his letters. The end of Empson's first missive to Ricks (a response to the latter's piece on Middleton) reads: 'However, after searching my mind for the limits of my agreement, I think you bring out some very important points; I must mind and not forget them' (*SL* 305). The act of interrogation is meant to imply a meeting of minds (as the dextrous shift from 'my mind' to 'I must mind' suggests). Dissent becomes a type of politeness. In response to John Wain's 'splendid praise' of his work, Empson explained that 'the best I can do by way of thanks is to say where I think it is wrong' (*SL* 638), and when he learned that H. W. Piper was also working on Coleridge, he wrote saying: 'Now that you have come across my book, I hope you will write telling me where you find it wrong' (*SL* 641). Though he sometimes finds others' arguments disagreeable, disagreement is a form of tribute.

Some of the most rewarding criticism on Empson has followed his lead, and has mirrored what he wrote of one of his own chief influences, I. A. Richards: 'the people influenced by him seem to have followed the beckoning of his style rather than his repeated instructions' (*SCW* 14). Reviewing *Seven Types*, Bonamy Dobrée wrote that 'though you can agree with and rejoice in Mr. Empson's main lines, you are moved to quarrel with him in detail on nearly every page . . . His active mind stimulates yours either to join him and outgo him, or else to refute him . . . [the book] will be a good friend to quarrel with on idle evenings.'[19] This cultivation of an ability to see in the round by arguing with Empson has been one of his most enduring legacies as a critic. Michael Wood has recently observed that 'Not least of the challenges Empson sets us is

[19] Bonamy Dobrée, 'Poetic Pitfalls', *Spectator*, 145 (29 Nov. 1930), 850–1.

where we are to stand if we want to contradict him.'[20] This appreciation itself follows the beckoning of Empson's style; as, for instance, when he pauses to praise and heckle Salvador de Madariaga, 'whose lively book on Hamlet has at least the merit of needing some effort to refute it' (*ES* 105).

It is hoped that *Some Versions of Empson* will be a good friend to quarrel with—an invitation to a round table as well as an attempt to go the rounds with Empson. The contributors do not always agree with him (or with each other), and their essays have been loosely arranged in pairs so as to emphasize their place in an ongoing dialogue. The first pair considers children: Deborah Bowman focuses on literary and familial argufying in Empson's poetry and criticism, while Adam Piette examines Piaget's theory of child logic and Empson's views on the responsibilities of the artist in wartime. The second pair turns to the East: via close analysis of Empson's translations of Chiyoko Hatakeyama's poems, Peter Robinson reconsiders why he stopped writing poetry; Jason Harding looks at the influence of China across the whole span of his career. The third pair dwells on Empson's protracted struggle with Christianity: Seamus Perry shows how attending to some versions of Empson's Coleridge can illuminate the relations between his early and late writings; Eric Griffiths considers the poetry alongside the prose to highlight the oversights as well as the insights of Empson's argufying mind. The fourth pair takes different kinds of Empsonian tone as its sounding board: Hugh Haughton explores the importance of the *Alice* books for Empson's poetry, as well as considering how his work revels in and ponders the fine line between sense and nonsense, while Matthew Creasy elucidates Empson's distrust and support of tact, and the way he blends social and class considerations with studies of semantic implication. The fifth pair examines theoretical engagements: Paul Fry revisits the critic's defence of intentionalism via a close look at his contretemps with Rosemund Tuve and W. K. Wimsatt; Christopher Norris argues that Empson's work has much to teach philosophers of semantics, and that it provides a much needed alternative to accounts of meaning, truth, and interpretation from Donald Davidson and others. The sixth pair considers sexual politics: Katy Price shows how sexual and scientific debates shed light on one another in Empson's poetry, and delves into the poet's early engagements with the new cosmology of Einstein and

[20] Michael Wood, 'William Empson', in *The Cambridge History of Literary Criticism*, vii. *Modernism and the New Criticism*, ed. A Walton Litz, Louis Menand, and Lawrence Rainey (Cambridge: Cambridge University Press, 2000), 219–34 (p. 234).

Eddington, while Susan Wolfson reveals the kinship of Empsonian reading and gender criticism by placing his work alongside that of Mary Wollstonecraft and examining his studies of Keats, Shakespeare, and Milton. The volume ends by giving Empson the last word. In 1970 he was interviewed by Christopher Norris and David Wilson, and discussed—among other things—the composition of his poetry and criticism, relations between theory and practice, fear of cows, students, intentionalism, Basic English, T. S. Eliot, imagery, Buddhism, the Beatles, parody, and the Queen. The interview, annotated by John Haffenden, is published here for the first time.

II

It may be worthwhile to end with a sort of final canter round the field. Empson sometimes saw things in the round in spite of himself—as he wrote of Milton: 'his style of attack is savagely whole-hearted, but his depth of historical knowledge and imaginative sympathy keep having unexpected effects' (*MG* 123). Those effects are also part of the experience of reading Empson, for he is keen to take sides yet frequently drawn to writing that does something more than that. He once wrote of 'the specific novel-reading pleasure . . . that of getting inside a life different from one's own and establishing kinship with it' (*RB* 7), and his prose often stages this disorienting yet rewarding sense of encounter. Ian MacKillop observed that 'Empson was a good commentator on what it is like *not* to grasp something, and, more than that, describe the sequential stages through which we pass, and which criticism should be allowed to track, before we "make sense".'[21] Making sense of something requires us to make decisions, yet a rounded sense of that 'something' will also often come from an ability to allow for hesitation and uncertainty. Empson's cognizance of this mixed state of affairs is one reason why he writes so well about journeys towards decisiveness.

Take one paragraph from a discussion about Virginia Woolf; he is considering *To the Lighthouse*, and how, 'by the very structure of the sentences, we are made to know what it felt like for the heroine to make up her mind':

[21] Ian MacKillop, 'Revisiting Empson: Successive Fireworks of Contradiction', *CCUE News*, 18 (Winter 2004), 13–15 (p. 15).

We arrive, for instance, with some phrase like 'and indeed' into a new sentence and new specious present. Long, irrelevant, delicious clauses recollect the ramifications of the situation (this part corresponds to the blurring of consciousness while the heroine waits a moment to know her own mind; and it is here, by the way, that one is told most of the story); then by a twist of thought some vivid and distant detail, which she is actually conscious of, and might have been expected to finish the sentence, turns her mind towards the surface. From then on the clauses become shorter; we move towards action by a series of leaps, each perhaps, showing what she would have done about something quite different, and just at the end, without effort, washed up by the last wave of this disturbance, like an obvious bit of grammar put in to round off the sentence, with a partly self-conscious, wholly charming humility in the heroine (how odd that the result of all this should be something so flat and domestic), we get the small useful thing she actually did do. (*A* 446)

This is characteristic of Empson's criticism, for it establishes kinship with the life of the character—and the life of the writing—by entering into and inhabiting the spirit it describes. As the heroine 'waits', so the parentheses offer their own delicious delay with 'by the way' comments; then, where Empson 'might have been expected to finish the sentence' (after the parentheses), his writing continues—in tune with the consciousness and the style he is observing. 'From then on the clauses become shorter' (as do Empson's). The second set of parentheses then holds the thought in a medium that feels very close to Woolf's own free indirect style—'how odd . . . ' is perhaps a blend of the heroine's and the critic's voice—and the slowly dawning sense of decision is embodied by the timing of Empson's own periodic sentence, as we finally 'get' the verb and the rounding off for which both the heroine and we have been searching.

The careless ease of such writing does not preclude a deep engagement with its subject, and is itself founded on what Woolf termed 'the power which adds the supreme flavour to existence—the power of taking hold of experience, of turning it round, slowly, in the light'.[22] This criticism has waited a moment to know its own mind as well as that of another, and it encourages us to do the same. Part of its magic comes from its being permeated by that vocabulary to which Empson is so often drawn ('A *twist* of thought . . . *turns* her mind . . . *round* off the sentence . . . *wholly* charming'), where twists and turns precede and enable a vision of things in the round, giving us the sense of an experience as a whole. I say 'us', for—like much of Empson's writing—this paragraph

[22] Virginia Woolf, *Mrs Dalloway* (1925), ed. Stella McNichol (London: Penguin, 2000), 86.

is structured around the first-person plural ('we arrive . . . we move . . . we get') even as it imagines and describes a feeling that is, in many ways, a form of isolation. In a study of Empson's poems, Paul Alpers paused to observe that 'Every one of the statements of isolation in the poems we have discussed conveys a sense of human community. The pronouns that continually appear are *we* and *you*.'[23] Indeed, take the first line of the first poem Empson ever 'thought worth keeping' ('The Ants')—'*We* tunnel through your noonday out to *you*' (*CP* 155; my italics)—a line book-ended by pronouns that elaborate at once a separation and a yearning for community. Or observe the dance of the pronouns in 'Aubade': the first use of the refrain 'The heart of standing is you cannot fly' sees the 'you' poised between the lonesome shrug of a speaker who is talking to and commiserating with himself, and the firmly committed tone of someone who is trying to extrapolate a rule out of his own specific experience. 'The Ants' moves from 'we' to 'you' and 'Aubade' circles in the opposite direction, as we arrive at the last line's small but significant revision to the refrain: 'The heart of standing is we cannot fly' (*CP* 69–70). Like many of Empson's 'we's, this one intimates both a predicament and a consolation; '*we* can none of us say more than this', yet in saying so, we can, on occasion, gain a dignity and a grace of style.

Empson felt that 'Chinese Ballad . . . clears the palate after a reading of my stuff' (*CP* 401), so it is perhaps appropriate to turn here last. The poem (a translation from Li Chi) is itself built on turns, and on a figure of speech that is particularly suited to Empson's roundly enquiring imagination: *antimetabole* (*anti*, 'in the opposite direction', and *metabole*, 'turning about'). The figure repeats words in successive clauses in reverse grammatical order; thus, 'Make *one of me and one of you* . . . They yet shall live *again*' and '*Again* make dolls of *you and me*'; 'So *your* flesh shall be *part of mine*' and '*part of mine* be *yours*' (*CP* 103; my italics). These yearnings and returnings are themselves a longing for union amid the threat of separation:

> Now he has seen the girl Hsiang-Hsiang,
>   Now back to the guerrilla band;
> And she goes with him down the vale
>   And pauses at the strand.
>
> The mud is yellow, deep, and thick,

[23] Paul Alpers, 'Empson on Pastoral', *New Literary History*, 10: 1 (Autumn 1978), 101–23; repr. in John Constable (ed.), *Critical Essays on William Empson* (Aldershot: Scolar Press, 1993), 496.

> And their feet stick, where the stream turns.
> 'Make me two models out of this,
> That clutches as it yearns.[']

In a typescript draft Empson wrote a 'possible footnote' that exemplified his ability to view things in the round, and to see a 'turn' from more than one angle: 'He crosses the stream at a bend because the swing of the current makes it broader and hence shallower there. But of course the point of the detail is that she is turning like the stream as well as sticking like the mud' (*CP* 402–3). This is one of those sprightly Empsonian 'of course's that George Fraser would have enjoyed—so much more than just a matter of course. This criticism, like the poem itself, displays the qualities to be valued in Empson's work, qualities that this collection of essays tries to emulate and explore. It would be hard to sum up what these qualities are, but Empson himself was a great master of summing-up. When trying to say what it was about a piece of George Bernard Shaw's criticism that moved and inspired him, he hit on a luminous description of his own work: 'so lucid, so penetrating, so bare, so full of decisive detail, so rewarding to the imagination' (*UB* 207).

2

Argufying and the Generation Gap

Deborah Bowman

In a letter of 1732, Thomas Bentley recorded a bitter argument with his uncle, Milton's editor Richard Bentley, over *Paradise Lost*: 'I told him I would never object again, since I saw he would not bear it . . . for I know he can't forbear talking of Milton, & I can't bear the nonsense & absurdities he puts upon him.'[1] Uncle and nephew differed in their interpretations of Milton, but a striking sequence of words in Thomas's letter shows a likeness: 'he would not bear . . . for I know he can't forbear . . . I can't bear.' Lack of patience seems to have been a family characteristic, the younger Bentley's inability to 'bear' his uncle's theories repeating the elder's inability to 'bear' objections to them; Thomas's 'for I know' partially prefiguring, in recognizing, Richard's inability to 'forbear' talking. Their exchange brings to the surface two tricky facts: first, that much forbearance is needed but not always used when dealing with forbears, both literary and familial, and second, that the consequent arguments may be as liable to demonstrate likenesses as differences.

Both of these facts are pertinent to William Empson's work. He was drawn, in both his poetry and prose, to the type of argument he described as 'argufying', 'the kind of arguing we do in ordinary life, usually to get our own way; I do not mean nagging by it, but just a not specially dignified sort of arguing' (*A* 167). Distinguishing this form of argument from 'thoroughly conscientious uses of logic', Empson's words 'ordinary life' and especially (and even though it

[1] Cited in J. K. Hale, *Thomas Bentley to Dr Pearce: New Light on Richard Bentley's Edition of Paradise Lost* (Wellington: Turnbull Library Record, 1981), 25–6.

is denied) 'nagging', suggest that rather than springing from a literary or academic context, argufying begins at home. That such altercations are 'not specially dignified' removes this kind of particular quarrel from more lofty and universal debate; the phrase suggests both the root of such disagreements in the individual quirks and irritations inherent in every ménage, and the danger, in such personal and unregulated involvements, that rather a lot of dirty washing may be hung out. At times, in fact, argufying appears close not only to the domestic, but 'a domestic': 'Argufying in poetry is not only mental; it also feels muscular. Saying "therefore" is like giving the reader a bang on the nose'; 'You can feel his elbows coming out as he jabs the argument home' (*A* 170, 171). The physical analogies show argufying as a way of arguing which attempts to find proximity through disagreement; reaching out, it expects to make contact with an adversary, driving arguments 'home' with a touchy familiarity. It is also, like domestic rows, emphatically vocal. The *OED*, in explaining the development of 'argufy' from 'argue', cites that of 'speechify' from 'speech', and Christopher Ricks traces argufying, 'the stylized combative courtesies within which passionate conviction may boisterously and rudely play', back to Empson's schoolboy debating at Winchester.[2] Many childhood familiarities, though—Sunday lunch with the folks as much as a classroom debate—encompass both quaint ceremony and bolshy shouting-matches. Argufying, like the slangy and down-to-earth family row, airs differences but relies upon common ground.

Empson first suggests argufying as a corrective to the conduct of Symbolist poetry, which he sees as 'completely out of touch with . . . fair public debate'; he contrasts its jabbing elbows with the Symbolists' indirect and 'hinting' articulations (*A* 168, 167). It can, however, make its points more subtly than his essay suggests. Marcel Proust, in his own attack on symbolism, indicates how:

Les symbolistes seront sans doute les premiers à nous accorder que ce que chaque mot garde . . . du charme de son origine ou de la grandeur de son passé, a sur notre imagination et sur notre sensibilité une puissance d'évocation au moins aussi grande que sa puissance de stricte signification. Ce sont des affinités anciennes et mystérieuses entre notre langage maternel et notre sensibilité qui . . . en font une sorte de musique latente que le poète peut faire résonner en nous . . . Il rajeunit un mot en le prenant

[2] Christopher Ricks, 'William Empson', *The Proceedings of the British Academy*, 71 (1985), 539–54 (p. 540).

dans une vielle acceptation, il réveille entre deux images disjointes des harmonies oubliées, à tout moment il nous fait respirer avec délices le parfum de la terre natale.[3]

Taking issue with the Symbolist desire to wipe language clean of its history, Proust points out that words already carry with them something more powerful than denotative meaning: sounded correctly, present speech can be made to resonate with the harmonics of past contexts and usages, and is less, not more, musical, if these are disregarded. These, too, are some of the noises that Empson hears in 'complex words', as a writer makes his language's different senses and strands of history jar and chime within it: 'The English [word] Dog' is a complicated chord, whose notes include 'cynicism', 'sexual freedom', and 'cheerful stoicism' (*SCW* 165, 174, 166). In *The Structure of Complex Words*, Empson sets out to examine 'the logic of these unnoticed propositions' (39), but what he finds in such 'vague rich intimate words' (158) is often, like argufying, and Proust's 'musique latente', 'not specifically logical' (252). And although Empson first establishes argufying as a refreshingly abrasive antidote to poetic smoke and mirrors, its out-loudness, heard in his own poetry and prose, frequently calls on the same resources to which Proust refers. At such times, as in Thomas Bentley's letter, the voices it raises make audible the 'harmonies oubliées' of a shared language which is not only 'maternel' but involved in more extensive familial, and societal, relations.

Empson recalled one such exchange with his mother:

She was scolding me because I wouldn't take my civil service examinations. She said I was wasting my life, what did I think I was going to do being a poet, and so on. Then the while denouncing my activities, she paused, always willing to be fair, and said, 'I will say, that poem about your Granny, William, now that showed decent feeling.' And I was greatly relieved by her saying this . . . She thought it was about her own mother, who actually was being rather a handful at the time, you see, and I meant it

[3] 'The symbolists will no doubt be the first to grant us that what each word preserves . . . of the charm of its origins or the splendour of its past, has a power of evocation over our imagination and our sensibility equally as great as its power of strict signification. It is these ancient and mysterious affinities between our mother tongue and our sensibility which make of it . . . a sort of latent music which the poet can make to resonate within us . . . He rejuvenates a word by taking it in its old sense, he reawakens forgotten harmonies between two disjointed images, he causes us continually to breathe in with delight the fragrance of our native land.' Marcel Proust, 'Contre l'obscurité', in *Contre Sainte-Beuve*, ed. Pierre Clarac and Yves Sandre (Paris: Gallimard, 1971), 390–5 (pp. 392–3). Translation from 'Against Obscurity', in *Against Sainte-Beuve and Other Essays*, trans. John Sturrock (Harmondsworth: Penguin, 1988), 135–9 (pp. 137–8).

about her. This cleared the matter up very much . . . The idea is that we—our ideas in common are so many, we agree on so many points—we somehow can't talk to each other, and why is that, it seems mysterious. (*CP* 193)

In mistaking the poem's subject, however, Mrs Empson inadvertently grasped its meaning: it is about the feelings of one generation for another, at once sensitive and irritable, feelings which are amply displayed in the quarrel during which the poem is mentioned. Empson's anecdote brings out the difficult similarity between mother and son, as while he had written it about his parent, as a reader of the poem she felt it true of hers. And, as Thomas Bentley expressed his difference of opinion with his uncle in language which brought them closer, the poise of Empson's words remembers those of his mother; he frames her pause from anger—' "I will say, that poem about your Granny, William, now that showed decent feeling" '—with a phrase which remembers her generous concession in a similar movement: 'Then the while denouncing my activities, she paused, always willing to be fair.' His 'fair'ness is descended from her own 'decent feeling', just as her 'I will say' modulates into his 'always willing'. His report of her accusation—'I was wasting my life'—echoes, and yet in echoing opposes, and yet in opposing fits together with, the first lines of the poem she mistook, and didn't: 'Ripeness is all; her in her cooling planet | Revere; do not presume to think her wasted' (*CP* 24). Her words mingle with his: when he reports the argument, there is more than a hint of free indirect style about its phrasing, in the quaint locution 'then the while denouncing', and the naggingly informal syntax of 'I was wasting my life, what did I think I was going to do being a poet'. Their difficulty is created in the image of other intergenerational tensions within the family, between Mrs Empson and her mother, for the son's 'being a poet' might feel very like his grandmother's 'being rather a handful'. Yet the incident confirms not only that he and his mother 'agree on so many points' but also their continuing distance and divergence from each other. It is, after all, based on a misprision, caused by the fact that 'we somehow can't talk to each other', and Empson's hearty summary—'This cleared the matter up very much'—is qualified by a persistent, syntactically loose, puzzlement: 'The idea is that we—our ideas in common are so many, we agree on so many points—we somehow can't talk to each other, and why is that, it seems mysterious.' The last line of 'To an Old Lady' brings together bafflement and clarity: 'And but in darkness is she visible' (*CP* 24).

'To an Old Lady' charts the often disputed territory between parent and child, the site of so many argufying encounters. Empson thinks feelingly about the puzzlements and insights inherent in the relationship between parents and their not-quite-adult children, in a clear-sighted navigation of what Ricks describes as the 'mysteriously vista'd' strait now 'trivialized as "the generation gap" '.[4] Imagining the past as not merely a foreign country but a different world, and himself as quite literally on another planet from his mother, Empson looks back on his mother's life with a clarity brought by distance:

> Ripeness is all; her in her cooling planet
> Revere; do not presume to think her wasted.
> Project her no projectile, plan nor man it;
> Gods cool in turn, by the sun long outlasted.

Clarity, but also tentativeness; it is with extreme delicacy that he introduces the matter of her age:

> Still stand uncalled-on her soul's appanage;
> Much social detail whose successor fades,
> Wit used to run a house and to play Bridge,
>
> (*CP* 24)

Each of these lines hints at decline, but admiringly, dauntedly. Stretching T. S. Eliot's poem 'Marina', Empson read into Eliot's phrase 'in a world of time beyond me' a drawn equivalence between 'an order in this world to be known by a later generation' and 'the life in heaven which is to be obtained after death'; Empson's poem sees how appropriate it is to wonder whether a mother sees her future in her children or herself (*A* 356). The lines can be read as a description of the narrowing horizons of an elderly woman, her 'appanage' (glossed as 'territory or property') now 'uncalled-on' by visitors, and her previously full 'social' life succeeded by a more 'faded' scene (nobody calls); the third line's 'used to' might be meant sadly—as Al Alvarez admitted he once thought—as part of the imperfect tense, personifying Wit into the alias of Mrs Empson in her former, more vigorous life.[5] A more specific meaning of 'appanage', however (territory or property 'such as might be provided for the maintenance of the young children of royalty') shifts the disappointment from a dwindling life to one which

[4] Ricks, 'William Empson', 540.

[5] A. Alvarez, 'A Style from a Despair: William Empson', *The Twentieth Century*, 161 (1957), 344–53 (p. 350).

hasn't yet lived up to its forerunner (cited in *CP* 196). Mrs Empson's legacy is then 'uncalled-on' by her children, who are not yet putting it to good use; they are also the 'successors' to her 'social detail', but are rather letting things go; they don't yet 'run a house', or do so without 'calling upon' their mother's 'wit'. The immediate effect on the poem's tone of these two sets of possible readings is that exasperation at the latter is a match for the sadness of the former, answering youthful pity with, 'Well, who are you to judge?' And there remains the possibility that both readings are true, in a double loss. The consideration of a son's life as in any way a continuation of his mother's makes his choices still more urgent; as one of her future lives, in wasting his own, he would also waste hers.

The poems in Empson's first volume were, he said, 'about the young man feeling frightened, frightened of women, frightened of jobs, frightened of everything, not knowing what he could possibly do' (cited in *CP* 118). The 'planet' seen from afar is not only his mother, but her world, ever more distant, and the poet's future is a place hardly more distinct. Empson finds himself stranded between them: 'Stars how much further from me fill my night. | Strange that she too should be inaccessible, | Who shares my sun.' The poem is brought round, as if settling into a new and wider orbit, by the family's gravitational pull, strong enough to withstand other impulses (the other worlds of a future) and allow for irregularities: 'you didn't realize what a strong support she was till you were in real trouble.'[6] 'Our ideas in common are so many', Empson concluded, after arguing with his mother, and began a gloss of 'To an Old Lady' by asserting that they were 'so completely in the same tradition' (cited in *CP* 194). His poem shows the common background of traditions, familial love and antagonism, as a reflection on the distance between a young man and his mother becomes a recognition that the notion of closeness might indicate degrees of resemblance rather than contact.

The quotation from *King Lear* with which Empson begins his poem acknowledges this. 'Ripeness is all': a son's words to his parent, in a work which lays out the wrenchings and comforts of relatedness, also point to a trans-generational context of sameness and difference: 'What, in ill thoughts again? Men must endure | Their going hence even as their coming hither. | Ripeness is all. Come on.'[7] Shakespeare brings together aged despair and infant wail. Edgar's

[6] Letter from Empson to Maxwell-Mahon (6 Nov. 1967), cited in *CP* 197.

[7] William Shakespeare, *The Tragedy of King Lear* (v. ii. 8–10), in *The Riverside Shakespeare*, ed. G. Blakemore Evans *et al* (Boston: Houghton Mifflin, 1974).

words both compete and keep company with his father's misery, reminding Gloucester that 'coming hither' into the world isn't all fun and games either. His lines recall a lecture on the same topic from Gloucester's contemporary and fellow father, Lear: 'Thou must be patient. We came crying hither: | Thou knowest, the first time that we smell the air | We wawl and cry' (IV. vi. 167). A sour reminder of generational distance—Gloucester and Edgar are at opposite ends of life, and their circumstances differ accordingly—the reflection tries hard to be comforting: they are, in some senses at least, in the same boat. And they must both, in the interim, 'come on'; the phrase's roughness and understanding, its impulses both to urge and to soothe, come out of Edgar's experience, rather than any sympathetic imagination, of wretchedness. The position of the first line's quotation, immediately after the title, could make it indicate a biased view ('To an old lady, ripeness is all') or, with the title read as an address, then give a considered opinion. 'Ripeness' might separate parent and child, as a reminder of the particular decays of age, or, meaning 'readiness', recall something they should both, in their own ways, try to achieve.

In considering the considerable life of Mrs Empson, then, the poem also thinks about the sorts of future life which Empson was at that time contemplating for himself. He has written of the poetic choices facing him at the time that 'an English poet struggled to emulate either the recent French or the English of 1590–1640' (*A* 428). 'Struggled' refers to the difficulty of writing, but also that of choosing the right style in which to write; to speak of 'either the recent French or the English of 1590–1640', as urgently as if they were options (*a*) and (*b*) on an exam paper, and as self-consciously as if they were the uniforms of mod and rocker, is only half-arch; fashion can be just this exact, and exacting. 'To an Old Lady' invokes some of the sartorial angst of generational conflict in the poet-spaceman's worry, 'Landing, you break a palace and seem odd': Muriel Bradbrook recalled that amongst Empson's generation at Cambridge 'our strongest term of disapprobation was "odd" ', and the word could at the time refer specifically to appearances (cited in *CP* 195). The *OED* gives as an example of sense 9.a of 'odd' ('that is not, or cannot be, reckoned, included, or co-ordinated with other things; not belonging to any particular total, set, or group; . . . unconnected, irregular; casual') the *Daily Telegraph*'s sniggering advice, from 1930, that 'the "odd" heavy tweed skirt that is worn in the English country can be left behind'. The *Telegraph*'s inverted commas suggest a slangy contempt relevant to Empson's situation; he might well have felt that the way he presented himself at home, Yokefleet Hall in Yorkshire, was entirely different from the way he appeared in Cambridge, and that this difference was a visible sign of his half-belonging to two separate worlds. It would be natural to fear looking inappropriate in either, a fear resulting in a feeling of really being 'odd'—'not belonging to any particular . . . set, or group'. The worry that he will 'break a palace and seem odd' now feels like a terror of gatecrashing in the wrong clothes and saying the wrong thing at the wrong time to the wrong person. In 'To an Old Lady' the speaker declares that he will keep his distance, and in this, Empson shows the same fine linguistic tact with which he reports the quarrel with his mother. Minding his language, he combines it with hers in a verbal double meaning which he loads with feeling: as he strains to describe the strangeness of his position, he finds a term—odd—which would be recognized as slang by some and still pass muster with his mother. In this way, a single syllable joins and divides them, summing up their 'indefinite' relationship, which at times (when they are 'at odds', perhaps) involves a feeling, on both their parts, of being 'unconnected'.

'To an Old Lady' makes its feelings known and its relations felt in other words. The poem's most puzzling line is 'Bees sting their need, the keeper's queen invader'; it breaks the poem's cosmic metaphor and disrupts its acoustic with a welter of assonance. Ricks remarks that 'we should . . . ask with some urgency what it is up to':[8] one of its tricks is to draw attention to the long, stressed vowel and its occurrence, outside this line, in descriptions of the young man's activities ('leap', 'seem', 'bees', 'need', 'keeper's', 'queen', 'see', 'reads'). In the third stanza it comes together in a poignant not-quite-rhyme with its unstressed, feminine counterpart:

> Watch while her ritual is still to see,
> Still stand her temples emptying in the sand
> Whose waves o'erthrew their crumbled tracery.

Empson admires his mother from a respectful and necessary distance; these similar sounds touch again in the penultimate stanza's admiring consideration of her abilities, 'She reads a compass certain of her pole', when Mrs Empson, though consulting only a compass, assumes an attribute of her literary son, and its associated sound, in the word 'read'. An alternative scansion—placing a heavy stress on 'she'—is less likely, both in its tone of peeved comparison and

[8] Christopher Ricks, 'Empson's Poetry', in Roma Gill (ed.), *William Empson: The Man and His Work* (London: Routledge & Kegan Paul, 1974), 145–207 (p. 180).

in that it would change the vowel-sound from short to long, feminine to masculine, making it a phrase all about Empson. In the last stanza, the line 'Strange that she too should be inaccessible' does lengthen this vowel, but the spondee 'she too' is a moment's reflection, a needy lingering rather than a doubly stressed competitive pout. In his state of flux the young man envies his mother her stable point of view, but also salutes her different ways of seeing, hearing, and speaking which have played a part, however subtly, in forming his own.

Another parent figure towards whom Empson felt similarly awed and guarded was Spenser, and in his description of their shared but distant languages, there again resonate his feelings for the Old Lady, and specifically his instruction 'her in her cooling planet | Revere':

> However rightly we may revere Spenser, he seems about the last man a modern poet would study to learn technique . . . We need to recognise that there is a considerable resistance to Spenser, which I partly feel myself; or at any rate a resistance to the process of soaking oneself in Spenser at great length, which is the only effective way of reading him. He is a separate world. (*A* 244)

Spenser is revered and resisted because he, like Mrs Empson, 'is a separate world'; Empson's writing about his literary predecessor draws on his feelings for, and the vocabulary he used to describe, his familial elder. The divide between the young man and all his parents, literary and familial, is a point of conflict and a cause for nostalgia; like his argufying, this crossover brings everyday experiences and habits into the exercise of criticism, and is felt and made evident through the sharing of language.

Empson's engagement with Tennyson involved a similar clash of literary personalities, but like his feelings for his mother, and unlike his relation to Spenser, it's brought to an acoustic resolution in which the writer, whilst feeling some 'resistance' to a predecessor, makes contact through the sounds of his verse. When Empson writes about Tennyson in critical prose, he certainly seems less than sympathetic. Taking Cleanth Brooks to task over the first two lines of *Tears, idle tears*, he denied that they simply frame a paradox: instead, he found the phrase 'Tears, idle tears, I know not what they mean, | Tears from the depths of some divine despair' to be 'good manners more than anything else; [Tennyson] describes the crying as it would appear to the world before he says what it means to him' (*A* 282).[9] His tone is comically opposed to that of

[9] *The Poems of Tennyson*, ed. Christopher Ricks, 2nd edn., 3 vols. (London: Longman, 1987), ii. 232, ll. 1–5.

his subject; although he wrote elsewhere, of the second line of *Tears, idle tears*, that 'it seems to me stupid not to feel the . . . line is beautiful', and defended it from a 'jeer' of Donald Davie's for 'accidental fuzziness', Empson's description does anything but echo the deliberately woozy out-of-body experience of Tennyson's poem (*A* 110). His remark has a brisk, pull-your-socks-up tone, impatient with too much brooding, which recurs when Empson complains about Tennyson's overuse of sound-effects. Calling this tendency 'mouldy wedding cake', he derides the Laureate's moony acoustic dwelling upon what he himself, reflecting upon *Tears, idle tears*, had called 'not real woe' but 'the "passion of the past" '.[10] Derides, but in doing so notices. When Empson refers to 'Tithonus' in the same quick-smart tone, as 'a poem in favour of the human practice of dying', this both reads well and misrepresents Tennyson; it is true, and sharp, but not the whole story, because Tennyson's whole story is precisely not sharp. Empson's remarks on Tennyson are both paraphrasings of, and reactions to, certain features of the poems, deliberately choosing to see what might 'appear to the world' rather than trying to get under the poet's particular skin. He seems to 'question the solemnity' not only of Brooks's paradox-hunting, but of *Tears, idle tears* itself, much as this seriousness is queried by Tennyson's own later comments on its lack of 'real woe': in his prose at least, Empson plays on the differences between his predecessor and himself.

His villanelles 'Missing Dates' and 'Villanelle', however, show another facet to this relationship, as they allude acoustically and syntactically to Tennyson's verse (*CP* 33, 79). The first line of 'Villanelle', and the third of 'Missing Dates', preserve a disembodied 'Death in life' which echoes the first line of 'Tithonus' ('The woods decay, the woods decay and fall') and also recalls the experience of self-estrangement in *Tears, idle tears*: 'It is the pain, it is the pain, endures'; 'The waste remains, the waste remains and kills.'[11] These lines brood assonantly, to an extent which makes the poems—as the villanelle repeats these lines which themselves contain repetitions—sound as if they have three and not two rhymes, on the long vowel-sound [eɪ]. The poems' remembering form, too, and their reflections on the suffering caused by what 'endures', or 'remains', chimes with Tennyson's poems. Empson remarked that 'the difficulty of writing a villanelle is to stop it from dying as it goes on', hearing the villanelle's tight rhyminess growing heavy as lines recur with a cumulative effect (as in

[10] Empson, 'Empson on Tennyson', *Tennyson Research Bulletin*, 4 (1984), 107–9 (p. 107); cited in *The Poems of Tennyson*, ii. 232.

[11] Ibid. ii. 607; *CP* 79, 33.

'Missing Dates', 'Slowly the poison the whole blood stream fills'); each new example of the rhyme means that, like Tithonus, it 'goes on', living to die another day.

Both 'waste' and 'pain' are part, and not part, of the sufferer. 'Tithonus' and *Tears, idle tears* probe feelings like loose teeth, exploring the ways in which your own emotions can seem foreign to you: the former's preoccupation is with the odd clinging otherness of nostalgia; in the latter Tithonus remembers—or thinks he remembers—'with what another heart | In days far-off, and with what other eyes | I used to watch—if I be he that watch'd—'.[12] It's apt, then, that these particular poems should infiltrate Empson's villanelles. What his criticism recoils from as the 'mouldy wedding cake' of Tennyson's gloomy assonances, his poetry understands and echoes, creating the moody 'salon nostalgia' which comes over both of his Miss Havishamesque villanelles.[13] In speaking his poetry, the Laureate was said to '[lengthen] out the vowel a in the words "great" and "lamentation" till the words seemed as if they had been spelt "greaat" and "lamentaation"'; Empson transfuses into and passes throughout his villanelles the sound from Tennyson's line which its author, too, liked to dwell upon.[14] In *Seven Types of Ambiguity* Empson had distinguished between the appreciative critic, who 'produces literary effects similar to the one he is appreciating', and the analytic critic, who 'is not repeating the effect; he may even be preventing it from happening again' (*STA* 287). 'The difficulty is,' he added, 'that they have all got to be both'; Empson's writing on Tennyson is both. The reaction of his 'analytic' prose, and his villanelles' 'appreciative' response, show two sides of argufying, as while his criticism can joke about the 'good manners' and 'mouldy wedding cake', of Tennyson's poetic texture, emphasizing its distance from his own temperament, his own verse comes to an accord, across the generations, with the Victorian poet's voice.

II

In *Paradise Lost*, another family separation is figured musically. Echoes of this rupture recur in Empson's own writing; and in *Some Versions of Pastoral*, he goes

[12] Tennyson, 'Tithonus', ll. 50–2.
[13] Geoffrey Hill, 'The Dream of Reason', *Essays in Criticism*, 14 (1964), 91–101 (p. 97).
[14] Cited in Norman Page (ed.), *Tennyson: Interviews and Recollections* (London: Macmillan, 1983), 63.

on to find hidden harmonies in its critical reception across the ages, which also reflect back on family relations. Milton's discord, though, is clear:

> No more of talk where God or angel guest
> With man, as with his friend, familiar used
> To sit indulgent, and with him partake
> Rural repast[15]

When his first family comes apart the shock is audible, and Milton 'now must change | These notes to tragic': it is as subtle and immense as the switch to a minor key.[16] His own music alters, losing the easy, unforced, and responsive likeness of the rhyme between 'guest' and 'used' (with 'repast' as a minor echo) which, as his rhymes often do, offers a précis of the situation: the inhabitants of Heaven 'used' to be Adam's regular dinner 'guests', but after the Fall, God and man just don't talk any more. *Paradise Lost* is a tale of leaving the nest; as Alastair Fowler notes, 'familiar' 'carries, in addition to its modern meaning, the sense, "on a family footing" '.[17] Satan's rebellion and man's disobedience mean that we are all products of a broken home, the generation gap between Man and his Father having become something more fundamental. Empson's reading of *Paradise Lost* looks at, and through, the ensuing cracks:

> so long as Milton is dealing with his first parents, it is fair to say that he has a pastoral sentiment about them. Adam's life is so far from ours that it is necessary to imagine him with dignity from a distance, and Milton seems both to have the double feeling of pastoral, that he is both inferior and superior to Adam, and to be sufficiently at home with it to turn it into poetry.
>
> We first see Paradise through the eyes of the entering Satan . . . Like him we are to feel aliens with a larger purpose; our sense of its pathos and perfection seems, as he does, to look down on it from above; the fall has now happened, and we must avoid this sort of thing in our own lives. (*SVP* 154)

Empson's writing relates those feelings associated with pastoral not only to 'our first parents', but also to parents and other family forerunners, important 'characters' in our own histories, to whom we look up and upon whom we look down. 'Pathos and perfection' seen and felt by an 'alien' aptly describes the view of Empson's mother taken in 'To an Old Lady', the poet peeping through a telescope, thinking of the damage he might do. She, too, is imagined

15 John Milton, *Paradise Lost*, ed. Alastair Fowler (Harlow: Longman, 1971), IX. 1–4.
16 Ibid. IX. 9.
17 Ibid. note to IX. 2.

'with dignity from a distance', but also with a certain condescension: the poet's examination of 'stars how much further from me', his checked impulse to 'project', implies that he has 'a larger purpose' than that of his mother, reflecting most children's determination to 'avoid this sort of thing in our own lives'.

Empson ends his essay by contemplating the pagan figures present in Milton's description of Eve's bower, though not in Christian Eden:

> Faunus haunting the bower, a ghost crying in the cold of Paradise, and the lusts of Pan sacred even in comparison to Eden. There is a Vergilian quality in the lines, haunting, indeed, a pathos not mentioned because it is the whole of the story. (*A* 115)

These chill ghosts, and the feelings Empson believes they give rise to, haunted those in 'To an Old Lady': her world was described as a 'cooling planet', and Empson seemed to seek out the same kind of foreign, vanishing tradition when he urged

> No, to your telescope; spy out the land;
> Watch while her ritual is still to see,
> Still stand her temples emptying in the sand
> Whose waves o'erthrew their crumbled tracery;

The o'erthrowing waves lead back to *Paradise Lost*, and the description of the fallen army of rebel angels, like

> scattered sedge
> Afloat, when with fierce winds Orion armed
> Hath vexed the Red Sea coast, whose waves o'erthrew
> Busiris and his Memphian chivalry[18]

Mrs Empson was not, as was Busiris, a mythical tyrant, but the allusion remembers that even the best mothers can feel like domestic dictators, whose absolute control is thrown over by the escape of growing up. Yet as Empson wrote, 'parents may be viewed with admiration so long as they do not impose on us their system of values'; his fascination with the foreign 'tracery' and 'ritual' of the past recalls Milton's own relish for the olde worlde exoticism of 'Memphian chivalry' (*SVP* 154). This is not triumph but partial yearning, which is what Empson sees, and hears, in the pastoral of *Paradise Lost*.

[18] Ibid. I. 304–7.

Milton's pastoral, writes Empson, is focused on Adam. Empson's own pastoral, in 'Milton and Bentley', centres on Richard Bentley. Bentley, as Empson's critical forerunner, is also a parent-figure, and Empson's attitude to him is one of filial embarrassment, argument, but also acknowledgement; he sets himself apart from the other 'English critics' who 'adopt a curious air of social superiority to Bentley; he is the Man who said the Tactless Thing' (*SVP* 123). In this, there is also filial resemblance; Robert Martin Adams notes that 'Empson's comments have been treated very much like Bentley's original emendations—as a *faux pas* with just enough oblique cleverness attached'.[19] The performance is a *faux pas de deux*: Empson himself finds—and it is this finding which opens the essay—that Bentley 'raised several important questions about Milton's use of language' (*SVP* 123). The essay itself, then, raises important questions about Empson's use of, and feelings about, his critical forebears.

Harold Bloom wrote, influentially, of the links between poetic and genetic parentage. Although *The Anxiety of Influence* seems at first to define his diagnosis against the critic's situation—'What gives pleasure to the critic in a reader may give anxiety to the poet in him . . . This . . . is the anxiety of influence'—literary criticism cannot escape him: 'we all suffer' from this complaint, he later claims, 'whether poets or not'.[20] In a sense Bloom presents critics as even more overshadowed than poets, pointing out that 'a critic has more parents. His precursors are poets and critics'; he then, however, goes on to argue that 'so are a poet's precursors'.[21] In following this line of non-argument, he ignores a quite different and peculiar respect in which critical descent, and dissent, might be distinguished from poetic influence and called more true to the biological model: while poets can to some extent choose their influencers, critics are expected—academic critics required—to take account of a much wider sweep of their past, and especially their immediate past. A poet isn't compelled to include in her work allusions to predecessors; a large proportion of critical writing, being academic, must consist of quotations and discussions of previous critical writing, as well as of literature.

Critics might, then, be more subject than poets to Bloom's doomy syndrome. One advantage of such an ever-present past, however, is that it's ever-*present*.

[19] Robert Martin Adams, 'Empson and Bentley: Something about Milton Too', *Partisan Review*, 21 (Mar.–Apr. 1954), 178–89 (p. 178).

[20] Harold Bloom, *The Anxiety of Influence: A Theory of Poetry*, 2nd edn. (New York: Oxford University Press, 1997), 25, 56.

[21] Ibid. 94.

When Empson considers Bentley, as when any critic deals with ancestors literary and critical, this business is conducted, as is traditional, largely in the historical present tense. 'Empson writes', I write; 'Bentley writes', writes Empson. And: 'Milton writes'. Roy Harris, however, has pointed out the problems of an oversimplified Western view of timeless literate continuity, 'the conclusion that when the bonds of communicational contact are not merely between one living individual and another, but—through writing—between past, present and future generations, the result is a superior form of social entity'; these problems lie, though, with the privileging of written over 'merely' oral history, and the social attitudes which have been associated with this position.[22] The 'social entity' Empson finds to be created by critical argument is different, distinguished partly by its argufying closeness to spoken exchange. For him, the case is less an instance of Bloom's Oedipus complex, and more one of prolonged sibling rivalries and alliances, in which considerations of brilliant literary pedigree make way for more ordinary negotiations of difficult resemblance.

Empson plunges straight into these noisy squabbles when he involves not only Milton, but Milton's critics and editors Richard Bentley and Zachary Pearce, who argued with each other and their subject in furious notes.[23] It may be that he is noting that Pearce and Bentley were in fact contemporaries, and so could have discussed the matter face to face, but Empson's essay brings their exchanges especially vividly, and vocally, into the present; he describes their exchange of fire as if it really were a conversation. His essay transforms print into speech, referring to 'Pearce's detailed replies' (*SVP* 124), 'a snort worthy of the nostrils of Milton himself' (126), Bentley's 'nagging' and 'complaint' (134). Sometimes, Empson will join in, as if very nearly present at their discussion: 'I am glad', he whispers to the audience, rather like David Attenborough, 'not to have to tell them what was evidently in Milton's mind' (129): although his not telling depends upon chronological distance, he manages to make it feel like a near thing. At one point, the voices of Milton, Bentley, Pearce, and Empson combine:

'Why may I not add one verse to *Milton*, as well as his Editor add so *many*?' inquires Bentley, with the innocent wilfulness of the great Victoria:

[22] Roy Harris, *Rethinking Writing* (London: Athlone, 2000), 4.

[23] Richard Bentley, *Dr Bentley's emendations on the twelve books of Milton's Paradise Lost* (London, 1732); Zachary Pearce, *A review of the text of Milton's Paradise lost: in which the chief of Dr Bentley's emendations are considered* (London, 1733).

> Him thus intent Ithuriel with his spear
> *Knowing no real toad durst there intrude*,
> Touch'd lightly.

It is the Doctor who dare intrude anywhere and will never whisper any harmful fancies. 'Here, you see, the Versification and Sentiment are quite of a Piece. How naturally does the Movement of the Line imitate the croaking of a Toad!' says Pearce. It is like dogs who cannot bear not to join in the singing. (128–9)

If Pearce's sound-effects ('*M*ove*m*ent . . . *im*itate', and 'cr*oa*king of a T*oa*d') are an harmonious accompaniment to the barber-shop chorus of Milton and Bentley, Empson chimes in with the pack as an echo or modulation of Bentley, repeating 'intrude', and adding his own descant in the jingling alliteration and rhyme of 'the Doctor who dare intrude anywhere'.

The variorum edition makes such critical exchange more vividly present as conversation; James McLaverty remarks of Pope's *Dunciad* that 'the notes to the Variorum are something like a talking bibliography'.[24] That Pope intended these entries to be imagined out loud is indicated by the instances when, as McLaverty notes, he 'uses typography to make its own comment', adding italics when citing (or misciting) real critical comments.[25] Such emphases are everywhere in Bentley, and Empson is quick to hear in them a spoken tone, which may not, however, have been what their author intended to emphasize. When Bentley writes 'Why may I not add one verse to *Milton*, as well as his Editor add so *many*?', his critic perceives not the balanced swing of rational argument, but a charmingly petulant stamp of the foot, indulged, but which perhaps should have been outgrown: 'the innocent wilfulness of the great Victoria'.

This comment shows exactly that pastoral combination of looking up to and down upon which is Empson's attitude to Bentley, and illustrates that continual competitiveness of critical writing which encourages the transformation of predecessors into peers: Bentley is a regal child, simple because he wrote in a simpler time (at least for literary critics). He's also somehow praiseworthy in the splendid wrongheadedness of his arguments, which, however, show other critics where to look. Empson picks up smartly upon Sir Walter Raleigh's comment on *Paradise Lost*: 'Sir Walter Raleigh said there could not have been a child in *Paradise Lost*, because one touch of common sense would have destroyed it; it was left to the great Doctor to take upon

[24] James McLaverty, *Pope, Print and Meaning* (Oxford: Oxford University Press, 2001), 95.
[25] Ibid. 96.

himself this important role' (*SVP* 126). In Empson's game of the Emperor's New Clothes Bentley plays the 'important roles' of both forerunner and playmate. The view of Bentley, 'the Man who said the Tactless Thing', as a perceptive infant, is one relished by Empson, not least because of his own 'inquiring' Alice-persona;[26] in the 'Preface to the Second Edition' of *Seven Types*, he boasts that 'my attitude in writing it was that an honest man erected the ignoring of "tact" into a point of honour' (*STA* 8). In 'Empson's Poetry' Ricks sees the writer's central concern as fathering, but Empson is more convincingly an *enfant terrible* than a Victorian paterfamilias. The critical tradition that allows predecessors to be argufied with as contemporaries gives this tendency free rein.

Perhaps the presentness of the argufying Variorum edition can be traced to the fact that the subject of its disputes is frequently the interpretation of words which have remained current in the language: this is how writers can be all contemporaries. On the other hand, footnoted explanations will pass out of critical fashion, and notes to Shakespeare, for instance, offer a sort of geological cross-section, preserving, along with 'the richness of the deposit of cross-reference and incidental detail', a richer silt of critical contribution (*STA* 68). This, Empson admits, is the soil from which *Seven Types* grew, writing that 'most of what I find to say about Shakespeare has been copied out of the Arden text. I believe, indeed, that I am using in a different way the material that three centuries of scholars and critics have collected' (*STA* 104). He brings to the Arden notes, though, the same sensitivities to tone that he brought to *Paradise Lost*:

> It is with a pretty turn of grammar . . . that the Arden editor insists on the variety of associations the word rooky had for an Elizabethan audience.
>
> This somewhat obscure epithet, however spelt (and it should be spelt *rouky*), does NOT mean 'murky' or 'dusky' (Roderick, quoted by Edward's *Canons of Criticism*, 1765): NOR 'damp', 'misty', 'steamy with exhalations' (Steevens, also Craig); NOR 'misty', 'gloomy' (Clar. Edn.); nor 'where its fellows are already assembled' (Mitford), and has NOTHING to do with the dialectic word 'roke' meaning 'mist', 'steam', etc. . . . the meaning here . . . I THINK, is simply the 'rouking' or perching wood, *i.e.*, where the rook (or crow) perches for the night. (*STA* 104–5)

And a pretty turn of typography, which Empson hears as he heard Bentley's, the long-dead editor 'insisting' through printed emphases. Empson's spotting of the negative grammar, and consequent use of the note, finds the same

[26] See Hugh Kenner, 'Alice in Empsonland', *Hudson Review*, 5 (Spring 1952), 137–44 (p. 141).

ghostly, hovering co-presences as he would later see in Eve's pagan-Christian bower, 'Not that fair field | Of Enna . . . nor that sweet grove . . . nor that Nyseian isle . . . Nor where Abassin kings their issue guard.'[27] You are not the same as your parents, but they are mysteriously half-present in you, which is one reason why they (and other family members) may haunt you. When Empson wrote that Milton's spectres had 'a pathos not mentioned because it is the whole of the story', he caught the nagging power of that negative, something defining because defined against.

This, in turn, rouses the ghost of Bloom. Paul Alpers has pointed out the difficulty for pastoral poetry of Bloom's idea of influence: if harking back to literary predecessors is liable to be classed as 'weak', then pastoral's backwards glances are its undoing.[28] But the strength of Empson's own pastoral writing—of his mother, of Milton, Bentley, and Pearce, of Tennyson, of the critics and editors of the Arden Shakespeare—is heard in the discovered consonances of argufying, its emphasis on the aural continuity of a 'langue maternelle' which provides a common home. Wordsworth demonstrates a similar quality, and the same syntactical shape, in his negative definition of the shepherds he remembered from childhood:

> Not such as in Arcadian fastnesses
> Sequestered handed down amongst themselves
> (So ancient poets sing) the golden age;
> Nor such—a second race, allied to these—
> As Shakespeare in the wood of Arden placed
> . . . .
> Nor such as Spenser fabled.[29]

The 1850 *Prelude* prefaces the passage above with another layer of definition, focusing on pastoral's companionable quality:

> Not such as Saturn ruled 'mid Latian wilds,
> With arts and laws so tempered, that their lives
> Left, even to us toiling in this late day,
> A bright tradition of the golden age[30]

[27] Milton, *Paradise Lost*, IV. 262–80.
[28] Paul Alpers, *What is Pastoral?* (Chicago: University of Chicago Press, 1996), 36–7.
[29] William Wordsworth, *The Prelude: 1799, 1805, 1850*, ed. Jonathan Wordsworth *et al* (New York: Norton, 1979), VIII. 183–91.
[30] Ibid. VIII. 129–32.

The stress on 'left' brings out the awkward mystery of this repeated 'Not such . . .' construction, not just in Wordsworth's setting but in those picked out by Empson in *Paradise Lost* and the Arden notes. Coming first, the word throws the line out of kilter. After this, it's a struggle to keep it running smoothly, just as the negative catalogue sways towards nostalgia, leaning on what isn't. But the meaning of 'left' is finely poised, including both what's departed, and what remains; its sound, too, takes the 'l' of 'lives', and modulates its 'v' into the softer 'f', smoothing it past the line-ending into the shadow of a further 'life'. If these shepherds, like Pan and the undertones of Shakespeare's wood, are no more, their clear echoes in myth, connotation, and 'tradition' persist. Naming these things in order to deny them is not necessarily, or not only, an act of futile rebellion: it might also be a leave-taking, a remembering, and a coming-to-terms. 'If you attack a view in any detail', wrote Empson,

> that proves you to have some sympathy with it; there is already a conflict in you which mirrors the conflict in which you take part . . . Only because you can foresee and enter into the opposing arguments can you answer them; only because it is interesting to you do you engage in argument about it. (*A* 83)

The reciting and turning away from implied in these negative catalogues, although not an explicit argument, is a mirroring, a way of entering into the past's 'separate worlds'. Considering Empson's pastoral as an alternative to theories that would make it 'weak', Alpers points to its historical specificity; the larger story, though, is that Empson's version of pastoral draws its strength from the argufying quality of his writing.

III

Introducing a topic over which he'd argued before, Empson used the phrase 'I was having a small controversy some while ago'; the idea that *having* an argument yourself (and not simply *making* one against someone else) is the prime activity of critics describes his ideal of criticism very well (*A* 159). The occasion for internal debate, though, may also be a revision or new edition of earlier work; Empson most often stages his revaluations as a generational conflict between himselves, again showing the domestic situation as a model for critical conduct. The 1947 Preface to *Seven Types* begins with an image of Old and Young Empson:

It seemed the best plan to work the old footnotes into the text, and make clear that all the footnotes in this edition are second thoughts written recently. Sometimes the footnotes disagree with the text above them; this may seem a fussy process, but I did not want to cut too much. Sir Max Beerbohm has a fine reflection on revising one of his early works; he said he tried to remember how angry he would have been when he wrote it if an elderly pedant had made corrections, and how certain he would have felt that the man was wrong. (*STA* 7)

Empson consolidates his old text so that he can 'make clear' his new differences of opinion with it, enjoying the two personae this gives him, and wanting to keep them separate. The standing-asides of his footnotes—they often begin 'I now think'—and the opportunity they give him to talk things through with himself, allow him greater freedom when considering possible interpretations and reinterpretations. He wrote of 'the chatty explanatory frame of mind which could annotate its own works', and his footnotes, as Bentley's to Milton, differ vocally from their main text, providing another voice gruffly muttering at the bottom of the page (*A* 83). Like Alice, he is 'fond . . . of taking both sides of an argument when talking to [him]self', and does this by allowing himself 'the advantages of being childish and grown-up at once' (*SVP* 216, 213).

Acting the old buffer, then, Empson is also a child at play. His idea of this activity, though, was at variance with contemporary theories of developmental psychology. In *The Structure of Complex Words* he notes that 'various child-psychologists have emphasized that a child only talks to itself, but surely what it really does is to play at having a conversation between two people' (*SCW* 65). This point reaches beyond the nursery. Empson's poem 'Your Teeth are Ivory Towers' (*CP* 67–8) names and quarrels with the child psychologist Jean Piaget, who wrote that children under the age of seven often speak in 'collective monologues' addressed to nobody in particular, and in which 'the words have no social function'.[31] The poem's rhymes are comically strained, but its point is serious: 'a Ba | Cordial in more than one direction | Can speak well to itself and yet please Pa'; 'more than one direction' indicates the dialogic quality of the child's play and its part in the dialogue between father and child, hinting strongly that this supposedly self-absorbed play is linked to, and in fact leads to, the ability to speak to and understand others. Empson compares Piaget's mistake with contemporary attacks on his own 'clotted kind of poetry', thick

[31] Jean Piaget, *Langage et la pensée chez l'enfant*, trans. Marjorie Warden as *The Language and Thought of the Child* (London: Kegan Paul, 1926), 16.

with multidirectional meanings; the analogy claims that such accusations of withdrawal into a self-absorbed cleverness miss the unambiguous link between ambiguity and attempts to understand other points of view (cited in *CP* 311). The same belief, and the same analogy, motivate an example he uses, more than once, to argue for argufying:

> one of the things the baby has to start learning is that other people really exist, and that its sense-data can be interpreted on that basis—if it doesn't do it it is mad; and there is no reason why the print of authors should be safe from this universal human necessity. (*SSS* 94–5)

> Among the first things a baby has to learn, and if it can't it's mad, is that other people really exist; if it couldn't feel 'Mum's cross' and so forth before it learned to speak, then it couldn't learn to speak. (*A* 124)[32]

This shows the importance Empson attached to the complex position of being part of a disagreement, as constituting our very first experiences of others; he traces back to it the very beginnings of language, and so finds it natural that it should recur in the context of thinking critically about language. What 'the print of authors' shares with the gurgling baby is a need to recognize 'that other people really exist', but specifically, both child and writer must also realize that these people may be 'cross' or at least at cross purposes with them. After a later relationship characterized by a different 'language problem', Empson traced the cross-currents of misunderstanding between himself and his Japanese girlfriend; an echo of the baby's progress, and the generation of his own argufying poetry and criticism, lingers in his ambiguous reflection on the good and the bad of conflict, political and erotic unrest: 'But as to risings, I can tell you why. | It is on contradiction that they grow' (*CP* 70).

[32] See also *A* 116.

3

Empson, Piaget, and Child Logic in Wartime

Adam Piette

Your Teeth are Ivory Towers

There are some critics say our verse is bad
Because Piaget's babies had the same affection,
Proved by interview. These young were mad,
They spoke not to Piaget but to themselves.

(*CP* 67)

The child psychologist Jean Piaget's interviews with children in the 1920s formed the basis of his research into the development of logic and reasoning in the human mind. Empson's defence of his own brand of metaphysical verse against the charge of escapism is well known. John Haffenden has shown, in the notes to the *Complete Poems*, the uses Empson makes of early Piaget to bolster his complex and witty disclaimer of escapism, in particular Piaget's theory of autism and collective monologue in the chatter of children at play in his first important work, *The Language and Thought of the Child* (1926). The Leavisite brickbat that metaphysical modernist poetry is wilfully egocentric and obscure, withdrawn from the social world of moral realities, self-indulgently revelling in redundantly puzzling language games, is cleverly related to Piaget on primitive child logic because of Leavis's turn against Empson after the Alice essay.

Haffenden is right to adduce the 1939 *Scrutiny* issue devoted to the relations between writer and politics in the light of the onset of war, since this neatly staged the views of some of the critics who were prepared to lambast the escapist tendencies of obscurantist poetry. The socialist-pacifist science fiction writer Olaf Stapledon argued that:

> in this crucial phase of man's career every creative writer who is tempted to choose the ivory tower should earnestly consider whether his work is likely to be so very valuable to the future that he is justified in denying the claims of the present.[1]

In the same symposium, the sturdily independent-minded, anarchist novelist Richard Church urged artists to resist scientific culture's standardization and 'centralization of control':

> This is an age of mass-production. What is the fastidious artist, or religious initiate to do about it? If he keeps out of the melée, will he escape? Can he find an ivory tower, and if he does will he be bombed or gently taxed out of it?[2]

Stapledon was to develop his ideas about the writer's responsibilities in the next issue, presumably picking up on Church's contribution, in the essay 'Escapism in Literature', which contrasted creative, propaganda, release, and escape writing. Creative writing is defined as a construction of 'universes of fiction which symbolize aspects of the actual universe'. Propaganda literature is the Auden group, the 'cause' the artist is serving 'irradiating and transforming his experience'. Release literature is roughly popular sensation fiction and surrealist texts which release 'pent-up forces in the personality'. Escape literature attracts the most opprobrium, the writer withdrawing from unpleasant reality:

> into some safe corner, where he can live in peace and occupy himself with activities unrelated to the vital struggles of his contemporary world; or else, unable to find actual escape, he solaces himself by constructing a dream world wherein he can live 'in imagination', a world after his own heart's desire . . . The escape motive is generally an unrecognized fear, which causes an unwitting incapacity to face up to reality. A morbid blindness, a self-protective and perversely creative blindness, not only blots out the obnoxious aspect of reality but also reconstructs the remaining characters into a coherent and lying image.[3]

[1] Olaf Stapledon, *Scrutiny*, 8: 2 (Sept. 1939), 155. Stapledon is using familiar Marxist rhetoric with the ivory tower slur—it was one of Earl Browder's favourite clichés.

[2] Richard Church, *Scrutiny*, 8: 2 (Sept. 1939), 133.

[3] Olaf Stapledon, 'Escapism in Literature', *Scrutiny*, 8: 3 (Dec. 1939), 298–308 (pp. 304–5).

Stapledon is primarily reacting against his own pacifism here, and defending himself against the too-easy implication that science fiction is escapist. Empson's sensitivity to *Scrutiny*'s moral condemnation of his criticism and poetry may have made him read those lines as a coded attack; but it is important to realize that 'Your Teeth are Ivory Towers' is written in direct engagement with Stapledon's (and Church's) response to the new *wartime* responsibilities of the writer.

It is clear that it is Stapledon's charge that escapist writing is 'self-protective' which most intrigues Empson, for the poem goes on to argue that childish autistic monologue, and the metaphysical-puzzling poetry that might resemble it, may actually be a true reflection of the ways people use defensiveness in ordinary life:

> Protection
> Indeed may safely grow less frank; a Ba
> Cordial in more than one direction
> Can speak well to itself and yet please Pa.
>
> (*CP* 67)

As Empson put it in his notes:

> Critics often say that modern poetry retires into an ivory tower, doesn't try to make contact with the reader, or escapes facing the problems of the time. I try to defend it by saying that there is a good deal of defence in ordinary life (talking or biting). A critic like Dr Leavis can speak with the same tone of moral outrage about an Escapist (sentimental) novel as a customs official would about *Lady Chatterley's Lover*, say; but this is being over-simple, I was claiming, is itself a way of escaping the complexity of the critic's problem. The relations of the artist to his society may include acting as safety valve or keeping the fresh eye, etc., of the child, and therefore can't be blamed out of hand for escapism or infantilism. (*CP* 310)

The pitching of 'complexity' against 'over-simple' goes to the heart of Empson's practice as critic and poet—to oversimplify the seemingly simple is itself an evasion from the complexities of responsible writing in the world.[4]

[4] The false opposition of simple and complex is the main focus, of course, of Empson's concerns in both *Some Versions of Pastoral* and *The Structure of Complex Words*. In both books, the key work of Empson's critical thinking is aimed at demonstrations of the dangers of oversimplifying seemingly simple words, such as 'honest', simple phrases and syntactical moves, such as the 'queerness' of the 'forces' in Macheath's question 'Was this well done?' (*SVP* 187–8), and apparently straightforward

The brilliance of the opening lines of 'Teeth' lies in the quiet assumption of the very clotted and metaphysical poetry being defended, and a turning round of the very idea of escapist poetry *as* itself a means of defending oneself against political accusation ('I try to *defend* it by saying that there is a good deal of *defence*'). The poem is a Sidneyean defence of poesy which is *about* defending oneself.[5] This is shadowed by the toothpaste joke implied by the title: our principal means of protection as biting animals, our teeth, themselves need protection, Gibbs Dentifrice. The ivory tower becomes comically the teeth in one's mouth, used both to harbour and shape the articulation of talk, talk to oneself, against one's critics, for one's own pleasure and for the incidental pleasure of those overhearing, and to bite when hungry or when fighting in close combat. In a further note, Empson shows that it is not just the Leavisites he is defending his own defensiveness against, but the Auden group socialists of the 1930s: ' "Your Teeth" defends this kind of poetry against the objection of the 'thirties, that poetry should make contact with the public and current problems; however, I have always admired the poets who did' (*CP* 311).[6] This note makes clear how important it was to Empson that readers did not oversimplify matters by splitting the world into dreamers and activists—a dream can be a form of oblique action in the contemporary world.

A poem for Empson was a forum where one could make up one's own mind, in the sense both of creatively inventing one's mind by positing many enemies, oppositional points of view, complexes of rival meanings; and in the sense of making a decision, making one's mind up about a problem or set of emotional difficulties and calls to responsible action. It is thus absurd to accuse the poems of being escapist since their concern is always from the outset with the imagining of as many constraints upon feeling oneself into the world as possible in order to test and discover true measures of resolution in and incorporation of the mind in the world. What might be sacrificed in such close engagement with the world and one's words in the world is the local contract

social categories such as the fool or child. Empson's own bluff and idiomatic diction is, as always, the issue here too. A typical example would be Empson's exploration of the triple implications, or 'whole set of tricks' embedded in Herbert's advocacy of a plain style (*SCW* 188).

[5] Defensiveness in Empson goes back a long way. See the remark in *STA*: 'The object of life is, after all, not to understand things, but to maintain one's defences and equilibrium and live as well as one can; it is not only maiden aunts who are placed like this' (*STA* 285).

[6] See John Haffenden's notes to 'Just a Smack at Auden' (*CP* 351–6).

with the reader, of course, and it is here that 'Teeth' is most mordant. The problem lies with the readership not the poet.

One of the most important ways 'Teeth' engages with the public and current problems, albeit obliquely, and it is the obliqueness of poetry's relation to contemporary culture which is at issue, is in its exploration of the writer's responsibilities in wartime. If the poem is reacting to the *Scrutiny* polemics about the duties of the writer in a nation at war, then its advocacy of the artist as child and safety valve are, obliquely, about that too. The machine the safety valve knows the worst of is culture as war machine. The child's-eye view of the world is a view that resists being misled by the propaganda of war, however locally necessary.[7]

And again, if, obliquely, the finesse of using Piaget comically to outwit the oversimplistic bombast of a Leavis has something to do with Leavis's contempt for the uses of Freud in the Alice essay,[8] then the poem is hinting that the artist's oblique attitude to a wartime culture is perhaps to be found in that very essay. It's not hard to find a figure for Alice as escapist—it is Alice as the Cheshire cat, symbol of the 'ideal of intellectual detachment':

> The famous cat is a very direct symbol of this ideal of intellectual detachment: all cats are detached, and since this one grins it is the amused observer. It can disappear because it can abstract itself from its surroundings into a more interesting inner world; it appears only as a head because it is almost a disembodied intelligence, and only as a grin because it can impose an atmosphere without being present. In frightening the king by the allowable act of looking at him it displays the soul-force of Mr. Ghandi; it is unbeheadable because its soul cannot be killed; and its influence brings about a short amnesty in the divided nature of the Queen and Duchess. Its cleverness makes it formidable—it has very long claws and a great many teeth—but Alice is particularly at home with it; she is the same sort of thing. (*SVP* 218)

And Empson, one might argue, is the same sort of thing. The poems may seem to withdraw or retreat into a more interesting world, but the retreat is an act of abstraction rather than an escape, for the mind is abstracting

[7] For Empson on the relations between the child's point of view and propaganda, see 'Statements in Words' chapter of *SCW* and the discussion of 'awful' in a joke which is 'anti-British propaganda': 'the persons who use this school-girl slang really do feel awe on the occasion; they feel the adult world to be cruel about meaningless rules' (60). In the same chapter, Cold War propagandistic use of the term 'treachery' depends on 'a breakdown of the reciprocity we learned as children—the word is used in one way about me and in another about you' (59).

[8] Leavis rejected the essay for *Scrutiny*.

itself into a mental space precisely in order to *have* a real impact on the world. This might be an abstract vantage point enabling the intelligence to prosper from the freedom to make one's mind up, from whence the mind's eye may gaze the more forcefully on the mad world of power. The act of looking is an attitude of soul whose influence is partly a function of the unassailable freedom from harm of a lasting work of art, partly due to Empsonian cleverness—his poems have teeth too and can bite, as 'Teeth' demonstrates, satirically in the mordancy of their play with the enemy's idiolects and idiocies—and partly because of the ethical power they have to bring about amnesties in divided natures; i.e. to arbitrate at the contact zone of heart and word between rival powers and points of view.

The Buddhist grin on the world smiles on the world's divided nature but is also a baring of teeth: this as protection against the world's power to hurt and as warning of the free play of the intellect upon the world's assumptions. Its possible applicability to the wartime context relating artist to culture is hinted at in the reference to Ghandi's soul-force: poetry and criticism, or a poetry of criticism, is not naively pacifist but positively non-violent in the sense of being detached from the world's power to kill. This detachment is identical with making a real home for art's formidable cleverness about power's motives, uses of language, deployment of unreasonable logic.

The childish escapism of an Alice or a Cheshire cat Empson poem is really an oblique way of getting a peep at the machinery of power:

> This sort of 'analysis' is a peep at machinery; the question for criticism is what is done with the machine . . . In [Dodgson's] sort of child-cult the child, though a means of imaginative escape, becomes the critic; Alice is the most reasonable and responsible person in the book. This is meant as charmingly pathetic about her as well as satire about her elders, and there is some implication that the sane man can take no other view of the world, even for controlling it, than the child does; but this is kept a good distance from sentimental infantilism. (*SVP* 221)

The child's view is sanely detached, capable of puzzling out the riddles of the men and women in power, clear-eyed enough to acknowledge the mind's own attraction to and repellence of the machinery generated by the chatter of the powerful. It is a means towards a mobile point of view that is free of a whole host of distortions, summed up by Empson as the wish:

> to be like [a child] in having fresh and vivid feelings and senses, in not knowing, expecting, or desiring evil, in not having an analytical mind, in having no sexual desires recognizable as such. (*SVP* 221)

The attitude is acknowledged as usually mixed up with 'a desire to be mothered and evade responsibility', with a complicating distaste 'not only for sexuality but for all the distortions of vision that go with a rich emotional life' (221), with the social faults of one's own culture and class in their figuring of the particular child personality adopted, as with the complacency of Alice's snobbery. But these are all risks taken in the eyes of the world being criticized: they are, in a sense, the things the world will say.[9] Nevertheless, they do not, very importantly, take away from the clarity of quick intuition afforded by the persona.

The child as artist *is* self-protective, but not according to the Stapledon formula, rather in the sense Empson sees operating in the Alice books. Other versions of pastoral stage a gloriously all-inclusive persona, 'the idea of including all sorts of men in yourself' to reconcile the self with nature and therefore gain power over it (210).

> The Alices are more self-protective: the dream cuts out the real world and the delicacy of the mood is felt to cut out the lower classes . . . There is a real feeling of isolation and yet just that is taken as the source of power. (210)

This does not make the artist miraculously free of the world at war. After all, Alice sings the eternal poetry of childhood only when locked into an uncomfortable ring of dancing complicity with the satirized warmongers:

> Yet it is the frank selfishness of the brothers, who being little boys are horrid, are made into a satire on war, and will only give her the hands free from hugging each other, that forces her into the ring with them that produces eternity. Even here this puts a subtle doubt into the eternities open to the child. (209–10)

It is because there must always be subtle and less than subtle doubts put into the artist's relation to wartime culture that it becomes of the utmost importance self-protectively to defend the frank though oblique isolation of the poet from the dance of war. The poet can only hope to marry the Cheshire grin with the song of war if she can artificially make up her mind as precisely *not* including the real world of power, *not* including the unreal assumption of

[9] As with the 'pretence of jeering, such as people imagine puts a child at ease' (*SCW* 116).

class interests alien to the ways the mind can make anything up, i.e. within the known conventions of the class, in Empson's case, the aristocratic class, into which he was born and bred.

If the trick is to make up a child mind capable of satirical bite and a honestly suasive display of fresh and vivid feelings and senses which may magically create amnesties in divided natures, then one begins to see why Empson may have been attracted to Piaget's work—it seems sensible to argue indeed that he was reading Piaget for the Alice essay. Uses of the child cult after Freud and Wyndham Lewis, it could be argued, had to acknowledge, as an act of isolating self-protectiveness, the sexualization of the child persona at the latency period as well as the potential charge of intellectual infantilism and escapism, whilst at the same time preserving the political-satirical intuitive logic and emotional power afforded by the detached view of the child-critic: 'the sane man can take no other view of the world.'[10] Dodgson saw the child as intellectually important according to the current scientific dogma of the day, specifically the post-Darwinian view of the child combining ontogeny (the development of the individual embodied self) with phylogeny (the development of the species)[11]—in studying the child one could map the ways the human body preserves traces of the development of the human species from its most distant origins. For a twentieth-century view of the child, we see Empson combining a Freudian view of the child as incorporating at the dream level the basic human family and their warring instincts (Alice is mother, father, child) with a soft Marxist view: Alice is a child of her class and its conventions. What liberates Alice from Darwin for Dodgson was the practical good sense and sanity of her scientific-poetic post-Romanticism, inherited from Wordsworth and Coleridge. What liberates Alice for Empson is her capacity for magical logic, a view he inherits from Piaget.

[10] The child cult is discussed at length by Wyndham Lewis in the first book of *Time and Western Man* which critiques the Bergsonian infantilism of the work of modernists such as Stein and Joyce, also found in the attack on the baby language and childish forms of behaviour in the character of Satters in *The Childermass*. Lewis is clearly influencing Empson between the wars in his choice of subjects and in the forms of 'childish' speech patterns and beliefs he chose to defend. Empson also believed the child cult to be the last refuge of pastoral once Puritanism had developed in the upper and lower classes (*SVP* 17–18).

[11] The so-called recapitulation theory developed by Von Baer which Empson brilliantly finds at work when Alice emerges from the bath of tears to discover the menagerie of more primitive life forms: 'ontogeny then repeats phylogeny' (*SVP* 204).

The child, for Piaget, begins as an entirely selfish creature of her own desires (I'm thinking of Piaget's babies as versions of Alice): each talks as mere talking to herself, a quasi-magical dreaming of the world as fabricated by human beings for the satisfaction of those desires. This magical autism is transformed into a pre-causal egocentricity between 2–3 and 7–8, the age of the collective monologue. But importantly, and remarkably quickly, from 7–8 to 10, the child has not only learnt to adapt the monologue into creative dialogue with her elders and peers, but has begun to formulate her own astoundingly original form of playful logic.[12] It is a vital part of Piaget's argument in *The Child's Conception of Physical Causality*, however, that the child's egocentricity is not a stage the human mind might be happy to have abandoned, but a way of assimilating and understanding the world which has its own force.[13] In Piaget's terms, child logic is characterized by 'transduction', an animist, dynamic, substantialist form of reasoning from particulars, subject to no general law, unaware of relativist or rival points of view, blissfully and magically unaware, in short, of the 'abstraction of relations common to all the terms', but free to reason 'simply from particular to particular'.[14] Empson saw affinities between transduction in child logic and the relation of false identity of 'A is B'—dependent on 'first imputing and then interpreting'—as analysed in the 'Statements in Words' chapter of *Structure of Complex Words*. 'A is B' logical moves are observable in Freudian transference and in the kinds of associative thinking theorized by Levy-Bruhl—the move is transductive for, as Empson puts it, 'Piaget's children are doing it all the time' (*SCW* 42). Piaget himself uses Levy-Bruhl to promote the analogy between child logic and the magical thinking of the 'primitive mind' in *The Child's Conception of Physical Causality*, and in the final paragraph of *Judgement and Reasoning in the Child*.[15]

The child, for Piaget, is simultaneously 'both closer to immediate observation and further removed from reality' than the adult.[16] The child is content to

[12] It would have been important to Empson that Alice is 7–7½ in the Alice books, and therefore in the creative dialogue phase—he mentions her age in the *SVP* essay when discussing whether Alice is roguish in the books, or sentimentalized by the later Dodgson: 'It depends', he writes, 'what you expect of a child of seven.' For Empson, as a 7 year old, she is 'pert', 'the underdog speaking up for itself' (208).

[13] Jean Piaget, *The Child's Conception of Physical Causality* (London: Routledge & Kegan Paul, 1930).

[14] Ibid. 304

[15] Ibid. 196. Jean Piaget, *Judgement and Reasoning in the Child* (London: Routledge & Kegan Paul, 1929).

[16] Piaget, *Physical Causality*, 253.

adopt in her mind 'the crude forms of actuality as they are presented in observation', entirely sacrificing logical coherence 'to fidelity to fact'.[17] The world is constructed according to random associations of very powerfully observed phenomena which become magically causal:

The moon follows us, the clouds that go with the rain, the heaviness and lightness of floating bodies—all these are phenomenistic associations at the start, which later on lead the child to say: the moon moves along because I do, the clouds are the cause of rain, floating is determined either by heaviness or by lightness, etc.[18]

At the same time, 'the child is far further away from reality in his thought than we are':

Reality is still overgrown with subjective adherences: it is alive and artificial; words, dreams, and thought reside in external objects: the world is filled with forces. Phenomenistic relations themselves take place against a background of dynamism, either magical or animistic. Thus the fact that the moon follows us is immediately interpreted by means of pre-relations, one of which makes the child think that he has power over the moon, the other that the moon is interested in him.[19]

For Empson, the child constructs the world in making up her own mind, observing the world with a power adults have forgotten, and making the world up as a field of forces which have to do with her. This double point of view is made up of utter pre-logical fidelity to particulars and facts combined with a magical, animistic sense of the world as filled with forces which are both subject to the observer's power and interested in that point of view. Empson argues that it is only by preserving this childish view that any point of view at all could be said to exist.

The *Pastoral* Alice essay had been very clear that this split in disposition—between a child's potential and what adult culture actually enables the human mind to do in the world—is a Romantic notion, depending, Empson argues:

on a feeling, whatever may have caused that in its turn, that no way of building up character, no intellectual system, can bring out all that is inherent in the human spirit, and therefore that there is more in the child than any man has been able to keep. (*SVP* 208–9)

[17] Ibid. [18] Ibid. [19] Ibid. 253–4.

Empson repeats this argument in his inaugural lecture at the University of Sheffield in 1954, defending the child cult from a Wyndham Lewis-like adversary:

> It is what has been so often attacked in later years as Child-cult, the literary man pretending to be a child to make himself look sweet; but I think the people who attacked this didn't recognize the merit of the child cult when it is good, and that is, basically, that every man has to be trained to do one thing or another, and there was more in his original nature than any social arrangement can reasonably be expected to develop in him, so that the child, even in a good society, can make the grown man feel ignorant and narrow. (*SSS* 202–3)

It was equally important to Empson that this Romantic notion colours, inevitably, what constitute the literary artist's duties and responsibilities: 'the world of the adult made it hard to be an artist; and they kept a sort of tap-root going down to their experience as children' (*SVP* 209). Piaget's theory of child logic saved Dodgsonian pastoral from becoming fossilizedly Victorian, in other words enabled its potential evolution into twentieth-century thinking, without necessarily soap-boxing the genre into 1930s-style propagandizing as proletarian pastoral.

Piaget's child was no apolitical creature, though. Just as Alice's logical independence of mind gave Dodgson the freedom to indulge in an unsentimental satire on war, so did Piaget's theory of child thinking spark off manners of defensive logic in Empson which brought wartime responsibilities, artist's logic, and experiences tap-rooted in childhood together as a way both of imagining and writing within and counter to wartime culture.

The analogy between the development of the mind from autistic-magical point of view to adult socialized coordination of many points of view is always shadowed or accompanied, in Empson, by the history of the development of the construction of the semantic meanings of words: 'I am assuming that we build such words [as *sense* and *sensibility*] by a primitive, or anyway not specifically logical, process of thought, and I must be careful to avoid saying that this makes the thought expressed by them necessarily fallacious' (*SCW* 252). Such care is indebted to Piaget, I would argue—we can feel that Piaget form of carefulness throughout Empson, as in the typical turn from *Structure*: 'the feeling is not merely primitive or illogical, indeed, it keeps us in contact with reality' (*SCW* 318).

The belief preceded Piaget, of course, as we see if we look at the wry and respectful references to the half-unconscious functioning of child judgement in *Seven Types*; for example: 'It is ordinary experience that our minds work like this; and we can often see our way through a situation, as it were practically, when it would be extremely hard to separate out all the elements of the judgement. Most children can play catch, and few are good at dynamics' (*STA* 11). Piaget helped Empson to understand childish notions and thought process *as* logical in ways that precede the laws and norms of adult logic, the socializing conventions of which assimilate individual feelings and senses into classifiable and normative points of view. A poet who isolates himself from the world can reclaim the powers of observation and sensitivity to the world as filled with forces that are foundationally necessary for any possible resistance to and influence upon standardizing culture. Such isolation retrieves an individual point of view, countering culture's power to dissolve individual thought into its own machinery of coordinated points of view.

What is interesting in Empson's strategic use of Piaget is the sense of urgency about self-protectiveness and childish logic in the run-up to wartime. If points of view are likely to be dissolved in ordinary culture, then how much more so in the perceived propagandized machine of wartime government. If selflessness is necessary in defending the nation at war, then it becomes even more important to preserve this specific mode of the imagination (not an escapist but a transductive point of view) as that which the nation ought to be defending if it is to count as a free nation worth defending. Such egocentricity and magical illusion may be accused of infantilism and escapism, but in its Alice form can equally generate an artificial identity which preserves the poet's power to observe and satirize, power to influence a madly warring culture, to make that culture acknowledge this vital point about its own secret best interests: located in the child's point of view, preserved into adulthood in the poet's credences and benign imagination.[20]

That Empson was impressed by Piaget's demonstration of child logic of this kind is clear from the late use of Piaget in *The Structure of Complex Words*, specifically

[20] For an example of the ways Empson feels it always necessary to move beyond the oversimplification involved in infantilizing the 'primitive' towards a more humane and complex view of childish/primitive forms of egocentricity, see *SCW* chapter 'Honest Numbers': 'The Freudian view of the primitive gift, if you drop its infantilism to take a wider view of the naivety of our selfishness, becomes "to show that you are willing to take your pleasure in that person's company"; there is some element of generosity in all social pleasures' (217–18).

in the essay on the primitive mind. There he uses Piaget's account of a 'wind-breath' theory in *The Child's Conception of Physical Causality*, i.e. in Empson's words, 'a queer idea of "participation" between wind inside and outside the body' which led the children to say 'that wind is produced by man, God, breath, or machines'. The crucial point, though, is that the children are still 'quite clear about the *difference* between wind and breath'. Piaget's stress on the children's 'quasi-identifying of wind and breath from a vague magical belief that they have connections of cause' is more reasonably modest and true, he argues, than Barfield's oversimple identification of the double meanings of words such as *pneuma* with primitive mythical beliefs (*SCW* 377). It is Barfield's oversimplifying which generates the patronizing attitude towards the 'primitive' and the 'childish'. For Empson, 'what we want from "primitive" language, if that is to explain the development of complex words, is a process that may work at any time, and therefore among ourselves, though perhaps feebly' (377). Very close to the centre of Empsonian ethics is this turn against assumptions of superiority through the cheating impersonality of critical distance. Selfish condescension and secret pride are all too often the real motivations fuelling acts of oversimplification of the relations between observer and subject: we must be ethically involved in the subjects of our enquiries—the processes observed have to be felt as still at work 'among ourselves'.

And it is among ourselves that the child's logic may be a necessary resource in the impending conflict of the Second World War, precisely because the logic enables a sweet faith in the queer idea of participation between inside and outside so needful if men and women are to defend themselves and their world (thus defending their very freedom to imagine and to dream) from external forces.[21] One of Piaget's children, the $8\frac{1}{2}$-year-old 'Ris', is interrogated 'by interview' on her beliefs about the origin of dreams:

Where do dreams come from?
From the night.
Where is the dream when you are dreaming?
In my bed.
Where?

[21] That the external forces might in certain cases be largely childish bugbears conjured by propaganda was less true then in the gathering storm of the Second World War than it is in more contemporary situations one could cite. Doubtless Empson's Alice would have seen through to this basic difference too.

In the room quite near, beside me.
Where does the dream come from?
From the night.
Should I see it, if I was near you?
No.
And do you see it?
No.
Then what is it? . . . Is it made of something or not of anything?
Of something.
Of paper?
(laughing) *No.*
Of what?
Of words.
And what are words?
Talking [en voix].
Where does the talking in the dream come from?
From the sky.
Where in the sky? . . . How is it made in the sky? . . . Does the dream come of itself or does something send it?
It comes by itself.
Why do we dream?
Because we think of something.

Ris's view is evidently advanced. But she identifies thought with speech [*la voix*] and continues to believe the dream comes from without:

What is talking [*la voix*] made of?
Air.
Where does it come from?
The air.
And the dream?
From the sky.[22]

One of the curious strengths of Piaget's children lies in the magical confidence they have that internal voices come from without, and that dreams are external phenomenon. This queer idea of participation testifies to a touching belief in the testable qualities of the outside world which helps to locate their own point of view, their own imaginative processes *out there in the sky.*[23] And

[22] The commentary is Piaget's. Italicized French indicates original formulation. *The Child's Conception of the World* (1929; St Albans: Paladin, 1973), 117–18.

[23] See 'Sense in *The Prelude*' for Empson on Wordsworth's exploration of the same trick of the child's mind (*SCW*, in particular 298).

it is this capacity to externalize self-evidently subjective states of mind which Empson mimes in 'Your Teeth' with the extended figure of the poet addressing the star, hoping one day to get a response, like Ris hearing voices from the sky. The reference to the star is also, of course, a wry response to Olaf Stapledon again—Stapledon's best-selling Wellsian scientific romance, *Star Maker*, had been published in 1937 to considerable acclaim. In the novel, the protagonist is transported telepathically throughout the universe, visiting planets, stars, aliens, and parallel universes, in a Dantescan-Miltonic tour of the heavens. His first intimation of the mystery of the universe's communication system occurs in the opening pages, on a hill in the suburbs, sick of the delirium of the world, struck by the vision of one star in the sky:

> Overhead, obscurity unveiled a star. One tremulous arrow of light, projected how many thousands of years ago, now stung my nerves with vision, and my heart with fear. For in such a universe as this what significance could there be in our fortuitous, our frail, our evanescent community?
>
> But now irrationally I was seized with a strange worship, not, surely of the star, that mere furnace which mere distance falsely sanctified, but of something other, which the dire contrast of the star and us signified to the heart. Yet what, what could thus be signified?[24]

As he travels, though, he discovers that his irrational feeling is confirmed by a vaster web of community: even nebulae and star systems can 'think', communicating through the wide web of cosmic telepathy, a network leading to the Star Maker himself. The novel is pointedly pacifist too, with visions of universal war in certain systems and universes announcing a potential world war in the skies. Empson's child and star offer a Piagetian response to Stapledon's star travel—you don't need a 'hypertelescopic imagination' to see what you see in scientific romance[25]—just *be* as a child can be, and talk to the stars of your choice. Evanescent community starts with the confidence of Ris dreaming from the sky, Alice talking to the ghost of her cat in the tree. Such irrationality is the basis, Piaget and Empson argue, of all subsequent rational thinking, of all kinds of kind imagination, of the very possibility of community with other minds.

The more interesting inner world is consubstantial with the world that is the case for the participatory intelligence. Ris is like Empson in her sturdily

[24] Olaf Stapledon, *Star Maker* (1937; London: Victor Gollancz, 1999), 2. [25] Ibid. 6.

logical-magical belief that her own mind bears some kind of relation, some kind relation to the real heavens above; like him perhaps because that is how poets dream of response from the absent, future-tense perhaps imaginary kind reader. But also he is like her in his defence of dreamwork and imaginative logic as a real form of understanding—for clearly in Kantian terms we are always at work half-creating what we perceive. It is also arguable that Empson's defence of the childish is itself a response to his difficult and complex relationship to the Auden group: at once admiring of their preparedness for war, and sceptical of their infantile boyishness, equated with 'playing at the child' in 'Just a Smack at Auden', as John Haffenden has shown in his notes to the poem (*CP* 351–6).[26] Piaget enables Empson somehow to salvage his own forms of intuitive logic as childlike and then to move towards a measure of war-preparedness without the wracked pacifist reaction of a Stapledon. Or rather to prove, at the same difficult level of engagement, that a childish statement of the real and generous connections between the sky of the world and the mind's deep feeling (as from an arrow of light stinging nerves with vision, and hearts with fear) might simultaneously avoid infantilism, substantiate a zone of free thinking worth defending, and liberate an active point of view (armed to the teeth) helpful to all defenders.

In a world set to destroy itself in a second world war through the unleashing of lethal polar enmities—'The poles define the surface and it rolls | Between their warring virtues' (*CP* 68)—the arts can hope to retain 'a steady hold on the controls' by just this act of childish faith in the world's kind responses, though seeming to evade the world by entering the world of dream. Just as Ris's dreams plot and then sustain a belief in the kindness of the sky, so poetry, especially in a time of warring evils, must plot and sustain a belief in the star's reply, without succumbing to the gloomy scientist romance of a Stapledon—rather as a poet assuming the crazy confidence that the public will understand his foreign forgotten language of the feelings, senses, close intuitive logic. Either that or condemn the adult population to the desperate

[26] Cf. Empson's 1940 review of Auden's *Another Time*: 'you're afraid on every page that a horrid false note of infantilism will poke up its head' (*CP* 356). And Empson's comment on the Auden: 'the work of Auden in preparing the public mind for the war to come, which was coming, had been extremely important' (*CP* 354). Significantly, it is Leavis's criticism of the Auden group ('that they're all talking like public schoolboys pretending to be workers') which Empson remembers. The triangle of Auden-Leavis-Empson which is set up in 'Teeth' is shadowing this other debate with the same triangle involved.

wit and unreal cheerfulness of survivors of the wreck in the last lines of 'Teeth', a beautiful anticipation of the Blitz spirit. It is a child's transductive logic, reasoning simply from particular to particular, capable of reading the sky as filled with forces connected to her dreams and dynamic with her own power too, which might indeed *enable* something resembling a Blitz spirit, free of propaganda, self-protective and defensive to the teeth, constituting a popular front against the enemy of such imagination.

As Empson observed in that other great poem about the importance of preserving a child's faith in its magical relations to an unchanging world, courage in an encroaching wartime has a lot to do with the child's ability both to stay in the room and speak from the sky. Empson had found courage enough to stay in China as a form of duty to his country whilst all those who ought to have stayed, the sympathizers, had cut and run. It is Alice's and Ris's simple, complex faith, logical and unsuperstitious, not escapist (like the false friends scuttling home) but also not escaping the implications of the queer idea of participation in one's nation's war so far from home, under other skies:

> Verse has been lectured to a treat
> Against Escape and being blah.
> It struck me trying not to fly
> Let them escape a bit too far.
> It is an aeronautic feat
> Called soaring, makes you quite a star
> (The Queen and Alice did) to try
> And keep yourself just where you are.
>
> ('Autumn in Nan-Yüeh', *CP* 93)

If the point is that it is somehow childish to believe you can be in flight and stuck in bed, then such childishness may in fact be much truer to the ways of the imagination as rooted in the real world than the fake platitudes shaping the slur identifying metaphysical modernist poetry with escapism. Those platitudes, Empson argues, are potentially more escapist in the (war) poet's sense than the soaring aeronautics of Alice on the chessboard. Because they shrink the mind down to a tiny world circumscribed by 'adult' logic of rational time and space, the real world of dark imaginations with their flying machines dispensing bombs is flown away from. It takes a child to be terrified of the sky. An adult can forget what the sky means and snuggle down self-appeased into the bomb shelter.

Similarly, a poet can participate in England's war just as well in Nan-Yüe as in London—because, childishly and logically too, she dreams it is the same dangerous sky she soars in. The world is full of forces. Written in jaunty Audenese, the poem may well also hold Auden up to judgement, a poet soon to be under suspicion too of running away, subject to flight's temptations in a fearful time. To escape war is impossible, however, the poem tells us, to the poet who is still in touch with the soaring, unbeheadable logic of the child, who knows, as the poet continues to know, the *difference* between staying and flying, yet stays though flying still, staying true to the aeronautic freedoms of the transductive imagination, its forces, views, and vivid particulars. To stay is to face the impending conflict with the fragile but true resources of the imagination still active along the tap-roots of the mind, there where the child still abides: to face it with Alice's 'cool courage' (*SVP* 233).

4

C. Hatakeyama and W.E.

Peter Robinson

I

When the facsimile edition of *The Waste Land* drafts was published in 1971, William Empson remarked in his review that 'The poem is inherently a mystery; I would never have believed that the Symbolist programme could be made to work at all, if it had not scored a few resounding triumphs, such as this' (*UB* 189). His problem of belief about French poetic theories from the later nineteenth century was fed by other beliefs about justifying critical or satirical views in literature. He explained: 'Being thus dubious about symbolism, I was one of the mugs who hoped that the story of the poem would be unveiled when the lost bits were restored; and I do find that the Introduction to this edition of the bits lets the story peep out' (189). Why the occluded story should be of importance to Empson is clarified later when, commenting on 'What are the roots that clutch, what branches grow | Out of this stony rubblish?',[1] he notes:

> a touch of the craving to scold may be observed in the poem here, with its assumption that the poet is nobler and purer than anything he contemplates. The French writers

[1] T. S. Eliot, *The Waste Land: A Facsimile and Transcript of the Original Drafts Including the Annotations of Ezra Pound*, ed. Valerie Eliot (London: Faber and Faber, 1971), 135.

who invented Symbolism seem never to have thought of turning it to the uses of a cats' tea-party; but then, if Eliot was imitating Dickens, he was bound to scold, and Dickens would have shown no mercy to a Hapsburg courtier. The difference is that Dickens had a plot, which allowed him to show adequate reasons for his scolding; it is true that the plot is often perfunctory—no admirer of *Oliver Twist* would try to detail the itinerary of the villain; but to scold without even a residual plot, as a Symbolist, is bound to feel self-regarding. (*UB* 191)[2]

You can justify the attitudes expressed in a work, however extreme or unlikely, through a narrative, or narrative-like, understanding of what is motivating them. The story of *The Waste Land*, in Empson's intuitive piecing together, turns out to be a family plot about conflicts involving T. S. Eliot's parents, and particularly his father, over the poet's decision to remain in England and marry.[3] This is, as *Using Biography*, the title of the book that collected the piece, underlines, a tale linking the action of the poetry to the author's life at the time of composition. The polemic of the last book Empson published in his lifetime was then, in short, that the rumoured death of authors and their intentions had been exaggerated. It was time to give our sleeping beauties the kiss of life.[4]

This being the belief of old Empson, there is reason to take heart from researches into the complex relations between life and art that can humanize literary studies by inviting a greater understanding of art's capacity to give pattern and significance to experience by allowing contrasts between the shaped artefact and the lives and contacts from which it emerged. The writer of *Using Biography* would, then, have welcomed such contributions as John Haffenden's in his exemplary notes and other apparatus to *The Complete Poems*, which also let stories peep out, and, with much candour, in his biography of this emblematic poet and literary critic.

One of the mysteries surrounding Empson's poetry involves explanations for why he stopped writing it. The main candidates to date have been those offered by Christopher Ricks and, in response, by the poet himself. Ricks thought that it was marrying and producing children that effectively extinguished the need to write verse.[5] The poetry had been written to address fearful contradictions

[2] See also the 1963 title essay in *A* 167–73.

[3] See *UB* 192–6, and Eliot, *Waste Land*, pp. xv–xvi, for the relevant passages from Valerie Eliot's Introduction.

[4] I reviewed the book: 'Family Affairs', *English*, 34: 150 (Autumn 1985), 270–8.

[5] See Christopher Ricks, 'William Empson: The Images and the Story', *The Force of Poetry* (Oxford: Oxford University Press, 1984), 189, 191 especially. Evidence connecting the decision to have children and war work is in 'Orwell at the BBC' (*A* 499).

involving such experiences, and when the fears had been overcome so had the urge. As an explanation this seems psychologically mechanical, and, at the same time, not sufficiently deep. The offered match between the skillfully explored subjects of some poems and their motivation seems too neat. The presenting symptom for the poetry as evidenced and explicated by Ricks is assumed to be the causal nexus; but there can be no guarantee that the disappearance of the apparent symptom means the end of the cause, should there be but one. Empson effectively rejected this explanation by avoiding his psychology. It was doing war work at the BBC that made him stop—and, by the by, his not liking attempted poems being written at the time.[6]

If I am inclined to believe the testimony of the poet, this hardly implies that Ricks's reading of the poetry is not illuminating, or that Empson's explanation wholly convinces. Other poets have written through bad patches; and Empson's understanding view in September 1940 of Thomas Hardy's poetry was that, however poor in individual cases, he needed it all to get through (*A* 421–3). Empson's colleague Louis MacNeice did propaganda broadcasting at the BBC, and kept producing verse.[7] At the end of his letter to Ricks, Empson comments: 'Reading this over, I see it is too glib, and some other process was probably at work earlier to make the poetry I hammered out strike me as unfit for publication' (*CP* 127–8). That sounds more like it: his critical intelligence was making him doubt the quality and suitability for publication of his poetry, a process that had begun at least five years before decisively resolving his conflicts about parenthood or marriage. Empson's afterthought, his suggestion of 'some other process probably at work earlier' (suspecting that his socio-political explanation may be, finally, as incomplete an explanation as Ricks's about fearing to bring children into the world) promises evidence for this 'other process' in the later poetry—and with reflexivity: what Empson 'hammered out' could 'strike' him back.[8]

Rather than retell the twice-told tale of Empson's epistolary exchanges with Chiyoko Hatakeyama, I attempt here to look again at issues surrounding Empson's letting poetry go—in the light of his ideas about scolding and story,

[6] See Empson's 19 Jan. 1975 letter to Ricks responding to the first publication of this essay, printed as Appendix 3 in *CP* 126–8.

[7] See John Stallworthy, *Louis MacNeice* (London: Faber and Faber, 1995), chs. 17–18, especially 291–2, 304.

[8] For other versions, see Christopher Norris, *William Empson and the Philosophy of Literary Criticism* (London: Athlone Press, 1978), 13–34, and Richard Pollott, 'The Poet's Repose: William Empson and the Faces of the Buddha', *PN Review*, 32: 3 (Jan.–Feb. 2006), 54–6.

and as illustrated by his versions of the three poems by C. Hatakeyama whose originals had not been seen, let alone published, before I was lucky enough to help unearth them on 17 May 2003.[9] That the story of Empson's correspondence and collaboration with this Japanese schoolteacher and amateur poet should connect with his views of T. S. Eliot's masterpiece can be indicated by a remark from one of his letters to her also discovered with the three poems. When sending her 'The Fool' from London on 9 July 1935, Empson wrote under the text that 'Perhaps the main difference I want to make in translating is to concentrate the ideas into fewer words—a thing present day English poetry is very anxious to do, perhaps too much' (cited in *WE1* 341). In that 'very anxious' and that brief second thought, 'perhaps too much', can be sensed his views about 'the Symbolist programme' and the story needed to give reasons for emotions and views compacted into the lines of barely plotted lyrics.

Empson was already thinking about the ethical problems of lyric poetry and its compression in the years when he became acquainted with Chiyoko Hatakeyama. In the magazine printing of 'Aubade', a poem which Empson noted had nothing to do with her (as the manuscripts discovered in North Japan and my *TLS* article amply demonstrated), the poet included a number of lines later cut for the book publication, which focus on precisely the expressions of attitude in poetry without sufficient contextual information, or story, to justify them or even make a decently balanced case:

> This is unjust to her without a prose book.
> A lyric from a fact is bound to cook.
> It was more grinding; it was much more slow.
> But still the point's not how much time it took.
> It seemed the best thing to be up and go.
>
> (*CP* 319)

There are reasons for hoping that in best cases it ain't necessarily so that 'A lyric from a fact is bound to cook'; but certainly when the prose book, a biography

[9] The story was first told in my 'Very Shrinking Behaviour', *Times Literary Supplement* (18 July 2003), 13–15. The insightful retelling is by John Haffenden in *WE1* 331–45, using material also absorbed from an unpublished longer version of my 'C. Hatakeyama [trans. W.E.]', *PN Review*, 31: 2 (Nov.–Dec. 2004), 55–60. The present chapter adapts the central passages from my second published article (ones not made use of in Haffenden's biography), but is substantially different in relating these three translations to Empson's abandonment of poetry, or, equally likely, to its abandonment of him.

or annotated edition of the poems, say, has been published, then readers are in a better position to reflect upon relationships between the raw situation and the cooked lyric. This cut verse hints at the possibility that problems with story, explanation, justification, and lyric compression are at the heart of Empson's stopping writing poems.

Finally, the third of Hatakeyama's lyrics, 'The Small Bird to the Big', is itself a farewell to writing poetry in English—though this story could only peep out once the original from which the translation indirectly derives had been discovered.[10] It is thus curiously related to one of Empson's mysterious poems, the one he said himself was about 'stopping writing poetry'—a phrase that effectively equivocates about destiny and choice, about whether this stopping was suffered or decided. Written during the Second World War, 'Let It Go' observes that 'The contradictions cover such a range' and 'You don't want madhouse and the whole thing there' (*CP* 99). It's always an idea to take poetry literally, at least at first. Empson's reasons for letting it go must have been that *they do*, and *you don't*. It's not difficult to appreciate from our own experience and Empson's work that 'The contradictions' could 'cover such a range'; but the wartime composition of the poem would suggest that these contradictions also related to global conflicts. Yet what means 'madhouse', a singular countable noun without an article, and what was 'the whole thing there'?

II

On 8 July 1934 William Empson left Tokyo on the NYK line Kashima Maru after his three years in Japan. While there, he had corresponded with a teacher at Hirosaki Girl's High School called Chiyoko Hatakeyama (1902–82).[11] In her early thirties, unmarried partly due to the misfortune of having lost her right arm at eight years old, she had developed an ambition to write poetry in English after studying Anglo-American Literature at Miyagi Jo Gakko, a

[10] Hatakeyama did not give up writing poetry in Japanese, though she did make no further attempts to have it published. 'Sekishu e no Banka' (Elegy to my Left Hand), a longer poem not yet translated into English, was written in the autumn of 1974. The Japanese text, together with other poems and essays, has recently appeared. Chiyoko Hatakeyama, *Sekishu e no Banka* (*Elegy to my Left Hand*) (Tokyo: Shupansha, 2005), contains an introductory essay by Chikako Saito.

[11] Hatakeyama's side of this correspondence, including all the poems that Empson saw and commented on, was published in the *Miyagi Gakuin Yearbook*, 10 (2003), 67–92.

women's college founded by missionaries in Sendai. Empson had been asked to brush up her English and comment on the poems by Hiroshi Hirai, a friend of hers and a student of Empson's at Tokyo University. Hatakeyama and Empson had met, briefly, on 26 March 1934 at his home in Shirokane, Sankocho, Tokyo, and then in the Ginza and Ueno on the following day. After his departure from her country, Hatakeyama made efforts to keep in touch with the person she saw as her poetry teacher. Two of her letters did find their way from the north of Japan to Empson in London. After receiving the second, he was moved to compose some lines more or less his own, and pen a reply.

The three-page letter dated 9 July 1935 sent from Marchmont Street begins by explaining that he had already received a letter from Hatakeyama in the north of Japan, but thought he would 'let the matter drop' (cited in *WE1* 338). She had evidently sent a second letter, including an English version of a poem that had first been drafted in Japanese. Empson enclosed the short poem called 'The Fool', because she had sent 'such a good poem', he explains, that 'I wrote one of my own from it which I enclose.' The poem she sent was her English translation of 'Baka' ('Fool'). What follows, in the absence of Hatakeyama's own rendering that has not survived, is a literal translation from the discovered Japanese original of 'such a good poem':

> A great fool who cannot hate the others,
> look!
> He strides through the town.
> Eyes sagacious-looking
> Mouths distorted by common sense,
> the object of their ridicule
> is just his individual body.
>
> As if there were no vault of heaven,
> as if there were no world beyond the sight,
> people's eyes and mouths
> demand an object to despise,
> to set in the frame of their common sense.
>
> Eyes swarming like maggots,
> lips laughing like poison flowers,
> look!
> Notwithstanding these, among them
> a great fool is strolling around.
>
> For him, the eyes of people are bright stars,

to his ears which are unclean
the derisive laughter sounds like delicate music,
and he goes on in dream-visions
staring far away beyond the sky.

The fool who doesn't know how to hate the others,
look!
He strides through the town.

8 November 1934[12]

After quoting this text, Haffenden comments: 'Empson felt so stimulated that he could not resist tinkering with it; he presently refashioned it as his own: tighter, more succinct, though scarcely less gnomic' (*WE1* 340). But Empson's acknowledged compression of the text she sent to him makes his version a good deal more gnomic. Hatakeyama's lines are clearly about a social misfit, an innocent or even idiotic person. 'Baka' is the word for 'stupid'—and it can be used with prejudicial force in certain situations. The ordinary people of the town, with their reassuring sagacity and common sense, confirm their social solidarity by having an outcast to mock. 'Baka' is an account of an unusual individual's defence against prejudicial group behaviour.

The idea of the poem, as with all three that Hatakeyama sent Empson, is to have her art transform an oppressive predicament into a survivable state of mind. Her fool is granted a striking role reversal. The townspeople are mocking and exclusive despite the existence, for the poet, of a heaven beyond the sight—we being said to be equal in the eyes of God. The eyes and lips surrounding the fool all mean him ill; but, like a holy fool, he does not have the animus to hate those that hate him. His state of mind—whether innocent or godlike—sees the beauty even in those that mock him. The paratactic structure and reiteration of Hatakeyama's poem, returning to a variant of its opening lines at the end, affirms that this is a regular and daily condition, a common experience for the fool who must live in a small town surrounded by such people.

Nor is it difficult to suspect the poem of having an autobiographical theme that has been distanced by identification with the experiences of this fool.

[12] For the Japanese text, and a commentary by Chikako Saito, see Hatakeyama, *Sekishu e no Banka*, 102–4. 'Baka' is the correct transliteration of the title, not 'Baku' as in *WE1* 339. Haffenden kindly attributes the literal translation to myself 'with Chikayo Saito and Eichi Hara'. The spelling of the Japanese given names should be 'Chikako' and 'Eiichi'. The translation is in fact, as noted in my articles, by Chikako Saito with help from Hara and myself.

The fact that it's the body of the fool being treated with ridicule, rather than his mental state, indicates one source of the poem's feeling—the poet's loss of her right arm in childhood. The fool's way of dealing with his enemies, turning the ugly into something beautiful, has much in common with the activities of artists—who are frequently made to feel outsiders in provincial societies—and with the spiritual powers of Christianity, in which believers are called to love their enemies and do good to those that hate them. In the nationalistic atmosphere of 1930s Japan, with its re-emphasized Shinto cult of the emperor as a god, the spiritual values of Christianity were those of socially marginal people whose religious sympathies were aligned with the 'foreign devils'. Furthermore, the reiterative structure of Hatakeyama's Japanese poem can express a dogged commitment to the values shown in the behaviour of the fool. The distancing of its expression by means of the 'baka' character also protects the poet from exposure—an observation only underlined by her Japanese poem's remaining unpublished until 2003 in all but its shortened and recast version by Empson:

> Describe the Fool who knows
> All but his foes.
> Wading through tears striding the covered sneers
> And against tide, he goes.
>
> Delighting in the freedom of those bounds
> Your scorn and even your reason are his aid.
> It is an absolute health that will not heal his wounds.
> Wisdom's the charger mounts him above shade,
>
> Hanged by suspense and eternally delayed.
> 'Your eyes are corpse-worms;
> Your lips poison-flowers.'
> They become stars, the eyes he thus transforms.
> All the lips' whispers are cool summer showers.
>
> (*CP* 71)

This is one of Empson's in that it characteristically seeks to condense narrated experience into resonantly ambiguous, aphoristic summations. While some of these are elucidated by the Japanese poem from which they derive ('Your scorn and even your reason are his aid'), others remain tantalizing. 'Wisdom's the charger mounts him above shade, | Hanged by suspense and eternally delayed' appears to work with the ambiguities of 'mounts' (horse-riding, or stamp collecting), so wisdom both rides him and exhibits him in the daylight, while subjecting him to a perpetual postponement, a hanging around, like an execution with rope, but this then proves the making of the Fool. Such a reading is easier to intuit from Empson's condensed phrases using the literal version of 'Baka' as a guide. In his letter to Hatakeyama, her translator is absolutely clear that he won't alter his text even if she says there are things in it she didn't mean. The status of Empson's 'The Fool' is made explicit by his claiming it as a poem of his own. Whatever she intended, he is sticking to his version.[13]

It's tempting to think that Hatakeyama might have been inspired by a Shakespearean character, given her practical familiarity with *Lear* (having played the part of the King in a fully staged English version at university, and written a poem called 'The Storm'). Despite the fact that Japanese has another word for this figure, her poem does imitate the theatrical reversal whereby it is the Fool in *Lear* who is allowed to express hard truths. If her poem has anything to do with the play she took part in, her title may be remembering the behaviour of the King—who, with the division of the kingdom, is rather a 'Fool who knows | All but his foes'. Yet, all things considered, the addition of a capital letter for 'Fool' in the collected versions of the text introduces a theatrical sense probably not intended by the Japanese poet. 'Baka' nevertheless contains phrases authorizing Empson's 'poison-flowers'. So it may be Hatakeyama who recalled Keats's 'Isabella; or The Pot of Basil' or Tennyson's *Maud*—sources for the lines in Haffenden's note for *The Collected Poems* (*CP* 324).

III

The final paragraph of his 9 July letter makes it clear how Empson thought he and Hatakeyama might continue to collaborate on a book of her poems rephrased by him (*WE1* 338–9). The evidence of Empson's oeuvre shows that Hatakeyama did attempt to respond with new poems for the proposed volume of translations whose surviving trace is the inclusion of the three poems attributed to her in *The Gathering Storm*. Hatakeyama sent two, or perhaps three, more pieces in addition to 'The Fool' during June 1936. One of these was 'Hankyo' ('Echo'):

[13] 'You see how we stand—if you didn't mean it I don't mean to alter my translation' (*WE1* 340–1).

Suddenly, a black shadow ran off.
It was my bad luck.

When he dug lines in my forehead,
when he stole the oil from my hair
with which to dye his own robe
I did giggle.
When he squeezed tears from my eyes
I would quietly close them and smile.
When he pierced my heart with a needle,
laughing, I would suck the gushing blood.
Perhaps finally that man was disgusted.

Suddenly, the black shadow ran off

I laughed out loud.
Thereupon
from mountains, from fields, from heaven
in every direction
my voice
came back ten-fold

April 1936[14]

This poem is also about how to address misfortune. If in the case of 'Baka' it was being considered different by small town people, here it is the personal sense of injustice in what has befallen the speaker that must be treated. Here too, a trace of Hatakeyama's childhood calamity can be sensed in the role of the speaker's shadow—one way that you can be reminded of your appearance without the aid of a mirror. This is perhaps why the shadow is her bad luck. Hatakeyama also recorded a nightmare in her diary during February 1929, one including a persecutory black shadow.[15]

Another possible source for 'Hankyo' is Ralph Hodgson's 'Thrown' from *The Last Blackbird and Other Lines* (1907). It too is a poem considering how bad fortune can be turned to advantage by an author:

I'm down, good Fate, you've won the race;
Bite deep and break a tooth in me;

[14] For the Japanese original, and a commentary by Chikako Saito, see Hatakeyama, *Sekishu e no Banka*, 168–70.

[15] Detail provided by Naoko Hatakeyama, whose help and kindness on numerous occasions I gratefully acknowledge.

> Now spit your poison in my face,
> And let me be;
> Leave me an hour and come again
> With insults new and further pain.
>
> For of your tooth I'll make a pen,
> And of your slaver ink, and will
> I bring a joy to being then
> To race you still:
> A laughing child with feathered heels
> Who shall outspeed your chariot wheels.[16]

These lines also invite the opponent to inflict suffering, to do his worst, precisely because this is what will be used to defeat him. Hatakeyama's poem shares with Hodgson's both the idea of cruelty transformed, and of running. Her work too contains unusual representations of a fortitude that could derive from Eastern or Western traditions, but bears resemblances to Jesus's teaching his followers to turn the other cheek. The speaker confronts her bad luck by seeking to enjoy it, or at least appear to do so. Building towards the masochistic image of the needle and the heart's blood, the poem's speaker attributes the shadow's running away to its being disgusted by this apparently perverse behaviour. The turn of the poem is given by the extraordinary image of the echo, which carries back to the speaker her triumph at having seemed to defeat her bad luck. The multiplication of the laughter in the echo could be considered mocking or ironic, as if it were now turned against the speaker, suggesting that this sense of success is an illusion—yet for the Japanese poem this would have to be counted a reader interpretation. Empson's version, however, builds such an idea into the translation (either because Hatakeyama had suggested it in her English version, or because the translator assumed the echo signified self-mockery).

As Haffenden pointed out in his note, Empson's translation was called 'Echo' in *Contemporary Poetry and Prose* no. 7, November 1936—a detail that helped in locating the original among Hatakeyama's surviving papers. Here is 'The Shadow', as it was then titled, when published in *The Gathering Storm*:

> It caught my eye, my shadow, as it ran,
> My bad luck, and it had a plan.

[16] Ralph Hodgson, *Collected Poems* (London: Macmillan, 1961), 35. Hatakeyama was an acquaintance of Hodgson and his wife. A greeting card sent to them by her for New Year 1938 has survived among his papers at Yale. I am grateful to John Hatcher for sharing this information.

Clearly new friends for play
Were what it wanted, since it went away.
I had often giggled when
It dug lines in my forehead,
Or stole oil from my hair to dye its gown.
Feeling it drive its needle through my heart
I had often laughed and enjoyed licking the blood.
You want to please your pets. I began
To fear it was disgusted, since it ran;

Unprepared on laughing to hear rise
Tenfolded echoes, scattering mimicries,
Come from the hills and fields and the far skies.

(*CP* 72)

Empson's translation is evidently much closer to the Japanese original than is 'The Fool'. Here he recasts a fairly close rendering of Hakeyama's Japanese. But there are differences. The translation attributes variant motives to the shadow, and these come from the formal obligation to put the poem into an approximation of rhyming couplets—a form Empson had suggested she practise in an undated letter from 1934.[17] Perhaps this form derives from Hatakeyama's lost translation. The shadow, which is still 'my bad luck', has a plan to get new friends. It is as if the speaker doesn't want contact with others, but her shadow does. The masochistic behaviour of the speaker is preserved in Empson's version; but the ordering of the information muffles the sense that this odd behaviour is done in direct response to what the shadow does, and is therefore an instance of a Christian resistance to misfortune, or to one's enemies. The distinctly Empsonian 'You want to please your pets' in 'The Shadow' has no source in 'Hankyo'. It is the most decisive intervention in preventing the responses of the speaker from seeming to be linked directly to the bad behaviour of the luck. The shadow, one's bad luck, has been transformed into a domestic creature that the speaker needs to indulge. All this softens the quite grim extremity of Hatakeyama's poem. Empson's word 'mimicries' also seems an addition without equivalent in the Japanese version. These echoes strangely answer the 'unprepared' speaker.

In their handling of variable line-lengths and semi-regular rhyming patterns, Empson's three translations are expert instances of compacted lyric writing in

[17] See *WE1* 333.

a mode that he didn't find occasion to exercise when composing on his own materials. His short, unrhymed, free-verse poems ('Note on Local Flora', 'The Beautiful Train', and 'Manchouli', for instance) have a more prosaic terseness, and when he uses regular metres and rhymes he is at his best when working on a larger scale. The final three lines of 'The Shadow'—with that poised final spondee 'far skies'—have a perfectly sure touch. Empson appears to be all but deleting the Christian dimension from Hatakeyama's poems, while making them more intriguing in their motivations. His version of her 'Echo' balances anguish and humour with a rhymed and cadenced assurance. This gives 'The Shadow' an aptly echoing close with its 'rise . . . mimicries . . . and . . . far skies'.

IV

'A little bird's soliloquy' is Hatakeyama's name for what Empson called 'The Small Bird to the Big'—but, since there are no articles in Japanese and what follows is not Hatakeyama's version, a more neutrally literal title might be 'Little bird's soliloquy'. Her manuscript draft is followed by a note that confirms the dedication of the poem to Empson implied in the fragment of a covering letter to him that survived among her papers:[18]

Fly high,
great hawk,
fly high, fly far and away
over mountains of night
into the eternal day.
From the sky it is your eye
views the world shown by the sun's audacious light
and the secret the moon tells in whispers.

It is the very eye small birds cower before.
When I hear the flutter of your wings above my head,
poor thing, I fold my wings,
hide with a shudder behind a twig
and listen to the sound.

But, when
beyond doubtful smoke over mountains,

[18] See *WE1* 342.

defying damp winds that ruffle skin and hair,
your wings magnificently wave,
from my eyes that push aside weakness and fear
flow tears of joy
and the sun shines over them.

Fly high, come, fly aloft,
great hawk,
my thought too will at least reach with your wings
to the place where you unlock the gates of Paradise
and pour light upon this shadowy globe.

August 1935

(Now that I am going to abandon writing poetry in English I would like to wish all the best for the bright future of my teacher W.E. I dedicate this to him.)[19]

Her note makes it possible to understand far better the relationship between the two birds in the translation. Empson's revision of the title, avoiding the namby-pamby adjective 'little' and making it less theatrical, may also be discreetly acknowledging the dedication's interpretive point. There is a copy of the first edition of *Seven Types of Ambiguity* in the Hatakeyama bookshelves, and her papers refer to the fact that she had read the work. At the start of chapter five, verses four to six of Shelley's 'To a Skylark' are cited. In Hatakeyama's copy of Q's *The Oxford Book of English Verse* (1930 printing), a slip of paper still marked the pages for 'To a Skylark' when I opened it in the family home.

'The Small Bird to the Big' may, then, have been influenced by Shelley's poem and Empson's debate with T. S. Eliot in *Seven Types of Ambiguity*:

The poem was probably written under the influence of the Keats *Nightingale* Ode, and for it to seem straightforward one must hold the main tenets of the Romantics. The skylark, I should have said before, is a very precise symbol of Shelley's view of the poet; it rises higher and higher, straight upwards, alone, always singing, always in effort, till becoming exhausted somewhere out of sight of the normal world it tumbles back in silence, and resumes a humble, isolated, and invisible existence somewhere in the middle of a field. (*STA* 188)

This passage, in turn, is a response to T. S. Eliot's conversation in Cambridge from February 1926. Ronald Schuchard notes in his Introduction to *The*

[19] For the Japanese original, and a commentary by Chikako Saito, see Hatakeyama, *Sekishu e no Banka*, 141–3.

Varieties of Metaphysical Poetry (1993), Eliot's Clark and Turnbull Lectures, that 'At the coffee-circle following Lecture VI, Empson also listened well to Eliot's discussion of Shelley's careless use of imagery in "To a Skylark" and in a chorus from *Hellas*. Four years later, the attentive Empson reconstructed the discussion in his *Seven Types of Ambiguity* (1930).' Schuchard concludes: 'Thus did Eliot unwittingly impress his critical imagination on Richards' dauntless student during the coffee meetings.'[20] An echo of that conversation over coffee had, some ten years later, reached as far as north-eastern Japan.

Hatakeyama divides the characteristic image of a striving Romantic poet into two different birds. One of them, the Empson hawk, is encouraged to rise higher and higher, to lead the way for lesser creatures, as, meanwhile, the small bird, Hatakeyama, is hiding below—'a humble, isolated, and invisible existence somewhere in the middle of a field' (a rice field, as it were). Shelley's second stanza has 'Higher still and higher | From the earth thou springest' and his fourth, cited by Empson, has 'Like a star of heaven, | In the broad daylight | Thou art unseen, but yet I hear thy shrill delight—'. Hatakeyama's poem invokes a rising: 'Fly up and away, great hawk, | To the eternal day of the abyss, | Belittling the night about the mountains.' It places the small bird in the position of Shelley's poet, lower down but able to hear and be influenced by the bird's flight: 'Then shall I weep with joy seeing your splendour, | Forget my cowardice, forget my weakness, | Feel the whole sunlight fall upon my tears.' Shelley's poem draws attention to his skylark's beneficial advice to the earth-bound writer: 'Better than all measures . . . Thy skill to poet were, thou scorner of the ground!' His last stanza begins with a call to be educated by the high bird: 'Teach me half the gladness | That thy brain must know' and ends: 'The world should listen then, as I am listening now.'[21] Hatakeyama's poem views the big bird as all but a god: 'I shall believe you a key to Paradise. | I shall believe you the chief light upon this dark grey world.' Both Shelley's poem and 'Little Bird's Soliloquy' come back to the word 'world' in their closing lines.

In the letter from Marchmont Street where he frankly doubts her chances of writing good English poetry, Empson is also at pains to repudiate the implications of devotion and idealization in her treating him as a teacher or *sensei* (*WE1* 338, 341). If Hatakeyama did tell Empson in her letter that 'A

[20] Ronald Schuchard's introduction to T. S. Eliot, *The Varieties of Metaphysical Poetry*, ed. R. Schuchard (London: Faber and Faber, 1993), 15.

[21] Percy Bysshe Shelley, *Poetical Works*, ed. Thomas Hutchinson, corrected by G. M. Matthews (Oxford: Oxford University Press, 1970), 602–3.

little bird's soliloquy' was a farewell to writing in English, he might have been able to intuit that the poem was dedicated to him. The poet's note reads: ' "The Small Bird" is merely a re-phrasing of Miss Hatakeyama's own English translation of her Japanese poem' (*CP* 324). Yet the poem bids farewell to an ambition Empson had sought to discourage, and her Japanese note says it was meant to be read as addressed by her to him. Even if he knew or suspected this, the 'large hawk' never let on in his notes for 'The Small Bird to the Big'. This story's being allowed to peep out has clarified the point of his translation, to my mind the best of the three, which Empson included in *The Gathering Storm*.

Hatakeyama's poem also makes it clear that the example of the big bird is what makes the smaller ones take fright. It has an autobiographical meaning elucidated by Empson's letter from Marchmont Street. The idea that a major writer can silence minor ones with an inimitable example is shadowed across and resisted in Keats's 'On First Looking into Chapman's Homer', another poem that Hatakeyama certainly knew. However, her lyric is designed to turn this negative influence—a direct result of Empson's advice that she should abandon all hope of writing good poetry in English—into a source of gratitude and of emulative inspiration. The big bird's flight is not meant to put the small bird's to shame, but to be something the small bird can take pleasure in, and can follow as showing the way to a heaven, and of showing how the life to be lived 'somewhere in the middle of a field', as Empson put it in his commentary on 'To a Skylark', can be transformed by the big bird's reflected light:

The Small Bird to the Big
Fly up and away, large hawk,
To the eternal day of the abyss,
Belittling the night about the mountains.
Your eyes that are our terror
Are well employed about the secrets of the moon
Or the larger betrayals of the noon-day.
Do not stay just above
So that I must hide shuddering under inadequate twigs.
Sail through the dry smoke of volcanoes
Or the damp clouds if they will better encourage your feathers.
Then shall I weep with joy seeing your splendour,
Forget my cowardice, forget my weakness,
Feel the whole sunlight fall upon my tears.

> I shall believe you a key to Paradise.
> I shall believe you the chief light upon this dark grey world.
>
> (*CP* 73)

In September 1936 Hatakeyama received a letter from the Shakespeare scholar Rintaro Fukuhara of Bunrika University, Tokyo, enclosing a letter from Empson and page 252 of the *Listener* for 5 August 1936. 'The Small Bird to the Big' is printed in the bottom right corner, surrounded by political commentary on Anglo-French relations and the threat of Fascism less than two weeks before the murder of García Lorca. The 'dark grey world' of her poem's close is, in its first publication anywhere, attributed with a daunting political context—the gathering storm itself.

The beautifully apt 'Belittling the night' at the opening of line three in 'The Small Bird to the Big' is either an odd phrase retained from Hatakeyama's lost English version or a lexical choice of Empson's prompted by the implications of the whole poem. The translator appears to ignore the fact that the poem has been addressed to him (it's hard to believe that Hatakeyama didn't indicate this in her lost covering letter, especially since she mentions its purpose in the surviving fragmentary draft).[22] Her translator makes the large bird into a symbol for the kinds of inspiration described in his passage devoted to the athetistical Shelley's idealization of the poet's role and the role of art. In this poem of Hatakeyama's there doesn't seem much direct Christianity—although once again the small bird's activity of converting a set back into an opportunity might have some relation to Jesus's teachings. Empson makes it into a poem about art and the inspiration of one's mentors—leaving more or less to one side the specifically Japanese characteristics of the master-pupil relationship. Hatakeyama's surviving papers make it likely that the publication of her 'Echo' in November 1936 was never communicated to her. She may also have died without knowing that Empson collected and reprinted his three translations of her poems. There were no copies of his poetry among her bookshelves.[23]

[22] '"A little bird's soliloquy" was written when I gave up my ambition of writing English verses.' Cited in *WE1* 342.

[23] Haffenden suggests that I perhaps made Hatakeyama 'seem more pathetic and abject than she was in life: as a self-responsible adult . . . she must have had opportunities to seek out editions of Empson's poetry if she so wanted' (*WE1* 345). Yet this may not take sufficiently into account the difficulty of finding *The Gathering Storm* in Japan during 1940, the high cost of buying or having English books imported, and the likelihood of other priorities for spare funds.

V

As noted above, John Haffenden remarked on the composition of 'The Fool': 'Empson felt so stimulated that he could not resist tinkering with it; he presently refashioned it as his own: tighter, more succinct, though scarcely less gnomic.' But, as I have shown, Empson's acknowledged compression of the text she sent makes his version distinctly more gnomic, and his note to the published translations offers no explicatory help. Haffenden also observes in his biography that the draft versions sent by Hatakeyama were worked on at a time when Empson 'was starting to run out of his own original poems' (*WE1* 341). These translations briefly freed the drought-struck poet to write a kind of poetry that is both like his and not like his. Haffenden is on an equally odd tack when he suggests that there could not be 'some sort of mixed marriage between the cultures' (339) in Empson's rewriting Hatakeyama, since that's what his texts have to be. One interest of these poems is that they are unlike both his new explanatory style and his later short lyric mode. They are story poems; but the story has been more than partially effaced in the compression. The fact that the translations are so much more effective as poems than the literal renditions of the Japanese cited above also presents a conundrum for views of what made a twentieth-century lyric good.

I want to conclude by reflecting on how the translations of Hatakeyama are different from lyrics like 'The Beautiful Train' and 'Manchouli', and are equally, and more obviously, different from poems that attempt both to describe a complex situation, and to justify values and behaviour as if from within it: 'Aubade', 'Letter VI: a marriage', and 'Autumn on Nan Yüeh'. The Hatakeyama translations, I would suggest, are situation poems like the latter three, but with a scale and a mystery (in Empson's translations) that link them to his few short imagistic poems. The fact that Empson felt inclined, in improving Hatakeyama's English versions as poems, to compress them and more than half-efface the situation, points to his dilemma between the compounding that poets must do to produce ringing and singing lines, and the thorough expounding that critics must do to justify their writing about poetry at all. Empson was of course among the inventors of this new kind of critical duty in *Seven Types of Ambiguity*. There are contradictions of sufficient range in the relationships between these activities of packing and unpacking to prompt the fear of that 'madhouse' which, as Wordsworth wrote, poets find when no longer young: 'We poets in our youth begin in gladness, | But thereof comes in the end despondency and madness.'[24]

One evident contrast with the Hatakeyama poems is provided by three of Empson's own late short lyrics. Though each has its stylistic character, not one of these is rhymed or cadenced as are the translations of her poems. 'The Beautiful Train' is Empson's nearest approach to Imagist writing.[25] It superimposes a memory of the ballet dancer Argentina upon the present fact of a Japanese train, rather as Pound had collocated his 'faces in the crowd' with some haiku-like 'Petals on a wet, black bough'. Pound's explanatory title 'In a Station of the Metro' has its equivalent in Empson's subtitle '(A Japanese one, in Manchuria, from Siberia southwards, September 1937)' (*CP* 83). The difference between the two is that where Pound excludes all authorial comment, Empson's poem constitutes an attempt to explain by means of the metaphoric superimposition and a final remark his self-contradictory appreciation of the aggressor's transport: 'And I a twister love what I abhor, | So firm, so burdened, on such light gay feet' (*CP* 83). The grammar seems to indicate that it is the 'I' which is 'So firm, so burdened'; but the semantics require that it's the train, and 'on such light gay feet'. This slight confusion may be the result of compression, or of inspirational drought; whichever, it allows the implication that the poet is spinning like a dancer too, 'a twister', and this is because he's being taken to his job in China thanks to the enemy. 'The Beautiful Train', despite its grace, is not quite able to evoke its occasion, integrate that with the interpretive metaphor, or fully explain the concluding self-distaste and self-division. By contrast, 'Manchouli' is a six-line explanation for a momentary lapse of emotional vigilance with barely enough description to occasion it: 'I find it normal, passing these great frontiers, | That you scan the crowds in rags eagerly each side | With awe.' This is as much of the situation as we are given. The poem returns to its pondering on how 'the nations seem real . . . seem sane' and concludes: 'I find it normal; | So too to extract false comfort from that word' (*CP* 84). The longest of the three, at ten lines, 'Note

[24] William Wordsworth, *Selected Poems*, ed. Damian Walford Davies (London: J. M. Dent, 1994), 305.

[25] For Empson on Imagism and its relation to the problems of scolding without explanatory plot, see his response to William Cookson's letter to the *Listener* about 'Argufying', *A* 171–2. Reviewing Empson and William Carlos Williams together in 1949, it was 'The Beautiful Train' that Robert Fitzgerald alighted upon to make his nearest comparison of these contrasting poets. See 'Bejeweled, The Great Sun', in John Constable (ed.), *Critical Essays on William Empson* (Aldershot: Scolar Press, 1993), 184–5.

on Local Flora' expresses a 'thirst' for revolutionary human change in lines so lacking in enjambed energy that the desire feels sapped in its expression (*CP* 56; there are punctuation-marked pauses at the end of all but the penultimate line). What makes the Hatakeyama poems different is their communicative urgency of matter, however compressed, and this derives from a sharp focus in their author's experience. Empson's later short lyrics, whether short on description, argument, or feeling, have the half-hearted air of marginal notes. His letting go was already taking hold.

The publishing history of 'Aubade', 'Letter VI: a marriage', and 'Autumn on Nan Yüeh' variously indicates difficulties with the achievement of an expansively narrating and commenting style that would get round the problems of unjustified scolding. I have already noted the cut that Empson made when republishing 'Aubade' after its longer magazine appearance in *Life and Letters Today* (1937). When it appeared there Empson wrote to the editor, Philip Herring, that 'The poem about a girl in Japan that you published left me entirely blank when I found it in the copy here. I feel only a vague embarrassment' (*CP* 316). It may be a coincidence that the poet admits to feeling 'entirely blank' here, and then in 'Let It Go' begins by affirming that 'It is this deep blankness is the real thing strange' (*CP* 99)—but it's an eloquent coincidence. The 'vague embarrassment' might have been about the literary quality of the poem, of course, but is more likely to have been connected with the fact that it comes transparently from his personal life, 'about a girl in Japan', as he notes. 'Aubade' is a poem that 'lets the story peep out' to such an extent he found himself inclined to note that 'C. Hatakeyama' was not the girl in his bed when the earthquake struck.

Such embarrassment is quite enough to explain why 'Letter VI: a marriage' remained unpublished until after the poet's death. The poem explores—with a winning frankness—Empson's idealizing, 'mad as a March hare' love for Desmond Lee, a fellow student at Cambridge who married on 23 March 1935:

> Rejoice where possible all hares of March
> And any daffodils not forced at this date.
> I too attempt an epithalamion
> Never to be thrust on your unwilling notice
> Still less before the public, annotated.
>   Life's not more strange than this traditional theme.
>
> (*CP* 61)

This opening verse not only raises the same issue of autobiographical poetry and explanation as the phrase 'unjust to her without a prose book', but adds to that the equally pressing issues of an interlocutor's feelings and the relations, in 1935, between public and private: 'Never to be thrust on your unwilling notice | Still less before the public, annotated.' What's more, in the first of the Spenser-like refrains that round off each of its variously straying verses, Empson deploys another of the words later used in 'Let It Go'. Here, 'Life's not more strange'; there, 'blankness is the real thing strange'. Yet it should be further noted that what will have made this poem unpublishable at the time of writing was not that it is about homosexual feeling, or that it has an autobiographical source, or that it has a living (but unnamed) interlocutor. What makes it unsuitable for publication in 1935 is its lucidity about these things—which points to the fact that its materials, however private, have, like those in 'Aubade', public and communal ramifications. If this were not so, then there would be no cause for embarrassment, vague or otherwise.[26] 'Autumn on Nan-Yüeh' is a bravura poem of 234 intricately rhymed lines reflecting on life with 'the exiled universities of Peking' during the Sino-Japanese war. Over twice as long as its nearest rival in Empson's published oeuvre, it proceeds by deploying an explicatory voice, much of the second stanza being, in effect, a long note on the final line of 'Aubade'—'The heart of standing is we cannot fly':

> And it is true I flew, I fled,
>   I ran about on hope, on trust,
> I felt I had escaped from They
>   Who sat on pedestals and fussed.
> But is it true one ought to dread
>   This timid flap, that shirk, that lust?
> We do not fly when we are clay.
>   We hope to fly when we are dust.
>
> (*CP* 91)

Haffenden calls this 'light verse' and 'owing more to Byron than to the social bards of the 1930s'—momentarily overlooking the fact that Auden, the

[26] Haffenden notes (p. xlv) that his edition of *The Complete Poems* does not contain 'The Wife is Praised', a 200-line poem begun during 1948 in Swinburne's 'Dolores' stanza about sexuality in marriage (see *WE2* 666–71). Since the poet did not attempt to place it during his lifetime, the estate did not authorize its publication.

leading bard among those poets, wrote a 'Letter to Lord Byron', one that is a good deal lighter than Empson's poem which has multiple meanings spun from the word 'fly' in the last two lines above. Haffenden's ever-fascinating notes to *The Complete Poems* make it clear that the poet's attempts to publish 'Autumn on Nan-Yüeh' in a magazine not only came to naught, but caused him to reflect upon the relationship of its style and content to the needs of the then current political situation. After Philip Herring rejected it, he sent it to Michael Roberts noting that 'I am afraid I have cut myself off from Life and Letters by sending them a long poem on China which wasn't sufficiently Leftwing . . . Very proper to have politics important now but suggests England is a bit grim' (*CP* 380). In contrasting so directly his 'somewhat prattling long poem' (380) with the appreciated social demands of red Herring's magazine, Empson appears to set the stage for the yet fiercer contradiction between poetry and the social demands on him when working for the BBC during the Second World War.

But why should he give up writing poetry because he was broadcasting propaganda? A poet can't honestly edit a poem to fit some political programme without sabotaging the relationship between imaginative responsiveness and verbal means.[27] The broadcaster of propaganda to enemy or occupied countries is required to subordinate a strict fidelity to the promptings of verbal conscience to the demands of the emergency situation. Empson met his future wife at what he liked to call 'the BBC Liar's School for training propagandists'.[28] When the matter of 'lying' makes an appearance in 'Aubade', in Empson's time-honoured love-poetry pun on being prone and mendacious, the intent of the line is to utter a truth about that moment: 'Some solid ground for lying could she show?' (*CP* 69). At the most general of levels, his poetry attempts to tell as much of the truth about life and life's situations as its structures

[27] Empson noted around 1941 that 'It is always hard to translate the wisdom of the literary into political plans.' See *CP* 353, where he also expresses a contradiction between his 1930s cultural beliefs and his poetic style: 'I agreed with the pylon poets . . . I just didn't know how to do this kind of poetry.'

[28] See *CP* 127. In his 'Orwell at the BBC' Empson notes that 'The Liars' School, I should perhaps explain, had only dealt with lies in passing, and only under the form of warning us against the methods of the enemy' (*A* 498). Orwell's commitment to the defeat of the Japanese *and* the liberation of India (497), or Empson's belief that Auden was 'right in refusing to become the laureate of Churchill' (496) exemplify, in their different ways, the contradictions and requirements to simplify for the war effort's sake, without our assuming that the 'Liars' School' writers were required merely and consciously to misinform.

will bear. Yet in the course of attempting such truth-telling he encountered a number of powerful contrary pressures. The contractions between public war effort utterance, and the already conflicted ethics of Empson's poetry could not be readily integrated.

In a draft letter to Herring after 'Autumn on Nan-Yüeh' had been rejected, the poet also relates the explanatory lucidity of this poem to his attempts to escape from the compounded complexities of his Cambridge style: 'My attempts at getting out of the narrowness of my early verse are painfully halfbaked' (*CP* 380). Again there is a problem with the relationship between raw life and cooked verse. The last line of the piece as it appeared in *The Gathering Storm* self-referentially comments on Empson's longest published poem: 'The streams will chatter as they flow.' This concluding phrase, in Haffenden's edition, faces the six-line 'Let It Go' whose fifth reads: 'The talk would talk and go so far aslant.' Haffenden's note on the line cites the poet's comments on Vaughan's 'streams both run and speak', indicating that the 'chatter' is also talk going aslant (*CP* 394). In the conflicted relationships between the public and the private, the demands of personal honesty and public economy with the truth, and the aesthetic or communicative losses and gains in either poetic compounding and expounding are generating the blank-making states of affairs that he would generalize with the line: 'The contradictions cover such a range.'

In the dedicatory note that she wrote at the foot of her Japanese poem 'Little Bird's Soliloquy', Chiyoko Hatakeyama had wished 'all the best for the bright future of my teacher W. E.' The sad fact, though, is that while Empson was indeed to have a bright future, it was not to be as a poet. Within two years of her sending that poem to him for his beautiful rewriting, he was involved in the exchanges with Philip Herring and Michael Roberts that would result in those self-doubting comments on his 'halfbaked' attempt to write in a style that escaped the limits of his early verse. He needed to be able to comment on life, to 'scold' as it were, while also avoiding the social and human faults he associated with scolding without a plot to explain the values being expressed. He had attempted to continue the anti-Symbolist programme of his argufying 'metaphysical' poetry, without the evident drawback of that style—a difficulty that could be accused of social faults similar to those held against the Symbolist compacting.[29] Though in his poetry Empson may have

[29] Empson will not have missed the bluntly expressed implications of MacNeice's review of *Poems*: 'In poetry we want a spareness and clarity . . . The clever fellows must wait to show off some

learned a style from a despair, he had then found that despair was not a style he wanted to live by.

What makes the early Empson poetry tricky to fathom is not the argufying, but the argufying in analogical metaphorical patterns that tend only to half-reveal and half-conceal the urgent themes powering the poems' dramatized emotion.[30] The writing of explanatory notes and justifications for them admitted his problem of method without being able to solve it in the terms of his poetic art. Committed to the natural idea that poets should write about what most immediately and urgently concerns them, Empson had, as it were, avoided being unfair by being hard to understand. When he attempted to be clear, he became, in the conditions obtaining at the time, barely publishable. It is in that acutely distressing combination of personal and political pressures, of the poetic need for compacting and truth-telling, and the social requirements for discretion or propaganda work, that we may begin to locate the 'contradictions', the 'madhouse', and 'the whole thing there'.

Yet if 'Little Bird's Soliloquy' and 'Let It Go' are both poems about giving up poetry, the similarity and difference between them is that they were saying farewell to the writing of poetry in English—a language that, in C. Hatakeyama's case, was not her mother tongue. Of the two who met briefly on 26 and 27 March 1934 in Tokyo, each was to encounter personal and social reasons for preferring either not to publish or not to write more poetry. Yet, of the two, it was to be the small bird who would continue, occasionally, to write lyrics that have now, finally, been enabled to fly up into the light of day—and among those who helped to make that happen I would like to end by gratefully acknowledging her first translator, the poet W. E.

other day.' He might also have reflected on the phrase in I. A. Richards's warmly positive review admiring 'lines that resound with an extraordinary and inexplicable passion'. Yet 'inexplicable' would surely not have been a virtue for a communally responsible poet opposing Symbolist hauteur. Citations from Constable (ed.), *Critical Essays*, 58, 76.

30 The exemplary researches of John Haffenden and, earlier, the critical insights of Christopher Ricks have also served to underline the unbridgeable gaps—in the poems themselves—between their occasioning concerns and their achieved styles. See, for an extreme example, the suicide connected with the close of 'Bacchus', *CP* 306–7 and *WE1* 415–21.

5

Empson and the Gifts of China

Jason Harding

> Attending there let us absorb the cultures of nations
> And dissolve into our judgement all their codes.
>
> 'Homage to the British Museum' (1932)
>
> A more heartening fact about the cultures of man
> Is their appalling stubbornness.
>
> 'Sonnet' (1942)[1]

William Empson cherished 'our strong and critical curiosity about alien modes of feeling, our need for the flying buttress of sympathy with systems other than our own' (*EG* 32). It was a belief that fuelled a sustained attempt to foster deeper understanding between the cultural traditions of Europe and Asia. However, after seven years as a university professor in China, Empson did not underestimate the difficulties of a rapprochement between two civilizations separated by what he conceived of as a profound difference of theology. John Haffenden's narrative of the extraordinary years Empson spent in China during the turbulent upheaval of the Sino-Japanese War (1937–9) and throughout the Civil War and the Communist takeover (1947–52) has transformed the context in which scholars and critics approach the worldliness of the later poetry and criticism, peppered with anecdote and offhand personal testimony. And yet, a decade of 'attending' to Asian cultures had taught Empson a tough

[1] *CP* 55, 101.

lesson about the 'appalling stubbornness' of one's own cultural formation. In fact, the problematic nature of adaptation to life in Chinese society is placed in striking relief in the case of Empson's intellectual and imaginative development. His comprehension of China, shaped at first through literary sources, had to confront a series of deconstructive jolts. Empson could not simply absorb Chinese culture like a traveller sipping tea, but nor did he arrogantly appropriate the idea of 'China' from Orientalist discourses—the situation is far more complex, requiring a detailed attention to the variegated references to China in his writings. The questions this chapter seeks to address are less concerned with what Empson *saw* or *felt* or *did* in China, than with what he *made* of these experiences in his literary criticism and poetry; in other words, how was Empson able to activate or transform his encounters with Chinese people, places, poetry, and politics in the domain of English literature. The focus here will be on concrete examples of his engagement with China: the concept of the East evident in the early critical writings; his poetic representation of China in *The Gathering Storm*; the impact of his two periods of residence in China on his later critical thinking; and concluding with the use of these experiences as part of a critique of the myopia of English literary critics.

'The wisdom of the East': Harmony in Conflict

Before Empson had ever set foot in Asia, a range of textual sources served to whet his appetite for an engagement with Chinese civilization. As an undergraduate he was influenced by senior members of Cambridge University, most notably Goldsworthy Lowes Dickinson, who sought to position China in the minds of an English audience as a repository of wisdom, tolerance, and tranquility.[2] This idealized vision of a harmonious, agrarian China and of the esoteric 'wisdom of the East' elided the poverty, misery, and political turmoil in the fledgling Chinese Republic.[3] Yet for Western liberal intellectuals, this conception of 'China' served as an alternative to the

[2] See E. M. Forster on Dickinson: 'In a life which contained much disillusionment, China never failed him . . . Politeness, gaiety, imagination, good taste—these he found or thought he found'; cited in E. M. Forster, *Goldsworthy Lowes Dickinson* (1934; London: Arnold, 1973), 117, 126.

[3] *The Wisdom of the East Series*, containing volumes on Chinese poetry and philosophy, edited by L. Cranmer-Byng *et al.*, had been steadily appearing from the publisher John Murray since 1904.

imperialism and industrialism that were often blamed for contributing to the devastation of the First World War. As a president of the Heretics Society, which had rewarded Dickinson with honorary membership, Empson moved in these circles of Cambridge liberal world-mindedness. Several of his contributions to the undergraduate magazine *Granta* reveal the impression of this intellectual milieu. After attending a Christian missionary lecture on China, Empson bought Rodney Gilbert's pamphlet *What's Wrong with China?* (1926). His review countered the slur that the Chinese were an 'inferior race'. On the contrary, Empson expressed a strong desire that the Chinese would absorb any assault emanating from the 'barbarian' Anglo-Saxons.[4] In fact, in his reviews for *Granta* he went to considerable lengths to suggest the West could learn greater moderation from the East. Reviewing a memoir by an exiled Chinese politician, Empson concluded that the 'maturity' of Chinese customs highlighted the West's 'lack of courtesy, restraint, and poise'. In a similar vein, in a review of Arthur Waley's translation of *The Tale of Genji*, he confessed to a feeling of 'our civilization's inferiority' to the graciousness of the East. More significantly, Empson praised the 'extraordinarily high' level of Waley's compendium of translations, *Poems from the Chinese* (*EG* 23, 55, 24).

It is instructive that it was Arthur Waley, rather than Ezra Pound, who introduced Empson to Chinese classical poetry. Waley's translations may have had (in the words of W. B. Yeats) 'more learning but less subtlety of rhythm' than Pound's *Cathay* (1915), yet they provided a poetic texture that Pound's ignorance of Mandarin could not supply: that is, approximations of the conventions of Chinese poetic tradition, together with allusions to the original socio-historical contexts of these poems.[5] It was Waley and not the 'Imagist' Pound who opened Empson's eyes to the abundance of multiple meanings in Chinese literature. *Seven Types of Ambiguity* quoted lines from Waley's translation of the poetry of Tao Qian to illustrate ambiguity of the first type; namely, 'comparisons with several points of likeness, antithesis with several points of difference'. Empson's analysis of the lines 'Swiftly the years, beyond recall. | Solemn the stillness of this spring morning' draws out 'the profundity of feeling' that emerges from the clash of different time-scales apprehended in a single experience.

[4] See 'Just a Blond', supplement to *EG*.

[5] W. B. Yeats, 'Introduction', *Oxford Book of Modern Verse* (Oxford: Oxford University Press, 1936), p. xl.

The detachment of the large perspective encourages a feeling 'that there is nothing to be done about life' and that 'it must be regarded from a peaceable and fatalistic point of view' whereas the smaller, more urgently engaged one causes the reader to 'consider the neighbouring space, an activity of the will, delicacies of social tone and your personality' (*STA* 43–4). Empson's minor misquotation of Waley's translation does not affect his argument.

Swiftly the years, beyond recall.
Solemn the stillness of this fair morning.
I will clothe myself in spring-clothing
And visit the slopes of the Eastern Hill.
By the mountain-stream a mist hovers,
Hovers a moment, then scatters.
There comes a wind blowing from the south
That brushes the fields of new corn.[6]

In a direct allusion to the Confucian *Analects*, Tao Qian's poem announces a search for personal happiness amidst the rejuvenated spring landscape.[7] The grandeur of seasonal change implicitly diminishes public or political ambition, suggesting a hope for spiritual renewal similar to Wordsworth's reflections on nature. Inevitably, Waley's version adds a faint romantic haze to Tao Qian's lyrical imagining of a passage from the *Analects*, but Empson has correctly seized upon the structural principle of antithesis crucial to Chinese poetry.[8] The impact of Waley's Chinese translations on the parsing of ambiguity has not received due attention. Empson later generously acknowledged a debt to Waley, claiming that the 'basic virtue of Waley's mind' was exemplified by 'a large capacity to accept the assumptions of any worldview, without assuming any merit for our own'.[9]

The terms of this praise are, of course, equally applicable to Empson's world-view. 'One reason I wanted to come East,' he informed I. A. Richards in 1932 'was to find out what teaching was like across so large a gulf' (*SL* 46). It was Richards's example as a visiting professor at Qinghua University in

[6] Arthur Waley, *Chinese Poems* (London: Unwin, 1961), 94.

[7] Tao Qian's poem alludes to a celebrated passage from the *Analects* (the first part of XI. 26) in which Confucius discusses with three interlocutors the meaning of happiness.

[8] 'There is a natural tendency in Chinese [poetry] towards antithesis'; James J. Y. Liu, *The Art of Chinese Poetry* (London: Routledge, 1962), 146.

[9] Empson, 'Waley's Courtesy', *New Statesman* (13 Mar. 1964), 410.

Peking that encouraged Empson to take up the life of a peripatetic teacher of English literature.[10] Furthermore, the reference to an educational 'gulf' was a response to Richards's teaching experiences. He had encountered difficulties communicating with his students at Qinghua, who had appeared to him 'nearly as far off as fishes in a tank'.[11] Chinese thought has often appeared puzzling from a Western point of view, although it exhibits—no less than Western thought—clearly articulated patterns of reasoning, prominent among which is a desire for group harmony in the face of social conflict.[12] Curiously, Richards had hoped to understand Chinese psychology by making a highly theoretical study of selected passages from a Confucian disciple, Mencius. His findings were published in *Mencius on the Mind* (1932), a work subtitled 'Experiments in Multiple Definition'. In brief, Richards concluded that Chinese philosophy eschewed the analytical logic of Western tradition in favour of a tacit appeal to shared social norms or values. Abstracted from their social conditions, Mencius's suasive 'gestures' presented formidable problems to the English translator. Richards proposed that these difficulties could be met by listing the full range of meanings covered by key Confucian concepts; for instance, the virtue *ren*. In effect, Richards suggested that the resonant ambiguities of Mencius's writings were more 'poetical' than philosophical. Arthur Waley's review of *Mencius on the Mind* contended that Richards had been misled by an inability to construe ancient Chinese idioms.[13] The controversies surrounding Richards's championing of the efficacy of Chinese-English 'multiple definition' played a crucial role in the development of Empson's critical theories. From the 1930s onwards, Empson's investigations into the prismatic meanings of 'complex words' (and their interconnections) was worked out as a refinement upon Richards's linguistic theory, incorporating a forthright rejection of the emotive theory of value venerating a Confucian 'stable poise'.[14]

[10] After his Cambridge fellowship was terminated, Empson initially told Richards: 'my impulses are not so powerful as to drive me to China.' However, within a few months he reported: 'it is fixed in my mind that I want to go to China' (*SL* 13–16).

[11] Transcribed in the diary of Dorothea Richards, 30 Nov. 1929, Richards Collection, Magdalene College, Cambridge.

[12] This point is amply demonstrated in Richard W. Hartzell, *Harmony in Conflict* (Taipei: Caves, 1988).

[13] Arthur Waley, 'Mencius on the Mind', *Times Literary Supplement* (15 Sept. 1932), 634.

[14] Lisa A. Rodensky's introduction to the 1995 Penguin editions of *Some Versions of Pastoral* and *The Structure of Complex Words* gives an account of the divergence between Empson and Richards.

The translations of Waley and the critical theories of Richards formed part of the interpretative matrix in which Empson wrestled with the challenge of comprehending and representing China. The compression of the complexities of cultural difference into more readily familiar forms is an invaluable shorthand. Evidently, when Empson lived in the East this textual engagement was overlaid with specific occurrences of the unfamiliar, 'strange' and anomalous on perceptual, linguistic, and intellectual levels, which obliged him to acknowledge the inadequacies of a predominantly textual approach to cultural dislocation. During the three years Empson taught in Tokyo, he strongly disliked Japanese imperialism and the crude ideological stereotypes deployed to justify this military expansion. Empson had accepted a post in Tokyo the day before he received an offer from Peking and this contingency would affect his preconceptions of Chinese society. Many Japanese held deeply unflattering prejudices regarding the Chinese. When the Japanese author of *Rashōmon* published a volume about his travels in China, they amounted to a virulent indictment of the Chinese as an indolent, disorganized, and hopelessly backward people. Empson was shocked when his students reacted chauvinistically to the 1932 battle for Shanghai (*SSS* 206). The necessity of maintaining one's mental equilibrium when confronted by 'conflict' (personal, cultural, political, military) is a cornerstone of Empson's writings. Such urgent, existential tensions understandably led to a degree of ambivalence about Sino-Japanese relations and an eirenic impulse that flattened or softened the differences between these contending Asian civilizations. In the spring of 1933, Empson had the opportunity to inspect China for himself, journeying to Mount Yüngang, north-west of Peking, in search of the massive Buddhist sculptures carved into the sandstone caves. Brooding upon the metaphysics expressed by these statues, he felt emboldened in *Some Versions of Pastoral* to offer the following epitome of Chinese mentality: 'In China the feeling that everything is everything so nothing is worth doing, natural to this mode of thought, was balanced by the Confucian stress on the exact performance of local duties and ceremonies' (*SVP* 24). This remark is consonant with the contrapuntal movements he had discerned in Waley's translations of Chinese poetry. Moreover, the interplay of Buddhist, Taoist, and Confucian traditions was always a feature of his reflections on developments in Chinese civilization. Still, when Empson was 'bowled over' by the Chinese Imperial treasures on display at Burlington House in 1935 there is little to suggest he had anything more than a slight acquaintance with Chinese society and behaviour.[15]

'The dragon hatched a cockatrice': War Poetry

Empson returned to China in August 1937 on a Japanese troop train. He arrived in the country with no linguistic preparation and only a rudimentary grasp of the contemporary political situation. Not surprisingly, the poem 'China'—a miniature essay on the wartime prospects of the Chinese people—deploys cultural stereotypes he had acquired before any direct contact with the Sino-Japanese War.

China

The dragon hatched a cockatrice
(Cheese crumbles and not many mites repair)
There is a Nature about this
(The spring and rawness tantalize the air)

Most proud of being most at ease
(The sea is the most solid ground)
Where comfort is on hands and knees
(The nations perch about around)

Red hills bleed naked into screes
(The classics are a single school—)
The few large trees are holy trees
(—They teach the nations how to rule)

They will not teach the Japanese
(They rule by music and by rites)
They are as like them as two peas
(All nations are untidy sights)

The serious music strains to squeeze
(The angel coolies sing like us—)
Duties, and literature, and fees
(—to lift an under-roaded bus)

The paddy-fields are wings of bees

[15] See Empson, 'The Gifts of China', *Sunday Times* (30 Sept. 1973). For catalogue details of the 1935 exhibition see Leigh Ashton (ed.), *Chinese Art* (London: Kegan Paul, 1935).

(The Great Wall as a dragon crawls—)
To one who flies or one who sees
(—the twisted contour of their walls)

A liver fluke of sheep agrees
Most rightly proud of her complacencies
With snail so well they make one piece
Most wrecked and longest of all histories.

(*CP* 90)

The poem proposes that the Japanese invaders are themselves the offspring of Chinese culture. The Confucian *Analects* taught good government on the basis of the observance of ceremonial rites, literature, and music, but the Japanese will no longer submit to the lessons of their former imperial overlords. China must rely upon her ancient defensive culture, symbolized by the Great Wall, in order to contain the occupying army, as she had once absorbed Mongol and Manchu conquerors. The present sight of China reveals a land in disorder, her hills symbolically 'bleeding' or crumbling as the Japanese soldiers swarm like parasitic mites feeding off a decaying animal, or more disgustingly, a sheep liver fluke that has penetrated and aims to reproduce with the host. 'China' is ultimately sanguine, even optimistic, about the future of Chinese civilization: 'Most wrecked and longest of all histories.' Having witnessed the corrosive effects of Japanese nationalism, Empson chose to underscore the similarities between China and Japan, drawing upon the rhetoric of '*dōbun—dōshu*' (common culture: common race). He wished for a peaceful admixture of these two great Asian civilizations—'two peas' albeit 'untidy sights' in time of war. Empson was mistaken to advocate passivity in the face of the Japanese onslaught, including the 'Rape of Nanjing'. Yet it is churlish to belittle his efforts to maintain an unbroken spirit of optimism as he endured the cold, cramped, and unhygienic conditions of a scholarly refugee during the Sino-Japanese War.[16]

'China' is marked by those vertiginous, associative leaps of logic characteristic of Empson's poetry. In that sense, it is a continuation of the witty, erudite, 'metaphysical' *Poems* (1935): the interwoven strands of argument and the analogy of the sheep liver fluke are a twentieth-century rewriting of a seventeenth-century conceit. It is a poetic at the opposite extreme from Pound's wartime collection, *Cathay* (1915), in which an exotic 'Oriental' aura

[16] For a thorough account of Empson's life with the exiled Peking universities, see *WE1* 432–536.

provides the context for a loose, sequence of images. 'China' is a tougher, intellectual poetry of 'argufying' closer to Chinese literary traditions. Empson apprehended from Waley's translations that Chinese classical poetry was rich in ambiguities. Just as Chinese characters convey a variety of homonyms—some of them contradictory—Empson's poem trades on fruitful aural puns. The line 'They rule by music and by rites' evokes both the authoritarian rituals of Confucian tradition and the 'rights' and corresponding duties of Chinese officials which they encode. Similarly, 'The serious music strains to squeeze' combines the double implication of soothing strains of melody with taut, physical endurance. The penultimate line declares 'they make one piece' as an aptly comforting future for two peoples wracked by war. As we have seen, the structural conventions of Chinese classical poetry encourage repetitions, parallels, and antitheses. 'China' switches between the long perspective of the antiquity of Chinese history and the local, present-day trauma inflicted by foreign invaders; it also straddles the gulf between the educated ruling classes and the peasant masses. Out of this dialectical movement emerges a lofty vision of harmony in the midst of conflict. The repeated long e's of the *a*-rhymes (for instance, ease—squeeze—agrees) reproduce the slow, strained, yet disciplined ritual Empson associated with Confucian government. The longevity of Chinese civilization itself exemplifies the cyclical spring renewal voiced in Empson's notes to the poem: 'The prolonged disorder of China made everything feel crumbling like cheese but with an effect of new growth trying to start as in inclement spring weather' (*CP* 373).

Empson's poetry was softened by sifting and reflecting upon his remarkable experiences in China. As J. H. Willis has pointed out, Empson's 'most autobiographical poem', namely 'Autumn on Nan-Yüeh', a lengthy, chatty excursion on the themes of 'flight, escapism, courage and political involvement', is characterized by 'the relaxed and conversational phrases of his later style'.[17] Like a number of the poems collected in *The Gathering Storm* (1940), it contemplates the dilemmas that arise when honour dictates standing one's ground, or when flight is the better part of valour. In fact, *flight* is a key word in the poem expressing a complex range of related meanings: wartime aerial bombardment; the migrations of displaced populations; political appeasement; and the elevated 'otherworldly' vantage point of the Buddhist and

[17] See J. H. Willis, *William Empson* (New York: Columbia University Press, 1969), 44.

Taoist monks, whose temples and monastic complexes—centres of scholarship, art, and religious culture—dotted the mountain summit of Nan-Yüeh. The poet's detached, wry perspective on the imminent global conflagration is combined with more pressing anxieties about teaching without essential resources, such as library books. Empson elaborated: 'men get curiously non-plussed | Searching the memory for a clue', completing the rhyme 'Let textual variants be discussed; | We teach a poem as it grew' (*CP* 92). His colleagues at Nan-Yüeh frequently recited Chinese classical poems from memory.[18] The trace of these recitations is apparent in the themes of Chinese poetry found in 'Autumn on Nan-Yüeh': the war-torn frontier; rapture with wine; and anecdotal parables and jokes from the origins of Chinese literary tradition.

The poem, of course, is also inflected by English traditions of 'wit' and 'pastoral'. Still, the effect is curious and arresting. As the Japanese began to bomb nearby Changsha, 'Autumn on Nan-Yüeh' closes with a sober meditation upon the Xiang River winding its way through maples and pines in the first chill of winter:

> We have had the Autumn here. But oh
> That lovely balcony is lost
> Just as the mountains take the snow.
> The soldiers will come here and train.
> The stream will chatter as they flow.
>
> (*CP* 97–8)

The chattering, flowing stream echoes Henry Vaughan's 'singing' streams that 'both run and speak'.[19] When contemplating the sacred Chinese mountain where the great Tang dynasty poet and wanderer Li Bai had composed, Empson is drawn to the life's flow of a seventeenth-century meditative poet in retreat from the English Civil War. Yet it would be strange if Empson's rapt contemplation of the Chinese landscape was not influenced by the paintings, calligraphic scrolls, silk tapestries, lacquered panels, and blue-and-white willow porcelain he had inspected in museums and galleries; or by those evocative mists and mountain streams he had encountered in Waley's translations of Chinese poetry. For example, compare Empson's version of pastoral with this

[18] See Empson's comments in 'A Comparison Between the British and Chinese Approach to Poetry', *P.E.N. News* (Nov. 1957), 18.

[19] Empson quoted the relevant lines from Vaughan's 'The Bird' in *STA* 205.

extract from Waley's rendering of the Tang poet Bo Ju-yi ruminating upon his wartime exile:

> This year there is war in An-hui,
> In every place soldiers are rushing to arms.
> Men of learning have been summoned to the Council Board;
> Only I, who have no talents at all,
> Am left in the mountains to play with the pebbles of the stream.[20]

Empson's meditation on the urgency of the great political issues of the day is set against the grand backdrop of the perennial cycles of nature, thus recalling his commentary upon the clash of time-scales in Waley's translation from Tao Qian. It is evidence of the rich confluence of intercultural sources that flow together in 'Autumn on Nan-Yüeh'.

Empson's poetic treatment of China adroitly resists the Orientalist appeal of the 'exotic East' as portrayed in the translations of Pound and Waley, both of whom were imaginative rather than actual voyagers to the East. This does not mean that Empson was able to express the 'real China' but his efforts to fathom the disconcerting effects of an alien environment bear a favourable comparison with Auden and Isherwood's account of their travels in China during the Sino-Japanese War.[21] Auden and Isherwood, as Au Dung and Y Hsiao Wu, embarked on their wartime journey in a fanfare of publicity and a spirit that Isherwood characterized as 'an irresponsible, schoolboyish feeling of excitement'.[22] 'Autumn on Nan-Yüeh' contained a 'smack' at Auden in the astringent asides on politically inspired 'Up the Boys' verses characteristic of 1930s English poetry. All the same, Empson supplemented his classes on seventeenth-century metaphysical poetry with more propagandist material; including the oratorical, allegorical didacticism of Auden's *Spain*.[23] In a letter home, Empson remarked that after 'all these beastly little lovers of the Far East have slunk off', he was resolved to make 'a reasonable show of not deserting the

[20] Waley, *Chinese Poems*, 146.

[21] For a stimulating account of Auden, Isherwood and Empson's dealings with the Sino-Japanese War, see Hugh Haughton, 'Journeys to War: Auden, Isherwood and Empson in China', in Douglas Kerr and Julia Kuehn (eds.), *Travellers in China* (Hong Kong: University of Hong Kong Press, 2007).

[22] See W. H. Auden and Christopher Isherwood, *Journey to a War* (London: Faber, 1939), 28–9.

[23] Empson's lectures on modern poetry were recalled by Wang Zuoliang in 'William Empson in Kunming', *Foreign Literatures*, 1 (1980), 2–3. I am grateful to Dr Yumei Hsu for her translation of the Chinese.

Chinese intellectuals entirely' (cited in *WE1* 502–3). In a pro-Chinese article published in 1940, he declared: 'getting the intellectuals out of Peking and making them look at "the interior" has been an obviously healthy change.'[24] The changes effected by Empson's wartime experiences can be gauged from his decision to recite to his Chinese colleagues Satan's stirring address to the fallen angels in *Paradise Lost* (*MG* 45; *WE1* 539–40). When pondering why this speech seemed so apposite in 1939, it is worth recalling another occasion recounted in *Milton's God* when Empson identified with Satan. During a stopover on his flight home, he climbed a hill and began a bout of screaming. Empson compared this hilltop crisis en route from China (itself a reflection of the crises *on* a mountain in China), with the despair, doubt, and loneliness felt by Satan on Mount Niphates (*MG* 67). Getting intellectuals into war zones—conflicts which generated primal screaming—precipitated infernal tensions which would reverberate throughout his subsequent writings.

'The confusion of a liberation': Criticism and Propaganda

The essays Empson began on Nan-Yüeh and pieced together in *The Structure of Complex Words* (1951) amounted to a rejection of the translation theory of 'multiple definition' advanced in *Mencius on the Mind.* Empson's investigation into the crystalline structures of key words was predicated upon the subtle interconnections of emotive and cognitive uses of poetic language—as determined by their immediate (socio-political) context. Or viewed from another angle, a good critic possesses a contextual understanding sufficient to explain implicit value judgements to a foreign reader. The unpacking of complex words was interrupted by Empson's Second World War duties at the Chinese Section of the BBC's Far Eastern Service, where he was chiefly responsible for radio broadcasts to China and propaganda features on China for the Home Service. Empson informed Richards he was 'definitely an all-time propaganda hack' (*SL* 133–6). An extant draft typescript of the BBC feature, 'China on the March', broadcast in April 1942, reveals how conscientiously he tackled these programmes. The broadcast was arranged in the form of round-table discussion among various Western observers of China's predicament.

[24] Empson, 'A Chinese University', *Life and Letters* (25 June 1940), 243.

Speaker 'E' (a teacher from a refugee Chinese university) voiced Empson's own opinions on the Chinese Communists and the Nationalist Government. 'E' took a long-term optimistic view of the evolution of Chinese democratic society following the eventual defeat of the Japanese. Further, 'E' drew on Empson's first-hand experience to suggest that the Chinese were uniting to achieve this common goal.[25] When he came to revise and expand his pre-war essays, Empson argued that propaganda habitually employs stereotypical spokesmen in order to 'sum up a complex matter briefly' (*SCW* 51, 58–9). This is not telling lies and Empson was, at any rate, sceptical of the efficacy of 'purely emotive' propaganda. He resisted Richards's thesis in *Mencius on the Mind* defending the social uses of a rhetoric imposing doctrines.

Empson had plenty of opportunity to ponder the impositions of political rhetoric when he returned to China in 1947 to resume his teaching position at National Peking University. Here he witnessed the six-week siege of Peking in 1948 and the Communist Liberation, including the proclamation of the People's Republic of China on 1 October 1949. *The Structure of Complex Words* was, in Empson's own words, 'greatly expanded and rewritten' between 1947 and 1951 in 'very agreeable circumstances in Peking' (*SCW*, pp. xxvii, xvi). If this remark sounds odd, an Australian acquaintance, the anthropologist C. P. Fitzgerald, has claimed that during the years of Empson's second stint in China, Peking was a wonderful place for foreign professors: 'The most delicious and happiest, pleasantest way of life you could have imagined anywhere.'[26] Empson played down the dangers of venturing beyond the city walls during the siege of Peking, in order to teach a weekly class on Shakespeare. 'When I was crossing the fighting lines during the siege of Peking' he remembered, 'a generous-minded peasant barred my way and said, pointing ahead: "That way lies death". "Not for me, I have a British passport" was the answer that sprang to the lips, and I was right' (*SL* 550). Chinese culture and beliefs could invoke defamiliarizing angles of comparison in the chapters he was writing for *The Structure of Complex Words*. Discussing the benefits of worldly renunciation in *King Lear*, Empson

[25] The typescript of 'China on the March' is among the Empson Papers in the Houghton Library, Harvard. Scripts of BBC radio programmes involving Empson and George Orwell are included in *Orwell: The War Broadcasts*, ed. W. J. West (London: Duckworth, 1985).

[26] Michael Hollington, 'Richards and Empson in China: The Recollections of Professor C. P. ("Possum") Fitzgerald', *AUMLA* (1996), 90–1. In 1950, Empson told John Hayward: 'There is still the beautiful city [Peking] and the charming good humour and the best food in the world' (*SL* 184).

argued that this is 'not too Buddhist an idea to occur to Shakespeare' (*SCW* 138). Asides of this sort perplexed less world-minded English critics. Shortly after the publication of *The Structure of Complex Words*, Frank Kermode said that he was puzzled by the reference to Buddhist meditation in Empson's essay on Marvell's 'The Garden'.[27] Empson replied, somewhat gruffly, that he was not suggesting Marvell had studied Buddhism, but rather: 'We have only two or three independent civilizations to compare, developing in parallel through thousands of years, it has a steadying effect to compare them.'[28] For Kermode, crossing swords with Empson in this period left one feeling the narrowness of one's own point of view. 'I think he was very conscious of the breadth and variety of his own experience,' he later reflected, 'and so thought us all narrow and tame, venturing our pathetic little audacities from positions of bourgeois security.'[29]

Undoubtedly no champion of bourgeois security, Empson had shared in the great sense of expectation surrounding the Communist liberation of China. He recorded, in a vivid eyewitness account, the excitement enveloping the triumphant entry of the Red Army (the People's Liberation Army) into Tiananmen Square.[30] Empson felt sympathetic towards the Communist soldiers during the siege and subsequent takeover: 'I was greatly struck by the beautiful evangelistic feelings of the troops, all consciously and confidently redeeming and redeemed', adding: 'I admired the feelings of many other Chinese during the following two years' (*MG* 255). He was extremely moved by the patriotic folk nationalism of a Peking University performance of the *Yellow River Cantata*.[31] In 1951, he produced a fine adaptation of a proto-Communist peasant ballad.[32] The poem, cast in what Empson called the 'international ballad metre', delightfully reworks Li Chi's country ballad about a separating wartime couple who intermix two clay dolls, a variation on the topoi of enforced farewells and stoicism found in Chinese classical poetry (Empson cites the example of Yuan poet Chao Meng-fu) (*CP* 400–1). Endurance was clearly a Chinese virtue that Empson admired and imitated.

[27] See Empson, 'The Argument of Marvell's "Garden"', *Essays in Criticism* (July 1952), 225–41.
[28] See Empson, 'The Critical Forum', *Essays in Criticism* (Jan. 1953), 114–20.
[29] Frank Kermode, *An Appetite for Poetry* (London: Fontana, 1990), 118.
[30] See 'Red on Red', *London Review of Books* (30 Sept. 1999), 66–7.
[31] 'I thought it hauntingly beautiful, all the more in the late dusk in the great square with a tense audience waiting for the liberation of the city'; Empson, 'Pei-Ta before the Siege', *Arrows* (Autumn 1961), 6.
[32] First published as 'Chinese Peasant Song', *Nine* (Summer-Autumn 1952), 316.

The impact of epochal events in Chinese history also had a palpable, if indirect, influence on his critical writing. Consider the provocatively offhand reference in *The Structure of Complex Words* to Cordelia's avoidable death: 'just the kind of thing that happens in the confusion of a "liberation"' (*SCW* 154). Empson knew everyday life under the conditions of a civil war and the sort of thing that can happen during a liberation. 'The "liberation" of the city [Peking],' he recalled 'was very snidely given that name, even by Europeans, though in Europe of course liberating a hen had come to mean stealing it for dinner.'[33] Cordelia's 'liberation' was a tragic delusion for Lear.[34] Empson's reflections upon this key word were soaked in experience, more so than those of Richards, who delighted to see China returning to former glories. He had accepted Empson's invitation to lecture in Peking after the inauguration of the People's Republic of China, but he remained sadly unaware of the manner in which the intellectual climate had begun to deteriorate under Communism.[35] Empson maintained that during his time at Peking University 'thought control' usually took the form of a tiresome 'nagging' from committees of colleagues and students, rather than the police terrors later initiated during the Cultural Revolution. He described this process as 'the dragooning of independent thought and the hysteria of the confession meetings' (*SSS* 217). Empson recalled his students in Peking with affectionate regret as 'dialectical materialists of course, their eyes shining with idealism' (*A* 118). He later claimed to have been resident in Peking during 'the honeymoon between the universities and the Communists, which was scarcely over when I left in 1952'.[36] Once again, he refused to gainsay what he had witnessed. 'It seems natural in England by this time to give a pretty gloomy jeer at the term "liberation"' he told his Sheffield colleagues and students at his inaugural lecture in 1953, yet his Peking students 'honestly did think they were liberated from serious danger when the Communist troops finally walked in' (*SSS* 214). Empson became extremely irritated with the CIA-funded *Encounter* magazine in 1955 when he felt it

[33] Empson, 'Pei-Ta before the Siege', 8.

[34] 'The power of the last speech comes from the repeated delusions, the boasting, the pretence that Cordelia is still alive' (*SCW* 151).

[35] According to George Watson, Richards claimed to be a 'great admirer' of Mao Tse-Tung throughout the years of the Cultural Revolution. See *Never Ones for Theory?* (Cambridge: Lutterworth, 2000).

[36] Empson, 'Pei-Ta before the Siege', 8.

deliberately misrepresented the political opinions of a Peking acquaintance, Fei Hsiao-Tung.[37]

When the Chinese Communist Government failed to renew his British Council teaching contract, Empson apparently reacted angrily, banging his fist on a table.[38] This may be true, but the news also undoubtedly provided a measure of relief. For one thing, Empson was having increasing difficulty communicating with his two sons, who were educated at a Chinese school.[39] His failure to speak Mandarin after seven years is arguably evidence of conflicted feelings about long-term adaptation to life in Communist China.[40] 'My impression of Empson abroad', observed Graham Hough, who met Empson several times in Asia, 'is always of an uncompromisingly English figure.'[41] According to Haffenden, Empson remained through his years of exile 'too much the Englishman ever to seek assimilation' (*WE1* 346). In fact, in a letter to Haffenden, Empson said that he had failed to integrate with Chinese society and had 'probably missed a great deal' (*SL* 672–3). Yet a first-hand awareness of the difficulties of acculturation can also be a powerful teacher. On the day before he was due to sail from China, Empson had his passport taken from him, without any explanation, leaving him to fret anxiously.[42] A fortnight later, aboard a P. & O. ship in Hong Kong finally bound for home, he sighed: 'It was like diving out of intense heat into a deep cool pool' (*SSS* 217). Nobody could suggest that Empson's years in China were easy, but in common with Milton's fiercely independent Satan, alienation and torment could be a source of knowledge and pride—a badge of integrity gestured to in controversies with less world-minded critics.

'The gifts of China': Buddhist Enlightenment

The most enduring legacy of Empson's sojourn in China was the tendency to draw upon thought-systems beyond the ambit of the Christian West,

[37] See *WE2* 237–71.

[38] See Mark Thompson, 'Letters to the Editor', *Times Literary Supplement* (8 July 2005), 15.

[39] See *SL* 184. According to Empson's eldest son, Mogador (b. 1942), the need to start an English education and fear over the possible escalation of the Korean War were the main reasons the Empsons left Peking in 1952. E-mail to Jason Harding, 10 Apr. 2006.

[40] For Empson's early impressions of the challenge, see 'Learning Chinese', *Night and Day* (19 Aug. 1937).

[41] See *London Review of Books* (4 July 1984), 16.

[42] Empson mentions this incident in *MG* 263–4.

achieving a double perspective conceptually (and apparently morally) broader and of greater complexity. In *Milton's God*, he delivered a sustained polemic against the Christian, or neo-Christian, orthodoxy that was, in his eyes, corrupting English literary criticism. It was an indictment founded upon detailed readings of the epic but also on pungently expressed personal testimony. On his return from Communist China, Empson informed readers, he had found neo-Christian assumptions 'widespread' (*MG* 230). This new orthodoxy, he felt, caused critics to misinterpret Milton's real intentions in *Paradise Lost*. Empson countered T. S. Eliot's assertion that Satan's rallying speech to his troops was devoid of rhetorical power. Had Empson not read this speech to his Chinese colleagues and pupils in 1939 and witnessed the thrilling effect it had on an audience susceptible to wartime propaganda?[43] Empson maintained that his wartime work for the BBC was an advantage in understanding the literary sophistication of a fellow wartime propagandist, Milton. Neo-Christians, venturing complacent pieties from positions of safety, could scarcely be expected to appreciate this point; nor did their fastidious sensibilities allow them to empathize with Satan's anguish on Mount Niphates: the torment of an aristocratic pride that, according to Empson, Milton depicted as very far from contemptible. Fit readers should, he argued, 'feel the agony of his ruined greatness' and also 'horror at the God who has deliberately reduced him to such a condition' (*MG* 69–70). Pride and honour, he declared with the assurance of a scion of landowning Yorkshire gentry, are aristocratic virtues that could lead to suffering, doubt, and despair. There is something decidedly cavalier about Empson's dismissal of a generation of bourgeois academic puritans.

The attack on the Christian God was underpinned by comparative anthropology. *Milton's God* argued that, unlike Chinese civilization, which had abandoned a craving for ritual human sacrifice to embrace Buddhism and Confucianism, the Christian West had regressed into the worship of a sadistic God who tortures and sacrifices his Son. Empson suggested the fundamental difference between the East and the West was not racial but theological.[44]

[43] '[Satan's speech] was received with fierce enthusiasm, but also with a mild groan from some of the older [Chinese] hands, who felt they had been having enough propaganda already' (*MG* 45).

[44] See *MG* 236–42. Note also: 'In the West, the supreme God is a person, in the East He is not . . . It is much the most fundamental line of division between the civilizations of the world, and we need to understand the people on the other side'; Empson, 'Ballet of the Far East', *Listener* (7 July 1937), 16.

There is little doubt his distaste for, and impatience with, the cruelty latent in Christian doctrine was exacerbated by the years he spent in China. Empson commented: 'it wasn't till I began teaching in a Christian country that I realized the active harm done by the religion' (*SL* 426). However, Empson was never as enthusiastic about Confucianism as Richards or Pound (in his eccentric fashion). By the time Empson arrived in China, Confucian thought was associated with the corruption and political reaction of the Qing dynasty. By contrast, Empson felt a profound sympathy with the teachings of the Buddha. John Haffenden has shown how extensive was Empson's engagement with Buddhism. He travelled in search of Buddhist sculpture at a time when Western art critics were groping towards a deeper understanding of its iconography. Empson was convinced by Alfred Foucher's theory that Buddhist art showed the impact of Hellenism.[45] In effect, he was seeking to bridge the theological 'gap' between East and West. In his introduction to a 1933 Japanese edition of T. S. Eliot's *Selected Essays*, Empson instructed his readers to think of Buddhism when Christian tradition was mentioned, or when Eliot attacked the romantic artist's self-expressive 'personality' (*A* 566–9). Empson was never a Buddhist disciple and he did not practise meditation; he said that he would not encourage his children to become disciples. None the less a respect for Buddhism is pervasive in his writings. It may even be that Buddhism was a factor behind his loss of interest in writing poetry. The poem 'Let it Go', published while Empson lived in Peking, announced an abandonment of any further analytical worrying at the intractable conflicts of selfhood:

The contradictions cover such a range.
  The talk would talk and go so far aslant.
    You don't want madhouse and the whole thing there.

(*CP* 99)

The renunciation of 'Let it Go' exemplifies Empson's belief that life is inadequate to the human spirit. The stoical endurance of 'Autumn on Nan-Yüeh' had superseded the witty, metaphysical passion of his earlier poetry. 'Let it Go' divests itself from an attachment to conflicted desires. Empson told Christopher Ricks: 'I just found in Peking I was writing some [poems] and it struck me they were bad, I didn't want to print them.' He

[45] See Alfred Foucher, *The Beginnings of Buddhist Art* (London: Humphrey Milford, 1917).

surmised: 'The motives which made me want to write had I suppose largely disappeared.'[46]

Haffenden has suggested that 'Let it Go' is essentially an argument in favour of 'moral and mental health'; but he doesn't add that the proposed balm is consistent with the precepts of Mahayana Buddhism (*RB* 23). In an early draft talk, Empson had referred to the Buddha's 'Fire Sermon' as 'a supreme example of the beauty of at any rate one sort of death wish in an almost pure form' (*A* 535).[47] He ameliorated this nihilism by mention of the attractions of Nirvana. 'The basic position', Empson explained 'is that Buddhists believe in abandoning selfhood, sometimes interpreted as merging oneself into the Absolute or the impersonal Godhead.'[48] The decision to reprint his own translation of the Buddha's 'Fire Sermon' as an epigraph to *Collected Poems* caused something of a stir in England. Empson responded to misunderstandings by saying: 'I think Buddhism much better than Christianity, because it managed to get away from the Neolithic craving to gloat over human sacrifice; but even so I feel that it should be applied cautiously.'[49] He informed his Sheffield students: 'Buddhism obviously deserves respect; for one thing, though not only, as an extreme; it needs to be remembered when one tries to survey what the human mind could think about a subject. But I naturally would not want to present myself as a believer by mistake.'[50] The exasperation displayed in Empson's replies was fuelled by the conviction that his audience was obstinately provincial. He put the matter bluntly: 'The Europeans have got to realize that Asia really exists' (*CP* 150).

'Would that somebody could tell adequately what Empson did through his long years in Peking!' exclaimed I. A. Richards in the 1974 Festschrift *William Empson: The Man and His Work* (cited in *CP* 150). In his meticulous biography, John Haffenden concluded: 'In a spiritual or intellectual sense at least, Empson's

[46] See Ian Hamilton (ed.), *The Modern Poet: Essays from The Review* (London: MacDonald, 1968), 177. Empson explained to Ricks he nursed himself 'back into literary work' by writing a book on the faces of the Buddha (*SL* 597).

[47] Empson commented: 'The early Buddhist position, not offering an argument for its assertion that all existence is suffering, cannot be refuted so easily; and I understand that scholars increasingly suspect it . . . of an assumption that Nirvana is not merely a blowing-out of a flame but a reabsorption into the Absolute' (*SCW* 424).

[48] Empson, 'Everything, Beggars, is on fire', *Arrows* (1957), 5.

[49] Empson, 'Mr Empson and the Fire Sermon', *Essays in Criticism* (Oct. 1956), 481.

[50] Empson, 'Everything, Beggars, is on fire', 6.

passionate interest in Buddhism and its iconography gave him a large part of the authority for his very presence in China' (*WE1* 448). We will be better able to assess the justice of this remark after Haffenden has edited the recently recovered manuscript of Empson's treatise on the faces of the Buddha. Buddhist iconography was without doubt a source of wisdom and comfort, a soothing effect mentioned by Empson in his review of the 1973 Chinese Exhibition at the Royal Academy, entitled 'the gifts of China'.[51] The 'gifts' bestowed by China complicated and unsettled the perspectives he had acquired through books. More than that, his experience of encounters with Chinese people and places opened challenging and invigorating new imaginative horizons. 'We have only two or three independent civilizations to compare', to repeat Empson's words to Kermode shortly after his return from Peking and 'it has a steadying effect to compare them'.[52] The professional trade of 'Eng. Lit.', he never ceased to warn, has a great need of these expansive world-views. His own years in China taught him about the necessity of maintaining one's balance when faced with conflicting socio-cultural values. 'It may be that the human mind can recognize actually incommensurable values,' Empson observed in *The Structure of Complex Words*, adding tellingly: 'the chief human value is to stand up between them, but I do not see how we could know that they were incommensurable till the calculation had been attempted' (*SCW* 421). Here the literary critic could be an invaluable guide. The importance of China to Empson across his career lends a particular richness to his oft quoted remark: 'The central purpose of reading imaginative literature is to grasp a wide variety of experience, imagining people with codes and customs very unlike our own' (*A* 218).

[51] 'The mature periods of Chinese art, and the introduction of Buddhism, take effect almost as soothers'; Empson, 'The Gifts of China', 27.

[52] Empson, 'The Critical Forum', 115.

6

Coleridge, Christ, and Contradiction in Empson

Seamus Perry

One of the questions that most interests admirers of Empson is the continuity, or otherwise, of his career. What does the intricate textual analysis of *Seven Types* for which Empson quickly became known (and in some quarters notorious: 'merely early William Empsonism' was not a term of praise in R. S. Crane's book)[1] have to do with the boisterous, sometimes knockabout, pugnacity of *Milton's God* and the essays on Donne and Marlowe and others, polemically preoccupied by the wickedness of the Christian God and the pernicious effects of neo-Christianity? Empson was quite aware that admirers of the early work thought his later stuff regrettably off-track, as though betraying some loss of due purpose or even magnanimity. Denis Donoghue shook his head ('an indisputable grandeur of spirit denies itself and becomes, when the theme is Christianity, pinched and nasty') and scolded the scion of Yokefleet Hall: 'Undermining a man's faith is not the work of a gentleman.'[2] Empson disputed any charge of gifts going to waste, needless to say: a breezy exasperation with such unenlightened times became a hallmark. 'I am glad of an opportunity to assure the reader that I do not look at it in that way myself', he wrote

[1] R. S. Crane, 'Criticism and Literary History', in his *The Idea of the Humanities and Other Essays Critical and Historical*, 2 vols. (Chicago: University of Chicago Press, 1967), ii. 39.

[2] Denis Donoghue, 'Some Versions of Empson', *Times Literary Supplement* (7 June 1974), 597–8 (p. 597).

in a 'Postscript' to Christopher Norris's 1978 monograph: 'I have not been entertaining myself with frippery in my old age; I have not even felt a change in my line of interest.'[3] Some of his most sympathetic critics have agreed: 'a moralist . . . from the beginning', says Roger Sale, and that sense of the career has been filled out most notably by Norris and Paul Fry, among others.[4] But Empson himself had to concede that, however urgent the obligation to undo the 'dirty nonsense' of contemporary Eng. Lit. (*A* 21), it did nevertheless feel 'less momentous than propounding a theory of Ambiguity', as though that were, in some respects anyway, a distinct sort of activity;[5] and if there was no hardening of heart exactly, such as Donoghue made out, then some change of heart surely did occur—'a shift, at least in emphasis, in Empson's sense of the world', as Christopher Ricks puts it, 'at one with his crusade against neo-Christianity . . . the new energies and emphases are very different'.[6]

Coleridge matters to both versions of Empson, though in diverse ways: sometimes, he is explicitly the object of criticism, a test case invoked to show Christianity's corrupting power, while at others his presence is profound but much more implicit, and often mediated through other authorities. Which Coleridge you find depends mostly on which period of Empson you're looking at; and getting a sense of how Empson's Coleridge changes may help to clarify some of the ways in which the late and the early Empson connect. (And there is a nicety here, which is that Empson's most extensive writings about Coleridge turn principally upon the radical discontinuity of *his* career,

[3] Christopher Norris, *William Empson and the Philosophy of Literary Criticism* (London: Athlone Press, 1978), 205.

[4] Roger Sale, 'The Achievement of William Empson', *Hudson Review*, 19: 3 (1966), 369–90 (p. 374); collected, in part, in John Constable (ed.), *Critical Essays on William Empson* (Aldershot: Scolar Press, 1993), 445–6 (p. 450). 'Empson's humanistic rationalism is present in his earliest writings, and forms a coherent and developing background to each of his books': Norris, *William Empson and the Philosophy of Literary Criticism*, 2. Paul H. Fry's book elegantly pursues its founding belief: 'the course of his work, from the earliest to the latest writings, is by no means discontinuous . . . at all times and in every context, what Empson says can be seen as a warning against the perils of renunciation': *William Empson: Prophet Against Sacrifice* (London: Routledge, 1991), pp. xiii, xiv.

[5] Norris, *William Empson and the Philosophy of Literary Criticism*, 206.

[6] Ricks, 'William Empson: The Images and the Story', in *The Force of Poetry* (Oxford: Oxford University Press, 1984), 179–243 (p. 194). Norris acknowledges a 'very marked change of tack': 'Introduction: Empson as Literary Theorist: From Ambiguity to Complex Words and Beyond', in Christopher Norris and Nigel Mapp (eds.), *William Empson: The Critical Achievement* (Cambridge: Cambridge University Press, 1993), 1–120 (p. 12). And see Empson's important letter, discussing the shape of his career, to Roger Sale (undated; c.1973): *SL* 546–51.

as Empson perceived it, a shift in opinions of which he took a very dim view.) I do not say that it was contemplating Coleridge that provoked Empson to his later mode, merely that his translation occurs within Coleridgean territory; and approaching Empson with Coleridge in mind brings usefully into the foreground some key concerns which might otherwise stay in the shadows.

I

The most detailed and involved treatment came relatively late, beginning with an essay on 'The Ancient Mariner' published in the *Critical Quarterly* in 1964; but the poem had drawn Empson long before that: the essay grew from some remarks in the chapter about Marvell in *Some Versions of Pastoral*. He returned to expand his argument in his Waynflete lectures, given in Oxford in 1972, which were otherwise taken up with attacking Helen Gardner's edition of Donne's *Elegies and Songs and Sonnets*; and he wrote up his thoughts as a long introduction to the selection of Coleridge's verse made with David Pirie and published with Faber that same year. A late essay, disputing the well-known interpretation of the poem by Robert Penn Warren, remained in typescript until rescued posthumously from Empson's papers by the tireless John Haffenden.[7]

'The Ancient Mariner' was important to the later Empson as an exemplary case of enlightened genius corrupted by Christian orthodoxy. In the *Critical Quarterly* piece, the corruption is largely the work of critics who, infected with a more general neo-Christian malaise, obtusely take the poem to be 'an allegory in favour of redemption by torment, the central tradition of Christianity'; Coleridge himself, though, was a committed Unitarian who 'disapproved of this plan for redemption'; and so the whole modern tradition of interpretation is based upon a grotesque misreading of the original poem. 'A student at Sheffield wrote in an essay for me that she would have hanged the Mariner from the yard-arm with her own hands', recalled Empson, testifying to the

[7] Empson, 'The Ancient Mariner', *Critical Quarterly*, 6: 4 (Winter 1964), 298–319 (collected in *A* 297–319). Introduction to *CV* 13–100. Empson's acknowledgement says: 'The substance of my Introduction here, together with some material about Donne making changes in his love-poems . . . constituted the Waynflete Lectures for 1972, sponsored by Magdalen College, Oxford' (*CV* 7). (This volume was reprinted in paperback as Samuel Taylor Coleridge, *Selected Poetry* (Manchester: Carcanet, 1989).) 'The Ancient Mariner: An Answer to Warren', *Kenyon Review*, 15: 1 (Winter 1993), 155–77 (collected in *SSS* 129–55).

ubiquity of the damage: 'I had to warn her that the External Examiner would consider this to be in the wrong tone of voice, but she was expressing the orthodox modern view' (*A*, 297). Empson briskly set about the orthodoxy. There is no crime committed and the albatross was shot for perfectly good reasons, although we are not told them plainly: it was killed 'for food', which was the right thing to do as supplies were needed badly: we know that the biscuits were full of worms (l. 65).[8] The smaller species of albatross, such as might fit round a neck, boils up to a decent soup that keeps off scurvy, Empson said he had been told—the sailors, who were voyaging into unknown seas, would have known that from the Atlantic voyager (*A* 300). The centre of the poem, whatever the critics maintain, is not a crime committed and then atoned for, as though in imitation of Christ; and we should properly be remarking of the Mariner, ' "How free from guilt he is, according to our own beliefs" ': 'It took a sad lack of sturdiness in the modern world, I think, to obscure this point altogether' (*A* 300). Just as *Othello* is not about jealousy but about unfounded jealousy, so 'The Ancient Mariner' is not about guilt but about 'uncaused guilt', or what Empson calls 'Neurotic Guilt', capitalizing the phrase as though to cite a recognized clinical condition (*A* 316, 305). A pervasive guiltiness hangs in the air waiting an occasion to condense, because of the ship's intrusion, at once courageous and terrible, into an unknown world: discovery and violation go inexorably together here as they did in the great maritime voyages, which had led in no time to the business of slavery against which Coleridge was speaking out magnificently in the years before composing the poem.

One immediate complication that Empson had to acknowledge was that, however noisy Coleridge's Unitarianism might have been outside the poem, 'The Ancient Mariner' manifestly goes out of its way to incorporate just the Christian cast of mind that its author deplored. The Mariner himself, a pre-Reformation man, is hardly likely to be a Unitarian; his language and attitudes seem entirely orthodox; he certainly considers what he did to be a crime, and his crewmates do too; and the moral he draws from the whole adventure and its protracted aftermath sounds remorselessly Godly: 'For the dear God, who loveth us, | He made and loveth all' (ll. 649–50). Empson saw

[8] References to the poem are taken from S. T. Coleridge, *Poems*, ed. John Beer (1963; rev. edn. London: Everyman, 1999). Unless otherwise stated, reference is made to the 1798 text published in *Lyrical Ballads*.

this, of course, and praised Coleridge for being 'historically correct' when he placed the habitual pieties in his character's mouth (*A* 315). Historical correctness brings with it the opportunity to judge the old fallacies. Empson heard in the moralizing lines 'an inadequate conclusion to so much lightning and despair' (*A* 310); and it is true that the worthy moral is uttered while the Mariner watches how, in church, 'each to his great father bends, | Old men, and babes, and loving friends, | And Youths, and Maidens gay' (ll. 640–2): if your nerves are already jangling, that does come across like something ghastly and crushing in Blake's *Songs of Experience.* A similarly artful dramatized inadequacy or incomprehension informs the poem at large: the Mariner has, naturally enough, been indoctrinated in the standard Christian formulae, and the work is properly a portrait in superstition—something like Wordsworth's contemporary poems 'The Thorn' and 'Goody Blake and Harry Gill' which deal more explicitly with the self-punishing dynamics of the neurotic mind. Like those poems, 'The Ancient Mariner' structures itself around a cognitive mismatch; it is mostly narrated by a man with the wrong end of the stick. Orthodox Christian structures of belief are present in the poem because they are present in the mind of the Mariner, in an exemplary sort of way, a set of powerful but wrong-headed notions with which he struggles to account for what he has gone through: as Empson says in the Introduction to *Coleridge's Verse*, 'he tries to apply the theology he has been taught to his baffling and heart-freezing experiences' (*CV* 31). It is not a Christian poem, then, but a poem about Christianity, in the sense that it is 'a kind of parody of the traditional struggle for atonement' (*A* 316). But the poem does more than expose, by irony, Christian error: there is a real spiritual good in the poem too, and I imagine Empson would have thought the performance very mean-spirited otherwise. For the whole thing genuinely does turn about a moment of redemption, just not redemption of a Christian kind (according to Empson anyway).

> Blue, glossy green, and velvet black
> They coil'd and swam; and every track
>   Was a flash of golden fire.
>
> O happy living things! no tongue
>   Their beauty might declare:
> A spring of love gusht from my heart,
>   And I bless'd them unaware!
>
> (ll. 271–7)

It is a saving glimpse of what Empson calls, plainly but profoundly, 'the variety of the world': like Lovejoy and Berlin, he understood such diversitarianism to be a 'basic impulse of the Romantics', one formed in reaction to the uniformitarian habits of their fathers (*A* 298).[9] The Mariner, secretly a better man than his culture had led him to believe, is 'astonished to find his inside admiring what his outside had thought disgusting': 'The snakes are absolutely other to him, like beings of another planet, and it is an alien part of his own mind which blesses them . . . I do not think there is any traditional Christian parallel to this' (*A* 311). The real moral of the poem then, though the Mariner's schooling won't allow him to grasp it, is not something about the restorative agency of suffering, but a vindication of pleasure in the world and the psychological health which that brings. Empson saw the Mariner's predicament speaking to young Coleridge with such special emphasis because living at loggerheads with yourself was Coleridge's habitual condition too; but where the Mariner is bewildered and lost, Coleridge is painfully self-aware of a life led at cross purposes to the doctrines that are meant to be organizing it, 'one moral code . . . dragging against another' (*A* 312). Empson had already scouted this out in *Pastoral*, where the Mariner's banal and well-meant summary was interpreted as a deft sleight of hand on Coleridge's part: 'knowing what the conventional phrases of modern Christianity ought to mean he thought he could shift to a conventional moral that needs to be based upon the real one' (*SVP* 101). The poem turns out to be something like Shakespeare's sonnets, which, '[f]ull as they are of Christian echoes . . . are concerned with an idea strong enough to be balanced against Christianity' (*SVP* 83). 'Delight in Nature when terrible gives one strength to control it', Empson offers as a truer moral than the Mariner's own (*A* 309), which is quoting himself, more or less, from *Pastoral*, where the point is glossed in this way: 'So long as the Mariner is horrified by the creatures of the calm he is their slave; he is set free to act, in the supreme verses of the poem, as soon as he delights

[9] See, for example, the chapter on 'Romanticism and the Principle of Plenitude' in A. O. Lovejoy, *The Great Chain of Being: A Study of the History of an Idea* (1936; repr. Cambridge, Mass.: Harvard University Press, 1961), 288–314. Berlin's conception of Romanticism is articulated in many places: e.g. his essay 'The Counter-Enlightenment' in *Against the Current: Essays in the History of Ideas*, ed. Henry Hardy (London: Hogarth Press, 1980), 1–24; and, at length, in *The Roots of Romanticism*, ed. Henry Hardy (London: Chatto & Windus, 1999), esp. 145–7. The pluralism of Empson and Berlin is usefully compared by Mark Thompson, 'Versions of Pluralism: William Empson, Isaiah Berlin, and the Cold War', *Literary Imagination*, 8: 1 (Winter 2006), 65–87.

in them' (*SVP* 101). So, unexpectedly, and unwittingly, the Mariner emerges as a hero of Empsonian pastoral, 'at once the representative figure and the exceptional one', in John Haffenden's expert phrase (*WE1* 384): the Mariner is an outcast and a kind of scapegoat, forever outside the society he exists to enlighten, 'the sacrifical image of doomed and noble isolation', in Christopher Norris's.[10]

The modern critics of 'The Ancient Mariner' also endorsed the bad Christian paradigms and thus, quite blind to the irony of the thing, got everything about the poem precisely upside down. And yet their inability to spot an organizing irony was not just a matter of being righteously obtuse: for, in fairness, Coleridge himself appeared on several occasions to endorse the Mariner's pious view of things. When *Lyrical Ballads* went into a second edition in 1800 he cut the archaisms (so reducing the sense of historical distance) and added an Argument at the head of the poem which spelt out a moral plainly enough: 'how the Ancient Mariner cruelly, and in contempt of the laws of hospitality, killed a Sea-bird.' Empson blames the changes, which he thinks generally for the worse, on the influence of Wordsworth who was fretting about the impact such an odd poem had had upon sales; but he also floats the idea, nicely, that Coleridge's revisions may have benefited from a kind of implicit jokiness that had been present from the poem's conception. He is very good on the larky holiday spirits in which the poem began, a lucrative skit on the vogue for chilling balladry ('maybe they laughed heartily on that walking-tour': *A* 301); and though the joke soon grew more complicated, the literary archaism of the first text ('The Ancyent Marinere') might linger in the olde-worlde manner of the Argument, as though the moral it announces were just as quaint. The Argument was not reprinted; but the marginal glosses that first appeared in the *Sybilline Leaves* version in 1817, and thereafter, imply the same version of events: 'The ancient Mariner inhospitably killeth the pious bird of good omen' (note to l. 79) and so on. In the *Critical Quarterly* article, Empson is ready to interpret 'pious bird' as 'a mild parsonical joke, an aside to relieve the boredom of the parents who overhear the children being taught not to pull poor pussy's tail', a matter of 'plugging the moral archly'—not the endorsement of a Christian moralism, that is to say, but something said to please the censorious ear of respectability, a little like the

[10] Christopher Norris's description of the pastoral hero: Norris, *William Empson and the Philosophy of Literary Criticism*, 177.

double irony that Empson admired in *Tom Jones* (*UB* 132–3). 'Still, he was not altering the story, and would not think he was altering the interpretation' (*A* 301–2).

By the time of the Introduction in 1972, however, the feeling has grown more embattled, and the possibility of enlightened joking has begun to fade away: the revised version of the essay is a darker thing altogether. Neo-Christians are still to blame for taking as the poem's moral precisely what the poem dramatizes as grossly wrong-headed; but now, chief among those critics is Coleridge himself. The older Coleridge, a worldly-wiser man, finally broken into Anglicanism, returns to the work of younger, enlightened, pantheistic Coleridge, and distorts his greatest work dreadfully. In the first version of the poem, 'What redeems the Mariner is the opposite of pious self-torture; it is the return of spontaneous delight in the beauty of the world'; but this healthy heterodoxy is covered over by omission and revision, especially by the pious marginal commentary, a 'parasitic growth' which Coleridge added, Empson suggests, while 'in a thorough revulsion against the whole doctrine of Nature, as well as an extremely bad nervous condition' (*CV* 35, 43, 42). The idea that the piety of the notes might share in a collusive sort of joke with the reader, sympathetic with, but superior to, the benighted pre-enlightenment mind of the Mariner, is still just about present: 'the glosses are supposed to be written by a remote old pedant', says Empson, allowing a dramatized dimension to them and even suggesting that we 'may sometimes suppose the enlightened Coleridge to laugh at him for it' (*CV* 47). 'If a reader is disgusted at the tone of pious unction suddenly adopted by the Mariner, he may without serious falsification regard Coleridge as writing a parody of it, with this purpose' (*CV* 78–9); but 'without serious falsification' is a thin edge for a defence to stand on, and generally there is not much sense in the later essay of old Coleridge's connection with the mind that had authored a freethinking masterpiece. The main feeling, on the contrary, is the bleaker one that, as Empson puts it, 'the old Coleridge has ratted on the young one' (*CV* 48). And in the response to Robert Penn Warren, written in the mid-1970s, an entrenched annoyance at Coleridge's betrayal of himself has grown stronger still: 'the bemused Coleridge who wrote Glosses in 1815 wanted to pretend that all his early poems had pious morals' (*SSS* 131). Older Coleridge is now held to be entirely complicit in the poem's 'destruction' because it was his writings that precipitated disaster in Eng. Lit. in the first place: he had himself 'invented the frame of mind dominant among critics in 1930–50' (*SSS* 155, 146)—which is to say, neo-Christian, Symbolist, anti-rational, contemptuous of narrative, and generally hag-ridden.

The account is brilliant, at once reckless and reasonable like the best of late Empson. As it happens, by bringing colonialism to bear on the poem it anticipates a lot of (rather less brilliant) modern criticism; yet for all that I don't think the piece is much celebrated in recent scholarship, which would doubtless have confirmed Empson's bleakest suspicions, especially since the great Bollingen edition has subsequently made available a lot of evidence that Empson could have claimed for his side. Coleridge 'did not believe the religion which was technically required of him', says Empson, meaning Anglican Christianity, and his essay tries to piece together Coleridge's reasons for disbelief, attributing to him a disinclination to publicize his 'basic religious objection' (*A* 313). In fact, the 1795 *Lectures on Politics and Religion* show a Coleridge not remotely shy of setting out his objections. His Unitarianism involved discounting as corruptions of the truth, among other things, the divinity of Jesus, Original Sin, the miraculous conception, free will, the Trinity, the Atonement, and the efficacy of prayer—indeed, as Basil Willey once mildly observed, most of Christianity's fundamental doctrines.[11] When he called himself a Christian Coleridge meant that he admired and sought to emulate Jesus, the chief practical result of which seems to have been the abolition of private property; but he was vehemently against 'Christianity' as it was taught in churches and schools and Cambridge University, and when he and his friends were planning their utopian settlement he sought to rule out any influence of '*Christianity*,—I mean—that mongrel whelp that goes under it's [*sic*] name'.[12] Unsurprisingly, rumours spread that he was an atheist, or a deist: Coleridge enjoyed evangelizing what he called 'the heterodoxy of Unitarianism'.[13] In the *Critical Quarterly* essay Empson says he can find only one place where the ground for Coleridge's objection to orthodoxy becomes clear (*A* 313), though he could have found old Coleridge in the *Table Talk*, youthful passion long spent, being perfectly candid about 'a strong sense of the repugnancy of the doctrine of vicarious atonement . . . and I thought nothing

[11] Basil Willey, *The Eighteenth Century Background: Studies on the Idea of Nature in the Thought of the Period* (London: Chatto & Windus, 1949), 188.

[12] S. T. Coleridge, *Collected Letters of Samuel Taylor Coleridge*, ed. Earl Leslie Griggs, 6 vols. (Oxford: Oxford University Press, 1956–71), i. 123.

[13] Ibid. i. 112–13, 153.

could counterbalance that'.[14] The 1795 lectures are plainly outspoken about 'the Doctrine of Atonement . . . as it is now held', denounced by Coleridge as 'perhaps the most irrational and gloomy Superstition that ever degraded the human mind'; and he has some splendid platform oratory against the idea that God's outraged sense of justice was somehow satisfied by the torments of Christ on the cross, the view set out by Bishop Butler for example.[15]

The God present in such gloomy doctrine is the Father figure Empson memorably described in *Milton's God* as 'the wickedest thing yet invented by the black heart of man' (*MG* 251). Coleridge does sometimes use a normal Christian language of Fatherhood, especially when solicitous ('the God of mercies, and father of all comfort',[16] and so forth); but in 'The Destiny of Nations' such rhetoric normally falters at once as fatherhood dissolves into a more instinctively appealing abstraction—'Eternal Father! King Omnipotent! | . . . the Will Absolute, the One, the Good!'—or disperses into a kind of omnific Spinozistic immanence: 'Glory to Thee, Father of Earth and Heaven! | All-conscious Presence of the Universe! | Nature's vast ever-acting Energy! | In will, in deed, Impulse of All to All!' ('Destiny of Nations', ll. 4–5; 459–62). And the sense of deity veers erratically in 'Religious Musings', similarly, between a 'great Father' and an impersonal idea of 'Nature's essence, mind, and energy'—'The SUPREME FAIR sole operant' (ll. 67; 55; 62): his Unitarian convictions are undercutting a more traditional sort of idiom here, as they do (in Empson's reading) in the 'Mariner'. Coleridge told a fellow Unitarian: 'the worship of one God becomes Idolatory when instead of the Eternal & Omnipresent, in whom we live, & move, & *have* our Being, we set up a distinct Jehovah tricked out in the *anthropomorphic* Attributes of Time & *Successive* Thoughts—& think of him, as a PERSON';[17] and in a slightly later letter he set out the point with heartfelt urgency: 'you were the first man, from whom I heard that article of my Faith distinctly enunciated, which is the nearest to my Heart, the pure fountain of all [my] moral & religious Feelings & [C]omforts—I mean, the absolute Impersonality of the [D]eity'[18] (quoted in *CV* 93). In time he changed his mind on the point, to be sure; but he was never blithe about the cost of the new position: looking back in *Biographia Literaria*,

[14] S. T. Coleridge, *Table Talk*, ed. Carl Woodring, 2 vols. (Princeton: Princeton University Press, 1990), i. 489.
[15] S. T. Coleridge, *Lectures 1795 on Politics and Religion*, ed. Lewis Patton and Peter Mann (Princeton: Princeton University Press, 1970), 204. Coleridge is drawing on Joseph Priestley.
[16] Coleridge, *Letters*, i. 239. [17] Ibid. ii. 893. [18] Ibid. ii. 1022–3.

he remarked coolly how it took him 'a very long time indeed' to 'reconcile personality with infinity', which suggests a tough battle to persuade himself he had pulled the trick off.[19]

This is all roundly Empsonian: no wonder he greeted young Coleridge with such warmth, for Coleridge must have seemed, like Marlowe, Marvell, and Dryden, to avow just the sort of freethinking deism of which Empson could approve.[20] The moral disaster of the mainstream Western tradition, as he argued at length in the last chapter of *Milton's God*, lay in its conception of the deity as a person, where 'India and China tended to conceive an Absolute'. Tricked out anthropomorphically, God naturally acquires a set of motives, and then the redemptive mechanism of the Crucifixion suddenly begins to feel perplexing, if not murky. Even the faithful consider it a profound mystery that God should be satisfied by his Son's suffering to extend a possibility of redemption to mankind: Empson sniffs out the bad old 'Neolithic craving for human sacrifice' (*MG* 241). By denying God His personality, thought Empson, the Unitarianism of Socinius had constituted the real Reformation, 'and it went down in blood' (*MG* 282). For the unreformed Christian poet, such as Milton or Herbert, moral decency could only be a matter of self-division, the better half of the mind resisting the appalling theology embraced by the worse. (Of Milton: 'his feelings continually cry out against his theory' (*SVP* 147).) So, Empson suggests, I suppose implausibly, that Milton has his God ready to do the decent thing at the millennium and to resign His personality altogether: He will turn Himself into something like 'the God of the Cambridge Platonists and suchlike mystical characters', 'dissolve into the landscape and become immanent only'—which sounds very like the kind of divine life to be found in the Unitarian space of a Coleridge conversation poem (*MG* 132, 133).[21] Reading the words of Milton's God, 'For regal Sceptre then no more shall need, | God shall be All in All,' [22] Empson took the phrase from Corinthians ('All in All') to mean 'the Absolute' (*MG* 135)—rather as Coleridge used 'All to All' in 'The Destiny of Nations', although he was acclaiming an immanence

[19] S. T. Coleridge, *Biographia Literaria*, ed. James Engell and Walter Jackson Bate, 2 vols. (Princeton: Princeton University Press, 1983), i. 201.

[20] Of Marlowe, 'the basic position is what was later called Deism; his "atheism" meant not believing that Jesus was God' (*FC* 166 n. 3). For Marvell and his belief in Natural Magic, see *UB* 3–27; and for Dryden's deism, *UB* 99–122. And see Fry, *William Empson*, 26.

[21] See John Haffenden's discussion of the point in *A* 30–1.

[22] *The Works of John Milton*, ed. F. A. Patterson, 18 vols. (New York: Columbia University Press, 1931–8), iii. 340.

already achieved and not merely one in hopeful prospect: 'God is every where, I have exclaimed, & works every where', as he wrote excitedly to Wedgwood.[23] Empson was testy about the 'shuffling' version of the doctrine put forward in 'Tintern Abbey' (*STA* 183); but his impatience is a mark of the seriousness with which he wished to regard the Spinozistic or (broadly speaking) Unitarian position at issue, which Wordsworth had acquired from his garrulous friend.[24] Elsewhere Empson could sound rather more approving: when he singles out from *Paradise Lost* one of God's incongruously hopeful lines about heavenly life, 'United as one individual Soul', Empson says it feels 'oddly like Wordsworth' (*MG* 104)—which is to say, in the circumstances, like a breath of fresh air.[25]

There is a well-known theological solution to the gloom of the Torture-God, of course: the Trinity. 'A Christian reader will be feeling that there is an obvious and decisive answer to such talk', Empson acknowledges in the closing section of *Milton's God*, namely, that '[t]he Father is in some sense identical with the Son': in that case the possibility of vicarious satisfaction could not arise, since the act would really be an act of self-sacrifice (*MG* 243). Elsewhere he reflected: 'I was often abashed, reading C. S. Lewis while I was writing *Milton's God*, by the awe and wonder with which he treats the doctrine of the Atonement as meaning that God himself endured torture for the sake of man . . . There can be no possible complaint against such a doctrine; it clears the Father absolutely, and deserves the astonishment with which Lewis surrounds it' (*UB* 119). But 'astonishment' here is close to 'incredulity', and, generally, Empson refused to see the Trinity as anything other than a piece of irrational fumbling designed to obscure a dreadful truth. Whatever his official position might have been, when Milton portrayed the Father and the Son as 'about as identical as a terrier and a camel' he was coming clean about something fundamental to the religion.[26] 'The doctrine of the Trinity is necessary', Empson explained brightly in his review of Eliot's booklet about Herbert, 'or the Father appears too evil' (*A* 257); and in *Milton's God*, the doctrine is similarly despatched as 'a means of deceiving good men into accepting evil; it is the double-talk by which Christians hide from themselves the insane wickedness of their God' (*MG* 245). 'Double-talk' there is clearly alluding to Orwell's 'double-think': Empson often makes a connection between Orwellian Newspeak and the double-minded claims of

[23] Coleridge, *Letters*, ii. 916. [24] See Norris, 'Empson as Literary Theorist', 61.
[25] See also Empson, 'Basic English and Wordsworth' (*A* 232–8).
[26] Empson, 'Correspondence' (reply to a review of *Milton's God*, by R. L. Brett), *Critical Quarterly*, 3 (1961), 368; collected in Constable (ed.), *Critical Essays*, 361.

Trinitarian theology—'that the Father and the Son both are and are not identical, and that you will go to Hell unless you believe both' and so forth (*MG* 246).[27] In his response to the Milton book Graham Hough complained that Empson 'brushes off the consubstantiality of the Son with the Father as a mere form of words': a brave man to criticize Empson, of all people, for dismissing verbal complexities, as John Haffenden says (*A* 27); but Hough was quite right. Empson's view of the matter is bracingly impatient with mystery, full of bright eighteenth-century light. (Karl Miller once astutely observed Empson's fondness for the word 'clear'.[28]) The same light shone in young Coleridge, who followed Joseph Priestley and other illuminati in his dismissive attitude towards religious incomprehensibility: in the 1795 lectures Coleridge refers to the Trinity as a 'thrice strange Union' while speaking scornfully of 'the wondrous Power of the Cross'.[29] 'One can hardly discuss whether a man believes this doctrine, because it is merely a thing which his mind can be induced to do', said Empson (*MG* 245): 'it is a set of verbal contradictions', he wrote in a letter to John Wain, and a man can 'only inure his mind to accepting them' (*SL* 639).

II

The Coleridge who makes himself felt in the mind of the young Empson picks up on a very different set of preoccupations. This is not the young Unitarian, but an older Coleridge: the literary thinker of *Biographia Literaria*; and he exerts his presence in a pervasive but usually implicit way, mediated most obviously through the writings and lectures of I. A. Richards.

Coleridgean assumptions about the work of poetry underwrote Richards's theorizing long before the book he explicitly devoted to Coleridge in 1934: in *Principles of Literary Criticism* (1924) he had described chapter fourteen of *Biographia* as 'that lumber-room of neglected wisdom which contains more hints towards a theory of poetry than all the rest ever written upon the subject'.[30] That is

[27] He discusses Orwell's novel in *MG* 234–6, and mentions it tellingly elsewhere (69, 245); and see, for example, 'Christianity and *1984*' in *A* 601–2; and *SL* 234–5. Paul Fry observes that Empson 'could never stop mentioning' *Nineteen Eighty-Four: William Empson*, 94.

[28] Karl Miller, 'Empson Agonistes', in Roma Gill (ed.) *William Empson: The Man and his Work*, (London: Routledge, 1974), 41–8 (p. 44).

[29] Coleridge, *Lectures 1795*, 207.

[30] I. A. Richards, *Principles of Literary Criticism*, 2nd edn. (London: Kegan Paul, 1934), 140.

pitching it high; but it is at least true that a great deal of Richards's thinking on the subject builds on Coleridge's gnomic assertion within that packed chapter that the imagination 'reveals itself in the balance or reconciliation of opposite or discordant qualities', so bringing (in Coleridge's words) 'the whole soul of man into activity, with the subordination of its faculties to each other, according to their relative worth and dignity'[31]—'whatever calls into consciousness the greatest number . . . in due proportion & perfect harmony with each other', as he spelt it out in a Notebook, 'is the noblest Poem'.[32] Richards called the famous passage about imagination 'Coleridge's greatest contribution to critical theory', one to which 'it is hard to add anything'.[33] He nevertheless managed to add a good deal, much of it seeking to remake Coleridge in the terms of his own quasi-Benthamite psychological idiom ('I write then as a Materialist trying to interpret before you the utterances of an extreme Idealist');[34] but for all the revisionism, the foundational axiom of Richards's theory, to which he returned repeatedly in the works of his Cambridge period, is wholly Coleridgean: poetry matters because it brings into balance the heterogeneity of your otherwise conflicting attitudes and interests. The good life, says Richards in *Science and Poetry* (1926), is when your interests 'come into play and remain in play with as little conflict among themselves as possible', a condition of being which is to be found in 'the experience of poetry': poetry effects 'the swinging back into equilibrium of these disturbed interests'.[35] One of the main *Principles of Literary Criticism*, similarly, is that '[t]he equilibrium of opposed impulses, which we suspect to be the ground-plan of the most valuable aesthetic responses, brings into play far more of our personality than is possible in experiences of a more defined emotion'—which John Haffenden has astutely identified as the cue for Empson's own ' "conflict" theory of poetry', as it is named in *Seven Types of Ambiguity* (*A* 48; *STA* 263).[36] 'The balance or reconciliation of opposite or discordant qualities': Muriel Bradbrook recalled of Cambridge in the late 1920s how 'Coleridge's definition of the poet's activity . . . could have been recited

[31] Coleridge, *Biographia*, ii. 16; 15–16.

[32] S. T. Coleridge, *The Notebooks of Samuel Taylor Coleridge*, ed. Kathleen Coburn *et al*, 5 vols. (Princeton: Princeton University Press, 1957–2001), iii. 3827.

[33] Richards, *Principles*, 242.

[34] I. A. Richards, *Coleridge on Imagination* (London: Kegan Paul, 1934), 19.

[35] I. A. Richards, *Science and Poetry*; in *Poetries and Sciences: A Reissue of* Science and Poetry *(1926, 1935) with Commentary* (London: Routledge, 1970), 38, 39, 28.

[36] Richards, *Principles*, 251.

by any pupil of Richards as surely as a Presbyterian could recite the Shorter Catechism'.[37] Certainly, the imprint of the fourteenth chapter, and of other favourite Coleridgean formulations, shows itself often enough in the young Empson, as when Shakespeare's wit is praised for 'variety in unity' (*STA* 122). The job of the artist is to 'repeat the audience in himself', he writes in *Pastoral*, and since the audience is naturally disorganized and disputatious, 'complex and ill-connected', this entails a further task, which he casts in an eminently Coleridgean spirit: 'to reconcile the opposites into a larger unity' or to 'suggest a balanced position', and so on (*SVP* 60, 56).[38]

'That all these good qualities should be brought together is a normal part of a good poem; indeed, it is a main part of the value of a poem, because they are so hard to bring together in life' (*STA* 140). Where Richards characteristically emphasizes balance and reconciliation, Empson tends to dwell on the oppositions and discords which are the imagination's prerequisites: a poem is often a more war-torn phenomenon in Empson's criticism than it is in Richards's; but they are working the same Coleridgean theme. An emphasis upon the conflicting raw materials might be the inevitable result of seeking to show the reconciliatory powers at work: as when Coleridge says at one point in *Biographia*, 'While I am attempting to explain this intimate coalition, I must suppose it dissolved'; but equally it might betray an intelligence that's just more at home with conflict and division than it is with their notional harmonic resolution.[39] 'I can tell you why people make revolutions: they feel a conflict and they don't know what they expect, and they make a revolution merely because they get so irritated' (*CP* 119). Alternatively, they make poems. If an attunement to contradictoriness lies at the centre of his sense of poetry, including his own poetry—a way 'of expressing an unresolved conflict', 'done

[37] Muriel Bradbrook, 'The Ambiguity of William Empson', in Gill (ed.), *William Empson*, 2–12 (p. 4). Bradbrook goes on to say: 'It was partly this definition of the poet and poetry, I would think, from which *Seven Types of Ambiguity* originated, although Empson himself in his preface names as "onlie begetter" I. A. Richards and for the method, Robert Graves's and Laura Riding's analysis of Sonnet CXXIX in *A Survey of Modernist Poetry* (1927)' (ibid).

[38] And, as with Coleridge, the principle implies that the more contradictions encompassed, the better: 'the idea that poetry is good in proportion as it is complicated, or simply hard to construe; it seems quite a common delusion, and always shocks me when expressed. And yet I suppose it is very near my own position; in any case it joins onto I. A. Richards's Theory of Value as the satisfaction of more impulses rather than less' (*A* 105).

[39] Coleridge, *Biographia*, i. 255. 'It may be said that the contradiction must somehow form a larger unity if the final effect is to be satisfying', Empson wrote in a footnote in *Seven Types*, 'But the onus of reconciliation can be laid very heavily on the receiving end' (*STA* 226 n.).

to prevent him from going mad' (*CP* 124, 123)—then that is because it is at the centre of his sense of life outside poetry too. (It was praise he was prepared to risk extending to the best of his own poems that they were 'complicated in the way that life really is' (*CP*, p. xxxix).) The Ricardsian poet possesses a composed inward balance; 'artists commonly live in muddles', Empson wrote, contrarily, in his copy of Richards's *Principles.*[40]

A poem, in miniature, like a life at large, involves 'maintaining oneself between contradictions that can't be solved by analysis', as the celebrated note to 'Bacchus' runs; and prominent among those contradictions, as the note continues, is 'the religious one about man being both animal and divine' (*CP* 290). That was a contradiction that the Trinitarian Christ lived out at a fabulous extreme. In later years, Empson would often maintain that his opposition to Christianity had always been firm and so obvious that it didn't need stating at the time: 'If there is any insincerity about the change in Empson', he wrote to Roger Sale in 1973, 'it comes in the first two books, where I did not explain that I thought the Father who was satisfied by the Crucifixion disgusting; but really, everyone I knew thought that already, and accepted reserve about it as mere politeness' (*SL* 547). But this is to simplify the oddly compelling role that Christianity actually plays in the first books, where Empson treats it with an intricacy and a fascination which belies any claim of simply unmitigated disgust—as, for example, where in the brief and brilliant reading of a stanza from 'Summer's Last Will and Testament' he speaks memorably of a 'specifically Christian fusion of . . . elements' (*STA* 141). The figure of Christ, especially, occurs in these books with a peculiar force as though gathering a set of preoccupations: in the conjunction of opposites that makes up his complicated Trinitarian identity, Christ lives out in an intense and archetypal way an Empsonian multiplicity, embodying (as Empson says when discussing Herbert's 'The Sacrifice') 'the most complicated and deeply-rooted notion of the human mind' (*STA* 270).

'Twixt devil and deep sea, man hacks his caves; | Birth, death; one, many; what is true, and seems': Empson glossed the lines, '"Man lives between the contradictory absolutes of philosophy, the one and the many, etc."' ('Arachne', *CP* 34, 220–1). Both the early books, *Seven Types of Ambiguity* and *Some Versions of Pastoral*, are, each in its own way, about the One and the Many, their mutual dependence and complication; and the incarnate Christ

[40] Norris, *William Empson and the Philosophy of Literary Criticism*, 177.

is the symbol of that philosophical imponderable: 'The supreme example of the problem of the One and Many was given by the Logos who was an individual man' (*SVP* 70). In the terms of the first book, a successful ambiguity is at once a unity of effect, and a unity made up of contradictory elements, properly giving 'room for alternative reactions' (*STA* 19); the multiplicity of the poetry speaks to and organizes a multiplicity within the reader: so, upon investigation, 'the godlike unity of the appreciator' turns out to be 'complex and ill-connected' (*STA* 60) and his experience only 'a sort of unity'—what Empson calls 'a unity like a crossroads' (*SVP* 77). In the terms of the second book, Christ is the exemplary pastoral hero, and he crops up all over the place in *Some Versions of Pastoral*: the pastoral figure is at once universal and yet incorrigibly particular, 'the general . . . given a sort of sacred local habitation', which makes Christ the prototype for all other instances (*SVP* 70)—such as 'the honest man' who, 'in achieving normality reconciles a contradiction and becomes a half-divine figure of pastoral' (*SCW* 196). In his lucid account of Empson and the idea of pastoral, Paul Alpers identifies Christ as the 'one hero', because he alone 'fully takes on the conflicts of other men and experiences them as his own':[41] he is picking up there on a point made by Roger Sale, who found in the contradictory figure of the hero-swain the epitome of 'a sensibility that can unify'.[42] In due imitation of Christ, contradictoriness is the stock-in-trade of much Christian poetry, and when *Seven Types* reaches its climax with the seventh type, the articulation of 'a fundamental division in the writer's mind', 'at once an indecision and a structure, like the symbol of the Cross', it is to Trinitarian poems by Crashaw, Hopkins, and Herbert that Empson gratefully turns (*STA* 225, 226), rising to a crescendo of oppositions in what Empson calls 'the final contradiction' as he discusses Herbert's 'The Sacrifice', as though crowning the book:

> the complete Christ; scapegoat and tragic hero; loved because hated; hated because godlike; freeing from torture because tortured; torturing his torturers because all-merciful; source of all strength to men because by accepting he exaggerates their weakness; and, because outcast, creating the possibility of society. (*STA* 269)

The contradictions cover such a range.

[41] Paul Alpers, 'Empson on Pastoral', *New Literary History*, 10: 1 (1978), 101–23 (p. 118).
[42] Sale, 'The Achievement of William Empson', 381.

The contradictoriness of the Christ myth becomes another Empsonian interest: jokes. (They were a Coleridgean fascination too.) Where the New Critics—who sometimes claimed filiation but whose paternity Empson vigorously denied—tended to see multiple meanings organized into specially aesthetic structures like 'irony' or 'paradox' or 'tension', Empson saw them working by less specialized machinery, such as jokes, which led a life outside literature too.[43] Jokes are doubtless very various, but one good sort depends upon a meeting or clash of opposites—perhaps within a particular word, as in a pun, or between attitudes or assumptions—and they involve your appreciation of difference while yet you apprehend the odd appropriateness of the conjunction: like an ambiguity or pastoral or irony, such a joke is a playing out of oneness and manyness, where 'incompatibles are joined', as in a myth (*SCW* 242). *Some Versions of Pastoral* speaks as much of jokes as it does of Christ—at one point, admiringly, of the possible 'richness of a joke', which evidently has something to do with the manifold richness he ascribes to Marvell elsewhere in the book: 'readiness for argument not pursued' (*SVP* 51, 118). But perhaps the most tantalizing appearance jokes make in Empson is in the effortlessly superior review he wrote in 1928 of *Words and Poetry* by George Rylands, which ended 'I believe myself poetry is written with the sort of joke you find in hymns' (*A* 69).[44] It is a showily private witticism; but there is a

[43] 'But I deny that a poem is a private self-subsisting world', he wrote to the *TLS* in response to a review (*MG* 286). See Jonathan Culler, 'for Empson ambiguities derive precisely from the continuity between language in poems and language in other situations': 'A Critic against the Christians' (review of *Using Biography*), *Times Literary Supplement* (23 Nov. 1984), 1327–8 (p. 1327). His own works have sometimes been taken to be jokes, or like jokes. '*Some Versions of Pastoral* is, I have said, an elaborate joke', says Samuel Hynes, *The Auden Generation: Literature and Politics in England in the 1930s* (London: Bodley Head, 1976), 172. When Geoffrey Strickland ventured to think it 'difficult not to believe that Mr Empson is not [*sic*] aware that his latest work [i.e. *The Structure of Complex Words*] is in many ways a solemn joke', Empson responded ferociously: 'The meanmindedness of anybody who can believe I did that feels to me quite sickening', *Mandrake*, 2: 10 (Autumn and Winter 1954–5), 320–31 (p. 330), and 2: 11 (Autumn and Winter 1955), 447–8 (p. 448) in Constable (ed.), *Critical Essays*, 298–308 (p. 307); and 309–10 (p. 309).

[44] Incidentally, Rylands suggests that poetry works in two main ways, by sound—'The letter S is valuable', he remarks at one point—and by the association of particular objects—'in themselves beautiful, poetic subjects [which] possess secondary emotional implications': *Words and Poetry*, introd. Lytton Strachey (London: Hogarth Press, 1928), 48, 65. These seem very like the two rival theories of which Empson disposes in the first chapter of *Seven Types*, namely 'Pure Sound' and 'Atmosphere', suggesting that it is Rylands, not mentioned in those pages, whom he has particularly in mind.

religious joke in *Some Versions of Pastoral* that might help a bit.[45] Empson quotes there a comical and unsettling passage from the Second Shepherd's Play in the Towneley cycle, in which Mak and his wife, a comic underplot to the proper nativity story, have hidden a stolen sheep in a cradle, pretending it is a newborn boy. The shepherds grow suspicious about the contents of the crib, and Mak's wife protests: 'If ever I you beguiled | May I eat this child, | That lies in this cradle.'[46] Empson calls this 'a powerful joke on the eating of Christ in the Sacrament' (*SVP* 30). The joke is partly that she is sending up a greater solemnity, of course; but what makes the joke peculiar and powerful is the way her low-life burlesque version of the nativity comes so weirdly close to the real thing, as though a version of it and not simply its parody: it is a choice example of the comedy of mock-heroic, about which Empson writes with special brilliance, in which 'the mutual comparison . . . elevates both parties' (*STA* 140). Pastoral, with its constitutive 'clash between style and theme', was always liable to 'become funny' (*SVP* 17); and there was permanently open in Empson's mind a connection between pastoral and the rich joke of mock-heroic:[47] for a mutually complicating juxtaposition of the elevated and the mundane is the stuff of both. It is also the stuff of Christ's incarnation within the Trinitarian scheme, in which an unimportant person is chosen to represent the author and judge of the universe: the proximity helps explain the odd compulsion in *Some Versions*, especially, to bring Christ in. So I like to think that the jokes that Empson enjoyed in hymns were unwitting pieces of mock-heroic, the contradictions of the theology coming together with cumbersome honesty—like, 'Born thy people to deliver, | Born a child and yet a King' ('Come thou long expected Jesus'), or 'Did e'er such love and sorrow meet, | Or thorns compose so rich a crown?' ('When I survey the

[45] Paul Fry suggests: 'the true occasion of poetry is the longing for the reciprocal attention of other minds, a longing made absurd in hymns by the non-existence of the other mind addressed but marking for that very reason the poignancy and urgency of all poetry projecting its words into silence', *William Empson*, 17.

[46] i.e. 'If euer I you begyld, | That I ete this chylde | That lygys in this credyll': 'Secunda Pastorum', ll. 536–8, in *The Wakefield Pageants in the Towneley Cycle*, ed. A. C. Cawley (Manchester: Manchester University Press, 1963), 43–63 (p. 57).

[47] If you choose an important person to serve as the representative of a class, he says in *Pastoral*, then 'the result is heroic', and 'if you choose an unimportant one it is pastoral' (*SVP* 70), which discreetly brings pastoral and mock-heroic into company. See Fry, *William Empson*, 96. The link between the two first books occurs in the third chapter of *Seven Types*: 'It is this (in some sense conscious) clash between different modes of feeling which is the normal source of pleasure in pastoral' (140).

wondrous cross'), or 'Praise we him, whose love divine | Gives his sacred Blood for wine, | Gives his Body for the feast, | Christ the victim, Christ the priest' ('At the Lamb's high feast we sing'), or 'That last night, at supper lying, | 'Mid the twelve, his chosen band, | Jesus, with the law complying, | Keeps the feast its rites demand; | Then, more precious food supplying, | Gives himself with his own hand' ('Now, my tongue, the mystery telling'). At such moments, the innate incompatibles of Christ's story—kingship and kinship, victory and victimhood, sovereignty and subjugation—get forced together in a blunt-witted and unyielding way which might well afford a certain hilarity to the discriminating. Anyway, religious jokes of a subtler kind feature at the climax of *Seven Types*. Of Crashaw's 'Hymn to Saint Teresa', in which the chastity of the saint is described in sexual language, Empson writes, 'You might think I was being merely malicious in this collocation; trying to defile a Holy Thought by making it into a Dirty Joke. But the two systems of thought are not as unlike as all that';[48] the reading of Hopkins's 'Windhover' turns about a pun in 'buckle'; and while Herbert's 'The Sacrifice' is not exactly a series of gags, the fraught paradox of its representation of Jesus is nevertheless said to exhibit 'a pathetic humour' (*STA* 255, 261, 269). The description of the seventh class of ambiguity, taken alone, might be the description of a good joke, as well as a Coleridgean reconciling of opposites: 'two opposed judgments are being held together and allowed to reconcile themselves, to stake out different territories, to find their own level, in the mind' (*STA* 253).

To put it in these terms is hardly to speak the quasi-scientific, psychologico-materialist language of Richards; but then Richards was not the only Coleridgean figure to influence the young Empson. T. S. Eliot had prominently quoted Coleridge on the imagination in his great essay on Marvell's wit, and had written in Coleridgean spirit of the poet's mind (in 'The Metaphysical Poets') as 'constantly amalgamating disparate experience'.[49] When he was asked to write about Eliot in 1948, Empson politely deflected the challenge of making an assessment, explaining that 'I do not know for certain how much of my own mind he invented' (*A* 361); and a critical intelligence primed to

[48] Coleridge said that 'Christabel' was inspired by Crashaw's 'Hymn'. Empson speculates that Coleridge gave up his poem because the 'combination of sexuality and desire for martyrdom [became] too nauseating', as though an inherited proximity to the Dirty Joke had grown too much (*A* 317).

[49] T. S. Eliot, 'Andrew Marvell' and 'The Metaphysical Poets', in *Homage to John Dryden: Three Essays on Poetry of the Seventeenth Century* (London: Hogarth Press, 1924), 34–46, 24–33 (pp. 40, 30).

discern contradictory elements within poetry was a substantial part of the invention.[50] I am not about to allege a covert neo-Christian past here, but by his own account Empson's student life was oddly ambiguous, as though moving between contradictions that weren't to be solved by analysis:

In the year I. A. Richards was tutoring me some of my friends at Cambridge (especially James Smith, who wrote well in the early volumes of *Scrutiny*) thought that his 'scientism' was philosophically very absurd, and I could usually, after my weekly hour with Richards, go and tell them some particularly absurd thing he had just said. They of course were following T. S. Eliot, early members of the neo-Christian movement. I really was much influenced by Richards, but I thought it proper to learn from both sides, and would probably have said that I was on the side opposed to him. I am not sure when I decided that he had been quite right.[51]

You might take one of the formulations from *The Structure of Complex Words* as an account of those Cambridge days: 'It may be that the human mind can recognise actually incommensurable values, and that the chief human value is to stand up between them' (*SCW* 421).

III

James Smith's review of *Ambiguity* (which appeared in the *Criterion*) was perhaps the most important Empson ever received; thirty-five years later, he said it was the only notice of the book he could remember (*SL* 395): he discussed the implications of the review at length in the preface to the second edition of 1947, taking it as a statement of the 'fundamental arguments against my approach' (*STA* 9), and it provoked some key pages in *Pastoral* too (70–1). Smith's main point of disagreement was over the assumption apparently made by Empson's book that multiplicity of meaning was the basis of poetry. 'The student of poetry . . . has as his first business the passing of a judgment of value', and here the teasing out of ambiguities was of

[50] He later came to believe Eliot a principal cause of what was wrong with modern letters: his 'crawling insinuations' against the Enlightenment had worked to 'poison our whole intellectual life', he told Peter Ure in 1966; but at the time of writing *Ambiguity*, anyway, as he recollected while writing to another correspondent, 'I am sure I hadn't started reacting against the views of Eliot etc.' (*SL* 422, 503).

[51] Empson, 'Comments', *Modern Language Quarterly*, 27 (1966), 257–8 (p. 257), in Constable (ed.), *Critical Essays*, 425–9 (p. 428). And see his memories of Richards in *A* 227, *SL* 501, and *WE1* 194–5.

no help: 'It is not his main, or even his immediate, concern that a word can be interpreted, that a sentence can be construed, in a large number of ways: if he make it his immediate concern, there is a danger that, in the enumeration of these ways, judgments of values will be forgotten.'[52] Smith, following the early theories of Eliot I suppose, sought to draw a distinction between the conflicts that characterized 'life itself' and the autonomous achievements of poetry, and there Empson would not follow him: 'When Mr James Smith objected to my dealing with "conflicts supposed to have raged within the author" I think he was overplaying his hand very seriously; he was striking at the roots of criticism, not at me' (*STA* 14); and, of course, should you accept that value resides (wherever else it also might) in the maintenance of one's poise between competing ethical or emotional claims, then the dichotomy in Smith's argument begins to look untenable.

But there is a broader charge at issue, and I think it is one that provoked Empson a good deal: that the explication of textual multiplicity serves to distract the critic from more firmly minded sorts of decision. The risk implicit in Richards's Coleridgean poetics, in which impulses are recognized, balanced, and reconciled, is what Richards himself recognizes as 'deadlock': in *Complex Words* Empson puzzles over the distinction Richards seeks to establish between 'a deadlock (which is bad) and a balance (which is good)' (*SCW* 425). A deadlock would be a kind of paralysis, preventing you from coming to the judgement needed for action, as in Coleridge's version of Prince Hamlet, which was Coleridge's own analysis of the dark side of his thought. An ideological critic such as Terry Eagleton is going to sound sharpest about the threat of a 'critical intelligence which in foregrounding ironic complexity evades certain necessarily univocal social commitments' and firmest about the moral claim of 'a plainer, committed writing prepared to sacrifice ambivalences in the cause of political responsibility;'[53] but while the manner is naturally very different, Empson too was sharply aware of the claims properly made upon the critical intelligence by social commitments. 'For Empson—in poetry and in prose—insists not only that we must stand up between incommensurable values, but also that we must move, act, do something', is how Ricks puts it:

[52] James Smith, 'On William Empson's "Seven Types of Ambiguity"', collected in *Shakespearian and Other Essays* (Cambridge: Cambridge University Press, 1974), 338–42 (p. 340).

[53] Terry Eagleton, 'The Critic as Clown,' in *Against the Grain: Essays 1975–1985* (London: Verso, 1986), 154.

'The refusal to act or to decide, however rich its contemplation of complexity, is an act of indecision; prolonged, it can have no end but paralysis and neurosis.'[54] Empson's late polemics about Christianity are seeking to do something and are passionately engaged, 'the most important work that came to hand': no wonder he was so irritated by being thought latterly cantankerous or dotty.[55]

Paul Fry says: 'He liked things clear and definite, and while he continued to mistrust the doxological pull of obvious solutions and received ideas, there is no doubt that the later Empson preferred his answers to scholarly riddles to have a hammering directness and simplicity.'[56] When he returned to consider his own earlier performances he could sound very impatient with youthful ingenuities—with his much-discussed account of 'The Sacrifice' in *Seven Types*, for instance: 'It strikes me now', he wrote in 1963, 'that my attitude was what I have come to call "neo-Christian"; happy to find such an extravagant specimen, I slapped the author on the back and egged him on to be even nastier' (*A* 257). That has the bracing singleness of mind that Fry describes, and which you come to enjoy as a hallmark of late Empson: it is the gift, above all, of cheerfully reductive paraphrase. For example, that the last line of Shelley's 'Ode to the West Wind', 'If Winter comes, can Spring be far behind?', means 'Though the Bourbons have got back their thrones, which is bad, the resulting exasperation will bring world revolution all the sooner, which is good' (*A* 323); or that a verse of Marvell can only mean that the author 'was still able to believe in fairies' (*UB* 12); or the delightful one-liner synopses of Coriolanus's speeches: ' "Pure fluke, old man", or "Aw, shucks" ' (*ES* 177).

The knowing, often comical, reductiveness of the later manner comes across, you could say, as the voice of someone devoting himself to *not being Empsonian*, but rather intent on reining in a possible plurality of sense and joining up with the class of 'prosy-minded readers' (*A* 302). The work of *Seven Types* is the direct opposite of such strategic single-mindedness: it piles up readings in multitudinous parallel, as Empson himself described the desired effect in his review of Rylands: 'Dazzled by the difficulty of holding it in your mind at once, you feel this at any rate is complicated enough' (*A* 69). Of the paraphrases in *Seven Types*, Empson said: 'I have myself usually said "either . . . or" when meaning "both . . . and" ' (*STA* 104); and the inclusive

[54] Ricks, 'William Empson: The Images and the Story', 185.
[55] Norris, *William Empson and the Philosophy of Literary Criticism*, 205.
[56] Fry, *William Empson*, 119.

logic of 'both . . . and' implies how well the pluralist inclination of Empson's reading tesselates with the pluralism of his world-view, and of his ethics—as in the 'generous scepticism' he praises, 'which can believe at once that people are and are not guilty . . . a very normal and essential method'. 'This sort of contradiction is at once understood in literature, because the process of understanding one's friends must always be riddled with such indecisions' (*STA* 65–6): the ambiguity of poetic language draws its life, and its justification, from the proper customary ambiguities of human judgement. But the later Empson grew increasingly keen to restrain the multiplicity that his famous method always promised to release. In the essay on *Hamlet*, for example, he is sure to emphasize that the play was both a good old-fashioned shocker and also an up-to-date piece of irony, a formative 'ambiguity' that was 'an essential part of the intention'; but on the other hand, 'an ambiguity' in the playing of Ophelia's scene with Hamlet 'would only confuse the production' and he hastens to rule it out (*ES* 91, 106). '[T]hese essays on Shakespeare, Donne and Joyce', as Norris says, and he could have added Coleridge to the list, 'stay clear of detailed verbal criticism and argue in the broadest commonsense terms that an author's "intention" is always the first thing to be considered';[57] but while the reform brings immense gains in the clarity of tendentious purpose, it may risk making something too narrow of 'intention'. Whatever its popular reputation for over-ingenious 'reading in', *Seven Types* was never anti-intentionalist: 'I would never have intentionally gone beyond the intention of an author, either in his consciousness or his unconsciousness' (*UB* 40).

The late account of 'The Ancient Mariner', for instance, sets after 'a straightforward reading of the poem' (*CV* 48), and describes a markedly single-minded piece; and then deplores Coleridge's pusillanimity in smudging it. There is very little of the mutual complication of contradictory elements, such as characterized the irony described so finely in *Seven Types of Ambiguity* and *Some Versions of Pastoral*: his reading of the 'Mariner' identifies a much starker kind of irony, by which the Mariner's Christian efforts to comprehend are undercut and exposed as a species of false consciousness. There seems, for example, no possibility that young Coleridge might indeed have been caught between kinds of religious consciousness; that the poem might be ambiguous, in the old way, organized about a structure and an indecision. Empson does entertain

[57] Norris, *William Empson and the Philosophy of Literary Criticism*, 51.

the idea that the pious noises in the poem are jokes, as I said a few pages back; but these feel leaner, less inclusive jokes than normally occur in the earlier criticism—'holy lies' that are, perhaps, more in the company of 'God's blood-curdling jokes' from *Milton's God* (*CV* 48; *MG*, 29). Anyhow, there is little sense that the jokes might have worked with a complicating pastoral mutuality and richness, something like the mock-heroic of Pope's 'Epistle to Burlington' where 'it is the admiration latent in a sneer which becomes available as a source of energy' (*STA* 154–5). Empson's emphasis upon the Unitarian background to the poem is brilliantly astute, but his insistence that Coleridge was writing a downright Unitarian poem that somehow got contaminated by Christianity seems a simpler—a more strongly minded and ethically committed, to be sure, but nevertheless a simpler—kind of reading than the earlier Empson would have appreciated, and to depend upon a reduced conception of Coleridge's intention. 'Good poetry is usually written from a background of conflict', he had said in the second edition of *Seven Types* (14); but his reading of the 'Mariner' plays down much sense of Coleridge's inward experience of the conflict at issue: the poem is rather a disguised piece of polemic and a contribution to a public controversy, rather than the expression of an internal controversy. Yet even a Coleridge intently set against Christianity might, according to the younger Empson, have properly gathered into himself the position he was ostensibly opposing, especially if he had been moved to articulate such a conflict in his poem: 'if you attack a view in any detail that proves you to have some sympathy with it; there is already a conflict in you which mirrors the conflict in which you take part' (*A* 83). Altogether, there is a shift in the place of contradiction visible in Empson, as though conditions had grown too difficult for old indulgences to continue, or a commotion had grown too painful to bear: 'The contradictions cover such a range . . . You don't want madhouse and the whole thing there' ('Let It Go', *CP* 99).

For the later Empson's more polemical purpose, the 'both . . . and' logic of ambiguity or pastoral is simply not so amenable. *The Structure of Complex Words* seems the transitional work here: ambiguity and pastoral each in their way work to establish equivalences between contradictory elements, and one of the main tasks of *Complex Words* is to set out the ways in which such statements of false identity ('A is B') operate. The encompassing purpose of the book is to show both how fundamental it is to the way the mind works, but also how the human mind has the purchase to manage it: 'Regarded simply as a bit of our mental equipment, it carries within itself a kind of recognition that the matter would bear looking into, or an impulse to do that later . . . we should make terms with the process rather than struggle to renounce it', as he put it elsewhere (*MG* 245). In its pursuit, *Complex Words* begins to move away from Empson's earlier sort of interest in contradiction and plurality, as he explained in a footnote: 'the term Ambiguity, which I used in a book title and as a kind of slogan, implying that the reader is left in doubt between two readings, is more or less superseded by the idea of a double meaning which is intended to be fitted into a definite structure' (*SCW* 103 n.). A greater inclination to be definite becomes more and more the tenor—chiefly thanks, I think, to a keen sense of the abuse to which, as he saw it, this 'bit of our mental equipment' can be put. A footnote in *Complex Words* turns again to *Nineteen Eighty-Four*, with its 'ghastly paradoxes' such as 'War is Peace', which fit the model of false identity very well, but to horrible effect: 'to be analysable doesn't make a bit of language good', Empson says, 'but it was never supposed to' (83 n.). As before, 'double-think' is really standing here for a thought crime more fundamental to the West—the doctrine of the Trinity, the most outrageous and corrupting of all assertions of false identity. The Trinity, by having two contradictory ideas simultaneously held in the mind, sought to disguise the unspeakable brutality of the Father: 'the mind so easily falls back on the primitive assurance that the Father and the Son both are and are not identical.' Empson thought the doctrine of the Trinity '[t]he most staggering misuse' of the human capacity to embrace at once contradictory elements (*MG* 245), and the principal obstacle to sweep out of the way before pursuing the case against Christianity. Well, I do not say that an interest in poetic ambiguity ushers you helplessly into the arms of Athanasius (or Big Brother), nor that Trinitarians are peculiarly obliged to discern multiple meanings in poetry. But the ability to contain in the one act of the mind quite diverse meanings was at the heart of Empson's understanding both of ambiguity and of pastoral, and he recognized in it 'a positive capacity of the human mind' (*SCW* 83 n.): the early books are wholly shaped by the testing awareness that 'human life is so much a matter of juggling with contradictory impulses', with ambiguity and pastoral less literary techniques than real-life skills for coping (*STA* 230). So, for Empson to dismiss the Trinity merely as 'a set of verbal contradictions' is to direct fire very close to home: is there not a manifest and telling proximity between the 'both . . . and' logic of the '"conflict" theory' of poetry and the 'both . . . and' nature of Trinitarian doctrine?[58] Empson's principled decision largely to abandon the rich pluralism of his early textual analysis was taken, I should say, because that pluralism seemed so readily to lure one (as, he came to think, it had occasionally lured him) into a frame of mind too prone to accept the 'both . . . and' contradictoriness, at once a structure and an indecision, of Trinitarianism—that egregious and shameful attempt to mollify the old monster. As he says in his footnote about Orwell: 'It is rather hard to see beforehand what a line of argument is letting you in for' (*SCW* 83 n.).

[58] 'His criticism does, in a sense, lay itself open to suggestive logic of religious paradox', says Norris: his own preference for *Complex Words* among Empson's works may lie in the way that book seeks to evade such openness—'the whole tempting logic of Christian paradox which his favourite kinds of language confront and subvert', ibid. 166, 141.

7

Empson's God

Eric Griffiths

Not wrongly moved by this dismaying scene
The thinkers like the nations getting caught
Joined in the organizing that they fought
To scorch all earth of all but one machine.

It can be swung, is what these hopers mean,
For all the loony hooters can be bought
On the small ball. It can then all be taught
And reconverted to be kind and clean.

A more heartening fact about the cultures of man
Is their appalling stubbornness. The sea
Is always calm ten fathoms down. The gigan-

-tic anthropological circus riotously
Holds open all its booths. The pygmy plan
Is one note each and the tune goes out free.

(*CP* 101)

As the poem starts, we find ourselves already in the thick of things, if, that is, we find ourselves at all, for there is no pronoun to show who it is who is, or should be, 'not wrongly moved'. An old habit of contrast, opposition even, helps us guess at a 'we' from the 'they' of 'they fought'. And yet old habits, however die-hard, are not a reliable guide amid the novelties to be expected from a poem first published as 'Machine Age' and so perhaps wondering, right up-to-date with Herbert Read, 'Has [the artist] any function in a machine age society?'[1] The syntax of the opening quatrain is coiled so tight it springs demands for reorientation on us phrase by phrase 'with a compactness which gives the mind several notions at one glance of the eye, with a unity like that of metaphor' (*STA* 274–5).

A selection of tolerable senses for lines 1–2 yields: 'to be moved at all by this scene would be wrong' ('Not wrongly *moved*'); 'impossible not to be moved by such a scene and therefore important to be moved only in the right direction' ('Not *wrongly* moved'); 'thinkers are not upset by such sights, they enjoy ("like" as verb) the mess that lesser mortals make'; 'thinkers resemble nation-states ("like" as adverb), they too fall for the lure of systems which promise unanimity and result in strife'. The 'thinkers' may be part of the 'scene' (one reason to be dismayed by it) or not (different grounds to blench), depending on whether the opening line pre-modifies them or post-modifies an ellipted subject such as 'I' or 'we', not to mention other candidates. All this teetering-about is apt to a 'dismaying scene', because 'dismay' comes from *desmayo*, Spanish for 'swoon'. Yet the poem doesn't keel over; it stays throughout its octave neat in syllabic count and rhyme-scheme, perfectly shaping up to become a Petrarchan sonnet, that venerable contraption of elaborately handled distress. Two methods of verbal organization—syntactic, prosodic—are at work though not exactly co-operating, and this brings into deep, stereoscopic focus the pivotal issue of actual 'organizing', that 'organizing' which is a mark and support of 'cultures' but whose drive can become hostile to 'cultures', especially in their vital plural.

Things get, or at least look, simpler as we go on. The syntax is tidier after the wrinkle of whether 'It' in 'It can be swung' refers to the 'one machine' or ranges more laxly back to 'all earth' (the answer is 'all earth'). Empson had already brought 'small' and 'ball' into relevant orbit, when rendering J. B. S. Haldane into Basic in 1935. Haldane's 'On Scales' set up several thought-experiments to demonstrate that 'the man in the street' can 'get clear in his mind about the chief discoveries of present-day science'.[2] Just imagine, he says encouragingly, the earth mapped on to a globe sixteen inches in circumference, and then imagine that globe reduced as much again as the earth was in becoming the globe we twirl and consult. 'Globe' doesn't feature in Basic's epitome

[1] The second (1934) citation in the *OED* for 'machine', 10.

[2] I quote from Empson's translation in *The Outlook of Science* (London: Kegan Paul, Trench, Trubner & Co., 1935), 59; Haldane's original is in *Possible Worlds and Other Essays* (London: Chatto & Windus, 1927).

of the English lexicon, so this supposition comes from Empson as 'the ball will be made as much smaller as the earth was made to get it down to the size of the ball'.[3] This is a shrinkage owed to 'thinkers' but the poem also records less abstract methods in the hands of 'nations' for scaling down the distance between people—more or less benignly at 'hooters' which appear in the idiosyncratic, Empsonian sense of 'radio-stations',[4] or drastically in 'scorch all earth' which bears in mind the recent impress of Japan on Chinese soil: 'Apparently a translation of Chinese *jiāotǔ* . . . scorched earth . . . "The populace . . . are still disturbed, in spite of official denials, by wild rumours of a 'scorched earth policy' of burning the city before the Japanese enter" ' (*OED*, first recorded use, quoting *The Times* of December 1937). The sonnet itself can serve as a device for putting big issues in dinky nutshells, as Empson does when he makes, with wry correctness, the *volta* between lines eight and nine carry the change of his drift against the bland hopes of those who would convert the world; the small formal manoeuvre outlines and fends off a global conversion. In the sestet, he then disorganizes the little room of his sonnet to tell against the tidy schemes he mistrusts; immediately after the prospect of world-renovation has been voiced at the converting 'turn', the lines straggle beyond the established, decasyllabic norm to unpredictable lengths, syntactic and prosodic units mismatch so 'gigan- | -tic' is the tussle between hygienic aspiration and what it seeks to handle. As regards making the world a better place, the poem probably draws again on the Basic versions of Haldane, who had envisaged the earth in his 'The Last Judgment' as 'at worst . . . only a small poisoned place in space, which might be made clean without much trouble'.[5]

There's been a buzz about the word 'globalization' from the 1960s on (in 1962, the *Spectator* called it a 'staggering concept'), but issues of territory and jurisdiction have hung, implicitly or explicitly, in the atmosphere ever since two groups, who had not previously been introduced, of creatures of the same species, for which there was not yet a name, sized each other up across the Great Rift Valley. Empires tend to identify themselves with the *orbis terrarum*, sometimes by real expansion and sometimes by the less arduous method of discounting what lies beyond their frontiers as a zone for the

[3] *The Outlook of Science*, 63.

[4] 'The Archbishop of Canterbury is to be allowed his whack on the hooter this evening', 1926 diary, referring to the primate's broadcast during the General Strike; quoted in *WE1* 127.

[5] *The Outlook of Science*, 102; the original has 'sterilized' for 'made clean'.

subhuman—barbarians, pagans, savages, round-eyes. 'Under the Christian emperors the ancient dream of universality transformed the pagan ambition to civilize the world into the analogous objective to convert literally all its inhabitants to Christianity. The single unifying body of law—the *koinos nomos*—thus became a single body of beliefs.'[6] Professor Pagden immediately nuances this distinction between secular and Christian devotions to some 'one machine' by adding that Roman *pietas* had long involved 'the complete fusion of the numinous and the political'. It could be shaded further by noting that wars 'of religion' in the aftermath of Rome were usually waged over questions of social cohesion, over religion 'as a body of believers rather than the more modern definition of a body of beliefs', as is shown by the exemplary fact that the Edict of Nantes 'mentions nothing about belief or doctrine. Like all the earlier edicts of pacification throughout the religious wars, beliefs were not mandated.'[7] Indeed, the principle of *cuius regio eius religio* (roughly: 'as for religion: what the king says, goes'), often invoked during politico-religious squabbles in the area hyperbolically known as 'Western Christendom', reveals how innovative the authorities were ready to be, how little restrained by attachment to such sacred texts as 'Render to Caesar the things that are Caesar's, and to God the things that are God's' (Mark 12 : 17; King James version). Nor did the strain between universal ideals and a respect for particularity just fade away when religion loosed its hold, whether as motive or alibi, on the imaginations of political projectors. The early advocates of enlightened, techno-sociological reform relished that 'organizing' which Empson's sonnet resists; witness their fondness for the word and its cognates, as in Saint-Simon's *De la réorganisation de la société europćene . . .* (1814), his campaigning journal, *L'Organisateur* (1819), or Comte's *Prospectus des travaux scientifiques nécessaires pour réorganiser la société* (1822). It is as if the human being, though officially a *zoon politikon,* achieves only with difficulty and rarely without violent detours through illusions of unanimity, the state of coexistence with his or her fellows for which they are adapted.[8]

[6] Anthony Pagden, *Lords of all the World: Ideologies of Empire in Spain, Britain and France c.1500–1800* (New Haven: Yale University Press, 1995), 29.

[7] Mack P. Holt, *The French Wars of Religion, 1562–1629,* 2nd edn. (Cambridge: Cambridge University Press, 2005), 2, 167.

[8] See the work of René Girard, which Empson unfortunately does not consider, on 'victimary unanimity' and the 'sacrificial mechanism'; *Violence and the Sacred* (1972; English trans., Baltimore: Johns Hopkins University Press, 1977), and *Things Hidden since the Foundation of the World* (1978; English trans., London: Athlone Press, 1987) are good places to start.

Empson's sonnet recoils specifically from the pressures to dragoon the world of the warring totalitarianisms and their 'very fascist picture' of humanity. He spoke out against this when he found it in Auden's poems of the time:

I can't myself feel that the race of man is like this at all. What is heartening about people is their appalling stubbornness and the strong roots of their various cultures, rather than the ease with which you can convert them and make them happy and good. (*A* 373)

The sonnet's pivotal notion and a cluster of its terms come together here two years before the poem. But though the prose anticipates the poem's crucial, provoking thought that we should find 'heartening' the very stubbornness which makes people hard to change, for better for worse, it doesn't flesh this enigmatic wisdom out as the poem does with its tissue of three words ('dismaying', 'heartening', 'appalling') which stem from the circulation of our blood and its vagaries: a 'dismay' is etymologically a swoon caused by loss of blood-flow to the brain; 'heartening' indicates cardiac reinvigoration after the syncope; to 'appal' comes from French, 'to grow pale', as when the blood abandons the face we turn to the world. In Empson's day, and when considering the 'roots' of 'cultures', there was much clamour about, as well as for, 'blood', so the delicacy with which he instils this metaphor through his lines is admirably tactful and courageous too. The poem also amplifies the mild chime 'at all . . . appalling' from the prose into 'all . . . all . . . small ball . . . all . . . appalling . . . always . . . all'. And that's only the half of it, for the same vowel in different spellings crops up in 'caught . . . organizing . . . fought . . . scorch . . . bought . . . taught . . . more'.

In his notes on the word 'all' in *Paradise Lost*, Empson tuned in to one aspect of Milton's fondness for this long vowel:

It seems to be suited to his temperament because he is an absolutist, an all-or-none man. All else is unimportant beside one thing, he is continually deciding . . . It is as suited to absolute love and self-sacrifice as to insane self-assertion. The self-centred man, in his turn, is not much interested in the variety of the world, and readily lumps it together as 'all'. . . . the vowel is the 'organ' note for which Milton is praised (*SCW* 101–2)

Milton is not just an 'all-or-none man', he's an 'all-or-or' man; it's the same 'organ' vowel in the totalizing of 'all' as in the disjunctive 'or'. Statistics show he had a slight preference for 'or' (886 times in *Paradise Lost*) over 'all' (847).

It's sometimes hard to tell, as Milton veers between 'all' and 'or', whether he is balanced or deadlocked between these possibles; 'certainly', as Empson said, 'his poetic style does not let us watch him in the process of deciding' (*MG* 12). The full gamut of the vowel from the universality of 'all' to the polarizing sectarianism of 'or', from 'fall' to 'restore', is a thumbnail of Milton's temperament and of one version of Christianity, the only one Empson wrote much about—commandeering, exclusionary and cleft. Milton might also be listed among the sonnet's brisk hopers who think they know a short way with stubbornness. *De doctrina christiana* begins by discarding the developments of Christian doctrine between 200 and 1500 as 'the corruptions of more than thirteen hundred years',[9] which he is about to correct all by his own work; similarly, 'even in the year of the Restoration he . . . was fantastical enough to think that the nation, agitated as it was, might be settled by a pamphlet, called *A ready and easy way to establish a Free Commonwealth*'.[10] People like Milton who admire themselves for decisiveness take little interest in the process of their own deciding, and may not even recognize such a process has taken time and place. This is, as Empson said of *Paradise Lost*, 'one of the more appalling things the human mind is liable to do' (*MG* 13). In many poems from *The Gathering Storm*, his own jumpy manner of apophthegms strung out along a dimensionless, transtemporal present tense—'The sea | is always calm', 'The pygmy plan | Is one note each'—does not clearly display his 'process of deciding' but asks us to work out how on earth he vaulted from A to Q.

Coming from Empson, 'appalling' can sound struck to the heart or camply aghast. Milton's God is 'appalling' (*SVP* 138) as are some historical events of the twentieth century (*ERL2* 118); *Finnegans Wake* ends up a 'titanic corpse' because of the 'appalling persistence' of Joyce's puns (*SCW* 66). On the other hand, listening to the entire Fire Sermon through each of its permutations 'is a pretty appalling experience' (*CP* 150), unlike Empson's own 'Bacchus' which is 'not appallingly long' (*CP* 293). Writing critically and 'in a state of moderate beer' to Charles Madge, he cheers himself by 'assuming that you are not appallingly sensitive' (*WE1* 431). When Empson came upon the word, when it came over him, it already had a two-faced capaciousness about it, though the *OED* dates

[9] Milton, *The Works of John Milton*, ed. F. A. Patterson, 18 vols. (New York: Columbia University Press, 1931–8), xiv. 3.

[10] Samuel Johnson, 'Life of Milton', in *Lives of the English Poets*, 2 vols. (London: Oxford University Press, 1906), i. 89.

the more light-hearted sense only from 1919 ('What appalling rot!', *Punch*). He may have picked it up, then, as he went through puberty, about the time he finalized his views on the 'traditional God of Christianity' (*MG* 10). He described the process by which affect was bleached from 'appal', and terms like 'awful', 'divine', 'hellish', in a comment on the similar history of 'quite' as that word became able to mean both 'extremely' and 'a bit':

> The historical change in *quite* has been explained as due to a process of 'fading'; that is to say, persons trying to emphasise their remarks frequently used *quite* in situations which were not really exciting, as the listeners could observe, so the listeners came to feel that the proper use of *quite* was to mark not really exciting situations. (*SCW* 25–6)

Traces of these over-emphases and of their unenthused reception linger on even in rationally clarified parlance; Basic English preserves the nineteenth-century suppleness of 'quite', as in Empson's 'quite straightforward' meaning 'completely straightfoward' and 'quite complex' meaning 'fairly complex'.[11] The 'process of deciding' what was and wasn't 'basic' to English was meticulously thought through but still occurred within the tousled history of human terms, amid processes like 'fading' which nobody decided to initiate.

The 'fading' which 'quite' and 'appalling' underwent results from inherently ambiguous effects of repetition, whether verbal or behavioural, for repetition may dig an attitude in or wear one out. 'If I've told you once, I've told you a thousand times' a parent admonishes a child and the child replies 'you have indeed told me a thousand times, mother, and that is why I can barely hear you any more'. These effects are foreseeable results of our sayings and doings (and in this respect, they are—however vast their eventual extent—our responsibility) but also beyond our control. They occur in all living discourses and bring about many changes which may be excitably described. 'The death of . . .' this or that, for instance, has often been announced and now arouses among the initiate no more than the concerned murmur which would greet 'we need a bit of a re-think here'. Ritual action and utterance can serve in the life of cult and culture as vaccines, controlled dosages of rote, against our tendency to exhaust our words, for ritual is 'first and foremost, a mode of paying attention' and 'precises ambiguities; it neither overcomes nor relaxes them'.[12] Empson was not at home in ritual circumstance. His accounts of

[11] *The Outlook of Science*, 59, 62.

[12] Jonathan Z. Smith, *To Take Place: Toward Theory in Ritual* (Chicago: University of Chicago Press, 1987), 103, 110.

religion and of devotional literature are startlingly bare of these considerations; though he studied Buddhist sculpture and shrines intently, he paid no such heed to their Christian equivalents. Had he done so, he might have been less quick to identify 'redemption by torment' as 'the central tradition of Christianity' (*A* 297), for in early Christian art 'among the symbols . . . none signifies suffering, death, or self-immolation. All stress victory, peace, and security in the face of adversity. . . . There is no place in the third century for a crucified Christ.'[13]

One of his better arguments against a Christian theologian comes when he rebukes Saint Augustine for regarding involuntary physical reactions—Eve's blushes, the obtrusive erection in the communal shower—as signs of fallenness: 'The independence of our feelings from our will, which he regards as the essence of being fallen, is our basic protection against the lethal convictions which so often capture our brains. If Milton had presented Adam and Eve as "self-controlled" to this extent they would have seemed like insects and been unable to fall' (*MG* 169). God would also have been able easily to reconvert them and make them kind and clean again in a trice by washing their brains. 'Appalling stubbornness' is another name for this 'basic protection', and under either alias gives a sign that culture is the form which biology takes, that rationality is actualized in human practices, or, to put it in another dialect, that the Word has become flesh. As he wrote of his own stubbornness to John Hayward, 'The advantage or perhaps limitation of being an obstinate man is that you don't have moral problems, only risks' (*SL* 185–6). An advantage *and* a limitation, like instinctive capacities which have become hard-wired in species over time and which are on the whole adaptively expedient but at times dangerously inflexible. The point also holds good if we consider the independence of our meanings from our will. For our words are 'ours' just as significantly where in their grain or implications they cross and thwart us as when we click them expertly into place according to plan, because even when they 'go against' us they attest to the processes of their formation, processes in which we, or people quite like us, have had a part.[14]

[13] Graydon F. Snyder, *Ante Pacem: Archaeological Evidence of Church Life before Constantine* (Macon, Ga.: Mercer University Press, 1985), 29.

[14] The commandment 'Honour thy father and mother' (Exodus 20: 12) is not only an ethical imperative but a rule of method when considering where thoughts come from; compare Wittgenstein: 'Every human being has parents . . . . Language did not emerge from some kind of

This is the element in which, if at all, our thought is 'free', something which even, or especially, 'freethinkers' need to bear in mind. Mary Douglas:

Merleau-Ponty supposed that the symbolic order makes men free of the constraints which apply to lower forms of life. It is a flattering refrain: each animal species is limited by its proper mode of being; its goals are set; its capacity to learn is limited; not so ours. Thanks to our unspecialised skills and thanks to our control of symbols, especially language, we can choose freely from an infinite range of goals. . . . The human mind, playing freely in symbolic worlds which it creates itself, must bear the weight of its freedom. Smugly tragic, the favourite theme goes on: free to be noble, free to embrace error, free to poison ourselves, free to extinguish our species. This familiar chant nowhere admits that symbolic life is not entirely free. It works through a medium of expression. The peculiar limitations set by the medium are worth examining.[15]

Empson was versed in these 'peculiar limitations', the residue of earlier false starts and premature conclusions, but gave them only intermittent weight. He acknowledged them when he said he wanted the word 'free' at the end of his sonnet to have 'the impact of a contradiction' (*CP* 397). The contradiction resembles 'the old rabbinic pun on the tablets of the Law being *hrt* (Ex 32.16), a syllabic formation capable of being pointed as either *harut*, "engraved", or *herut*, "free" '.[16] He might have been vexed by such a comparison because he inclined to dismissiveness as regards the Hebrew scriptures.[17] Still, his poem has the effect of the rabbinic pun when it exhales at its last the long vowel of 'free' as into infinitely open air though it can send out the tune of the final rhyme loud and clear only by putting an antiquated, poetical stress on 'riotous-lee', relying on an old convention just as it envisages release from constraint, as if backsliding to what has gone before even as it speaks of wishing to set out for the uncharted. The phonetic strain on 'free' is itself taut rather than overburdened and makes in its small, adept challenge to voicing a recognition like that which he wrote large over the second edition of his magnanimous work on complex words: 'The idea that the theorist is not part of the world

ratiocination', *On Certainty*, ed. G. E. M. Anscombe and G. H. von Wright, trans. Denis Paul and G. E. M. Anscombe (Oxford: Basil Blackwell, 1974), 29e, 62e.

[15] Mary Douglas, *Implicit Meanings: Essays in Anthropology* (London: Routledge & Kegan Paul, 1975), 211–12.

[16] Jonathan Z. Smith, *Drudgery Divine: On the Comparison of Early Christianities and the Religions of Late Antiquity* (London: RoutledgeCurzon, 1990), 54.

[17] For example, 'the Old Testament is a rag-bag' (*MG* 115) or 'the Bronze Age literature to which [Milton] had nailed his conscience' (*MG* 199).

he examines is one of the deepest sources of error, and crops up all over the place' (*SCW*, p. xxxi).

He also felt the tug of other loyalties, towards a rationalized future and a fiercely professed though sketchy notion of progress. He remained one of his sonnet's 'hopers', or at least fairly sympathetic to a hope like that of H. G. Wells who foresaw that 'By 2200 almost everyone was able to make use of Basic for talking and writing.'[18] 'BASIC' was an acronym—'British American Scientific International Commercial'—as well as a vision; the acronym hints at a debatable, corporate agenda, though the debate goes differently, depending on whether it is conducted in Basic or not. Had Wells proved right, there would have been victims in the triumph of such near-universal skill. Haldane's memory of his own beginnings, for example, with its towering figures 'about the height of Giant Pope and Giant Pagan in the illustrated *Pilgrim's Progress* of my childhood' would have dimmed down to ahistorical, generic baddies 'about as high as the great bad men who kept attacking the good man, in the stories we had as boys';[19] a sharp and maturely informed sense of dilemma—'Perhaps the greatest tragedy of our age is the misapplication of science'—would have gone soppy: 'Possibly the saddest thing in our day is the fact that science is put to such wrong uses.'[20] Translation always carries risk, of course, but when it seeks to be part of a transvaluation too, assessment of whether the risk is worth taking depends trickily on which set of values, 'original' or 'target', is to measure the outcome. As Empson finely said, 'the term "values" . . . has the serious function of helping us to recognise the variety of the world. The chief use of reading imaginative literature is to make you grasp that different people act on different ethical beliefs' (*ERL2* 97). Yet no term can tell you how high a value to set on variety itself, and that is just what is at issue between those who are keen on some 'one machine' and those still devoted to a disorganized toolbox handy for all sorts of odd ends. Grasping how people act on differing beliefs (let alone the culturally more intricate issue of how they fail to act on their beliefs) is a long haul which Empson does well to compare to 'reading imaginative literature', because both involve more than knowledge of an abstractable set of doctrines, a 'more' which includes finding one's way round someone else's world, its contours, pace, sore points, and long-accrued tilt, where it frays as well as how it seems to him or her to hang together.

[18] 'Put into Basic' from *The Shape of Things to Come* on the title-verso of Empson's other 1935 selection from Haldane, *Science and Well-Being* (London: Kegan Paul, Trench, Trubner & Co., 1935).

[19] *Possible Worlds*, 18; *Outlook of Science*, 45

[20] *Possible Worlds*, 190; *Science and Well-Being*, 69.

These are things we come to understand about a poem, say, by attending to its textures and shape, place in a traditional process, the pleasures which it has on offer, as Empson so vividly did; we come to understand them about a religion through attending to its calendar of ritual observances, buildings, the ramified forms of life among its laity as well as the edicts of its officials, as Empson did not, or not much. The rationalist in him feels sure that 'what I am saying is just ordinary world opinion' and leaves himself open to the deserved retort 'you're simply Terrible for sitting in your own world and thinking out what flaws in the other man can explain his not thinking and writing as you like'.[21]

In her novel, *Mr Fortune's Maggot*, written just before she became a friend of Empson's, Sylvia Townsend Warner imagines a missionary who feels called to bring the Gospel to the inhabitants of a remote island, Fanua. He is a nice man (he writes Petrarchan sonnets) but hopefully adrift amid the variety of terms. He hears that the islanders 'only worship one god' and is cheered but wary, only to find 'on further questioning . . . that the islanders worshipped one god each',[22] like Empson's pygmies with their 'one note each'. It is no easier for Fortune to convey what it is for him to believe his beliefs than it is for him to apprehend the fit of their beliefs with their world, because his own creed, like theirs, transpires through detailed and unsystematized practice, as he realizes when trying to give scripture lessons:

> In the middle of an account of Christ's entry into Jerusalem Mr Fortune would find himself obliged to break off and describe a donkey. This would lead naturally to the sands of Western-super-Mare, and a short account of bathing-machines; and that afternoon he would take his pupil down to the beach and show him how English children turned sand out of buckets, and built castles with a moat around them. Moats might lead to the Feudal System . . .[23]

and so on and on. Mr Fortune's struggles to translate 'donkey' provide evidence for one of Empson's guiding insights, 'Much of our thinking has to be done in a summary practical way, trusting to a general sense of the whole situation in the background' (*SCW* 1), for the difficulties of the missionary's position arise when he tries to spell out what was 'summary', to make explicit

[21] The retort is Rosemond Tuve's (*SL* 199).

[22] Sylvia Townsend Warner, *Mr Fortune's Maggot* (1927; repr. London: Virago, 1978), 26. I am grateful to Peter Swaab for giving me a copy of the book.

[23] Ibid. 57.

'a general sense of [his] whole situation'. Anybody might be daunted by such a task. The second page of *The Structure of Complex Words* rephrases 'a general sense of the whole situation in the background' as 'what is in the background of the mind, or in the subconsciousness'. This psychologistic slant is something Empson picked up, like the divergent implications of 'appalling', from the air around him, and it distorts many of his attempts to grasp the variety of differing beliefs, in particular of differing religious beliefs. I blame I. A. Richards, agreeing with whom is the source of almost all the thoughtlessness in Empson, except the minor instances brought on through boyish zeal or simple Hampsteadfastness. The 'background' relevant to explaining 'donkey', a background which may cause trouble or become a place where they could meet, lies not in Mr Fortune's mind nor in the islander's. The 'background of the mind' is, from one point of view, a long way back into something that might not yet be 'mind' exactly, and, from another, not in individual 'mental space' at all but in the 'interdividual and ethnological domains'[24] between the missionary and his pupil as they build their castles on the edge of the sand.

In considering religions, 'regardless of whether we are studying myths from literate or non-literate cultures, we are dealing with *historical processes of reinterpetation*, with tradition'.[25] Creation may or may not be *ex nihilo* but revelation never is so original; there must be something before revelation, because revelation is always revelation to someone, someone by definition as yet more or less unpersuaded, in the dark, whether a person or a previous dispensation. What is revealed may be strikingly new but the language through which the revelation comes has to be the more or less faded language of those to whom the revelation is being made and who will need long practice in translation before their old words have reliably learned the new tricks. Empson strenuously resisted the 'word-magic' which makes out that words are indelibly dyed with past usage, 'saturated with the experience' of previous living as if with an hereditary taint, and therefore 'very insanitary, poisoned or bewitched' (*SCW*, p. xxix). He was right to resist, on the grounds both of what we know about semantic change and of what we must believe if we want to keep thinking of ourselves as subjects capable of change. Yet he treated the diction of Christian theology, especially terms like 'sacrifice', 'ransom', 'redeem', as both unambiguous and impervious to alteration of

[24] Girard, *Things Hidden*, 18. [25] Smith, *Drudgery Divine*, 107.

sense while the world in and to which they were uttered altered round them. His polemical writing remained oddly innocent of the implications of his own great discoveries in method, with the result that the 'background' against which teachings develop dropped from view and he thought too little of 'how the faces of God are formed in the social process of sorting out the world'.[26] Because revelation is always thus addressed in their tongue to a people busy with other things and likely to be stiff-necked, it 'must start out from the sphere of error and carry error over into truth. . . . To convince somebody that he is in error, it is not enough to state the truth, but rather we must find the *path* from error to truth.'[27] This is not something Empson in his controversies with the 'neo-Christians' bothered to do; he was more 'anxious to make my beliefs clear' (*MG* 9) than to get clear about his own beliefs, not to mention other people's.

The interpersonal and processive character of religion eludes a psychology fixed on the individual and his or her state of mind. Empson saw this point in the case of Dylan Thomas, who

> felt struck down by guilt though by his own principles he had done no wrong . . . it was easy to reflect that he had done wrong by the principles of the hostess of Fern Hill, his peasant aunt. A psychologist (as I understand) finds this trivial because it does not involve the mechanisms of the deep Unconscious, and indeed it is more like 'split personality'—one moral code goes on dragging against another. But it is the most prominent cause of mental upset among present-day educated people, and I think psychologists belittle it because they dislike admitting that there can be genuine rational disagreement about a moral question. (*A* 312)

He thinks too broadly ill of a vaguely characterized 'psychologist' here, while continuing to rely on offcuts from a clinical vocabulary (' "split personality" ', 'mental upset'), but the flicker of scepticism about the limitations of psychology as he knew it makes a pleasant change from his frequent airy borrowing of unexamined clinical notions.[28] The 'loony hooters' of his sonnet sounds like a slur dressed up as a diagnosis to bypass 'genuine rational disagreement', though we could hope that phrase is merely impersonating for a moment, as Empson liked to, some rampaging buffer. His prose is less easily excused: 'loony

[26] Mary Douglas, *Risk and Blame: Essays in Cultural Theory* (London: Routledge, 1992), 251.

[27] Ludwig Wittgenstein, *Remarks on Frazer's 'Golden Bough'*, ed. Rush Rhees (Retford: Brynmill Press, 1979), 1; the translation is mine.

[28] See, for example, his reliance in letters on 'neurotic', as when spotting Frank Kermode's 'neurotic sex-horror' or the 'neurotic' *pudeur* of 'Americans' (*SL* 271, 392).

aspiration or high-mindedness' (*ERL2* 25) is a probing joke but 'the mental disease of Eliot's "tradition"' (*ERL2* 135) has short-circuited argument and soared into the heady ether of sounding-off.[29]

Trouble like that between Dylan Thomas and his aunt can occur anywhere in the human family, for generation gaps model the disparities which arise from uneven development between and within nations. Conversation across language-families is as vulnerable to minor slips and big misapprehension as a dispute between neighbours. When Buddhism moved from India to China, it underwent multiple refraction, not only because Chinese in contrast to the Indian languages is uninflected and lacks a systematized grammar, but because Chinese ears were alerted by their preceding Taoism and Confucianism to hear the Buddha's teachings through a transformative acoustic—'For example, "Husband supports wife" became "The husband controls his wife".'[30] So too, 'I will be atonement for you' was a 'popular formula' between Jews when Jesus lived, used to express 'solidarity' with the afflicted and 'a readiness to take over suffering in cases of sorrow or disaster'.[31] It meant then something like what we now mean by 'I'm with you all the way' or 'I'm here for you', which is far from what it sounds like when part of Anselm's technical account of vicarious atonement, against which Empson seethed. Teaching has to try to bridge, however ropily, the 'incalculable gap' between those who are confident they have something to pass on and those who are less sure there's anything they need to learn, between 'the Gospel that is preached and the Gospel that is heard'.[32] Nor do these pitfalls gape only for the pious of various stripe; Comte in the struggle to get his social engineering off the ground felt 'opposed at every moment by language, by the need for new expressions, freed from the theological and metaphysical character under whose influence our languages

[29] It had been 'the deluge of Mr Eliot's tradition' on the previous page but Empson had warmed to his theme as he wrote.

[30] Arthur F. Wright, *Buddhism in Chinese History* (Stanford, Calif.: Stanford University Press, 1959), 37. For analogous warps from the history of Christianity in Mesoamerica, see Inga Clendinnen, *Aztecs: An Interpretation* (Cambridge: Cambridge University Press, 1991), 74; and Anthony Pagden, *The Fall of Natural Man: The American Indian and the Origins of Comparative Ethnology* (Cambridge: Cambridge University Press, 1982), 158.

[31] Martin Hengel, *The Atonement: The Origins of the Doctrine in the New Testament* (1980), trans. John Bowden (London: SCM Press, 1981), 64.

[32] Barbara M. Boal, *Human Sacrifice and Religious Change: The Khonds* (New Delhi: Inter-India Publications, 1997), 302; it is a pity Empson did not know this book with its richly detailed story of how an Indian hill-people came to give up human sacrifice in the mid-nineteenth century.

are formed'.[33] Such expressions might have been handy for Comte but they would have puzzled those whom he planned to enlighten.

We are slow learners as political animals and our teachers in such matters (who have often forgotten what learning involves so long is it since they concluded they themselves had no more to learn) tend to briskness. Hence our history of what once seemed bright ideas now evaporated by the mysterious ardours of garbling. As Ian Hacking puts it with incisive plainness, 'we have not got clear in our minds, yet, the interaction between expert knowledge and the behavior of troubled people'.[34] Hacking's exquisitely timed ', yet,' breathes an irreducible hope, Empsonian in spirit because it does not capitulate to 'word-magic' or 'appalling stubbornness', and yet manages not to reduce the dimensions of the challenge we present to ourselves, as Empson does when he writes as if the distressing friction of 'one moral code . . . dragging against another' is most signally felt 'among present-day educated people'. Such codes have been dragging against each other for ages and at all points on the educational scale; their drag is an integral part of hominization and inseparable from the progress to which Empson nailed his conscience. The drag occurs because we don't all change at the same speed, nor can we change all elements of our selves with equal ease. This too is part of the 'variety of the world', and of the variety within a religion. Religions have what Empson loftily called 'degraded popularised forms' (*A* 569), as do other cultural formations, such as scientific theories. Indeed, all teachings undergo dilution, clotting, refraction, strait-lacing, and the like as they go about their business in the world. Empson supposed, as far as concerns Christianity, that this happens because of what the teachings are, whereas reflection on the similar fate which has waited on empirical hypotheses shows that how they are taught also affects their reception and dispersal.[35] But teachers of all kinds are professionally inclined to concentrate on the 'what' rather than the 'how' of dissemination; such a focus saves them having to think about their pupils. Empson's arguments about Christianity, and his comparisons of Christianity and Buddhism, are seriously

[33] Letter of Dec. 1824, quoted in Mary Pickering, *Auguste Comte: An Intellectual Biography* (Cambridge: Cambridge University Press, 1993), 330.

[34] Ian Hacking, *Mad Travellers: Reflections on the Reality of Transient Mental Illnesses* (London: Free Association Books, 1999).

[35] See, for example, Haldane on 'deeds done in America in the name of eugenics' which were 'about as much justified by science as were the proceedings of the Inquisition by the gospels', *Possible Worlds*, 144, or Empson's own sloppy remarks about 'Darwinism' (*A* 558).

short of attention to the differential strata of reception,[36] and skewed by the sharp practice of setting elite versions of one faith against less intellectually refined manifestations of the other. The terrain of actual disparities across which progress has to be made if made at all vanishes, because when Empson is most determinedly forward looking, history shrinks to his wishes, as if it were an ideally smooth conveyor belt down which improvement reliably trundles.

His specific charge against Christianity is that, 'among the various universal religions' which began the great task of 'giving up human sacrifice', 'Christianity is the only one which ratted on the progress . . . This is what is the matter with it' (*MG* 241). Not all cases of failure or backsliding are instances of 'ratting'. Only an individual, or a quasi-individual such as a legal entity, can 'rat' but 'Christianity' is not that kind of thing. A Coleridge (*A* 305) or a Luther (*FC* 48) may 'rat' when he turns his mind from the direction in which Empson thinks he should be facing. Yet when the 'modern world' undergoes 'disastrous changes . . . often reverting to earlier conditions' (*FC* 53), he doesn't berate it for having ratted on the progress of which it itself is the result, preferring the therapeutic balm of 'reverting'. He suffered on and off from that strain of age-ism ('dark ages', 'machine age') which infects cultural historians and which he himself so sharply caricatured—'the idea that everyone held the same opinion at a given date, "the opinion of the time"' and which is 'disproved as soon as you open a history book and find a lot of them killing each other because they disagreed' (*ERL2* 114). He had an excessively intellectualized notion of why people kill each other. He forgot his own excellent gibe, though, in his incantations against the 'Bronze Age' or 'Neolithic' practice of human sacrifice, a practice not only outrageous but long outmoded according to his roster of ages, as if sheer passage of time had wiped away the impetus towards such atrocity within human groups, an impetus he left unexplored and which he could not have understood within the terms of an individualistic psychology, nor even correctly identified by those apotropaic cries of 'sadism' which he enjoyed in his later years. The world he lived in was not as goodnatured as he was; in March 1980, the *Times* of India reported on a swathe of propitiatory slaughter in Cooch Behar, Karnatka, and elsewhere, querulously wondering 'how is it possible that in the industrial age

[36] By contrast, he wrote perceptively to Richards about the need 'to consider how far a philosophical word is meant to be read differently by different readers, people at different stages of acceptance of the philosophy' (*SL* 34). But that was in 1930.

children in our country can be slaughtered like cattle, in order to appease some deity?'[37] But persistences like that (and they are legion) need real and not rhetorical questioning, questioning among other things of what a slogan like 'the industrial age', serviceable to the state and its 'organizing', in fact means.

By temperament and upbringing, Empson was not a congenial reader for the Scriptures which he thought 'ratted' on the universalizing energies released by 'giving up human sacrifice' so that 'thinkers felt free to consider what was just and good for all men' (*MG* 241). (Again those 'thinkers' feeling 'free'.) This is perhaps why he rarely quotes the sacred writings in his wrangling with Christianity. Both his broad commitment to progress and his thin sense of how beliefs eventuate in practice made him averse to the recognition that '[the Bible] is a process under way, a text in travail; it is not a chronologically progressive process, but a struggle that advances and retreats.'[38] Judaeo-Christianity is the religion of the hyphen, a hyphen which may figure as the rope in a tug-of-war, a shared yoke, a sign of affiliation as in a double-barrelled name, or the first stroke of what will become a directional arrow. It is an unusual religion in the integrity it self-consciously accords (in some of its versions, though not Milton's) to the dynamic of its own development, but not unusual among world religions in needing to be treated as a transhistorical and transcultural reciprocity, a 'process of deciding' not a set of decided doctrines which get unproblematically 'followed'. Sir Charles Eliot remarks in the book from which Empson learned about Buddhism:[39] 'You cannot separate Hinduism from Buddhism, for without it Hinduism could not have assumed its medieval shape and some forms of Buddhism, such as Lamaism, countenance Brahmanic deities and ceremonies.'[40] Just such a separation was what Empson resorted to when making over Buddhism in his preferred image, for he regarded Hinduism as 'Ancient Night' (*MG* 239) from which the Enlightened One had made a clean break. Being a capacious writer, he found it in himself also to express more weighed and inquisitive understandings of human development, as when, properly impressed by the vast stretch of evolution, he remarked 'reverence *ought* to be aroused by the thought that so long and large a process has recently

[37] Quoted in Nigel Davies, *Human Sacrifice in History and Today* (London: Macmillan, 1981), 93.

[38] René Girard, in Robert G. Hamerton-Kelly (ed.), *Violent Origins: Walter Burkert, René Girard and Jonathan K. Smith on Ritual Killing and Cultural Formation* (Stanford, Calif.: Stanford University Press, 1987), 141.

[39] Empson acknowledges his debt in *MG* 239.

[40] Charles Eliot, *Hinduism and Buddhism: An Historical Sketch*, 3 vols. (London: Edward Arnold, 1921), i, p. xi.

produced ourselves who can describe it' and identified such 'reverence' as an element of 'genuine religious feeling' (*MG* 131). The argument between Empson and the 'neo-Christians' on this point is not, as each side liked to pretend for the sake of a doughty stand to hector the other from, about whether progress happens but about how it happens, at what pace, and with what uniformity of sweep.

A religion grows like a drama; it starts in disparities of belief and sympathy as between initiates and the unconverted, proceeds through strife and accommodations with the *status quo ante*, and is always marked by uneven development as fervour or humour varies among its followers. Judaeo-Christianity is very dramatic, in that many of its scriptures tell stories and do that telling largely through dialogue (the recurrent 'and Jesus answering said' of the Gospels). A congregation might be thought of as an audience with more than spectatorial duties; what is true of the variety of attitudes and commitment in the group holds good also for the individuals within the fold, for 'the mind is complex and ill-connected like an audience, and it is as surprising in one case as the other that a sort of unity can be produced by a play' (*SVP* 60) or by preaching and cult. There is always a temptation, for opponents as well as adherents, to exaggerate this 'sort of unity' into a delusive unanimity, stirring for those who claim to feel it and easily disdained by those who don't. Writing about the Jacobethan theatre, Empson was alert to these variances in an audience's beliefs though he wavered about whether and when he gave them their due. He made some of his best jokes against scholars who pretend that audiences in the past were all of one mind—'These audiences after all were made up of simple people, so they had to agree with T. S. Eliot, because they didn't know any better' (*ERL2* 190)—but could not keep a steady eye on the fact of diversity, writing in one essay both that 'I am assuming that the audiences of the first period of Elizabethan drama thought revenge wicked' (*ERL2* 26) and that 'an audience would not have only one opinion, but would broadly agree on feeling that, while revenge was nearly always very wicked, a point might come where it was almost inevitable' (*ERL2* 36).[41] Plays, like religions, get much of their dynamism from the fact that those who listen to them are not in perfect harmony with each other or themselves; you don't find many dramatic masterpieces embodying debates about whether or not what goes

[41] See, for a further instance of Empson's unreliable short-term memory as to what he was arguing within a single essay, *ERL2* 126 and *ERL2* 139.

up really *must* come down, religions are designed to tackle thorny issues. Once this is realized, Empson's assurance in calculating the evils which are to Christianity's discredit proves to be empty, relying as it does on an impoverished notion of how doctrine goes into practice. Bad behaviour in medieval Europe is not 'plainly likely to be the result of implementing, in a high-powered way, the basic doctrines of Christianity' (*A* 624); even while we admire the polemicist's slick phrasing—the double-act of 'plainly likely' with its familiar combo of overpitch and paltering—we notice how thinly he describes the 'implementing', how little he suspects the 'high-powered' while scapegoating 'Christianity'. It is remarkable what the high-powered can turn to advantage when so inclined; Buddhism is a peaceable teaching, yet it served the Sui and T'ang dynasties' drive to recruit more soldiers for their armies.[42]

Religion is never the only power in town but stands, as Mary Douglas says in her calm way, 'in a sophisticated engagement with the social world'.[43] Empson was well aware of this, and knew about how 'we ran | Christ and the magnificent milord | As rival pets' (*CP* 67), but, when he's raging, Christianity takes the brunt of his vehemence and the magnificent milord for some reason goes out scot-free. This seems to me unrealistic about what we have to fear, but then I'm a Stalinist, at least in the sense of thinking Stalin's jolly-brutal question—'Oho! The Pope ! how many divisions has *he* got?'[44]—a good one. A characteristic Empsonian account of the history of Christianity runs: 'the religion of love produced appalling cruelties when made a governmental institution, but it seems arguable that the ideas of Jesus himself got fatally connected under the stress of persecution with the official and moneymaking cult of blood sacrifice, which he had tried to combat' (*CP* 362). Syntax lends its curve to Empson's bias; he could equally have written 'Governmental institutions, in partnership with the religion of love, produced appalling cruelties', though that was not his style. Various irreligions kept up an impressive production of cruelties while he wrote, and the 'stress of persecution' was undergone as well as imposed by Christians, but you do not hear about that sort of thing from Empson. The state in his story usually has clean hands, without even needing to wash them, as Pontius Pilate had to.

His case against historical Christianity is also mounted on a shaky preoccupation with human sacrifice, which is only one point on the broader spectrum

[42] Wright, *Buddhism*, 74–5. [43] Douglas, *Risk and Blame*, 241.

[44] As reported in Winston S. Churchill, *The Second World War*, 6 vols. (London: Cassell, 1948–54), i. 105.

of horrors that anthropologists term 'ritual killing'. In ancient China, as in the royal cemetery at Ur, a monarch's attendants were buried alive with their lord when he died. They were not sacrificial victims, who are treated for their ritual interim as beings of great moment. On the contrary, they mattered only as they had mattered to him and so went under with him: 'A feature special to China was a little cavity, hollowed out at the lowest level of all and reserved for the dead man's favourite cat or lapdog or occasionally a favoured human.'[45] Kings' favours as well as gods' are ambiguous gifts. Ritual killing includes ceremonial suicide as well as murder, for a husband's favours too may come at a price if you happen to be a widow where *sati* is customary, like one of the 8,134 women who were burned alive in Bengal alone between 1815 and 1828.[46] A one-sided diet of examples is a main source of Empson's anthropological malaise. When a witch, a heretic, or a dissident goes to the flames, he crackles with indignation, yet he passes in cool silence over the ashes of these women immolated on the altar of what was thought of as conjugal love. Human sacrifice was a fetchingly lurid debating-point in his campaign against the Christians; it was, though, truly puerile as the overwhelming focus of his concern if he hoped to fathom and to counter 'the wickedest thing yet invented by the black heart of man' (*MG* 251). 'Giving up human sacrifice' may have assisted 'thinkers . . . to consider what was just and good for all men' but all that thinking did not help the countless baby girls across India and China who have died (and die as you read) in ditches or buckets or strangled by the hearth and given drab and hurried burial at the edge of a village.[47] They were beneath consideration.

Just as sacrifice is too sharp a pencil-beam to pick out the full range of what people like us can achieve by way of the seriously appalling, so too Empson's paradigm of cruelty—sadistic gloating over torture—is a stagey thing, more suited to the manufacture of rhetorical *frisson* than inquiry into, let alone coping with, our ills. For decades he railed against God the Father and the 'satisfaction' or 'sadistic pleasure' Empson imagined him taking 'in watching the crucifixion' (*A* 622), admitting only in 1972, and then with a reluctant wince, that the term 'satisfaction' as used in theological jargon refers not to a psychological state but to a legal condition. It pained him

[45] Davies, *Human Sacrifice in History*, 38. The Mesopotamian burials are discussed in A. R. W. Green, *The Role of Human Sacrifice in the Ancient Near East* (Missoula, Mont.: Scholars Press, 1975).
[46] Davies, *Human Sacrifice in History*, 124.
[47] Further information is available at www.gendercide.org/case_infanticide.html.

to come clean about the complexity of 'satisfaction', for once he admitted the institutional sense of the term, he ought in conscience to have given up the pleasures of detecting sadistic motives in every individual who assents to Anselm's account of atonement. He also lost the smashing pun by which the 'satisfaction' of the Father *is* 'the satisfaction of an impulse to inflict pain'; such 'satisfaction' *is* 'an elementary evil . . . a remarkable object, carrying the only inherent or metaphysical evil in the world', and so 'what Christians are worshipping . . . *is* literally the Devil' (*MG* 260; my emphasis). This was a terrific showdown for *Milton's God*, like the scenes in which Poirot unmasks the meek, paid companion in the corner as the fiend who's all along been strangling everyone within reach, but Poirot's accusations usually rest on observed evidence, not on the pretence that a complex word is not complex. Empson is loose about 'sadism' too, another of his casual borrowings from the confident dawn of psychopathology, for not even he, I suppose, wished to attribute sexual appetites to the Christian God. When he was teased with characteristic penetration by Christopher Ricks, who pointed out that a masochistic God would be no improvement on a sadistic one, he admitted 'these terms are very question-begging anyway and cover a multitude of sins' and mentioned that, in revising his essay on Dryden, 'wherever I found *sadistic* I put "bad" ' (*SL* 595). There's something bad, though not sadistic, about a writer's style if you can systematically replace one of those words with the other in his prose. Then we find that 'when I say [Hugh Kenner is] wicked, what I mean is I disagree with his fundamental attitudes' (*CP* 121). If 'bad' and 'wicked' are more or less synonyms, this allows us to write an equation for Empson's controversial style: ' "sadistic" = "I don't agree with it" ', which is to say 'my opponents are perverts, there's no arguing with their horrid proclivities; I shall therefore treat them in the manner traditionally reserved for perverts, with jeers and bullying and the occasional touch of pity.' This is actually also how Milton's God conducts himself. A 'rational ethic' is one that 'anybody . . . who hasn't been specially perverted' (*MG* 259) will assent to; those who disagree with Empson, the sadists, are suffering from 'a very specialised form of disease' (*A* 561). There's 'genuine rational disagreement about a moral question' for you. '*Il n'y a guère que le sadisme qui donne un fondement dans la vie à l'esthétique du mélodrame*', as Proust recognized, a basis not only in life but in the study of culture as Empson in this respect practised it. Proust had a keener feeling for the cruelty we need to bear in mind if we are to guard against depravity, when he wrote of '*cette indifférence aux souffrances qu'on cause et qui, quelques autres noms qu'on lui donne, est la forme terrible et permanente de la cruauté*'.[48] Metaphysical evil does not appear with the showy fascinations of the regrettable Marquis, but in a continuous, unruffled disregard for the value and values of our fellow creatures, like that of Falstaff for the 'pittifull Rascalls' he had recruited ('good enough to tosse: foode for Powder, foode for Powder: they'le fill a Pit, as well as better'[49]) with his breezy pun on 'pittifull' and 'fill a Pit', or in the kindred accents of the papal legate at the siege of Béziers in 1209 who, when asked by the soldiers how they were to tell Cathars from Catholics so as to be sure to massacre only heretics, replied 'Kill the whole lot of them, God will know which ones are His'.

Empson was gentle with Swinburne:

> normally he only wrote well about his appalling ideas about sex, which is all about one side torturing the other. Very remote from my own ambitions in bed, but somehow it was what he wrote well about . . . Mr Eliot . . . said it was all about nothing, whereas it was about this slightly appalling thing . . .
>
> When with flame all around him aspirant
> Stood flushed as a harp-player stands
> The implacable beautiful tyrant
> Rose-crowned having death in his hands.
>
> (*CP* 122)

Nero's placid indifference to the suffering he caused finds its match in Swinburne's verse which jogs at a soothing trot over the realities it renders so palatable. A rhyme like 'aspirant' | 'tyrant'—elsewhere in 'Dolores', Swinburne asks us to mouth (and to stomach) 'Virgin' | 'purge in'; 'bedrape us' | 'Priapus'; 'doff it' | 'prophet'—does not ask for or get the laugh a similar rhyme would raise in Byron, who was alert to the foolery and shock that can come from grating against each other discrepant codes of vocal conduct and the variance of lives they imply. Swinburne's poem is monolithically solemn, and his rhymes are those of a bully, indurated by habit to a victim's squirms; they do not crow over the language as they push it around, they take it imperturbably for granted as counting for nothing when compared with his delights. The rhymes effect a lyric anaesthesia, as phrasing does elsewhere in the poem at 'live torches', where a reader has to resist the mellifluous drone

[48] Marcel Proust, *À la recherche du temps perdu*, ed. Jean-Yves Tadié, 4 vols. (Paris: Gallimard, 1987), i. 163.

[49] William Shakespeare, *The First Part of King Henry the Fourth*, Folio, ll. 2440–1.

to realize the words mean 'light cast by people burning to death', or as syntax does in

> when temples were built
> And the hair of the sacrifice braided
> And the blood of the sacrifice spilt[50]

where the triple alignment of ellipted passives smoothes over the vital differences between a hairdo and execution, so that it sounds as if blood can be unspilled as easily as hair unbraided.

These are neo-Roman lines and as much to be deplored as neo-Christian 'sadism', though 'a more satisfactory case can be made for the Roman upper class being callously indifferent to physical suffering than for their being actively sadistic'.[51] As usual with things 'neo-', they seem flimsily decorative and muddled in purpose when compared with what they pretend to revive. Swinburne flounces where Martial cuts to the chase in his *Book about Shows* in praise of Vespasian's 'hunting theatre' (known later as the Colosseum)—'non fuit hoc artis, sed pietatis opus' ('this was a work, not of art, but of *pietas*'). Martial's tenth suavely blood-curdled epigram Falstaffianly joshes a man torn apart by a bear[52] in that adventure playground completed by Titus with spoils from the destruction of the Temple at Jerusalem. There were hundreds of these amphitheatres across the Empire by 200 CE, and 'when Constantine, the first Christian emperor, came to power . . . his legislation against gladiatorial shows seems to have had about as much visible effect as a thirty-mile-an-hour speed limit at the outskirts of a British town.'[53] So much for even high-powered implementation of basic Christian teaching. Empson needs to occlude such realities because they mess up his tidy account of the Western European appetite for spectacles of pain as a sheerly logical consequence of the doctrine of vicarious atonement. Though he considered the Incas and the Aztecs 'essential test cases' for the study of religion (*A* 621), he neglected evidence from those cases which would have cast doubt on his belief that public torture as 'an admitted pleasure for a crowd' (*A* 619) was a specifically Christian practice. The Aztecs were literally appalling—they not

[50] Charles Swinburne, 'Dolores', ll. 244 and 402–4, in *Swinburne: Poems and Ballads*, ed. Morse Peckham (Indianapolis: Bobbs-Merrill, 1970).

[51] A. W. Lintott, *Violence in Republican Rome* (Oxford: Oxford University Press, 1968), 44.

[52] *Martial: Epigrams*, ed. D. R. Shackleton Bailey, 2 vols. (Cambridge, Mass.: Harvard University Press, 1993), i. 24, 19.

[53] Keith Hopkins and Mary Beard, *The Colosseum* (London: Profile Books, 2005), 153.

only exsanguinated their victims and drank their blood, but prepared them for sacrifice by whitening their faces with chalk. Nor was it St Anselm's God who served the conquistadors, imperial and indifferent like their Mexica victims, as a role model, but the musical emperor of Rome:

It is said that, while the Spaniards were slaughtering the five or six thousand men gathered in the courtyard, their commander regaled his men with snatches of:

> Nero watched from Tarpey's height
> the flames engulf Rome's awful might;
> children and ancients shout in pain,
> he all regards with cold disdain.[54]

It is an important question for students of cultures what you can tell about a people from their songs or other works of art. This is not a question Empson dwelt on. He trusted in *Paradise Lost* as a representative document for the understanding of Christianity and relied on literature and literary academics to supply most of the other evidence he felt he needed. He ends his great sonnet with a snatch of pygmy song, perhaps because pygmies had been said by Paracelsus to have no souls,[55] and so could stand as instances of freedom from the maw of any converting machine, or perhaps because in March 1929 he had played Tom Thumb in Fielding's *The Tragedy of Tragedies*:

Thumb. I know not where, nor how, nor what I am,
  I'm so transported, I have lost my self.
Hunc. Forbid it, all the Stars; for you're so small,
  That were you lost, you'd find your self no more.[56]

Maybe he remembered Huncamunca's blank verse internal rhyme of 'all' and 'small' when writing the 'small ball. It can then all be taught' in his last sonnet. Rhymes amid blank verse are formally discrepant; they jar like one system of organizing struggling to make its way through the cogs of another. They persist throughout *Paradise Lost,* like an old tune Milton can't shake from his

[54] Bartolomé de las Casas, OP, *A Short Account of the Destruction of the Indies* (1552), ed. and trans. Nigel Griffin (London: Penguin Books, 1992), 47. Some Roman Catholic writers in conquering Spain took more 'Roman' and others more 'Catholic' attitudes to the depradations of the one, imperial machine; see Pagden, *Lords of all the World*, 58.

[55] In his *Liber de nymphis, sylphis, pygmaeis et salamandris . . .*; Empson refers to this work in *FC* 103, but may not have known it in 1942.

[56] I quote the text from Simon Trussler (ed.), *Burlesque Plays of the Eighteenth Century* (Oxford: Oxford University Press, 1969), 167.

ear or a superstition he has not yet managed to uproot. They may have vexed him because independent of his will, but they are part of the 'somehow' which enabled him to 'keep somehow alive', underneath his 'downright horrible' and horribly downright 'conception of God', the 'breadth and generosity' Empson generously praised in him (*MG* 276–7). Little disparities like these can sound out the not-to-be-forgotten presence of a 'process of deciding' between systems, an ongoing reinterpretation of how we orient ourselves which in its small way shadows revelation's drift. Empson rightly said of Milton that 'he was a better stylist because he was so quaintly liable to leave loopholes for misinterpretation' (*SL* 606); this cannot be said of his own self-stultified controversial writing, whose shrill ease has sealed itself within a tight circle of talismanic instances and reiterated terms. The realized discrepancy between at least two systems offers a release from lethal convictions; it is a good way to keep a certain 'God' or 'one machine' at bay. As Mary Douglas writes: 'The problem of freedom is the problem of how to divest our categories of their halo of eternal truth. Here there is a chink of hope. For, mercifully, the system of classification never fits.'[57]

Such a chink appears in Empson's sonnet at the strain of 'gigan- | -tic anthropological circus', where the outreach of the hyphen shows the duress of so blithe a spectatorial attitude. The one-machinists are to be feared, but absolute pluralists are also in a risky business; they should themselves fear they might cease to be a working part of the world because they are no more than entertained visitors to it, for an 'emphasis on difference, diversity, oddity, discontinuity, incommensurability and so on' has left them 'with little more to say than that elsewhere things are otherwise and culture is as culture does'.[58] Empson was perhaps wrong to take his pygmies and their singing 'one note each' as an emblem of liberal unconcern for group cohesion, of how we might do well to abandon grand schemes, devote ourselves each to our own thing, and trust, to progress or to providence, for the outcome. In pygmy society, 'teaching of skills is mostly from parent to child of the same sex, and social customs are pressed on each individual homogeneously by all members of the group. These mechanisms of cultural transmission generate the most conservative cultural situations and leave least room for acceptance of internal or external innovation.'[59] They live mostly by hunting

[57] Douglas, *Implicit Meanings*, 215.

[58] Clifford Geertz, *Available Light: Anthropological Reflections on Philosophical Subjects* (Princeton: Princeton University Press, 2000), 50.

[59] Luigi Luca Cavalli (ed.), *African Pygmies* (Orlando, Fla.: Academic Press, 1986), 422.

and their 'necessarily cooperative food-getting techniques stress the social good as against the individual good'.[60] Their music, especially the hunting-songs which employ the 'hoquet' technique[61] that Empson admired, is 'highly integrative' and 'recreates the intensive cooperative patterns required by the hunt'.[62] When Mbuti pygmy boys are initiated into manhood (at about nine to twelve years old), they are circumcised, whipped each morning, and, in the intervals of ritual song, kept silent by stuffing leaves into their mouths.[63] If you saw the pygmies only as features in a circus, you'd never guess what had gone into their song; you need to imagine the forest in which they sing to hear the sense of their tunes. Something similar is true of the development of religious doctrines.

Empson's 'gigan- | -tic' hyphen, with what it hints of dragging codes, looks like the hyphen in 'Judaeo-Christianity'. There is a contrariety in these pointings, but the contrariety bears the thrust and counter-thrust from which an arch is sprung. When young, Empson responded with a torrential insight into the meaning of such signs:

> A contradiction of this kind may be meaningless, but can never be a blank; it has at least stated the subject which is under discussion, and has given a sort of intensity to it such as one finds in a gridiron pattern in architecture because it gives prominence neither to the horizontals nor to the verticals . . . it is at once an indecision and a structure, like the symbol of the Cross. . . . You might relate it to the difference of sound heard by the two ears, which decides where the sound is coming from, or to the stereoscopic contradictions that imply a dimension. (*STA* 225–6)

Athanasius was also describing a symbolic process, 'at once an indecision and a structure', when he spoke of the hyphen Christ made with his arms on the Cross:

> How could He have called us if He had not been crucified, for it is only on the cross that a man dies with arms outstretched? Here, again, we see the fitness of His death and of those outstretched arms: it was that He might draw His ancient people with the one and the Gentiles with the other, and join both together in Him.[64]

[60] Colin M. Turnbull, *The Mbuti Pygmies: Change and Adaptation* (New York: Holt, Rinehart and Winston, 1983), 20.

[61] It is also found in thirteenth-century polyphony and was much disliked by Pope John XXII.

[62] Turnbull, *The Mbuti Pygmies*, 51.

[63] You can see the silenced boys at www7.nationalgeographic.com/ngm/0509/feature5/gallery2.html. I owe this fact, and indeed most of what I know about pygmies, to Martin McLean.

[64] Athanasius, *De incarnatione verbi dei*, ed. and trans. 'a religious of C.S.M.V.' (1944; rev. edn. New York: St Vladimir's Seminary Press, 1996), 55.

Nobody can predict with confidence when such an offered embrace may start to feel like strangulation; there are no rules for knowing such things, let alone a calculus. But that the Cross was always and only just the chief of Christianity's 'incessant advertisements for torture' (*MG* 260) may still be doubted after all Empson's outcry. Any process, judged by those who are embarked on it, will seem at times riven with indecision; the same process, inspected by an outsider who has freeze-framed it at one stage or another, takes on the stability of a structure. 'A religion is the story that a group tells to explain where it has come from, where it is going, what it is, in accord with God's plan.'[65] The Cross recalls a point of departure (which is why Empson thought it encouraged backsliding towards a sacrificial regime) and indicates a direction to pursue (and so looks to the impatient like an incitement not only to clean up the world but to tidy it away). My own sense is, it was and is a sign of what our hopes are quite likely to cost us.

[65] Jacob Neusner, *Judaism when Christianity Began: A Survey of Belief and Practice* (Louisville, Ky.: Westminster John Knox Press, 2002), 1.

8

Alice and Ulysses's Bough: Nonsense in Empson

Hugh Haughton

I

Empson's essay on Lewis Carroll's *Alice* books, 'The Child as Swain', is probably the single most influential essay on those nineteenth-century classics, and one of the great essays of twentieth-century literary criticism. Freudian psychoanalysis, Surrealism, and literary modernism, had all opened new doors on to the peculiar territory of nonsense colonized by Carroll and Lear, with authors as different as James Joyce, T. S. Eliot, Louis Aragon, Breton, and Nabokov, taking up their legacy. Dodgson is an avatar of the father figure of *Finnegans Wake* and T. S. Eliot projected a book called *Inventions of the March Hare*. Robert Graves, who had briefly touched on nonsense in *English Poetry* and *Poetic Unreason*, described Alice in 1925 as 'that prime heroine of our nation' and the Carroll centenary of 1933 witnessed a resurgence of interest in his work.[1] This may have helped trigger Empson's essay, with its claim that 'the books are so frankly about growing up that there is no great

[1] Robert Graves, 'Alice' (1925), in *The Complete Poems*, ed. Beryl Graves and Dunstan Ward (London: Penguin, 2003), 217.

discovery in translating them into Freudian terms; it seems only the proper exegesis of a classic even where it would be a shock to the author' (*SVP* 203). Nevertheless, Alice was already a prime heroine for Empson, and remained so, as I hope to show.

'The Child as Swain' is the culminating chapter of *Some Versions of Pastoral*, and argues that the Romantic shift of pastoral on to childhood underlies the complex play of Carroll's nonsense. Reading the books as being about 'growing up' involved Empson in an early use of biography, as he drew on Dodgson's life and the intellectual contexts of post-Romantic, post-Darwinian England, to make sense of the jokes and twists which thread Alice's journey down the rabbit hole and through the looking-glass. *Some Versions* takes us on a critical journey from 'Proletarian Literature' via Shakespearian drama and Miltonic epic to *Alice*, expounding the parodic double of the heroic mode exemplified by 'comic relief' in Shakespeare, Gay's mock-epic *The Beggar's Opera*, and, climactically, Carroll. Defining pastoral in gleefully heterodox terms as the trick of 'putting the complex into the simple', the study finds a new complexity in many places, including the familiar *Alice* books, which, though never thought of as 'simple' exactly, had hitherto been protected by from any sustained analysis the *cordon sanitaire* of 'nonsense' (*SVP* 25).

As far as I know Empson didn't return to Alice or nonsense literature elsewhere in his critical writing. I want to suggest, however, that far from being a one-off virtuoso performance, 'The Child as Swain' taps into some of the main currents of his thinking and that nonsense is a central concern for a poet and critic interested in pursuing the multiplying senses of sense.

Lewis Carroll crops up, albeit fleetingly, early on in Empson's critical and creative career. The first critical reference to the *Alice* books occurs in an essay in the *Cambridge Review* in 1928, where he noted that 'The Christ in films (except for the one that reduced him to his halo, like the Cheshire cat) is always dog-like.'[2] This gives a nonsensical edge to the film iconography of Christ, and rather uncannily combines a series of interests that he would develop later: Christianity, nonsense, and the symbolic role of dogs. In miniature, the joke seems to sow the seed of *Milton's God*, 'The Child as Swain', and the essay on 'Timon's Dog' in *Some Complex Words*. Likewise in 'Three Stories', his

[2] Empson, 'The King of Kings', *Cambridge Review* (19 Oct. 1928), cited in *WE1* 139.

knockabout undergraduate play of 1927, which is a mock-heroic combination of Noel Coward and *Dracula*, Empson calls up Carroll in the context of a spoof on recent philosophy:

GERALD: Can't you see the two things don't *mean* the same?
MARGERY: Things don't *mean* things, Gerald, you know you aren't allowed to use that word.
GERALD: Sorry. I mean they don't refer to the same reference.
MARGERY: Of course they couldn't have just the same reference, Gerald, or we couldn't tell them apart.
GERALD: Margery, I am crying to you for help, I open my inmost heart to you, and all you do is to sit with your head in a cupboard and talk like the Mad Teaparty.
MARGERY: But I told you I agree with you, Gerald. I'm just filling in the time while you're thinking what to say next, getting the *quotations* in order and what not.
GERALD: (*screaming*) Fish.
MARGERY: Anyway, you ought to talk like the Mad Teaparty: he was a very intellectual man.
GERALD: What *you* said wasn't. It was perfect nonsense, they might perfectly well have exactly the same reference and quite different—

(*RB* 87)

This jokes on 'nonsense' and meaning in the era of *The Meaning of Meaning* but also tunes into Carroll's philosophical comedy. Gerald's dismissive reference to Margery as going on like the 'Mad Teaparty' is trumped by her comeback, 'you ought to talk like the Mad Teaparty', with its non-sequitur slide from the Mad Hatter to his author ('he was a very intellectual man'). 'It was perfect nonsense, they might perfectly well . . . ' sounds the kind of thing the Red Queen might say while Gerald's obscure cry of 'Fish' (presumably meaning something like 'Poppycock') recalls the fact that, as Empson wrote in *Some Versions*, 'everything seems to break up' in *Wonderland* when she realizes 'all the poems are about fish' (*SVP* 214). Gerald, the chief protagonist of his farce, also tells a nonsensical story about James the keeper, who 'told the lunatic he'd better come down and throw him up the tower, because after all anybody could throw him down'. Humpty-Dumpty-style, he says 'That's what they call a triumph of psychoanalysis, that is' (recalling the remark of Carroll's egghead, 'That's what you call a History of England, that is') (*RB* 97).[3] Margery tells

[3] Lewis Carroll, *Alice's Adventures in Wonderland and Through the Looking-Glass*, ed. Hugh Haughton (London: Penguin, 1998), 183.

Gerald that he behaves 'like a monster' who won't 'see any sense in it!' and the whole sketch veers sense and nonsense, farcical action and parodic explanation, in Carroll's way.

Empson was also a 'very intellectual man', as the show's Cambridge undergraduate audience no doubt knew. In 'The Child as Swain' he says 'the famous cat is a very direct symbol' of the idea of 'intellectual detachment', explaining that 'all cats are detached, and since this one grins it is the amused observer'. He also, however, says 'its cleverness makes it formidable—it has very long claws and a great many teeth—but Alice is particularly at home with it; she is the same sort of thing' (*SVP* 218). These early references suggest that, even as an undergraduate, with a starring role in the ADC and *Granta*, Empson was at home with nonsense. Perhaps he also felt 'the same sort of thing' as the Cheshire Cat. His later account of the White Queen in *Through the Looking-Glass* combines exegetical brilliance with an inwardness with Carroll and his creations that suggests the kind of familiarity he shows in his criticism of Milton and Shakespeare:

> The Queen is a very inclusive figure. 'Looking before and after' with the plaintive tone of universal altruism she lives chiefly backwards, in history; the necessary darkness of growth, the mysteries of self-knowledge, the self-contradictions of the will, the antinomies of philosophy, the very Looking-Glass itself, impose this; nor is it mere weakness to attempt to resolve them only in the direct impulse of the child. Gathering the more dream-rushes, her love for man becomes the more universal, herself the more like a porcupine. Knitting with more and more needles she tries to control life by a more and more complex intellectual apparatus (*SVP* 232)

The proposition 'her love for man becomes the more universal, herself the more like a porcupine' generates something of the queer logic we find in Empson's poetry, while his account of 'the helplessness of the intellect, which claims to rule so much' reflects an ambivalent rationality that goes to the heart of his own work, with its mixture of 'complex intellectual apparatus' and awareness of human irrationality. 'The Child as Swain', with its Freudian poignancy and panache, suggests that the dialect—or dialectics—of nonsense has an intimate bearing on his own work.[4]

[4] Hugh Kenner argues that Empson's 'charm has always depended on a sort of Alice-persona: the cool-headed quizzer of semantic monsters, seeking to adequate his understanding to the verdicts of his tastes.' He adds that it is 'no accident that his finest piece of sustained writing is his exegesis of *Alice*', 'Alice in Empsonland', *Hudson Review*, 5 (Spring 1952), 137.

II

In this context, it seems revealing that Alice crops up in at least two of his poems. The first of these, 'The Scales', opens with an allusion to Carroll's heroine that recalls the devotion to the mock-heroic played out in *Some Versions of Pastoral*:

> The proper scale would pat you on the head
> But Alice showed her pup Ulysses' bough
> Well from behind a thistle, wise with dread;
>
> And though your gulf-sprung mountains I allow
> (Snow-puppy curves, rose-solemn dado band)
> Charming for nurse, I am not nurse just now.
>
> (*CP* 35)

The 'nurse' in the background suggests the Victorian or Edwardian nursery, but the poem appears to be addressed to a contemporary girl friend. The 'you' who might, given the 'proper scale', expect to be patted on the head with affectionate patronage like a 'pup', looms gigantically in the poet's mind, as if her presumably childlike body had expanded monstrously to include 'gulf-sprung mountains'. She not only makes the speaker feel small but tiny. Indeed she makes him feel both like a girl and a child, identifying him, rather than the female addressee, with Alice.

The poem turns on the bewildering problems of scale Alice experiences in her early adventures down the rabbit hole, which Empson called 'the most spontaneous and "subconscious" part of the books' (*SVP* 204). It recalls the incident when Alice ponders the problem of how 'to grow to the right size again' and is confronted by 'an enormous puppy'. She has recently escaped from being cooped up in the White Rabbit's house, a place where she had found herself in danger of being squashed to death due to her gigantic size, but she is now so small that she is in danger of being done in by a pet she is simultaneously protective of and terrified by:

> 'Poor little thing!', said Alice in a coaxing tone, and she tried to whistle to it; but she was terribly frightened all the time at the thought that it might be hungry, in which case it would be very likely to eat her up in spite of all her coaxing.
>
> Hardly knowing what she did, she picked up a little bit of stick and held it out to the puppy: whereupon the puppy jumped into the air off all its feet at once, with a yelp

of delight, and rushed at the stick and made believe to worry it: then Alice dodged behind a great thistle, to keep herself from being run over.[5]

Alice is caught between two different perspectives on the dog, which is both 'poor little' puppy and dangerous beast. Not being her 'proper' size, and therefore unable to see it in perspective, she is 'terribly frightened'. In this respect, she is like the mouse in 'The Pool of Tears', who is offended by Alice's affectionate references to her cat Dinah, who may be a cuddly pet for Alice but is predator to the mouse.

Like Bunyan, of whom he wrote 'Usual for a man | Of Bunyan's courage to respect fear', Empson respects fear (*CP* 76). Indeed his respect for fear is one of the major sources of his poetry, as in 'Courage means Running' itself, 'Aubade' where 'It seemed the best thing to be up and go' (*CP* 69), 'Reflections from Rochester', with its opening quotation 'From fear to fear, successively betrayed' (*CP* 75), and 'Reflections from Anita Loos' where we hear that 'It is not human to feel safely placed' (*CP* 85). Alice is certainly not 'safely placed' at this particular juncture, and indeed is never 'safely placed' in the unstable world she travels through. She is always either changing size or up against changing rules and viewpoints. In 'The Child as Swain', Empson compares 'the changes of relative size' in the book to those in Gulliver which are directed to the 'impersonal eye', exciting 'Wonder but of a scientific sort'. By contrast, Carroll appeals to the fact that children 'like to think of being so small that they could hide from grown-ups and so big that they could control them, and to do this dramatizes the great topic of growing up, which both Alices keep to consistently' (*SVP* 212–14).

'The Scales' is about growing up too, but when Empson writes that 'Alice showed her pup Ulysses' bough' he is playing with other kinds of change too. He later described the poem as 'an excuse to a woman for not showing enough love', and the reference to 'Ulysses' bough' brings in quite a different range of feelings.[6] It refers, of course, to the incident where the recently shipwrecked Ulysses picks up an olive branch to hide his nakedness while approaching Nausicaa and her female companions on the beach. Making Alice's 'little bit of stick' into this particular bough plays some strange reversals. Is the child hiding her own nakedness here, or the adult, and which sex is the protagonist? Is this a comment on Dodgson with his urge to identify with pre-adolescent

[5] Carroll, *Alice's Adventures*, 37.
[6] Empson, *William Empson Reading Selected Poems* (Hull: Marvell Press: *Listen* LPV 3, 1961).

girls like Alice and photograph them in 'nature's costume'? Or on Empson's simultaneous identification with the nude Ulysses among the women and Alice with the puppy? Comparing the different kinds of exposure experienced by a miniature Alice and naked Greek hero, the poem generates a feeling of crossed wires, of cross-gendered and cross-genre embarrassment. The male speaker, like a confused version of Eliot's Tiresias, imagines himself as Carroll's fictional heroine and her nurse (he is 'not nurse just now') while also hiding his penis behind a bough. Commenting on Dodgson's ambivalent attitude towards children, Empson said that 'he, like Alice, wanted to get the advantages of being childish and grown-up at once' (*SVP* 213). The telescoping of Alice's twig and Ulysses' fig leaf suggests a comparable ambivalence about sex and growing up. He speaks of her being 'wise with dread' and we might remember that a 'voice of dread' is heard in the opening poem of *Through the Looking-Glass*, where Carroll says 'Come, hearken then, ere voice of dread | With bitter tidings laden, | Shall summon to unwelcome bed | A melancholy maiden! | We are but older children, dear, | Who fret to find our bedtime near.'[7] Commenting on this in the essay, Empson wrote that 'the marriage-bed was more likely to be the end of the maiden than the grave, and the metaphor firmly implied treats them as identical' (*SVP* 215). As a result he thought the poem was 'obviously more a joke against Dodgson than anything else'. Likewise, in calling Alice 'wise with dread', 'The Scales' is making more of a joke against Empson than anything else. The essay recalls his 'believing I should have to die in order to grow up, and thinking the prospect very disagreeable' and argues for a 'connexion in Dodgon's mind between the death of childhood and the development of sex' (214). Perhaps there's a trace of something similar in 'The Scales', with its switchback between childhood and adulthood, puppy love and puppy terror.

The opening brings together Empson's presumed adult addressee, the 7-year-old heroine of Carroll's story, and the hero of *The Odyssey* and Tennyson's 'Ulysses'. Explaining the references in the notes to *Poems* (1935) the poet lists 'Alice in Wonderland, Ulysses appearing to Nausicaa, and the jackal sandhole through which the heroes escaped in Rider Haggard's *King Solomon's Mines*'.[8] This yokes together a Victorian children's book, a classical epic, and a *fin-de-siècle* Imperialist yarn presumably read in his schooldays. The poem's subject is also closer to home. Empson, in one of many explanations, noted

[7] Carroll, *Alice's Adventures*, 117.

[8] Empson, *Poems* (London: Chatto & Windus, 1935), 45.

'*Scales*—in the sense of the first estimate of size which decides what kind of tool to use; an excuse to a woman for not showing enough love' (cited in *CP* 223–4). Ulysses' bough was a kind of fig leaf, but 'What kind of tool' suggests what a fig leaf is supposed to hide. There are boughs in *Through the Looking-Glass* where the Live Flowers speak of a tree that goes 'Bough-wough', explaining 'That is why its branches are called boughs' (the puppy might have triggered this cross-reference in the poet, and in the essay Empson represents 'the willow-tree that said Bough-Wough' as 'a symbol of hopeless love' (*SVP* 228)).[9] Calling the twig a 'bough', however, especially in the context of 'Ulysses', also signals what he calls his interest 'in Freud and Frazer, in traces of the primitive, and all that' (*A* 253). In his discussion of double-plots he alludes to *The Golden Bough* while arguing that the idea of 'the Sacrificial Hero as Dying God' is 'mixed up in the brew' of pastoral (*SVP* 23–4). Like *Some Versions*, the juxtaposition of Alice and Ulysses' bough sets up equations across very different scales of 'weight' and height but also value. Ulysses crops up elsewhere in *Some Versions* in the context of 'double-plots', where Empson speaks of 'the whole Pelion of theory ranged through the speeches of Ulysses' in relation to *Troilus and Cressida*'s principle of 'large-scale indefinite juxtaposition' (34–5). Like *Troilus* and Empson's critical study, the poem, with its Dantean *terza rima*, depends on the 'indefinite juxtaposition' of epic and nonsense.

It ends with a play on geographical scale, with the remark that 'to sea Nile only brings | Delta and indecision, who instead | Far back up country does enormous things'. If this draws on the African Imperial Gothic of *King Solomon's Mines*, the tributaries of allusion have sources in Carroll too. They may recall Haggard, Speke, and Cleopatra, but also Alice's involuntary parody of Isaac Watts' hymn, 'How doth the little crocodile | Improve his shining tail, | And pour the waters of the Nile on every golden scale!'[10] This gives us not only the Nile but more 'scales', not the 'golden mean' but 'every golden scale' of the crocodile. 'Far back up country' suggests the upper Nile Delta and the interior of Africa but also the world of childhood, which is 'far back' in a different sense. Empson explained the Romantic view of childhood to mean 'that there is more in the child than any man has been able to keep. (The child is a microcosm like Donne's world, and Alice too is a stoic.)' (*SVP* 209). Something comparable seems to be at work here, as the 'enormous things' of the anterior

[9] Carroll, *Alice's Adventures*, 137. [10] Ibid. 19.

and interior world (the world of ABC) end up in the adult world as 'delta and indecision'.

'To make the dream-story from which *Wonderland* was elaborated seem Freudian', Empson wrote, 'one has only to tell it', and the same is true of his poem (*SVP* 216). It juxtaposes the nursery, with its 'dado', and the Alps and Nile. John Haffenden quotes John Howard Willis to the effect that 'Freudian interpretation of the passage, involving trains, tunnels, height, curves and fingers, seems possible since Empson's note clearly equates the girl and the mountain or castle'.[11] There may be a subterranean analogy between Empson and Dodgson at work here, with the high-wire tension between 'sense' (in the sense of sensuality) and nonsense. The poem recreates the intimacy of 'careful fingers' which 'meet through castle sand', calling up not only trains 'climbing tunnels' but the seaside holidays Carroll enjoyed and parodied in 'The Walrus and the Carpenter'. Trains loom large in *Alice*, as do 'preserved kings' and 'tunnels'. The reference to the 'gulf-sprung mountains' might also recall the Red Queen's relentlessly comparative, 'I could show you hills in comparison with which you'd call that a valley.'[12] Likewise, though the 'tunnels' may hide 'Solomon's gems', they also suggest Alice's underground corridor and the Freudian interplay in Carroll between adult fantasy and childhood, and the poet's uneasy relationship to both. As poet and critic Empson makes it his business to map the 'enormous things' involved in small-scale operations, a skill that makes him naturally kin to Alice, equipped with 'Ulysses' bough'. Alluding to the fact that Alice has 'become a patron saint of the Surrealists', he observes 'they do not go in for Comic Primness, a sort of reserve of force, which is her chief charm' (*SVP* 221). A comparable mock-heroic Comic Decorousness is one of his.

III

John Haffenden's edition of *The Complete Poems* gives us a clearer idea of Empson's development as a poet than the old *Collected Poems*. He did not emerge fully fledged as a 1930s Donne in modern dress, though he very nearly did. Preceding and scattered around early metaphysical puzzle-poems such as 'The Ants' are

[11] John Howard Willis, 'The Poetry of William Empson' (unpublished Ph.D. dissertation, Columbia University, New York, 1967), quoted in *CP* 224.

[12] Carroll, *Alice's Adventures*, 140.

spoofs, parodies, bagatelles, and experiments, which are puzzling in a different way. They confirm the sense that from the outset Empson's poetic universe borders on the comic. As poet and critic, he is committed to making sense of the world but consistently aware of its absurdity. In the prefatory note to *Collected Poems* (1984), he said:

> Much of the verse here is about the strangeness of the world, in which we are often tripped up and made helpless, and the first thing to do in that situation is to understand it. In such a case, it is usual for some to laugh and others not. I was feeling very earnest when I was snapped, though the effect is comical; and this makes it a suitable lead-in for the poems. (*CP* 114)

Though not 'comic poems', Empson's are full of effects that are 'comical'. His criticism puts the jokes back into the cosmic epic of *Paradise Lost* and his poems put the jokes into modern cosmology. 'Landing, you break some palace and seem odd,' he says in 'To an Old Lady' (*CP* 24) and many of his best lines, like this one, break oddly like jokes.

From the outset Empson was interested in the kinship between jokes and poetry. In a 1928 review of George Rylands's *Words and Poetry* he asserted 'I believe myself poetry is written with the sort of joke you find in hymns' (*A* 67). To make sense of this Wildean claim, you have to rethink the relation between poetry and jokes, but also hymns, (a kind of poetry not normally associated with jokes) parentheses. Though this is a good joke about hymns, Empson's own verse often jokingly trespasses on their territory. Carroll deplored any joking that treated Christianity without proper reverence, but, nevertheless, Alice's 'How doth the little crocodile' parodies Isaac Watts's 'How doth the little busy bee', and its joke on the hymn is a deadly serious one, akin to Blake's 'Tyger' as a response to his 'Lamb'.[13] In fact Empson's earliest poem is a ferocious joke against a kind of hymn. Its heroine responds to her Mother's evening prayer 'Four angels guard you' with a skimming pillow aimed at the angels, and it ends with her Alice-like defiance:

> Mother, shocked, gasped feebly 'Anne!!!'
> (A pillow disabled the water-can.)
> Said Anne, 'I won't have things in white
> Chant prayers about my bed all night.'
>
> (*CP* 4)

[13] Empson comments that 'children who aren't forced to learn Dr Watts can't get the same thrill from the parodies of him as the original children did' (*SVP* 227).

Written when Empson was 13, it parodies just the kind of 'nursery charm' travestied in 'How doth the little crocodile' and shows comparable independence.[14]

Empson's undergraduate poetry was attuned to comic as well as cosmic effects. His first published poem was 'Poem about a Ball in the Nineteenth Century', which he later described as 'a bit of romantic description imitating Gertrude Stein'.[15] It opens with airy and feathery virtuosity:

Feather, feather, if it was a feather, feathers for fair, or to be fair, aroused. Round to be airy, feather, if it was airy, very, aviary, fairy, peacock, and to be well surrounded. Well-aired, amoving, to peacock, cared-for, share dancing inner to be among aware. Peacock around, peacock to care for dancing, an air, fairing, will he become, to stare. Peacock around, rounded, to turn the wearer, turning in air, peacock and I declare, to wear for dancing, to be among, to have become preferred. (*CP* 18)

In *Through the Looking-Glass* the Sheep cries 'Feather! Feather!' and Empson's nonsensical prose poem takes its cue from Alice's retort, '*Why* do you say "Feather" so often . . . I'm not a bird.'[16] Indeed, with its lunatic dance of sound, it might be described as a kind of Peacock Quadrille ('Will you, wo'n't you, will you, wo'n't you, will you join the dance?'). There is vertiginous play on ambiguity—with 'feathers for fair', 'to be fair', and 'fairing' all turning on different senses of the word 'fair', but also playing on the punning 'air' in 'airy', 'well-aired', and 'in air' and drawing on the same core of sound as 'aviary', 'cared-for', 'shared', 'stare', 'wear', and 'declare'. Later the dance becomes crazier and faster, with 'dancing being begun turning together' and that ocular 'stare' evoking 'a feathered peacock on the stair'. We hear of 'Moving and to make one the pair', but if there is a 'pair' at this Victorian ball, there are no obvious females. Perhaps we should see it as a camp version of Sitwell's 'Parade' manner, a mock-heroic homoerotic celebration of the male as peacock ('Will he be there, can he be there, be there?'). In *The Structure of Complex Words* Empson set out to counter I. A. Richards's claim that 'the Emotions given by words in poetry are independent of their Sense', and the entire book is a justification of the claim that poetry is never independent of 'the Sense', however weird or complex it may be (*SCW* 6). 'Poem about a Ball' reads like an experiment to test the 'Pure Poetry' theory he was attacking in *Seven Types of Ambiguity* and he said that 'no other poem . . . disregards meaning

[14] 'I think the traditional God of Christianity very wicked, and have done since I was at school, where nearly all my little playmates felt the same' (*MG* 10).

[15] Empson, *Reading Selected Poems*.

[16] Carroll, *Alice's Adventures*, 177.

in the sense that this one does'.[17] It gives air to a taste for nonsense, but still keeps an ear, not for Frost's sound of sense, but the play of multiple senses.

The Complete Poems reprints a number of comparable playful undergraduate performances, including 'Two centos', a satirical squib called 'Une Brioche pour Cerbère', and 'Address to a tennis-player', a Joycean complement to 'Poem about a Ball in the Nineteenth Century'. There's also a spoof 'Fragment', which apes modernist rhetoric in a nonsensical key ('Desperate ladders, mid bison, weeps') and 'Newly Discovered War Poems', a revue-style parody of First World War poetry from *Granta* ('Mud, oh, my God! Oh, my God! mud. | Oh, my mud! | Ping.'), with the comic 'ping' mimicking the fatal bullet (*CP* 133–4). 'Address to a tennis-player' opens in Hopkinsian vein, 'Gracious are you still unaltered, halted, untired no larger, Peter', but goes on to some rather rocky punning with ' "So long" and so long after, laughter and after all no, thou art Peter, upon this rock I build' (*CP* 19).[18] This is a camp parody of Hopkinsian grandeur, as the structural Christian 'rock' shifts to 'Peter Pan, Scarborough Rock' and references to a rock that will 'shock St Paul's dean and chapeetre'. 'Peter' is a slang word for penis, and Empson refers to his 'cock cocked amidden promptly crew to tears, grew to dears', making nonsense of Peter, the presumed tennis-player, as well as playing mischievously on his Christian names, indeed Christian names as such (with 'Simple to Simon Peter' combining 'Simple Simon' with 'Simon Peter', and 'mock wearing Christopher renamed' reminding us of people named after the renamed Christ-bearing saint). 'St Paul's dean' recalls John Donne, but the poem ends, not with the cross, but with 'hot cross buns'.

Similar mock-heroic, mock-Christian play runs through 'New World Bistres', which seems to parody the metaphysical poetry Empson was lovingly expounding in *Seven Types*: 'Oh socketed too deep, oh more than tears, | Than any faint unhurrying resurrection, | That even rain, manna (the manner born, | The man born of the manor, and that bourne | No traveller returns') (*CP* 20). Empson was indeed 'born of the manor' in Yorkshire, but leery of manna. If this punning is almost too much to be born, it plays off myth and nonsense, like later more serious poems, suggesting Empson needed both.

[17] Empson, *Poems* (1935), 41.

[18] Commenting on Johnson's remark on Shakespeare's love of 'quibbles', Empson said 'To relate a taste for puns with the author's sexual constitution, one would have to consider what a variety of notions of manliness then held sway' (*STA* 111).

'Two centos' is an example of a form which generates a poetic conundrum by way of mandarin parody of familiar poetic material. As a collage of quotations, it draws sentences that made sense in other contexts into a new situation, where the fun is in the mix of mishmash and miss-match which creates an incongruous sense of congruity or congruous sense of incongruity. So, sense is turned into nonsense, which in turn generates a kind of baffled sense. Conflict is at the centre of Empson's theory of ambiguity, and like the riddle, the puzzle, the conundrum, and the paradox, 'Nonsense' is—or can be—a site of conflict, as his reading of *Alice* demonstrates. 'Two centos' generates a sense of friction between its component parts while mimicking a sense of coherence which it also travesties.

i.
At Algezir, and will in overplus,
Their herdsmen, well content to think thee page, divided.
Tell Isabel the queen, I looked not thus
Leander, Mr Ekenhead and I did.

ii.
of them that are overcome with. Woe
stay me with flagons, civilly delight.
So lovers contracts, images of those,
so be I equalled with, as dark as night.

Do thy worst, blind Cupid, dark amid the blaze of. Woe
to the crown of pride, and Phineus prophets old,
did cry To-whoo To-whoo, and the sun did shine so
(the lords and owners of, poor Toms-a) cold.

(*CP* 8)

As Empson's footnotes tell us, this Frankensteinian monster is derived from limbs and fragments from the biblical authors of Genesis, Isaiah, and Song of Solomon, and the canonical English poets Chaucer, Shakespeare, Marlowe, Donne, Milton, Pope, Wordsworth, and Byron. As an early squib, it is one of the few poems in the awesomely annotated *Complete Poems* which doesn't inspire editorial notes. None the less, it is striking that the poets cannibalized in this nonsense cento are the ones closest to Empson's heart.

The poems quoted are (with the exception of *Don Juan*) poems of high seriousness. Extracts from the Bible and Milton's biblical epic mix with scraps from the tragic Renaissance dramas of *Edward II*, *King Lear*, and *Samson*

Agonistes, while phrases from Donne's love poems and Shakespeare's sonnets (an example of 'will in overplus') are spliced with splinters of mock-lyric by the Romantics Wordsworth and Byron. The material quoted is intensely charged, but the manner is characteristically Empsonian. The lines 'So lovers contracts, images of those, | so be I equalled with, as dark as night', not only comically telescope Donne, Milton, and Shakespeare, but have something of the vertiginously contracted oddity of Empson poems like 'High Dive'.

Love and madness, however, are at the heart of the scholastic play of this surprisingly dark squib. 'As dark as night' comes from one of the last sonnets to the Dark Lady ('My love is as a fever longing still'), a poem in which the disillusioned speaker fears for his sanity as well as cursing his lover: 'Past cure I am, now reason is past care, | And frantic made with evermore unrest; | My thoughts and my discourse as madmen's are, | At random from the truth vainly expressed.' Though he had thought her bright, his love is 'black as hell, as dark as night'.[19] The cento too is full of 'discourse' that might seem as 'random' as that of 'madmen', and includes not only the speech of lovers (Solomon's 'stay me with flagons', Shakespeare's sonnets, Donne's love poems) but a series of apparently mad figures, including Edgar as mad Tom in *King Lear* and the 'Idiot Boy' of Wordsworth's ballad, both of whom are joined in the final rhyme 'cold'. Edgar's 'Poor Tom's a cold' and the idiot boy's 'the sun it shone so cold' converge after the bracket, while also incorporating the coldness of the boy of Sonnet 94, who is himself 'as stone, | Unmoved, cold, and to temptation slow'. Discussing Alice later, Empson noted that 'The Idiot Boy of Wordsworth is too milky a moonlit creature to be at home with Nature as she was deplored by the Carpenter' (*SVP* 232–3). Like *Hamlet*'s 'reason in madness', the derangement of 'Two centos' turns on fear of nature and women. If madness connects the idiot boy to Edgar on the heath, blindness links many of the other disjointed phrases.

'Do thy worst, blind Cupid, dark amid the blaze of' yokes together two stark cases of literary blindness, Shakespeare's Gloucester and Milton's Samson. This remembers the misogynistic ranting of the mad Lear crying out to blind Gloucester ('Dost thou squinny at me? No, do thy worst, blind Cupid; I'll not love'), and also the blind Samson who at the opening of Milton's play exclaims 'O dark, dark, dark, amid the blaze of noon, | Irrecoverably dark, total

[19] William Shakespeare, Sonnet 147, *Shakespeare's Sonnets*, ed. Katherine Duncan-Jones (London: Arden, 1997), 411.

eclipse.' Milton recurs in the quoted phrase 'and Phineus prophets old', which comes from his appeal to prototypical blind prophets ('blind Maeonides, | And Tiresias and Phineus prophets old'). In other words the scraps of love poems by Donne and Solomon lead, after the phrase from Shakespeare's sonnet, into a mélange of blindness, darkness, coldness, and madness. It is a case of Eliot's 'These fragments I have shored against my ruins.'[20]

It is not clear whether this is how we are meant to construe the poem, but once the reader re-contextualizes the fragments, what at first seems nonsensically disparate generates a sense of uncanny convergence. Quoting and mimicking the playful allusiveness of Byron ('Leander, Mr Ekenhead, and I did'), Empson's centos bring together figures distracted to near madness by a sense of contradiction. The effect is of a literary mad-song, pitched at that pitch of nonsense we find in *King Lear*, and subliminally linked by the thread of misogyny we find in Marlowe, the Shakespeare sonnets, *Lear*, and Milton's Samson. In *Some Versions* Empson meditates on the way Milton's descriptions of Eden form 'our main subsequent poetic tradition of Nature', and describes Collins's *Ode to Evening* as 'a cento from Milton' (*SVP* 145). His own 'Two centos' documents a tradition that provides the poetic compost for his own brand of metaphysical poetry.

'Two centos' is an extreme case, but, like other early poems, it revels in the fine line between sense and nonsense. Empson moved on from the high jinks of the earliest work, but his poetry continued to thrive on the mock-heroic space between jokes and religious, philosophical, and moral beliefs. In many of his best poems and lines, there is a sense of dizzying complexity and joking oddity. 'Invitation to Juno', for example, begins 'Lucretius could not credit centaurs; | Such bicycle he deemed asynchronous' (*CP* 12), a proposition that can be decoded sensibly but has an indelibly comic ring, especially since this notion of the 'asynchronous' is 'anachronistic'. Lucretius may have had views on cycles and centaurs but couldn't have viewed centaurs as bikes. Likewise in 'Notes on Local Flora', the remark that 'I knew the Phoenix was a vegetable', while making complete sense in a poem about a flower that will 'ripen only in a forest fire', sounds absurd in the face of the weighty iconographic tradition which assumes it was an animal (*CP* 56). The opening of 'Homage to the British Museum', 'There is a Supreme God in the ethnological section', has a comparable effect (*CP* 55). We all recognize the jarring between the local

[20] T. S. Eliot, *The Complete Poems and Plays of T. S. Eliot* (London: Faber, 1969), 75.

divinity and the larger ethnological context when 'A hollow toad shape, faced with a blank shield' is described as a Supreme God, whose belly includes 'the Pantheon'. The irony, however, goes unnervingly in all directions. It re-situates not only the African toad God, but the Christian 'Supreme God' and the classical 'pantheon', jarring against the apparently value-free cultural relativism of the British Museum. The nonsense ring to the proposition 'There is a Supreme God in the ethnological section' recoils back on the proposition 'There is a Supreme God', giving the poem's account of religion a more vertiginous reach than the initial irony covers. It is a version of the puzzle of the One and the Many that lies at the centre of Empson's criticism of literary treatments of Christian theology that climaxes in *Milton's God.*

'Dissatisfaction with Metaphysics' is a modern 'metaphysical' poem on the model of Donne, in which the poet looks back at earlier cosmological models, including Judaic and Islamic ones. Opening with a view 'High over Mecca' of 'Allah's prophet's corpse' as the 'centre of the universe', he combines it with an account of Ptolomaic cosmology in a way that highlights the strangeness of both: 'How smooth his epicycles round him run, | Whose hearth is cold, and all his wives undone' (*CP* 17). As he does so, he generates a critique of 'Infinity', as traditionally conceived, that generates a sense of vertiginous nonsense. The strain is a measure of the poet's intellectual dissatisfaction with it:

> Two mirrors with Infinity to dine
> Drink him below the table when they please.
> Adam and Eve breed still their dotted line,
> Repeated incest, a plain series.
> Their trick is all philosophers' disease.
>
> (*CP*, 17)

There is comedy in this satirical development of the conceits of Donne and Marvell, with the flat 'dotted line' used to describe the progeny of Adam and Eve. The idea of 'Infinity' getting drunk at the dinner table, works as a bathetic demonstration of the infinite regression implicit in infinity. In his notes, Empson said the 'two mirrors have any number of reflections (the self-conscious mind)', and John Haffenden points us towards the 'Child as Swain' where Empson says that '*Wonderland* is a dream, but the *Looking-Glass* is self-consciousness' (*SVP* 206). The poem was first published in 1928, two years after T. S. Eliot's Clark lectures on 'The Metaphysical Poetry of the Seventeenth Century', where Eliot wrote that 'there are not wanting voices to declare that the present age is a metaphysical age'.[21] It might be read as a self-conscious commentary on the impossibility of modern metaphysical poetry.

Theology, cosmology, and nonsense converge giddily in many other poems, as in 'Earth has Shrunk in the Wash' (*CP* 39). In 'Rolling the Lawn', for example, the poet portrays himself absurdly as 'Holding the Holy Roller at the slope | (The English fetish, not the Texas Pope)' (*CP* 16), while in 'Part of Mandevil's Travels', he says, in another set of brackets, '(Paradise, like Bohemia, has no coast; | Of bombs and bowlers it has power to boast . . .)' (*CP* 26), and in 'The Extasie' he says 'We stand on the reflections of our feet. | Unsupported, we do not know whether to fall upwards or downwards' (*CP* 28). In such lines, physics meets metaphysics in unlikely places, and with unexpected results.

'Aubade', a poem about a potentially catastrophic emergency, is also about standing and falling. It describes lovers caught in the aftermath of an earthquake, and its choric line, 'The heart of standing is you cannot fly' combines grandeur with riddling oddity (*CP* 69). With its 'comic primness', this is just the kind of thing the Red Queen would say ('The heart of standing is you cannot fly, child.'). The eerie appeal to the multiple senses of standing and flying alongside the strange play on 'the heart' in 'the heart of standing', is both bizarre and oracular, especially set against the no-nonsense resolution of 'It seemed the best thing to be up and go.' The fact that standing and going look like opposite courses of action gives the phrase an air of paradox. If it appeals to common sense in an uncommon situation, it also gives all the terms of the equation a ring of nonsense. Likewise in 'Advice', a poem that plays on the idea of common-sense authoritativeness, we come cross the sentence 'Crash is a cloth but poisons are all greens' (*CP* 88), which would not be out of place in a Surrealist poem. The notes tell us that 'Crash' is a 'pleasant coarse canvas-like material; the only point of the pun is the idea that what seems smashing may turn out quite healthy' (*CP* 370). Though lines like these 'make sense', they expose the contradictory senses at work in their kind of sense. He goes on to refer to 'The great and good, more murderously scabbed, | No dug-out on whose lawns could spoil no game', moving from the clichéd 'great and good' to a tangle of negatives which satirizes their stoicism. The suggestion is that war and war-games can't be allowed to spoil the grandees' croquet lawns (as

[21] T. S. Eliot, *The Varieties of Metaphysical Poetry*, ed. Ronald Schuchard (London: Faber and Faber, 1993), 43.

in *Alice*), but also that neither war nor games are really games ('no game'). 'It is on contradiction that they grow', he remarks in 'Aubade', and such lines, like the jokes in *Alice*, confirm not only the 'strangeness of the world' but also the strangeness of the thinking about the world going on in the poem.

All these poems are 'teasers', and Empson also wrote a poem with that title. Asked by Christopher Ricks what 'The Teasers' was about, he replied that it had originally been longer and that he didn't like what he was saying, 'so I cut it down to rags so that it does not make sense, you can't find out what it is about. Of course, these powerful minds in the business of criticism, they're fascinated by something that doesn't make sense' (cited in *CP* 117). All the same he thought it a 'beautiful metrical invention' and liked the way it 'sings so'. An oracular rather than teasingly nonsensical poem, it announces at the outset 'Not but they die, the teasers and the dream, | Not but they die, | and tell the careful flood | To give them what they clamour for and why' (*CP* 86). As when faced with the pronominal indeterminacy of Carroll's 'They told me you had been to her, | And mentioned me to him', the reader can't tell what or who 'the teasers' are, nor what or who 'they' and 'them' are.[22] 'Not but they die' is a grammatical impossibility, suggesting a condensation of something like 'It's not that they die' or 'It's not only that they die', but with a 'but' that won't fall into line. Similarly, you can 'give them what they clamour for' but cannot give them 'what they clamour for and why', as it says. Later, the poem deploys comparable grammatical impossibilities when it says 'the short view | Could be so long it saw where it began' (which is not unlike the Red Queen's hills turning into valleys) and 'Remember what you once wanted to do | And will want to have done when the time came' (where the 'will want to have done' logically suggests the future 'when the time comes' rather than the past, 'when the time came'). The poem climaxes with the magnificent claim that 'short sight | Is the magnifiying glass able for the flame'. This plays off the sense that 'magnifying glasses' help the short-sighted to see better with the contrary meaning that by concentrating the rays of the sun they can generate fire. Our impulse, like those of the 'powerful minds' Empson talks of, must be to seek oracular sense in this, however difficult. The poem is about 'teasers', 'terrors', and 'dreams', as *Alice in Wonderland* and psychoanalysis are. All tease the conscious mind by deploying devices for not making sense. Empson doesn't want us to be teased out of but into thought,

[22] Carroll, *Alice's Adventures*, 105.

of course, and the riddling power of 'The Teasers' is that it can not quite be reduced to his un-riddling style of commentary. The 'nonsense' element is a sign of resistance to the sovereignty of the irrational (it suggests 'there's something absurd about this') but also, to that of the rational.

'"A girl can't go on laughing all the time"', he wrote in 'Reflections from Anita Loos' (*CP* 85), and Empson became wary of the giddy playfulness of the early work. Nevertheless 'Letter VI: a marriage', his improvised epithalamion, opens 'Rejoice where possible all hares of March' (*CP* 61), recalling both Christopher Smart and the March Hare, and Alice herself pops up once more in China in his verse letter, 'Autumn on Nan-Yüeh' (*CP* 91–8), written during the Sino-Japanese War. His earlier Asian emergency poem said that 'The heart of standing is you cannot fly', and this letter-style poem is about flying in many senses. Written when Empson was teaching on a 'holy mountain' with the exiled universities of Peking during the Japanese invasion, it begins 'If flight's as general as this | And every movement starts a wing'. It goes on to refer to many means of aerial flight, invoking planes, 'Pegasi', 'witches', and 'Phoebus' car', while also playing on the idea of 'flight' as 'escape'. At the literal level, it refers to the escape of the staff and students from the invading Japanese but, more generally, covers the sense that higher education itself is a necessary flight from more 'useful' activity. It's in this rather desperate context that Alice and the Red Queen make an appearance:

Verse has been lectured to a treat
  Against Escape and being blah.
It struck me trying not to fly
  Let them escape a bit too far.
It is an aeronautic feat
  Called soaring, makes you quite a star
(The Queen and Alice did) to try
  And keep yourself just where you are.
But who was bold enough to meet
  Exactly who on Phoebus' car
Slung on a Blimp to be a spy
  I ask before I cry Hurrah?

(*CP* 93)

Alice and the Queen, of course, 'went so fast that at last they seemed to skim through the air, hardly touching the ground with their feet, till suddenly, just as Alice was getting quite exhausted, they stopped, and she found herself sitting on the ground, breathless and giddy'.[23] Empson's 'aeronautic feat' no doubt includes a punning reference to those pedestrian 'feet'. Surprised to find she is exactly where she started, Alice exclaims 'Everything's just as it was!', to which the Queen replies 'Of course it is!' When Alice explains that in her country 'you'd generally get to somewhere else—if you ran very fast for a long time as we've been doing', the monarch is not impressed: "A slow sort of country!" said the Queen. 'Now, *here*, you see, it takes all the running *you* can do, to keep in the same place. If you want to get somewhere else, you must run at least twice as fast as that!" The suggestion is that in the 'other country' China, as in through the Looking-Glass, it is an 'aeronautic feat' for Empson and the other refugee academics to stay where they are, teaching on the mountain. To keep on with the ordinary business of education ('to keep in the same place') is an impressive achievement. Given the satirical allusion to the Leavisite distrust of 'Escape', he might also be suggesting that it is quite a feat to be true to the flight of verse. You have to expend a lot of energy and agility to stay true to the conditions you are working under even where you don't obviously travel anywhere new. Putting 'Escape and being blah' together makes a nonsense of Leavis and others, while the rhyme of 'star' and 'you are' (in the above extract) recalls 'Twinkle, twinkle, little star | How I wonder what you are', a romantic poem parodied in Carroll's 'Twinkle, twinkle, little bat! | How I wonder what you're at'.[24] Carroll's *Alice* books might be seen as instances of literature as 'Escape and being blah' ('blah', according to the *OED*, was originally US slang meaning 'nonsense, humbug'), but here, as in the essay, Empson makes it clear how serious the forces at work in them are. Alice and the Queen consort easily enough with the poetic machinery of that Miltonic 'Phoebus' car', and the comparison itself is, in the circumstances, an 'aeronautic feat' (reminding us Empson wrote an essay called 'Donne the Spaceman').[25]

Empson had written of the 'cool courage' of Alice, and his defence of 'Escape' in 'Autumn on Nan-Yüeh' shows 'cool courage' too (*SVP* 233). Despite its avowed dislike of Auden-style 'verses about "Up the Boys"', the poem has a witty, Audenesque air, and handles the wartime debates about education, philosophy, and literature with bravery as well as bravura. Once again, the idea of the Dream, central to the *Alice* books, recurs, and in a Freudian context:

[23] Ibid. 142. [24] Ibid. 63. [25] See *ERL1* 78–128.

Indeed I finally agree
  You do in practice have to say
This crude talk about Escape
  Cannot be theorized away.
Yeats is adroit enough to see
  His old word Dream must now leave play
For dreams in quite another shape,
  And Freud, and that his word can stay.

(*CP*, 94)

The poem invokes Freud as the figure who changed the way we see dreams and gave Yeats's 'old word' a new currency. The *Alice* essay is one of the most adroit applications of the new Freudian analysis of dreams to literary texts, and the poem, written a couple of years later, draws on its symbolic capital. Empson had said 'Death is never far out of sight in the books', and the same must have been true in wartime Nan-Yüeh (*SVP* 228). 'And as to fleeing, that we may', he says, and Alice and the Queen help him keep his composure in flight from the invading Japanese. 'Autumn at Nan-Yüeh' is one of Empson's last poems, so that, though he began as a Cambridge poet, he ended up as a Chinese one. It is fitting that in both roles he was accompanied by Alice.[26]

IV

In 'A Toast' for Empson on his retirement, W. H. Auden took issue with his 'conceit' that Milton's God is 'our Christian one', but went on to ask: 'Who, though, but you has pondered so deeply on Alice?'[27] Empson's pondering on Alice formed the concluding chapter of *Some Versions of Pastoral*, a study that, under its blandly generic title, set a Cheshire cat among the generically minded pigeons. Where the reader might have expected a treatment of *Arcadia* or *The Winter's Tale* or *Michael*, we get discussions of Soviet theory, Tudor history plays, Shakespeare sonnets, the critical reception of Milton, and John Gay's mock-heroic opera. In fact, the emphasis on rural subject-matter and shepherds

[26] For a fuller reading of the poem, see my 'Journeys to War: Auden, Isherwood and Empson in China', in Douglas Kerr and Julia Kuehn (eds.), *Travellers in China* (Hong Kong: University of Hong Kong Press, 2007).

[27] W. H. Auden, 'A Toast', in Roma Gill (ed.), *William Empson: The Man and His Work* (London: Routledge & Kegan Paul, 1974), 1.

established by Theocritus and Virgil is almost entirely ignored for something else, a demonstration of 'the ways in which the pastoral process of putting the complex into the simple (in itself a great help to the concentration needed for poetry) and the resulting social ideas have been used in English literature' (*SVP* 25).

Characteristically Empson doesn't ponder the aspects of *Alice* that are conventionally pastoral: the Oxford river trip, the 'golden afternoon', the Marvellian garden of live flowers, the 'cool and shady' wood of no names. There *is* a play on pastoral in Carroll's texts, as on Romantic medievalism, with Carroll's nonsensical Kings and Queens, Knights and Gryphon, travestying the Pre-Raphaelite iconography of the day. His pastoral settings don't offer a rural alternative to the world of sophisticated Victorian culture, however, but a mirror-image of it. The river in *Looking-Glass* emerges from and merges back into a shop, Alice arrives in the wood of no names after travelling by train, the garden is inhabited by playing cards, and Alice's dream reflects the everyday world of contemporary Oxford. This makes it a perfect instance of putting the culturally sophisticated into the apparently archaic and idyllic.

Though Empson does not pursue it, there is a sense in which not only *Alice* but children's literature itself is a new version of pastoral. You can see this in near-contemporary books like *The Water Babies, The Ring and the Book*, and *At the Back of the North Wind*, as well as later ones like *Treasure Island, The Jungle Book, Huck Finn, Peter Pan*, and *The Phoenix and the Carpet*. These are all metamorphoses of classical pastoral in which the child is the new universal 'primitive'. Huck Finn, Peter Pan, Jim, and Mowgli, like Alice, are bouncing versions of the Child as Swain, albeit closer to 'Nature' in an obvious way and beyond the pale of Victorian culture. If traditional pastoral was understood to be an attempt to restore or recall the Golden Age, post-Wordsworthian children's literature is bound up with a myth of childhood as a potential Eden from which we fall in growing up. This underpins work as different as J. K. Rowling's Harry Potter books, Philip Pulman's *Dark Materials* trilogy, and David Almond's *Skellig*.

The Wordsworthian story of 'growing up' as a secular fall is the source of much of the puzzling force of the *Alice* books. There are no children in Milton's Eden, of course, and during his discussion of Bentley's emendations, Empson quotes Raleigh's observation that 'there could not have been a child in *Paradise Lost*, because one touch of common sense would have destroyed it' (*SVP* 126). The notion of childhood as Edenically privileged is certainly at work in the *Alice* books, but it is an Eden invaded and possessed by crotchety adults, where the child is the spokesperson for 'common sense'. As Empson says, 'in this sort of child-cult the child, though a means of imaginative escape, becomes the critic; Alice is the most reasonable and responsible person in the book' (*SVP* 221). Empson doesn't compare *Alice* to Milton, but elsewhere smuggles a touch of Carrollian nonsense into *Paradise Lost.* Commenting on Bentley's objections to 'Uriel, gliding through the Eev'n | On a Sun beam', he says 'what was evidently in Milton's mind' was 'that the angel is sliding, choosing a safe gradient, down a nearly *even* sunbeam; like the White Knight on the poker' (*SVP* 129–30). Here, associating Uriel's aeronautic feat with the White Knight's poker has something of the same liberatingly mock-heroic effect as associating Alice with Ulysses' bough.[28]

The Fall finds its way into the *Alice* essay too. Discussing the heroine's conversation with the caterpillar, Empson notes the 'connexion between death and the development of sex', cutting between the Miltonic Eden and Wonderland:

> Alice knows several reasons why she should object to growing up, and does not at all like being an obvious angel, a head out of contact with its body that has to come down from the sky, and gets mistaken for the Paradisal serpent of the knowledge of good and evil, and by the pigeon of the Annunciation, too. But she can only make herself smaller for reasons of tact or proportion; the triumphant close of *Wonderland* is that she has outgrown her fancies and can afford to wake and despise them. (*SVP* 215)

This moves brilliantly between nonsense and epic, Alice and the 'pigeon of the Annunciation', with the same counter-decorous wit as 'The Scales'. At such points critic and poet converge, with his keen sense of the uses of nonsense to negotiate the boundaries between human and cosmic, sanity and madness. When the Cheshire Cat, responding to Alice's remark that 'I don't want to go among mad people' says 'we're all mad here', the magnificently sane Alice keeps her composure. Empson observes, however, that at the end of *Wonderland* Alice 'is a grown queen and has acquired the conventional dignities of her insane world; suddenly she admits their insanity, refuses to be a grown queen, and destroys them' (233). Noting that 'much of the technique of rudeness of the Mad Hatter has been learned from Hamlet', he concludes: 'It is the

[28] Nonsense returns in *Milton's God*, where Empson attacks C. S. Lewis for jeering at Satan's 'disbelieving his creation' and 'saying he is beginning to incur the Doom of Nonsense, so he thinks he just growed, like Topsy'. He suggests Lewis 'treats creation by a personal God as the only theory of origin which is not mere jabberwocky' (*MG* 88–9).

ground-bass of this kinship with insanity, I think, that makes it so clear that the books are not trifling, and the cool courage with which Alice accepts madmen that gives them their strength' (233).

Bringing Hamlet and Carroll together in this way opens up the boundaries between scales and genres, what is serious and 'trifling'. Empson elsewhere proves a great critic of *King Lear*, a play where 'The Fool sings some nonsense verses', as he noted in *Seven Types*, and the borderline of nonsense, like that between sanity and madness, is repeatedly crossed (*STA* 67). The same connections are at work in 'Let it go', a poem 'about stopping writing poetry':

> The contradictions cover such a range.
> The talk would talk and go so far aslant.
> You don't want madhouse and the whole thing there.
>
> (*CP* 99)

The tactic of Empson's criticism is to read poetry in terms of contradictions that also cover such a range. In *Seven Types of Ambiguity* he argued that 'good poetry is usually written from a background of conflict', but noted that in modern times, 'the effort of writing a good bit of verse has been carried through almost as a clinical thing; it was done only to save a man's own sanity' (14, 9). If he feared that his critical method 'could lead to a shocking amount of nonsense', his own beautifully 'aslant' poetry, with its giddy play on the border of nonsense, was a way of covering the contradictions between rationality and irrationality. Like Alice he 'doesn't want to go among mad people', but, like her, his voice of beleaguered English rationality goes hand in hand with a conscious 'kinship with insanity' that lend his poetry its intellectual charge and sane comic charm.

9

Empson's Tact

Matthew Creasy

William Empson is not famous for his tact. When the poet and social commentator Charles Madge asked for his appraisal of some unpublished literary critical material in March 1936, Empson did not pull his punches. He listed Madge's strengths, then rounded upon his weaknesses: 'the shape of the book I think is bloody insolent . . . I advise you very heartily not to publish this as it stands.' Commenting on these harsh judgements, Empson noted:

> I smack this out in a state of moderate beer assuming that you are not appallingly sensitive. The difficult thing would be to say it tactfully, but I don't believe you are as neurotic as your piece of writing. (*WE1* 431)

Tact is fraught with questions of tone and social context difficult to judge. Empson seems to add insult ('neurotic') to injury, but John Haffenden records that Madge kept this letter by him till he died (although he chose not to publish his typescript). Perhaps he appreciated the directness, or perhaps he relished Empson's beery tactless approach as proof of their friendship. Rather than his tact, Empson has been better known for the 'directness, bluntness, and lack of assumption or disguise' which George Fraser claims characterize 'his writing and . . . his personal manners. He is what one expects him, from his writings, to be.'[1]

[1] George Fraser, 'The Man within the Name: William Empson as Poet, Critic, and Friend', in Roma Gill (ed.), *William Empson: The Man and his Work* (London: Routledge & Kegan Paul, 1974), 53.

A drafted essay from 1930 confirms some continuity between Empson's behaviour in private and his public role as poet and critic: 'personally,' he announced 'I am attracted by the notion of a hearty indifference to one's own and other people's feelings, when a fragment of the truth is in question' (*A* 83). From this perspective, his apparent lack of tact should be seen as a matter of principle rather than an excess of alcohol or a social failure. He imagines himself as 'The Man who said the Tactless Thing'. This phrase is used in *Some Versions of Pastoral* to describe Dr Richard Bentley from the perspective of his detractors, but Empson admires Bentley:

> English critics adopt a curious air of social superiority to Bentley; he is the Man who said the Tactless Thing. There seems no doubt that he raised several important questions about Milton's use of language, that no one could answer them at the time, and that it is still worth while to look for the answer. (*SVP* 123)

The tactless critic is able to 'blow the gaff' (a phrase Empson nourishes in *The Structure of Complex Words*), addressing matters or speaking truths other critics will not broach because of social convention, timidity, or an excessive regard for tact.[2] Fraser even attributes Empson's influence as critic to a similar 'plain directness of manner'.[3]

Empson summed up his position in 1947, whilst revising *Seven Types of Ambiguity*. In a preface to the second edition, he asserts: 'My attitude in writing it was that an honest man erected the ignoring of "tact" into a point of honour' (*STA* 8). Following Fraser, Robert Adams suggests that this remark is a key to Empson's career. It anticipates his brusque dealings with the neo-Christians in the 1950s and his campaign against 'Wimsatt's Law'—the attempt to forbid consideration of authorial intention from criticism.[4] But this repudiation makes it curious that 'tact' should play such an important role in Empson's appreciation of Andrew Marvell elsewhere in *Seven Types*. He uses the word to describe the technicalities of Marvell's wordplay with admiration. A pun on 'sweet chordage' as physical constraint and musical harmony in 'The Dialogue between the Resolved Soul and Created Pleasure' is at just the right juncture between etymological truth and verbal wit. For Empson, 'it is partly this tact which makes Marvell's puns charming and not detached from his poetry'

[2] See *SCW* 166, 168, 224, 235, 239, 308, and esp. 166 n.
[3] Fraser, 'The Man within the Name', 53.
[4] Robert M. Adams, 'Hero of the Word', *New York Review of Books*, 32: 6 (11 Apr. 1986), 32–5.

(*STA* 131). Similar praise is accorded to less playful details in Marvell's work when Empson describes the sensibilities of the reading public:

It is tactful, when making an obscure reference, to arrange that the verse shall be intelligible even when the reference is not understood. Thus many conceits are prepared to be treated as subdued conceits, though in themselves they have been fully worked out. (197)

Empson is describing an allusion to 'The brotherless Heliades' who 'melt . . . in amber tears' in 'The Nymph Complaining'. His critical response to Marvell has recently been rightfully praised by Christopher Ricks for exercising a similar 'tact' in critical judgement to Marvell's own delicate and assured handling of his allusive materials.[5] Empson urges that the lines are still beautiful if you don't know that the sisters of Phaeton were transformed into poplar trees dripping 'amber tears' for his death. But he also argues that once this knowledge has been acquired the couplet becomes 'justified' and the reader becomes involved in a 'witty, sensitive and cultured' community with the poet (198).

Empson's claim, therefore, to ignore tact is demonstrably false. He refers to 'tact' or its cognates four more times in *Seven Types* and I count five further occurrences in *Some Versions of Pastoral*, nine in *Milton's God*, nine in *The Structure of Complex Words*, and nine in *Using Biography*. The word and its associations are important to the major works of criticism that Empson assembled for publication in his lifetime. 'Tact' may not be an obvious part of his critical vocabulary, but it has a significance within Empson's work that is betrayed by his attempt to rewrite the history of *Seven Types* in his preface to the second edition. He is not, I think, disingenuous here. Although Paul Fry describes the 'remarkable self-awareness in this sentence', there is an inconsistency about the values of tact within Empson's work which is not wholly intended.[6] His reference to the 'ignoring of "tact" ' combines the contradictory implications that Empson ignored tact (consciously turned away from it) and that he cultivated ignorance of its existence (pushed it from consciousness). Fry compares Empson's reference to tact with the seventh type of ambiguity, 'when the two meanings of the word, the two values of the ambiguity, are the two opposite meanings defined from the context, so that the total effect is to

[5] Christopher Ricks, *Allusion to the Poets* (Oxford: Oxford University Press, 2002), 2.

[6] Paul H. Fry, *William Empson: Prophet Against Sacrifice* (London: Routledge, 1991), 29.

show a fundamental division in the writer's mind'.[7] In *Seven Types* tact acquires a similar double value as the object of suspicion and as an epithet of praise. His concept of ambiguity and his theory of complex words both shed light on the word 'tact', which has a richness that arises from conflicting values within Empson and within the word itself. Examination of these references to tact in his work reveals how much 'other people's feelings' matter to his criticism and I shall conclude by arguing that tact is, in fact, one of Empson's strengths as a critic—both in his preparedness to exercise it on behalf of others and because of the motives that shape his distrust of it under certain conditions.

The *OED* lists three active meanings of the word relevant to this essay:

1. The sense of touch; touch.
2. A keen faculty of perception or discrimination likened to the sense of touch.
3. Ready and delicate sense of what is fitting and proper in dealing with others, so as to avoid giving offence, or win good will; skill or judgement in dealing with men or negotiating difficult or delicate situations; the faculty of saying or doing the right thing at the right time.[8]

Empson usually has (3) in mind and this understanding of tact as a form of social grace is clearly the chief meaning of the word in modern usage, but (1) and (2) are important to understanding the concept. (This is why I have listed (2) separately, rather than follow *OED* which records it as a subheading of (1).) They are listed here in chronological order and each new sense derives from the previous meaning. For example, in July 1802, Coleridge wrote to William Sotheby:

> a great Poet must be, implicitè if not explicitè, a profound Metaphysician. He may not have it in logical coherence, in his Brain & Tongue; but he must have it by *Tact* / for all sounds, & forms of human nature he must have the *ear* of a wild Arab listening in the silent Desart, the eye of the North American Indian tracing the footsteps of an Enemy upon the Leaves that strew the Forest—; the *Touch* of a Blind Man feeling the face of a darling Child.[9]

[7] Ibid. 32, quoting *STA* 225.

[8] *OED* lists two further technical usages of 'tact': 'a stroke in beating time' and 'B. F. Skinner's term for an utterance which is evoked by an object . . . and reinforces the learning of a response'.

[9] S. T. Coleridge, *Collected Letters of Samuel Taylor Coleridge*, ed. Earl Leslie Griggs, 6 vols. (Oxford: Oxford University Press, 1956–1971), ii. 810. I am indebted to Veronika Ruttkay for this example and to her unpublished discussion of Coleridge's 'poetics of feeling'.

The examples in this letter enact a shift from tact's original meaning, derived from the Latin *tactus* ('to touch') to a more figurative meaning.[10] Coleridge cites the different physical senses, culminating with the blind man's 'touch' (1)—his ability to discriminate his child's face from others (2) using the sense of touch at the end of his fingers. This process of figurative transference prefigures the modern meaning of tact (3). *OED* illustrates (2) by citing another letter from Coleridge to Sotheby in 1802 which contains the warning: 'You . . . must needs have a better tact of what will offend that class of readers.' Feeling your way through the senses (2) has become figuratively feeling your way through a social situation to avoid giving offence (3).

These shifts within the meaning of 'tact' and their historical associations are generally reminiscent of Empson's exploration of similar linguistic shifts within his complex words. But tact's specific transition from physical perception to social grace is also comparable to the findings from his investigation of the key terms 'sense' and 'feeling' in *The Structure of Complex Words*. In 'Sense and Sensibility' and 'Sensible and Candid', Empson charts the transition from physical perception to mental act in the word 'sense' and, again, the exchange of values implied by the use of 'feeling' to mean physical sensation and to mean emotion (*SCW* 250–69, 306–10). Coleridge's blind man illustrates the point. With the Duke of Gloucester from *King Lear* in the background ('I see it feelingly' (IV. v. 143)), the blind man feels with his senses in order to recognize his child, while feeling with emotion delight at his 'darling'.

One consequence of their comparable complex structure is that the meanings of 'feeling' and 'sense' may overlap, as Empson explains:

> Both of them (and *sensation* too) are concerned with both knowledge and emotion; a feeling of impending doom is very like a sense of one. The choice between using one or the other is I think often made on rather obscure grounds of tact. 'A sense of' impending doom claims that there is really something there to feel, though your interpretation of it may be wrong, whereas 'a feeling of it' admits that you may be wholly mistaken. (*SCW* 301)

This passage identifies a significant role for tact within literary criticism as a tool for seeking out the different implications of these two words. Empson calls explicitly upon this function of tact again in his exploration of dictionary definitions. Too often, he complains, dictionaries supply synonyms in place

[10] This seems to have occurred at the end of the eighteenth century: *OED*'s first citation for (2) dates from 1797.

of accurate description, failing to discriminate between important nuances. 'The effect' of listing *COD*'s definitions of 'damage', 'harm', 'hurt', 'injury', and 'injure', Empson argues,

> is of a stage army marching round and round, put a little out of order each time to make the repetition less obvious. One real point of distinction seems to be whether or not someone is blamed . . . Surely there must be some process of literary tact in play by which we can make sense of this if we try. (*SCW* 408)

This reference to 'some process of literary tact' subtly combines the different meanings of 'tact' as both the faculty of discrimination (2) and the observation of social graces (3). So 'literary tact' might be able to feel (by touch) a way into clearer understanding of the words in question. It might also separate the sense of the words without rendering one word obsolete (and thus a social outcast). Empson wishes to separate the meanings of these words with the kind of sensitivity and discrimination more usually associated with the exercise of tact in dealings with people. But equally tact may be needed to avoid offending or ridiculing Fowler, the dictionary's editor, in the execution of this task.

The overlap here between tact (2) and (3) is rich with possibility, but Empson still seems suspicious of the word and its ideological implications when he refers to the 'rather obscure grounds' which inform the exercise of tact. I shall argue that one of Empson's strengths as a critic is his ability to combine verbal analysis with social judgement, but the overlap between (2) and (3) may be the source of prejudice too. Matthew Arnold identifies 'tact' as one of the literary critic's necessary qualifications:

> The critic of poetry should have the finest tact, the nicest moderation, the most free, flexible, and elastic spirit imaginable; he should be indeed the 'ondoyant and divers', the *undulating and diverse* being of Montaigne.[11]

Empson and Arnold seem in agreement. As the heightened sensibilities which entitle the critic to pass judgement on artistic matters, tact (2) is predominant here. But the possibility and proximity of tact (3), which implies a social situation, raises the prospect that the critic is qualified by social standing, rather than critical acuity. Tact is a guiding principle for Arnold. His 'touchstone' theory of poetic value recalls the word's etymological roots:

[11] Matthew Arnold, 'On Translating Homer: Last Words', in *On the Classical Tradition*, ed. R. H. Super (Ann Arbor: University of Michigan, 1960), 174.

> Indeed there can be no more useful help for discovering what poetry belongs to the class of the truly excellent, and can therefore do us most good, than to have always in one's mind lines and expressions of the great masters, and to apply them as a touchstone to other poetry. Of course we are not to require this other poetry to resemble them; it may be very dissimilar. But if we have any tact we shall find them, when we have lodged them well in our minds, an infallible touchstone for detecting the presence or absence of high poetic quality, and also the degree of this quality, in all other poetry which we may place beside them.[12]

Arnold's references to 'tact' waver between imaginative critical perception (2) and social capability of judgement (3). The conditional phrase 'if we have any tact', which he repeats later in the essay, reinforces this effect. The formula is exclusive—only someone with the requisite tact will respond appropriately—and, I think, its gesture towards inclusion ('any tact') is false. Tact is not really in question for Arnold. He is confident that all right-minded readers feel and respond in this way. So what is objectionable is not Arnold's critical judgements, but his attempts to dress them up as universal and the social snobbery that peeks from his superlatives ('finest', 'nicest', 'most free').

This informs Empson's suspicion of tact. In *Some Versions of Pastoral* he notes the 'curious air of social superiority' adopted by Bentley's critics and in *Milton's God* he is scathing towards critics who bypass questions of critical or moral judgement by making similar appeal to social convention. Those critics who do not confront the theological difficulties posed by Milton's depiction of God are acting as if: 'His God is somehow "embarrassing"; indeed, almost all the contestants have used that coy word, with its comforting suggestion of a merely social blunder' (*MG* 9). In fulfilment of his admiration for Bentley, much of *Milton's God* is conceived as a defence of the 'tactless' depiction of God in *Paradise Lost* (*MG* 13).[13] This disdain for covert social judgement helps to account for Empson's rejection of tact in his preface to *Seven Types* on the grounds that it is not quite 'honest'. He fears that displays of tact may turn out to be a matter of tactics, rather than genuine feeling.

Elsewhere, remarking Peachum's treatment of Macheath in *The Beggar's Opera*, he noted that 'all politeness has an element of irony' (*SVP* 185). The outward forms of respect may hide insolence or simply keep someone at a distance, but Empson's references to 'tact' embody a particular heightened

[12] Matthew Arnold, 'The Study of Poetry', in *English Literature and Irish Politics*, ed. R. H. Super (Ann Arbor: University of Michigan, 1973), 168.

[13] See also *MG* 66, 143, 168, 169,180.

and fundamental worry of this kind about the relative sincerity of tactful behaviour. It underlies his denunciation of Hugh Kenner's account of the relationship between Stephen Dedalus and Leopold Bloom on the grounds that: 'There is a strong smell of tact here' (*UB* 256). Empson attacks Kenner for failing to acknowledge that the solution to *Ulysses* lies in Bloom's secret voyeuristic desire to watch Stephen have sex with Molly Bloom (this erotic experience will excite him enough to engender an heir). But the disdainful reference to 'tact' does not simply imply that Kenner misunderstands or overlooks Joyce's intentions (as Empson understands them), but that he deliberately withholds information, manipulating his readers. R. L. Brett refers to 'that fine instinct in the management of men which is commonly called tact'.[14] But even those who value 'fine instincts' will resist being managed, especially when it involves withholding the full truth of a situation from someone. Empson, for example, remarked the 'tactful coolness' with which he felt Christopher Norris had dismissed his later critical work, as if this were merely a way of appeasing him in his old age.[15]

The possibility of such manipulation is on Empson's mind when he describes 'people who kept tactfully silent' about Andrew Marvell's sexuality (*UB* 15), or when he refers to the 'wise tact' of stars separated by 'dark spaces' regarding his own love affairs in 'Letter I' (*CP* 31). Suggestively, each of these instances relates to sexual matters, making tact seem like a form of euphemism since it involves cushioning a blow or hiding the facts. Such refusal to touch upon particular matters may be disloyal to the etymological roots of tact. For once again the overlap between senses (2) and (3) of tact is significant. When Coleridge describes the blind man 'feeling the face of a darling Child', he implies that emotion and touch ('feeling') mix by unthinking instinct. In comparison, tact (3) means being sufficiently aware of a social situation to judge what it is appropriate (or inappropriate) to say. Awareness of self is involved, along with awareness of others and awareness of self in relation to others. Empson's occasional hostility to such tact betrays a fear that this awareness may decline into self-regard or mere self-preservation.

The historical point at which the English language admitted the social merits of tact into meaning is illuminating here. This linguistic shift coincides with the latter end of the philosophical and cultural interest in theories of

[14] Cited in *OED*.

[15] William Empson, 'Postscript', in Christopher Norris, *William Empson and the Philosophy of Literary Criticism* (London: Athlone Press, 1978), 205.

'politeness' during the eighteenth century.[16] This is, according to Theodor Adorno, the 'precise historical hour' of tact.[17] Just as the vogue for conduct manuals was fuelled by English translations of French works, so *OED* indicates that tact (3) is a French import, citing Dugald Stewart's *Outline of Moral Philosophy* (1797) which refers to: 'The use made in the French tongue of the word Tact, to denote that delicate sense of propriety which enables a man to feel his way in the difficult intercourse of polished society.' A source of snobbery (although not intrinsically snobbish) 'polished society' provides an important grounding to the values of tact.

For Adorno, however, the end of the eighteenth century is characterized by the glitter of 'polish' without the values of 'society'. It marks the collapse of absolutism, which divested 'the forms of hierarchical respect and consideration' of their 'economic basis and their menacing power'. The effects are mixed. On the one hand this liberates tact from 'compulsion': an 'emancipated tact' becomes possible, which is genuinely responsive to the particular needs of individuals and particular situations rather than being guided by 'form'. And yet, claims Adorno, this leaves no standard by which to measure the success of tact:

> The question as to someone's health, no longer required and expected by upbringing, becomes inquisitive or injurious, silence on sensitive subjects empty indifference, as soon as there is no rule to indicate what is and is not to be discussed. Thus individuals begin, not without reason, to react antagonistically to tact: a certain kind of politeness, for example, gives them less the feeling of being addressed as human beings, than an inkling of their inhuman conditions, and the polite run the risk of seeming impolite by continuing to exercise politeness, as a superseded privilege.[18]

While the nineteenth century may have seen the decline of 'politeness' as a specific philosophical, political, and social ideal, Andrew St George and Marjorie Morgan clearly demonstrate that social convention ('form') did not disappear.[19] If anything, St George argues, the Victorian etiquette books which

[16] See Lawrence Klein, *Shaftesbury and the Culture of Politeness* (Cambridge: Cambridge University Press, 1994); Philip Carter, *Men and the Emergence of Polite Society* (Edinburgh: Pearson, 2001); and Norbert Elias, *The Civilising Process* (1978–82), trans. Edmund Jephcott (Oxford: Blackwell, 1994).

[17] Theodor Adorno, 'On the Dialectic of Tact', in *Minima Moralia* (1951), trans. E. F. N. Jephcott (London: Verso, 2005), 36.

[18] Ibid. 36–7.

[19] See Marjorie Morgan, *Manners, Morals and Class in England, 1774–1858* (Basingstoke: Macmillan, 1994); and Andrew St George, *The Descent of Manners: Etiquette, Rules and the Victorians* (London: Chatto & Windus, 1993).

succeeded eighteenth-century conduct manuals were more rigidly defining and restrictive about the exact nature of appropriate social conduct.[20] This does, however, chime with Adorno's claim that historical forces have eroded the possibilities for genuine human interaction. For it may imply that the rituals of politeness have declined to mere form, that rules substitute for feeling response. Tact becomes, in H.D.'s deliberately insipid words, reduced to 'a code of behaviour | . . . only a sort of politeness'.[21]

Empson shares Adorno's fear that the nineteenth century had allowed tact to degenerate into empty form. In *The Structure of Complex Words* he denounces 'the Victorian fear of outspokenness' and observed: 'I think indeed that the Victorians were not ready enough to approve the good qualities of being "ready to blow the gaff" and "frank to yourself about your own desires".' Tact becomes a means of valuing the status quo over sincerity. Characteristically, this remark, from his account of 'honest' in *Othello*, is followed by an admission that when he first began to consider the play, 'I did not at the time think about the word "honest" at all' (*SCW* 235–6, 307). His assault upon 'the Victorians' allows us to see that Empson's denunciation of 'tact' in the 1947 preface to *Seven Types* has the flavour of a manifesto. By rejecting tact, Empson (in retrospect) sets up his own iconoclastic Modernist credentials.

The nub of this intergenerational conflict with regard to *Seven Types* lies in the nature and style of Empson's close reading approach. Upon its publication his literary critical manners were severely criticized by F. L. Lucas, who took particular exception to his analysis of George Herbert's 'Affliction (I)'. Empson had summarized Herbert's decision to remain in the Church rather than pursue a more glamorous career ('Ah, my dear God! though I am clean forgot, | Let me not love Thee, if I love Thee not' (ll. 65–6)), using the paraphrase 'Damn me if I don't stick to the parsonage' (*STA* 216).

The significant point about this sort of thing, which was praised to the skies by stupefied reviewers, is not, I think, that so far from meaning all four things at once the passage does not mean any of them; nor yet that one of the explanations is not even English; nor yet that so much ingenuity is squandered on a Philistine frivolity; but that the attitude to poetry involved is so curiously vulgar. And if there is one thing fatal to

[20] St George, *The Descent of Manners*, 1–44.

[21] H.D. [Hilda Doolittle], 'R.A.F.: XI.', in *Collected Poems 1912–1941*, ed. Louis L. Martz (Manchester: Carcanet, 1984), 490.

the writing or the appreciation of poetry it is surely vulgarity. Men have written well with, in the ordinary sense, bad enough morals; but not with bad manners.[22]

It is odd to describe Empson's 'bad manners' as 'so curiously vulgar', since his perceived lack of critical tact presumably marks the limit of Lucas's curiosity. Perhaps he finds it curious that a Cambridge-educated member of the upper classes should behave in a 'vulgar' way, or perhaps it erects a verbal wall of protection for Lucas, implying that all vulgarity is curious if you are well mannered. Yet the way Empson's vulgar paraphrase of Herbert encapsulates the range of meaning that he describes *is* curious. 'Damn me' is both an imperative (God should send Herbert to hell if he doesn't fulfil his vocation) and a hearty colloquial phrase. Herbert is imagined as challenging God and submitting to him at the same time. He is putting a brave face on things and facing them frankly and with honesty. This form of 'vulgarity' is eloquent about complex matters.[23]

Lucas's reference to 'Philistine frivolity' evokes the same connotations of snobbery as those implicit in Matthew Arnold's account of 'tact'. His appeal to 'vulgarity' connects matters of literary taste and judgement to the conventions of social interaction and standards of behaviour associated with class. A footnote citing Lucas and this accusation of 'vulgarity' appeared in the same edition of *Seven Types* as Empson's explicit rejection of tact (*STA* 216). His preface, then, may be taken as a retort to Lucas. This might account for the quotation marks Empson places around the word 'tact', which hold it in such disdain. Under fire, renouncing tact might seem a good idea, although, I would argue, mistaken about his own strengths as a critic.

This language of manners obscures Lucas's general complaint about Empson's methods of close reading. One of the reasons that tact is important to *Seven Types* is the possibility (raised by its detractors) that verbal analysis—spelling out associations and implications in explicit detail—might violate the integrity of a literary work. Clearly aware of this as a possible objection, Empson raises it himself in the first and last chapters of the book using the language of 'tact'. He remarks that: 'these analytical methods are usually employed casually and piecemeal, with an implication that the critic has shown tact by going no

[22] F. L. Lucas, *The Decline and Fall of the Romantic Ideal* (Cambridge; Cambridge University Press, 1936), 228.

[23] Empson answered Lucas and similar objections offered by John Carey at length and in detail in an edition of the *New Statesman* from 13 Aug. 1976. This is quoted in *WE1* 620.

further' (282). 'Tact' here may imply that such critics show false delicacy, or it may acknowledge that his material requires some sensitivity. For this remains a source of concern to him throughout *Seven Types*. Empson makes a point of identifying potential flaws in his argument and repeatedly concedes that some readers will find his methods inappropriate to poems as 'evidently delicate and slender' as a sonnet by Shakespeare (*STA* 166). He worries about 'libelling' John Donne (173), makes self-conscious excuses for being 'verbose' (162), and laments that:

> During the eighteenth century English poets were trying to be honest, straightforward, sensible, grammatical and plain; thus it is now my business to try and outwit these poor wretches, and to applaud them for qualities in their writings which they would have been horrified to discover. (91)

Such open confession represents one aspect of a tactless style. It is a means of 'being frank to yourself' (and your readers). Oddly it reverses the original grounds for concern. In place of 'honest', 'plain', and tactless statements, close analysis here supplies something artful and complex. The implication is that Empson does not accept that he is stating anything the poems do not already contain. However, he does concede that the tactless critic may expose meanings that an author may have wanted to keep in the background or that were not consciously intended. During his analysis of Donne's 'A Valediction: Forbidding Weeping', he observes: 'The language of the poem is shot through with a suspicion which for once he is too delicate or too preoccupied to state unambiguously, that when he is gone she will be unfaithful to him' (166–7). This is faithful to what Empson considers as Donne's (unusual) reluctance to bring up infidelity. He shows here a kind of sensitivity that Lucas and his detractors overlook when they accuse him of pursuing analytic methods without regards for the poet's intentions or sensibilities. A concern with the degree of licence proper to verbal analysis is at the heart of Empson's project. It is integral to the structure of *Seven Types* as it moves from conscious forms of ambiguous expression in the early chapters towards the exposure of ambiguities indicating unconscious or unintended conflicts later in the book.

Empson's awareness of objections to his methods clearly pre-dates critical responses such as Lucas's hostility. His openness about the possibility of such objections is part of the tactless style he adopts in *Seven Types*, exemplified by the famous 'barking dogs' passage:

Critics, as 'barking dogs,' on this view, are of two sorts: those who merely relieve themselves against the flower of beauty, and those, less continent, who afterwards scratch it up. I myself, I must confess, aspire to the second of these classes; unexplained beauty arouses an irritation in me, a sense that this would be a good place to scratch; the reasons that make a line of verse likely to give pleasure, I believe, are like the reasons for anything else; one can reason about them; and while it may be true that the roots of beauty ought not to be violated, it seems to me very arrogant of the appreciative critic to think that he could do this, if he chose, by a little scratching. (28)

Although the frequency with which he defends his enterprise indicates some underlying anxiety, this passage suggests that Empson's self-confidence was not completely shaken. In answer to the accusation that verbal analysis is 'the refuge of the emotionally sterile', he retorts 'that is only to say that analysis is often done badly' (35).

Empson probably became familiar with objections to close reading before writing *Seven Types* through the work of his Cambridge mentor, I. A. Richards, who had observed that: 'If we propose to look closely into the mental processes active in the reading of poetry a certain reluctance or squeamishness will often be felt. "We murder to dissect", someone will murmur.'[24] Richards's solution was to dismiss this attitude as 'prejudice': 'All respectable poetry invites close reading.' He indicates that, with good manners, the limits of criticism could be determined by 'the reader's discretion'.[25] Both Empson and Richards appeal to social metaphors in response to this 'squeamishness' about close reading. Richards hopes that gentlemanly conduct will resolve it, whereas Empson's reference to 'tact' ('the critic has shown tact by going no further') indicates that gentlemanly conduct may be at odds with the truth. At the same time, in comparison with Richards, he indicates that the critic's duty towards 'unexplained beauty' overrides this consideration.

Both critics suggest that close reading forces us to contemplate unpleasant truths about our 'mental processes'. Empson argues that this is particularly relevant when contemplating works of art which are 'independent of the moral code which their public accepts and is dependent on':

Under these rather special circumstances one should try to prevent people from having to analyse their reactions, with all the tact at one's disposal; nor are they so special as might appear. The object of life, after all, is not to understand things, but

[24] I. A. Richards, *Practical Criticism* (1929; London: Routledge, 1964), 322. [25] Ibid. 203.

to maintain one's defences and equilibrium and live as well as one can; it is not only maiden aunts who are placed like this. (*STA* 284–5)

The reference to 'maiden aunts' recalls the 'Victorian fear of outspokenness' that Empson later criticized in *Complex Words*. He is not unsympathetic to their predicament, imagining specific circumstances under which it might arise, but his choice of words hints at neurosis or complacency. This is confirmed by John Middleton Murry's criticisms of *Seven Types*:

a poem is a poem not least by virtue of its power to ward off these vagaries of the intellect. It is to some degree an incantation, a word of immediate power, compelling the wandering mind to response of a certain order; and only so far as the receiving mind restrains its speculations within the limits of this order is it speculating about the poem at all.[26]

Murry offers this in defence of his own view that 'the poem and the words which compose the poem are not the same thing': it is some 'organic whole' which suffers when its individual 'parts' are subject to scrutiny.[27] He wishes, like the 'maiden aunts', to sustain a state of comfortable intellectual numbness where the mind wanders within cosy limits.

Empson's reference to the 'tact' with which maiden aunts need to be handled indicates that it might be rude to point out truths or thoughts that are already present either in the back of the mind or as unspoken assumptions. On this view, which seems indebted to Freud's *Civilisation and its Discontents*, society depends on the repression of common thoughts or feelings which it has deemed unacceptable. Tact becomes part of the general social conventions which keep unruly desires in check. Empson acknowledged this in a letter from 1940:

In any tolerable society, whatever its political arrangement, you will have a variety of people meeting each other, and therefore Politeness will be necessary, and to maintain Politeness is liable to involve serious sacrifices. Yet they are worth it; if only because Politeness is the outward sign of more serious values less often called on. (*A* 458)

In this context, tact can be seen as part of the 'serious sacrifices' associated with 'Politeness'. It arises from the demands imposed by living in close proximity to other people. While these remarks form an unpublished riposte to

[26] J. Middleton Murry, 'Analytical Criticism', *Times Literary Supplement* (18 Dec. 1930), in John Constable (ed.), *Critical Essays on William Empson* (Aldershot: Scolar Press, 1993), 30.
[27] Ibid.

D. W. Harding's argument that Jane Austen is unconsciously opposed to the values of middle- and upper-class society, Empson also finds himself standing up for the values of politeness, not as a mere fiction but as 'the outward sign' of deeper commitments.

Tact, I think, has a similar value within Empson's work too, as an index upon 'serious values'. It does not simply reflect his concern about the propriety of his close reading. He had specifically attacked the idea, defended by Murry, that poetry is a form of 'incantation' in his arguments against the 'Pure Sound' theory of poetry (*STA* 28). But Murry's views are more generally antithetical to Empson's commitment to critical reasoning about the intellectual content of literature and his resistance as a poet to what he perceived as the dominance of Symbolism. Looking back in 1963, he recalled his early affection for Donne:

> I can see now that I really liked him because he argued, whereas the others felt that this side of him need handling tactfully, because he did not fit the Symbolist theory . . . [T]he anti-intellectual movement, which has been one of the causes of Symbolism, tells you that thinking is sordid or low-class. What I want to say amounts to a revolt against Symbolism. (*A* 167)

Just as he had attacked Milton's critics, Empson indicts the social snobbery of those critics of Donne who treat intellection as 'sordid or low-class'. Murry's empty pretensions to precision ('to some degree . . . a certain order') screen a similar snobbery which motivates his preference for refined vagueness. Empson's resistance to Murry and to Symbolism is of a piece with his remarks about 'barking dogs', with its repetitive insistence upon the values of 'reasons' and reasoning. His remarks about Donne indicate that Empson idealized the tactless approach because it so nearly approximates to his lifelong concern with the value of talking (and arguing) things through.

Yet Empson's sensitivity to objections to his analyses—his frank awareness of the opposite point of view—is also a source of critical strength. ('This is generally true;' he wrote in 1930, 'if you attack a view in any detail that proves you to have some sympathy with it' (*A* 83).) It enlivens his reading of *Measure for Measure*, and Claudio's description of 'a prone and speechlesse dialect' (I. ii. 185) in Isabella's 'youth', which might 'move' Angelo to pardon him:

> The last half-line makes its point calmly, with an air of knowing about such cases; and, indeed, I feel very indelicate in explaining Claudio's meaning. It is difficult to put the workings of the mind into a daylight which alters their proportions without an air either of accusation or of ribaldry; he is making no moral judgement of his sister's

character, and only thinking that as a weapon against Angelo she is well worth being given a try. (*STA* 236–7)

Empson's methods aim to expose the complicated semantic possibilities that arise in the reader's mind when confronted with ambiguous utterance. He shares this interest in 'the mental processes active in the reading of poetry' with his mentor, Richards. But this reference to 'the workings of the mind' is itself richly and characteristically ambiguous. His analysis hovers delicately between the imagined mind of Claudio, who may be judging Isabella or contemplating some form of moral prostitution for her, and the mind of the reader, who may be prurient in detecting such implications or justified in piercing Claudio's drift.

In other words, the passage exercises verbal discrimination (tact (2)) and social awareness (tact (3)) in benign and revealing forms. It is no accident that so many of Empson's examples in subsequent work, such as *The Structure of Complex Words*—including his repeated analyses of words such as 'delicate', 'quite', and 'honest'—should mix social and class considerations with exploration of semantic implication. The richness of tact as a concept stems from its social embeddedness, the way that the particular wording of an utterance impinges upon a social situation. Empson's attempts to spell things out, from *Seven Types* onward, are redolent with the heightened social awareness demanded by tact. One reason for this is his strong sense of the acts of writing, reading, and criticizing literature as social occasions. This position is stated explicitly towards the beginning of *The Structure of Complex Words*: 'Language is essentially a social product, and much concerned with social relations, but we tend to hide this in our forms of speech so as to appear to utter impersonal truths' (*SCW* 18). Much of Empson's charm as a critic stems from his turn away from 'impersonal truths' towards the personal. Murial Bradbrook recognized this, writing in favour of his 'inclusively human speech', both as a virtue of Empson's stylistic practice and his sensitivities as a critic:

> Nearly all the examples in *Seven Types of Ambiguity* come from lyric and dramatic poetry, where very often a complex human situation may be presented in its own terms, not transformed by being embodied in a scene. The truth about relationships is found to be rarely pure and never simple.[28]

[28] M. C. Bradbook, 'The Ambiguity of William Empson', in Gill (ed.), *William Empson, The Man and his Work*, 6.

This sheds further light on Empson's account of *Measure for Measure*. Unpicking what Claudio has to say about Isabella is potentially embarrassing because in this scene Shakespeare begins to unfold the degree to which a brother might be prepared to make use of his sister as a sexual object in order to save his neck. The question of relative tact is thus closely linked to Empson's capacity to respond imaginatively to writers and their imagined creations.

Poetry occupies a special position for Empson within this response to language as a 'social product'. Tact emerges as intrinsic to the resonance of a poet's words upon the page within the reader's ear. Richards describes the delicacy of judgement involved in this process:

> The poet has to find some equivalent for the gestures and intonations which in ordinary speech so often look after this whole matter, and this translation may at times ask for special discernment and tolerance in the reader.[29]

Tact, as 'the subjective counterpart of tone', has an important part to play here.[30] But, for Empson, there is often a resonant, tactful resistance within language itself to explicit statement. 'Poetry', he explains 'has powerful means of imposing its own assumptions':

> A single word, dropped where it comes most easily, without being stressed, and as if to fill out the sentence, may signal to the reader what he is meant to be taking for granted; if it is already in his mind the word will seem natural enough and will not act as an unnecessary signal. Once it has gained its point, on further readings, it will take for granted that you always took it for granted; only very delicate people are as tactful in this matter as the printed page. (*STA* 22)

The Structure of Complex Words unpicks the hyper-refinement of 'delicate people', so it may be difficult to keep away from these remarks the negative implications associated with some forms of 'tactful' behaviour discussed earlier. But I don't think Empson is suggesting that the printed word equivocates: he is genuinely admiring and pleased that it is his responsibility as a critic and poet to work in this tact-filled medium.

Of course such admiration for tact may leave it unclear where we find ourselves in relation to the suspicion and hostility towards it described earlier. The effect of Empson's references to tact is similar to his description of Edgar's 'confused rich phrase' in *King Lear* (*SCW* 140). He means that Edgar's

[29] Richards, *Practical Criticism*, 208–9. [30] Ibid. 184.

response to his father's plight is confused because he doesn't know quite what he thinks or feels and is therefore faced with different courses of action or possible interpretation. His words are 'rich' with moral possibilities and considerations. Similarly, his speech is 'confused' (the meanings of words overlap) and therefore 'rich' with meanings. The 'rich' moral complexity makes for interesting 'rich' verbal complexity. The speaker's moral confusion generates semantic confusion. Empson's poetry gives fullest expression to conflicted feelings about 'tact' in 'This Last Pain':

> Feign then what's by a decent tact believed
> And act that state is only so conceived,
> And build an edifice of form
> For house where phantoms may keep warm.
>
> (*CP* 53)

The collocation and internal rhyme of 'tact' with 'feign' and 'act' invoke the view of tact as a form of deceit in response to social pressure and yet 'decent tact' suggests other possibilities. Empson's notes explain that the poem is about being able to imagine ideal conditions, states of being, or modes of behaviour that are thwarted by ordinary human fallibility and the conditions of life. Under such conditions, 'decent' might mean behaving well by exercising tact or that the tact is sufficient to the circumstances, but it cannot help raising the prospect of indecent or malign forms of tact. A 'decent' person would behave tactfully in this way, but it is not possible to behave well unconsciously once you appreciate the circumstances described in the poem. It becomes necessary to 'feign' what a really good, 'decent' person would do. Adopting a 'decent tact' means pretending not to notice someone's failure or pretending that the attempt to realize an ideal might actually succeed. Empson later declared himself shocked by readings which understood this as an exhortation to pose and treat all systems of value as equally compromised:

> Somebody told me it was like Oscar Wilde saying that you ought to wear a mask and then you'll grow into your mask. This seemed to me positively embarrassing. I didn't want to be like Oscar Wilde in this business of being affected, and I couldn't see why it was different. I felt uneasy about it.[31]

Yet this poem acknowledges the concepts of posture and imposture in the way that it sets 'decent tact' in tension with belief. It is difficult to square 'tact'

[31] 'William Empson in Conversation with Christopher Ricks', quoted in *CP* 258.

with belief because the delicacy of tact requires too conscious an awareness of what might offend. The very possibility of behaving tactfully has become a problem: it represents the kind of ideal whose passing the poem laments.

John Haffenden's anecdote illustrates how, even where seemingly least tactful, Empson had no desire to trample upon the feelings of others: 'When invited to dinner by another colleague, he responded, "No, to tell the truth, I don't like your wife's cooking."—adding, to soften the blow: "Come to think of it, I don't like my wife's cooking either"' (*WE1* 10). The joke is on Empson as much as the wives. Although he was intolerant of unnecessary obfuscation or double-dealing, his repeated praise for tact indicates that Empson never gave up on it. I think his writing is hopeful that plain speaking needn't be incommensurate with tact and consideration for others. 'The main purpose of reading imaginative literature', he wrote in 1973, 'is to grasp a wide variety of experience, imagining people with codes and customs very unlike our own' (*A* 218). Empson's suspicion of tact stems from honourable motives, but his denunciations are mistaken about the importance of 'other people's feelings' to his work. A humane ability to disentangle meaning and retain regard for the wider social situation represents Empson's true tact and his critical achievement.

10

Hermeneutic Circling: Empson, Rosemund Tuve, and the 'Wimsatt Law'

Paul H. Fry

In 'The Marriage of Marvell', William Empson challenges a 1939 article by one Fred Tupper claiming that Marvell never married his housekeeper. The dispute is full of side issues, and when at length Empson tires of all the parry and thrust, he turns on his opponent: 'The fatal weakness of Tupper', says Empson, 'is that he has no sense of character' (*UB* 51). This round assertion makes the point I want to come back to in the end. For Empson, to grasp an intention is to have a sense of character, to know, like the magistrate Fielding, what a certain person would think or do in certain circumstances.[1] The wonderfully Dickensian Tupper is a character who has no sense of character: in the spirit of this observation we infer that the critic is to approach an author or author's character (e.g. Joyce's Bloom) just as a novelist divines the motives of a character. But of course that is easier said than done, even for Empson, whose humanism always quickly brings us face to face with this vexed topic but does not always clarify it.[2] He might admit this much, his position by the

[1] See *A* 182, and *UB* 155.

[2] I am no pioneer in discussing intention in Empson. The most careful work to date is Haffenden's Introduction in *A* 10–22, and Christopher Norris, 'Introduction: Empson as Literary

time of *Using Biography* having become emphatic yet not doctrinaire: whatever it is possible to know about intentions we are obliged as humanists to discover. To be sure, there is not much here for the theorist of intention; but it is well to remember, in considering Empson or anyone else on intention, that hermeneutic defenses of intentionality are much more likely to be ethical than epistemological. The issue turns out to be whether one *ought* to seek out intentions, not whether or on what grounds one infallibly *can* do so. As Empson himself declared: 'I would not mind agreeing, as a verbal formula, that the intention of an author can always only be guessed at, so long as it is also agreed that the guess, after collating the relevant information, should always be made' (*CV* 15).

By way of canvassing Empson's intentionalism anew, I had wanted to revisit his controversy with Rosemund Tuve about Herbert's 'The Sacrifice' because I happen to possess some manuscript copies related to it—an exchange of four letters between these critics, and a MS continuation of Empson's *Kenyon Review* response to Tuve (reprinted in *A* 250–5)—and also because when I sent him these copies Richard Strier made such interesting use of them in a chapter on Empson and Tuve in his book, *Resistant Structures*, to which I am much indebted.[3] I now see that there are less roundabout ways of getting where I want to go, but I think this will still do, just as I think it will still be worth while to talk about Empson's view of W. K. Wimsatt (and Monroe Beardsley, his co-author), even though it is not wholly accurate. I propose to make the following argument: for Empson, an intention must be inferred from a fully realized specific person, historically situated yet not just a composite of handy historical facts. This person must furthermore be the right sort of person, someone who acts forthrightly on the basis of coherent values, preferably a well-born republican or a 'pastoral' republican like Macheath in *The Beggar's Opera* (*SVP* 159). If these requirements are not met, it is to be feared that the author's or character's intention will remain obscure or corrupted.

Theorist: From Ambiguity to Complex Words and Beyond', in Norris and Nigel Mapp (eds.), *William Empson: The Critical Achievement* (Cambridge: Cambridge University Press, 1993), 31–8. Earlier thoughts of my own will be found in Paul H. Fry, *William Empson: Prophet Against Sacrifice* (London: Routledge, 1993), 68–71.

[3] Richard Strier, *Resistant Structures: Particularity, Radicalism, and Renaissance Texts* (Berkeley: University of California Press, 1995), 13–26. The typescript letters in my possession, cited by Strier (23 n.), with the unpublished continuation of the *Kenyon Review* essay, were photocopied by John Hollander, who had them from Tuve herself when they taught together at Connecticut College. See *SL* 188–99.

Now, apart from the obvious hermeneutic circularity of half-perceiving and half-creating the coherence of some well-judged agent's likely behavior (what Tupper can't do), the trouble with this sturdy opinion is that in holding it Empson accepts the strongest rationale there is for what he always calls 'the Wimsatt Law' (see, for instance, *UB*, p. vii). Whenever he throws up his hands and professes honest bafflement in the face of some shifty-eyed confusion, he perforce implicitly questions whether intention can be the cornerstone of hermeneutic theory.

With that preview, consider what is gained when one insists on the autonomous individuality of the intending authorial subject. Perhaps surprisingly, what is gained is not necessarily an interpretive victory. Anyone who reads the seventh chapter of *Seven Types* alongside Tuve's argument[4] will be hard put to decide a winner, and candor may just incline one toward Tuve. Empson himself later admits that the Frazerian underpinning of his approach to Herbert's ambivalence about sacrifice may have become a bit of a bore (*A* 253), and he is somewhat less patient with Freud too in 1950 than he was in 1930. (Notably, though, adherence to a Frazerian or Freudian reading of Herbert's intention makes Herbert himself less an autonomous individual than a repository of syncretistically observable lore.) No, Empson's victory in this controversy is not interpretive but ethical. Richard Strier perhaps likes Empson's reading of Herbert better than I do, and certainly there is much to like, but I would say the impressive part of Empson's reading arises not so much from the ad hoc insights for which every chapter of *Seven Types* is justly famous as from his principled openness as a reader—if indeed one sets aside the non-Christian dogmas borrowed from Frazer and Freud. Yet this openness in turn has somewhat narrow limits, as we shall see.

Empson insists on political and religious grounds that an early modern poet (as we now call poets like Herbert just for this reason) does not have to be a mouthpiece for the persistence of medieval tradition, in this case the Liturgy of Good Friday Reproaches. His most emphatic declaration of this point comes in his letter to Tuve of February 1953: 'I can never understand why critics who claim to be historical think they show expertise by getting their dates wrong and claiming that Renaissance writers were really Medieval ones' (*SL* 196). This of course is hardly fair to Tuve, yet the strain of defending her position is

[4] See *STA* 225–70 and Rosemund Tuve, 'On Herbert's "Sacrifice"', *Kenyon Review*, 12 (1950), 52–75.

shown in the rather startling way she puts it in her letter to Empson of a week earlier: 'I'd be burned alive before I'd cut down the meaning of GH's poem to that of a previous poem.' Well and good, though a still later Empson wouldn't let her taste for martyrdom pass in silence; but what she says she is doing instead, earlier in this same sentence, seems scarcely different from cutting down the poem. She is using her erudition, she says, to show that Herbert's poem is 'an explicit expression of' the 'tradition' in question. It is hard to know what that amounts to if not aligning the poem with the Holy Week Liturgy, albeit ne'er so well exprest ('It's good poetry,' she says in a sentence isolated between long paragraphs in the first letter). Empson's only claim is that Herbert had an individual and above all independent way of thinking about the crucifixion, which is surely true. The best justice that can be done to Tuve's position, by contrast, is to say that she is trying to distinguish between the personal inflection of a received opinion and the actual divergence of viewpoint argued for by Empson—who can point for his part to the known variety of Renaissance opinions about the Trinity and raise his own more and more insistent question, after his return from China, whether any honest poet can ignore the sadism of Christianity's central event.

Thus while Empson is right to insist that Herbert was entitled to his own views and almost certainly had them, Tuve is right to point out that Herbert's opinions may not have been those of the early or the late Empson. It remains the case, also, that while both critics argue from intention, neither has confirmed the existence of other minds by imputing to their poet an intention markedly differing from their own—or in Tuve's case an intention other than the intentional structure of a tradition that at the very least she takes seriously. It is Tuve who scores this point against Empson in her first letter: 'if you located H's originality in his unconsciously taking a position liker your own, that would put me off'—as obviously it has done. This shrewd hit needs to be modified in Empson's defense (although there are a few loopy turns of thought in *Using Biography* and *Faustus and the Censors* that seem to justify it fully): in the later rounds even of this particular dispute, he shows that he does not think all the Renaissance poets he likes agree with him fully when he grants that Herbert's view of Christianity was not as tormented as he continued to believe Milton's was.

He refuses to think, however, that Herbert could keep what a Marxist would call the internal contradictions of Christianity completely out of his mind in deference to the unequivocal collective voice of the old Liturgy. In this context Empson scores an incisive theoretical point of his own in his typescript continuation of the *Kenyon Review* letter—a point that today's hermeneutic traditionalist might well heed: 'What Rosemund Tuve is doing . . . is to arrive with a great fanfare of trumpets at the surface meaning of the poem, the part that was meant to be quite obvious at the time, and then promulgate a new law that anybody who thinks there is a secondary meaning must be grossly ignorant of this surface meaning' (*SL* 192). He then neatly anticipates the educational doomsters' argument of our own time, while rightly diagnosing its tone: 'These critics no doubt have a real fear, from their teaching experience, that the obvious may become forgotten in a new barbarism; but I find something totalitarian in their methods of fighting it, only delusively strong for defense, and hopeless for sustaining a tradition' (*SL* 193).

With all this said, however, it needs to be admitted that the issue between Empson and Tuve is not really whether Herbert's intentions are relevant to an understanding of the poem because both just take that for granted. Both insist firmly that intentions are relevant (even a surface meaning for Empson is '*meant* to be obvious'), and both claim to know what those intentions are. Still, we have already seen where it is that they differ as theorists of intention. In taking for granted from *Seven Types* forward the presence of secondary and additional meanings in literature, Empson for the most part openly acknowledges that some aspects of intention may be beyond an author's conscious control. As he says in the *Kenyon Review* continuation, '[The critic] should entirely concentrate on how the poem was meant to take effect by its author and did take effect on its first readers. But this formula includes the way in which it took effect on them without their knowing it, and that opens an Aladdin's Cave of a positively limestone extent and complexity' (*A* 254). Perhaps unwittingly echoing the Romantic tradition of hermeneutic philosophy from Friedrich Schleiermacher forward, Empson suggests that understanding the past requires divination as a supplement to philology.[5] Empson likewise echoes the opinion, pervasive in this same tradition, that we can know more about a text than its author did.[6] As Empson says at the end of the typescript continuation, 'I claim to know . . . what was going on in Herbert's mind when he wrote [the poem,]

[5] See Friedrich Schleiermacher, *Hermeneutics and Criticism and Other Writings* (1838), ed. Andrew Bowie (Cambridge: Cambridge University Press, 1998), esp. 92–3, 194–8.

[6] In review of this idea, see Hans-Georg Gadamer, *Truth and Method*, trans. Garrett Burden and John Cumming (New York: Crossroad, 1982), 263.

without his knowledge and against his intention' (*SL* 194)—meaning, I take it, against his conscious intention.

Now, as we have seen, Tuve, if only to avoid seeming naive, does not positively deny the existence of unconscious intention, she only suspects others of calling attention to it to ride a hobby-horse of their own. But in her first letter to Empson she bridles at the passage I have just quoted, making the familiar argument that there is no known way of finding falsifiable 'evidence' for the sort of intention Empson has in mind, and claiming further that an 'antithetical' intention—she uses the word—can be refuted by philology. This shows that for her the distinction between subconscious or preconscious thought on the one hand and the unconscious on the other is not as great as perhaps it needs to be. Preconscious thought contains nothing antithetical to what is conscious and must therefore be consistent or continuous with the appealed-to philological record. Unconscious thought on Tuve's view is a quicksand best avoided, yet if one considers it at all it must needs likewise be stocked (because all views repeat prior views) with traditionally expressed ideas—in Herbert's case, perhaps, Gnostic or black-magical ideas. Empson stands accused of stocking Herbert's unconscious anachronistically and arbitrarily because, Tuve says, there are no such ideas in the archive.

This in itself seems untrue, for what that is worth. Empson rightly claims to find such ideas in the Bible itself and probably suspects he could find them elsewhere if he took the trouble. In more recent times all he would have had to do, with many others, was wave the works of Christopher Hill and his school under the noses of the traditionalists. But this is only to say that Empson was enough of an Eng. Lit. man himself (as he called such people) to feel uncomfortable without an archive of some sort, and increasingly he did not relish the charge of anachronism, hence the second thoughts about Frazer and Freud. But after all, the deeper argument is surely that the ideas he finds in 'The Sacrifice' *need not* have been written down anywhere else. They need not be part of any tradition, whether they are conscious or unconscious, but may be the products of an independent, autonomous mind, hence confirmations of the humanist faith that guided Empson's whole career, the faith that ties his career together for those who read both his early and late work. To concede that all of Herbert's thoughts must have been part of the record would be to concede likewise not only that all human thoughts must have been written down but that no one could ever have an idea or a feeling for the first time.

These are deep waters, as Empson often admits, too deep, as we shall see, for a staunch intentionalist to swim in comfortably. But we have come closer to seeing why, for Empson, intention must be individual and independent if it is to have any value at all. There is no need to call it a rebellious intention, although we know how important freethinking is to Empson, because his wish to link intention to autonomous judgement need amount only to a simple definition of originality—not even showy originality at that, just independence from herd instinct and dogma. As is often pointed out, Empson is surprisingly vehement in disagreeing with the *Keywords* of Raymond Williams (who must have seemed sympathetic politically), and the reason is just this belief in the possibility of independence. Countering Williams's argument that the word 'interest' has always carried an economic connotation, Empson remarks simply that he can find no trace of that connotation in Jane Austen (*A* 185). In linguistic terms, Empson's point drives a wedge between the sociolectical sense of words, the sense in which all users in a given community perforce use them the same way, and the idiolectical sense that confirms our independence of will, *if only* at the level of indifference to, or even ignorance of, the way others use the word.

But that 'if only' poses a problem, and shows that after all Williams stood on pretty firm ground. It would seem on reflection that the only person who could defy the sociolect (some sociolect) in using a word is Mrs Malaprop, the person who is merely ignorant of how the word is used by others. 'Allegories of the old Nile' are certainly idiolectical (and 'signify' beyond what she can know), but their preposterousness makes them the exception that proves the sociolectical rule, and scarcely proves the independence of her intention because what she *means* to say is merely what anyone else would say. This sobering realization may account in part for the dazzling complexity of *The Structure of Complex Words,* which struggles to find other ways of saying we can use words independently while showing how unlikely it is that we will. We are on the brink of needing to interpret the intention of irony (lacking in Mrs Malaprop), which Empson attempts in his review of Wayne Booth and returns to in 'Tom Jones': A says to B something cutting about C in code which C can either ignore, thus appearing a fool, or acknowledge and thus stand guilty as charged (see *A* 178–9, and *UB* 132).[7] Jane Austen, an ironist central to the

[7] Closely related to this scenario is the one developed by Henry Louis Gates on the agency of indirection in the traditional African and African-American theory and practice of 'Signifyin(g)'.

Booth canon, may indeed be suspected of knowing as much as Williams knows about the word 'interest', and ironically assigning it an economics-neutral meaning. But can we know that she does this? Plenty of Austen readers would probably disagree with Empson that her word 'interest' lacks an economic sense. Empson himself says that the economic sense of the word must have seemed 'remote' to her because she was a good ironist in related respects and would have used the economic sense if she could (*A* 185). Interpretation of Empson's ABC formula is evidently an Aladdin's cave, either because C or B or both of them may be oblivious to A's code or because A may not be aware of speaking in code or indeed may not be speaking in code. If we take A here to be an author and B to be the reader of A's allegedly ironic book about C and C to be the reader of A's allegedly derisory book about himself, we can see the difficulties involved. These difficulties are compounded, as Empson admits in his late Dryden essay, by the compression of verse: 'The heroic couplet is perhaps a narrow instrument, but [Dryden's] mastery of it is so great that it betrays feelings he had meant to conceal—or else, its merit is that even while expressing one part of his mind forcibly it expresses contrasted feelings which he is only pretending to conceal' (*UB* 111).

With this 'or else', it is time to turn to the Wimsatt Law, I hope with the realization that Empson has not succeeding in repealing it. 'The Intentional Fallacy' by Wimsatt and Beardsley is in one respect irritatingly inconsistent: it veers in a more or less unexamined way between discussing the relevance of intention as a criterion for evaluation and discussing the relevance of intention as a criterion for interpretation. Of course, as Empson would have been poised to recognize, the authors probably saw a subterranean connection between these topics in supposing that what they call the 'success' of a poem hinges on the complexity of the coherence with which it can be interpreted.[8] Viewed from outside the aesthetic bounds of this supposition, however, Wimsatt and Beardsley are certainly inconsistent, and in addition to this they are daring beyond anything said in their time when in the seventh footnote to this essay they announce that 'the history of words *after* a poem is written may

The relation among A, B, and C are the relation among the monkey, the lion, and the elephant in the Signifying Monkey songs. Gates, *The Signifying Monkey: A Theory of Afro-American Literary Criticism* (New York: Oxford University Press, 1988), 54–9. Like Empson, Gates wishes to 'give a voice' to textual meaning by according it the drama of human agency.

[8] W. K. Wimsatt and Monroe Beardsley, *The Verbal Icon: Studies in the Meaning of Poetry* (New York: Noonday, 1964), 4.

contribute meanings which if relevant to the original pattern should not be ruled out by a scruple about intention'.[9] This allows us to say very interesting things about Mark Akenside's 'The great Creator rais'd his plastic arm' (*The Pleasures of Imagination*, 1744) or Yeats's 'and those that build them again are gay' ('Lapis Lazuli'), perhaps thereby refuting the argument of Steven Knapp and Walter Benn Michaels in 'Against Theory' that text and intention cannot be separated.[10] We know very well that these anachronistic meanings cannot be intended, yet we can argue that such meanings augment rather than undermine the meaning of the poems in which they appear. Yet it certainly does blow the gaff, as Empson would say, fully in alliance here with Tuve, on the kind of enterprise Wimsatt and Beardsley are engaged in. Coherence for them is the connection of textual parts as a purposive manifold, while coherence for an intentionalist—in so far as coherence is required—is a guiding idea purposefully connecting these parts.

It was because of this lurking formalism in the Wimsatt Law that Empson kept inveighing against it. He was either too impatient to read the essay carefully, however, or else ('or else!') he deliberately distorted it in order to avoid admitting his basic agreement with its premisses.[11] The fact is, Wimsatt and Beardsley give Empson just about all, or at least a great deal, of the latitude he could desire. The Wimsatt Law (if there is one) does not state, as Empson claims in the preface to *Using Biography*, that 'no reader can ever grasp the intention of the author' (p. vii). Rather, the authors distinguish between 'extrinsic', stated intentions and various sorts of 'intrinsic' evidence for meaning, much of which corresponds to what some at least would call intention.[12] Their argument turns on the Kantian paradox about the public and the private: the semantics of word use is in the public domain but intrinsic to the text, whereas extrinsic information about circumstances and opinions surrounding the composition of the poem are 'private and idiosyncratic', hence off limits for the interpreter.[13] Empson of course would not and does not avoid using such information, always trusting to his judgement of 'character'. Yet even here Wimsatt and Beardsley seem, up to a point, to accommodate

[9] Ibid. 281 n.

[10] See Knapp and Michaels, in W. J. T. Mitchell (ed.), *Against Theory: Literary Studies and the New Pragmatism* (Chicago: University of Chicago Press, 1985), 11–18.

[11] Certainly the latter, as on one occasion Empson takes note of Wimsatt's allowance for authorial idiolect (to be discussed below), but he then immediately dismisses it as an aberration from an inflexible viewpoint. See *A* 124.

[12] Wimsatt and Beardsley, *Verbal Icon*, 10–11.

[13] Ibid. 10.

him: they acknowledge a third, intermediate category of evidence for meaning which precisely involves the author's 'character': 'evidence about the character of the author or about private or semiprivate meanings attached to words or topics by an author or by a coterie of which he is a member.'[14] They sum up as follows: 'The use of biographical evidence need not involve intentionalism, because while it may be evidence of what the author intended, it may also be evidence of the meaning of his words and the dramatic character of his utterance.'[15]

As to Empson's 'no reader can ever grasp the intention of an author', then—to return to that—Wimsatt and Beardsley do not generalize about what a reader might be able to do in this respect, whether by sound or unsound means, but if they did one imagines they would say that no readers can *know* whether they have grasped the intention of an author. Very possibly readers have done so in this or that case, very possibly indeed they have stumbled on the truth by appealing improperly to extrinsic evidence, but they will never know for sure, and in many cases they will not even know with reasonable certainty. And the important thing in any case, for Wimsatt and Beardsley, is that intention, whatever it may be, is not meaning. Or more precisely, intention, should one be interested in it (and Empson is) can only be inferred from meaning. I have mentioned Empson's anti-formalism, and characterized it at length elsewhere,[16] but in this case he needs to appeal to form in pursuit of his own goal. As he says in a letter quoted by John Haffenden: '"Intention can only be known as it is shown"' (*A* 13). If the coherence valued by formalism is lacking, in other words, no controlling intention can be inferred with confidence, although local intentions—rather more Empson's specialty—can still be chased down by isolating a passage (or biographical episode) and treating it as though it were an accomplished whole.

In attacking the Wimsatt Law as though it were a caveat against appealing to human agency, Empson seems almost to announce a public reconciliation or at least compromise with Tuve: 'A student of literature ought to be trying all the time to empathize with the author (and of course the assumptions and conventions by which the author felt himself bound); to tell him that he can not even partially succeed is about the most harmful thing you can do' (*UB*, p. viii). Yet I hope to have shown that Empson's passionate humanism seems

[14] Wimsatt and Beardsley, *Verbal Icon*, 10–11. [15] Ibid. 11.
[16] Fry, *Prophet Against Sacrifice*, 55–87.

to indicate a far more fundamental disagreement than he can actually sustain. 'The Intentional Fallacy' arises from a formalistic premiss (complexity of coherence in the text as a whole equals value), and the footnote I mentioned is extravagant almost beyond comparison from the standpoint of any historicist textual critic, yet the offending essay is by and large written in the vein of broad common sense with which the sensible and unblindered Empson is simply powerless to disagree in any fundamental way. He does not feel that literature necessarily reconciles, or need reconcile, conflicting feelings (the seventh type of ambiguity, illustrated by 'The Sacrifice', is reserved for unresolved conflict), and for the most part he has little interest in the New Critics' emphasis on the text as a unified object, but these are the only key points on which he differs.

Repeatedly, indeed, he seems to agree. In the typescript continuation to the *Kenyon Review* letter, in the very act of attacking the Intentional Fallacy once again, Empson writes, '[the reader] ought to be ready to decide that good intentions haven't been enough to make the result good' (*SL* 191), wholly agreeing with Wimsatt and Beardsley's evaluative premiss that the only criterion for the 'success' of a poem is its internal coherence—a concept for which perhaps the Husserlian notion of 'intentional structure' can be seen as equivalent, but which does not at all correspond to the determinate invocation of a biographical intention. Quoting a passage from Yeats's *A Vision* as a possible gloss for the 'Byzantium' poems, Empson concludes 'This is rather misleading' (*UB* 165). Wimsatt and Beardsley would agree, or would say rather that we cannot know except on intrinsic grounds whether it is misleading or not, but in any case they would find Empson's rejection of this kind of evidence sufficiently guarded. Of the later T. S. Eliot, whom Wimsatt and Beardsley chide for having once explained in notes what he intended passages in a poem to mean,[17] Empson writes, no doubt conscious of having himself once written a complex unpublished essay on annotation with *The Waste Land* notes chiefly in mind (see *A* 70–87), '[Eliot] spoke about the poetry indeed, as if his father or his son had written it; sturdy in defense, but with no authority to expound' (*UB* 199). Empson in this passage means primarily that this was Eliot's conversational way of evading responsibility for the anti-Semitism and other offenses in his poems, but he must also mean, at the same time, that Eliot had arrived in

[17] Wimsatt and Beardsley, *Verbal Icon*, 14–17.

the end at Wimsatt's view of his own early assumption of authority as a commentator.

It is not clear to me in view of such passages, then (and there are many others), just where the crucial divergence lies in theory between Empson's intermittent caution in judging intention and Wimsatt's cautious willingness to accept certain sorts of intention as evidence, even though there is indeed a vast, justly admired ethical difference in Empson's championship of the integrity and heroic independence of human cultural performance. We know of course that there *are* intentions; we must even agree with Knapp and Michaels that all utterance *qua* utterance is perforce intended,[18] and Empson is at least at times as cautious in claiming to know *what* such intentions are as any anti-intentionalist could wish him to be. Yet there remains a difficulty, even for an intentionalism as qualified as Empson's is. It is telling that he has two ways of expressing his frequent appeal to the efforts of babies to learn the intentions of others. Sometimes he says the baby for its own good needs to learn *that* Mum's cross (e.g. *A* 124), and this no one would deny, as no one would deny that it's just human nature, socio-biologically understood or otherwise, to look for intentions; but crossness is not so much an intention as the behavioral equivalent of a textual feature; with a little practice you can just *read* Mum's crossness. It is a very different matter, though, when on another occasion Empson says the baby needs to learn *why* Mum's cross (*UB*, p. vii).[19] We agree that that would be a useful thing to learn while wondering whether anyone has ever really succeeded in doing so. In other words, to infer an intention involves two bits of guesswork, not just one, and it needs to be added that one sometimes needs to move from the 'why' to the 'that' rather than the other way around. For example, in contrast with the case of Mum being cross: in trying to decide whether a conventional-seeming yet somehow anomalous literary passage is intended to be ironic (the opening of Lucan's *Pharsalia*, for example), I cannot conclude *that* it is ironic until I can see *why* the author might have wished to make it ironic. Various sorts of contextual evidence may allow me to learn why or to see that there is no good reason, after which I can reasonably guess that it is or is not ironic.

[18] Knapp and Michaels, *Against Theory*, 13 ff.

[19] Eric Griffiths too sees the difficulty in deciding *why* Mum's cross, but he points out that in judging a person we in fact have more clues than we have in judging the intention of a text. See Griffiths, *The Printed Voice of Victorian Poetry* (Oxford: Oxford University Press, 1989), 86–7.

These complications make the humanism of the intentionalist all the more strained, while no less admirable.[20] When we think about minds differing from our own, we may 'understand what they are saying' without knowing why they are saying it (or vice versa), or we may have to confess that we do not understand anything about what they are saying fully, or at all. This touches on T. S. Eliot's point, while discussing the relation between understanding and belief, in saying he understood and agreed with Dante, he disagreed with Lucretius but understood him (with similar remarks about Goethe), and he neither believed *nor* understood Keats's line, 'Beauty is truth, truth beauty'.[21] The case of Lucretius is meant to be the interesting one, and Eliot realizes that it is controversial, especially in the 'Note to Section II' of the Dante essay, which is more skeptical about bracketing belief in understanding than the main text is. It may not be enough to say that you understand your opponent's argument (you find it coherent); you need also to understand the opponent's *point of view,* and if you understood that thoroughly (that is, if you found it coherent and plausible), the chances are that you might think yourself obliged, rightly or wrongly, to accept the argument you began by opposing. One is inclined to say that Eliot could not understand *why* Lucretius was a materialist, hence did not fully understand him after all, otherwise he would have agreed with him. That Rosemund Tuve understood Herbert's poem in a certain way follows from her belief in his commitment to the medieval liturgical tradition. That Empson understood the poem in a different way follows from his belief that no intelligent person in the 'early modern' world could possibly ignore the contradictions of Christianity. In each case there is a basis in agreement, in belief, even if they put it into the poem themselves.

Tuve, in short, is a historicist confined exclusively as she supposes to philological evidence, while Empson despite shunning anachronism believes that we need to merge our own historical horizon (what we now know and believe) with that of the text we read, combining philology with hermeneutic

[20] In revisiting Empson's intentionalism, I have ignored the argument that he is an avatar of deconstruction, which I treat seriously but skeptically elsewhere (*Prophet Against Sacrifice*, 56–61), because outside a humanist viewpoint like his own—wherever there is doubt, that is, about the relation of a stable human subject to meaning—disputes about intention are obviously irrelevant.

[21] T. S. Eliot, 'Dante' (1929), *Selected Essays 1917–1932* (New York: Harcourt, 1932), 218–20, 229–31 (the 'Note to Section II').

divination.[22] Both these positions entail a fervent, ethical appeal to the dignity of human intentions and the duty of the critic to understand them. And yet, as the frustrated tone of their correspondence indicates, these two views (unlike the views of Empson and Wimsatt) are fully opposed and incompatible. Let me put two passages alongside each other to indicate what I mean. The first is from E. D. Hirsch's second book in defense of intentionalism, *The Aims of Interpretation*, and corresponds to Tuve's position as she would herself wish to describe it: 'Kant held it to be a foundation of moral action that men should be conceived as ends in themselves, not as instruments of other men. This imperative is transferable to the words of men because speech is an extension and expression of men in the social domain, and also because when we fail to conjoin a man's intention to his words we lose the soul of speech.'[23] Empson of course would deny that he has ignored Herbert's intention, but Tuve accuses him of anachronism at the least, so that part of Hirsch's assertion too would appeal to her. Hirsch believes that a historicist account of other minds (bracketing one's own views) is possible, and that one can therefore know other minds. How 'other' Herbert's mind is to Tuve's remains a question to us, but not to her, and she rests her case wholly on the philological record.

Here by contrast, then, in Empson's corner as I believe, is an equally impassioned ethical *attack* on historicism by Hans-Georg Gadamer in *Truth and Method*:

> We think we understand when we see the past from a historical standpoint, i.e., place ourselves in the historical situation and seek to reconstruct the historical horizon. In fact, however, we have given up the claim to find, in the past, any truth valid and intelligible for ourselves. Thus this acknowledgment of the otherness of the other, which makes him the object of objective knowledge, involves the fundamental suspension of his claim to truth.[24]

Clearly Gadamer's 'merger of horizons' (*Horizontsverschmelzung*) severely limits our hope of knowing minds that differ greatly from our own. It helps that they differ a little, as that anomaly in their text which causes us to be 'pulled up short', as Gadamer puts it,[25] forces an adjustment of our personal horizon

[22] It is true that he insists in both of his letters to Tuve that he is not biased by his hostility to religion; but this is only to imply that his open hostility is covertly yet authentically present in past devotional authors.

[23] E. D. Hirsch, *The Aims of Interpretation* (Chicago: University of Chicago Press, 1976), 90.

[24] Gadamer, *Truth and Method*, 270. [25] Ibid. 237.

that enables sympathetic understanding at its furthest reach. This reach is not perhaps very extensive (hence Gadamer's argument that we need the continuity of 'the classical' to understand each other[26]), but it is clear-sighted; one knows by this means, or tries to know, what part of oneself one puts into the understanding of others. It remains unclear to Tuve as an interpreter that she too has some form of belief invested in Herbert, and I am inclined to say therefore that just in so far as Empson knows his own beliefs to matter in reading Herbert his self-awareness is greater than Tuve's, as also there is greater flexibility in his ability to understand *why*, owing to his own views, he thinks Herbert ambivalent about the crucifixion, not just *that* he thinks it.

If we stand back a little from Empson's late biographical exercises we shall see a pattern emerging that will make us wonder whether he ever really fathomed or even thought he could fathom the intention of other minds fundamentally differing from his own. We don't doubt for a moment that unlike Tupper he was a good though opinionated judge of character; the reason we don't doubt this is that we gladly agree with Empson in liking, admiring, and recognizing the lineaments of the character he judges well, even though it is to a large extent the character he sees in the mirror. We agree likewise, showing him in this though to be an incautious anti-intentionalist, that whenever he says an intention remains unclear he has professed to identify, simply in taking this view, a character flaw in the author or fictitious character at hand.

To Empson, an unclear intention is an oblivious dishonesty arising from the inauthentic or insecure position in the world of someone who may believe himself sincere. Such a personage has simply taken up an untenable position, hence cannot be understood, except *as* a flawed character. The incredible complexity of the argument concerning Marvell with which I began is unavoidable because Empson must skirt so close to the belief held by many, including Tupper, that Marvell was just such a person, however splendid his poetical gifts. It is as though Empson chose Marvell as a test case, as the most difficult possible use of biography, and felt that if he could triumph over Tupper he could do anything. He always lets his opponent supply the evidence for his own case (he was already doing this with Tuve); and even if it is true that he lacked the patience to comb through the archive himself, as his detractors say, he presumed plausibly enough that any diligent person would be capable of unearthing the appropriate facts—which he might as well make

[26] Ibid. 253–8.

use of—but that only he had the empathetic power to explain them. Yet after all, while the Marvell essays are wonderful reading, as Dickensian as he says Tupper's scenario is (*UB* 61), and as much part of what Empson calls 'the high summer of the detective story' (*UB* 67), they leave us as uncertain about anything to do with Marvell as we were before. Marvell just wasn't the sort of person whose likeness can be found in the composite portrait of honorable if scruffy Englishness that Empson builds up through his analysis of complex words like 'wit', 'fool', 'dog', 'honest', and 'sense'.[27]

Merely to survey the contents of *Using Biography*: even in Marvell there is sometimes republicanism and a companionable bisexuality to allege; in Dryden the strain of negotiating the landmines of Restoration politics and religion (resembling the Cold War world Empson found on returning from China) and a homoerotic attachment; in Fielding and his hero, bluff, rather wishful approximations of himself; in Yeats, a puzzle in textual criticism that can make Yeats a materialist interested in storytelling (not a quasi-Christian), but is weakened by the need to confess that the mystical symbolism remains baffling; in Eliot (Empson's Lucretius, antagonistic but admirably intelligible) the most powerful influence on his and his contemporaries' youthful tastes; and in Joyce and Bloom the full-scale opportunity to explore the companionability of sharing a wife. I don't want to make too much of Empson's class allegiance and his equal liking for the critique of his class in what he calls pastoral, and in any case I've said quite a bit about that in my book and elsewhere.[28] But in between the hearty, sometimes bisexual squire and the plain-spoken, sometimes bisexual proletarian (no longer commonplace types once the sexual theme is factored in), together with such persons as a Rosemund Tuve might suspect Empson of commandeering for this group—in between these types difficulties do arise. It seems right to end with Empson's remark about Rochester: 'Only in real high life could a man learn to talk so that anybody could understand him at once' (*A* 275). Possibly so, but in that case Empson would have to agree that the Wimsatt Law had better be kept handy for the rest of us so that we need not anchor our understanding in intention; and we are left wondering too whether a clear intention is really individual and independent or whether, in so far as there is such a thing, it is not a social attribute after all, like an accent or a college tie.

[27] See *SCW*, chs. 3, 5–6, 7–8, 9–11, 12–15, respectively.

[28] See *Prophet Against Sacrifice*, 29–46, and also Fry, 'Empson's Satan: An Ambiguous Character of the Seventh Type', in Norris and Mapp (eds.), *The Critical Achievement*, 156–69.

11

The Machinery of a Rich and Full Response: Empson as Philosopher-Critic

Christopher Norris

I Analysis and its Discontents

Empson was never much given to 'philosophy' in the various forms that achieved academic prominence during the period (roughly 1930 to 1970) when his work nevertheless engaged a whole range of distinctly philosophical interests and concerns. Nor was he well disposed towards 'theory' in the sense of that term which took hold among mainly French-influenced literary intellectuals from the early 1970s on but which first emerged—and had already attracted Empson's hostile notice—with the American New Criticism some three decades earlier. All the same he was a highly original theorist and philosopher-critic—without rival in this country at least since Coleridge—and one whose contributions have been drastically undervalued, in part no doubt through his own keenness to abjure any credit (or blame) in that regard but also through his habit of adopting positions strongly at odds with just about every tenet of 'advanced' theoretical wisdom.

In this essay I shall put the case that philosophers—especially workers in the field of philosophical semantics—have a great deal to learn from *Seven Types of Ambiguity* and *The Structure of Complex Words.* I shall also suggest (with an eye to certain recent 'post-analytic' developments) that Empson provides a much-needed alternative approach to issues of meaning, truth, and interpretation. In particular he points a promising way forward from the impasse arrived at by a thinker like Donald Davidson who adopts a minimalist semantics—or a 'no-theory theory of meaning'—by way of escape from what he now regards (having once been very much a part of it) as the endgame project of old-style analytic philosophy.[1] For it is widely held that this project has stalled on the sheer impossibility of producing a truth-based compositional semantics for natural language, that is, some means of individuating beliefs and assigning truth- (or falsehood-) values while respecting the need to interpret speakers on a Davidsonian 'Principle of Charity' that maximizes mutual understanding.[2] Since this book will most likely find its main readership among those with a primary interest in literature and literary criticism rather than philosophy I shall have more to say about these topics and developments as the argument goes along.

Stephen Schiffer takes the gloomiest possible view in his book *Remnants of Meaning*.[3] Having started out firmly committed to the programme of Intention-Based Semantics, Schiffer now despairs of carrying that programme through.[4] For there is—he concludes—no adequate or non-circular method for determining (1) the propositional content of beliefs; (2) the reference (or extensional scope) of their various constituent terms; (3) their compositional structure expressed in logico-semantic form; and (4) speaker's or utterance meaning, the latter construed as a relation that obtains between various attitudes (primarily that of holding-true) and belief-content as specified by items (1) to (3) above. Schiffer is undecided, at the end of all this, whether his own attitude is more aptly characterized as 'defeatist' or 'despairing'. At any rate he lacks Davidson's breezy assurance that 'wit, luck, and wisdom'—plus

[1] Donald Davidson, 'A Nice Derangement of Epitaphs', in R. Grandy and R. Warner (eds.), *Philosophical Grounds of Rationality: Intentions, Categories, Ends* (Oxford: Oxford University Press, 1986), 157–74. For further discussion see Christopher Norris, *Resources of Realism: Prospects for 'Post-Analytic' Philosophy* (London: Macmillan, 1997).

[2] On the 'Principle of Charity', see Davidson, 'On the Very Idea of a Conceptual Scheme', in *Inquiries into Truth and Interpretation* (Oxford: Oxford University Press, 1984), 183–98.

[3] Stephen Schiffer, *Remnants of Meaning* (Cambridge, Mass.: MIT Press, 1987).

[4] Stephen Schiffer, *Meaning* (Oxford: Clarendon Press, 1972).

the occasional 'passing theory'—are all that is required for communicative uptake in the absence of anything that could properly be described as knowing, possessing, or sharing a language.[5] Still there is a sense in which Davidson and Schiffer have travelled the same road of increasing disenchantment with the prospects once offered by a truth-based theory of meaning and interpretation. Thus in Davidson it takes the form of certain throwaway pronouncements (e.g., famously, 'there is no such thing as a language'[6]) coupled with the idea that we can best get along—from one speech-occurrence to the next—through an ad hoc mixture of charity, guesswork, and sheer adhockery.

So it is that he can treat Sheridan's Mrs Malaprop as a set-piece example of what goes on when we encounter some novel or hitherto unmet-with item of usage. For, according to Davidson, there is a difference only of degree between the sorts of allowance we can learn to make in cases of chronic malapropism and the sorts of localized adjustment that are always required in order to construct a 'passing theory' for this or that particular utterance in context. His point—briefly put—is that *every* such utterance will need interpreting with due regard to certain specific (uniquely occurrent) factors such as social setting, idiolectal variation, peculiarities of tone, shared background knowledge, or circumstantial cues and clues. In which case there is no point trying to come up with a generalized account (or 'prior theory') of what it takes for speaker and interpreter to converge on a shared understanding of the utterance in question. For this must always be subject to a law of sharply diminishing returns, that is to say, a situation such that the theory's usefulness for practical purposes varies inversely with the scale or scope of its proposed application. Thus it is in the very nature of a passing theory to work just once—for some particular utterance-in-context—and lay no claim to any higher degree of trans-contextual validity. By the same token, in so far as prior theories have any use at all, they will need to be applied in the default mode or as working hypotheses that may always turn out to offer little or no guidance in matters of communicative uptake. And so it follows—on Davidson's minimalist-semantic account—that prior theories are pretty much redundant and passing theories just a stopgap expedient whose field of application is always, of necessity, 'vanishingly small'.[7]

There could hardly be a greater contrast than that between Empson's prolific insights as a close reader of texts and the exiguous resources currently on offer

[5] Davidson, 'A Nice Derangement', 173. [6] Ibid. 174. [7] Ibid. 172.

from post-analytic philosophers like Schiffer and Davidson. Perhaps it will be said that this comparison is wildly off the point since philosophical semantics and literary criticism are two quite distinct activities with differing standards as to what should count as a valid interpretative insight. However, *The Structure of Complex Words* is, among other things, a sustained and highly resourceful attempt to work out the details of a logico-semantic theory applicable not only to literary texts but to all forms of natural language or communicative utterance. Indeed—as I shall argue—it achieves just what Schiffer despairs of achieving, that is, an intention-based and logically articulated theory of semantic content fully adequate to meet the various kinds of objection (on grounds of circularity, redundancy, or failure to individuate beliefs and objects of belief) that have lately been brought against it. This is why, as Empson comments in a footnote to *Complex Words*, 'the term Ambiguity, which I used in a book title and as a kind of slogan, implying that the reader is left in doubt between two readings, is more or less superseded by the idea of a double meaning which is intended to be fitted into a definite structure' (*SCW* 103 n.). Moreover, his approach helps to show just how much is left unaccounted for by Davidson's prior theory/passing theory distinction. For there is evidence that Davidson had read some parts of the book—in particular its chapter on metaphor—and that his own idea for that distinction came from Empson's broadly parallel treatment of the 'head sense'/'chief sense' pair, the one taken as referring to the dominant (received or commonplace) usage of a word at any given time, the other to its salient meaning in context as conveyed by the various types of logico-semantic 'equation'.[8] However, the resemblance turns out to have sharp limits since Empson exhibits a far greater interest in the way these senses may interact so as to generate complex structures of meaning beyond anything dreamt of in Davidson's minimalist theory.

Empson's advantage as a literary critic is that he can take passages of poems and offer just the kind of minutely detailed analysis that a close reading makes possible. However, one can gain some idea of what is involved from the following piece of more abstract and generalized commentary:

> If 'p and $-p$' could only be resolved in one way into: 'If $a = a_1$, then p; if $a = a_2$ then $-p$', it would at least put two statements into one. In many cases the subsidiary uses of language limit very sharply the possible interpretations, and the ambiguity is only

[8] Davidson, 'What Metaphors Mean', in *Inquiries into Truth and Interpretation*, 245–64, especially 52 n. and 263 n.

of this sensible sort. But it is evident that any degree of complexity of meaning can be extracted by 'interpreting' a contradiction; any $_xa_1$ and $_xa_2$ may be selected, that can be attached to some $_xa$ arising out of *p*; and any such pair may then be read the other way round, as 'If $_xa = {}_xa_2$, then *p*; if $_xa = {}_xa_1$, then $-p$'. The original contradiction has thus been resolved into an indefinite number of contradictions: 'If $a = {}_xa_y$, then *p* and $-p$', to each of which the same process may again be applied. (*STA* 231)

It is by means of such complex but logically accountable operations, Empson thinks, that we can make a fair shot at understanding what is involved in the more complicated cases of seventh-type ambiguity. Yet there remains, beyond this, a need to acknowledge that some such cases may put up resistance at a deeper level, a stage where the logical resources run out or give rise to a potentially infinite regress for which 'paradox' seems the only available term. And it is here that a further principle comes into play, that is, a recognition that some sorts of deep-laid difficulty may lack any adequate resolution (or even any means of intelligible statement) in logico-semantic terms, and yet possess a 'fair title to humanity' when judged against a larger background of motives, beliefs, and desires (*STA* 230). As I have said, Davidson's minimalist-semantic approach finds no room for any of this and indeed makes a cardinal point of denying that such complexities of logical meaning and structure have any significant role to play in the process of everyday communicative uptake. The contrast comes out in the above-quoted passage from *Seven Types* where Empson can be seen to make a first stab at expressing ideas about the role of logical analysis in relation to poetic language which he then takes up and develops to a much greater level of refinement in *The Structure of Complex Words*. Hence his characteristic stress on the sheer complexity of what must be assumed to go on in even the most apparently straightforward or simple act of communication.

Of course these are not the sorts of case that Empson is chiefly concerned with when discussing ambiguities of the seventh type, instances of extreme (often depth-psychological) conflict which cannot be resolved by any such appeal to our normative sense-making habits of thought. Nevertheless, he thinks, that logico-semantic 'machinery' must still be engaged at some point, if only as a set of background assumptions against which to interpret other, more complex or extravagant examples of the kind. For we shall do the speaker (or the poet) less than justice by working on a Davidsonian principle which offers them a licence to indulge or exploit such deviant modes of expression just so long as we can hit on some 'passing theory'—perhaps like the New Critics' rhetoric of paradox, irony, and so forth—by which to construe their meaning from case to case.[9] But if applied in Davidsonian blanket fashion that principle fails to take adequate account of the various ways in which speakers may fail to make sense—even on the most resourceful logico-semantic interpretation—for reasons which may yet be within reach of sympathetic understanding since they have more to do with the puzzles and paradoxes of human life in general. Hence the well-known (even notorious) passage towards the end of *Seven Types* where Empson remarks that '[t]he object of life, after all, is not to understand things, but to maintain one's defences and equilibrium and live as well as one can; it is not only maiden aunts who are placed like this' (*STA* 285). It is not just the offhand reference to maiden aunts that has made this passage difficult to swallow even for Empson's best-willed exegetes. It is also the untypical suggestion—at odds with the whole tenor of his argument in *Seven Types*—that (as Empson puts it in the previous sentence) 'under these rather special circumstances one should try to prevent people from having to analyse their reactions, with all the tact at one's disposal; nor are they so special as they might appear' (284–5). And indeed he goes on straight away to retract what may appear too large a concession ('since I am saying the best I can for the enemy') and to reaffirm the virtues of an analytic method that would come out very firmly against the retreat—widespread among literary critics at that time—into postures of reactive anti-intellectualism under the banner of 'appreciative' criticism.[10]

Still one can read the passage as a somewhat caricatural version of Empson's principle of humanity, that is, his belief that verbal analysis in the logico-semantic mode may not take us far enough towards achieving a complex, intelligent, and (above all) a humanly adequate response.[11] For the main purpose of having such 'machinery' (*STA* 291) is to understand both its

[9] See for instance Cleanth Brooks, *The Well Wrought Urn: Studies in the Structure of Poetry* (New York: Harcourt Bruce, 1947), and W. K. Wimsatt, *The Verbal Icon: Studies in the Meaning of Poetry* (Lexington, Ky.: University of Kentucky Press, 1954). For Empson's often hostile response to the New Criticism—even (or especially) when it claimed Empsonian warrant for its various methods and doctrines—see various items collected in *A*, especially 67–189. The New Critical reaction may be gauged from the various doctrinal misgivings expressed in John Crowe Ransom, 'Mr. Empson's Muddles', *Southern Review*, 4:2 (1938–9), 322–39.

[10] For a classic exchange along these lines, see Empson, 'O Miselle Passer', *The Oxford Outlook*, 10 (1930), 470–8, and John Sparrow, 'Practical Criticism: A Reply to Mr. Empson', ibid. 598–607.

[11] For further discussion of 'Charity' and 'Humanity' as principles of interpretation, see Davidson, 'On the Very Idea of a Conceptual Scheme', and also Richard Grandy, 'Reference, Meaning, and Belief', *Journal of Philosophy*, 70 (1973), 439–52.

operative scope and its limits when applied to certain sorts of utterance. On the one hand there is no making sense of language unless we assume that speakers and interpreters have a range of semantic, grammatical, and logical resources at their disposal that cannot be explained—although they may be vaguely presupposed—by a theory of the Davidsonian type. On the other hand there is much to be said about the subtlety, the range, and the communicative power of certain deviant—illogical, contradictory, or paradoxical—forms of expression that should none the less register as meaningful on any adequate account. In such cases what is required is a working sense, on the critic's or interpreter's part, of how speakers may often find themselves placed—like those unfortunate maiden aunts—in predicaments (whether verbal, social, or ethical) that involve the appeal to some larger background of shared human experience. Even so, one must first have run through all the various 'sensible' interpretations, including the attempt (as Empson describes it in the above-cited passage of wire-drawn logical analysis) to discover some rational means of resolving them without falling back prematurely on talk of 'paradox', depth-psychological conflict, and the like. This process is perhaps best thought of, he suggests, as belonging to that preconscious (rather than unconscious) level where we manage to 'talk straight ahead and get the grammar in order' (*SCW* 104). If so, then we need not be driven to suppose that there exists any ultimate, unbridgeable gulf between seventh-type ambiguities and those familiar (if rarely examined) operations which underlie our everyday performance as speakers and interpreters of language. Yet there is another, complementary side to this argument: that what actually occurs in these instances of 'straightforward' communicative uptake may well turn out, upon closer analysis, to involve much more than we are usually aware of when engaged in such familiar activities. In which case, as Empson puts it, '[t]hings temporarily or permanently inexplicable are not to be thought of as essentially different from things that can be explained in some terms that you happen to have at your disposal; nor can you have any reason to think them likely to be different unless there is a great deal about the inexplicable things that you already know' (*STA* 290–1).

On the face of it this sentence itself contains so many paradoxes as almost to qualify for inclusion in Empson's Seventh Type. Thus one might well ask how 'things permanently inexplicable' can all the same be treated as not differing—or not in any 'essential' way—from things which lend themselves to explanation in currently available terms. Or again, how we could already know a great deal in respect of those mysterious 'things' while continuing to regard them as somehow (even 'temporarily') beyond our grasp. Still one can see what Empson is driving at, perhaps—if this is not too circular or question-begging a claim—precisely on account of that obscure though practical knowledge to which the sentence appeals. Again the point can best be brought out by contrast with Davidson's minimalist-semantic approach. For on his account, when speakers apparently go off the rails—start uttering non sequiturs, logical absurdities, malapropisms, and the like—we can best (most charitably) construe their words by suspending all that otiose logico-semantic or lexico-grammatical 'machinery' and going straight for what Empson calls the 'most sensible' interpretation. And if this means treating them rather like *idiots* in the root (etymological) sense of that term—that is, as using words in so peculiar, aberrant, or idiomatic a way as to require a 'passing theory' for every such utterance—then in Davidson's view it is a small price to pay for making their beliefs come out true and their expressions meaningful for us good-willed interpreters. Yet clearly there is a sense in which this 'charitable' default mechanism operates more as a selective override control, that is, as a device for routinely ignoring the sense of what they say in order to avoid problems of linguistic grasp on our own (i.e. the interpreter's) side. Thus the real beneficiaries of Davidson's prescription for optimizing truth-content are those who find themselves strategically placed—on whatever social, cultural, or more specialized philosophical grounds—for deciding just where the line should be drawn between normal and abnormal or deviant forms of utterance. In the latter case his argument tends to work out as a licence for making what we will of their words—irrespective of grammatical or logico-semantic content—so as to construe them most fully in accord with our own best notions of rationally warranted belief.

In short, there is a kind of inverse law which holds that utterer's meaning should always be optimized *by the interpreter's lights* even—or especially—where this requires that we minimize its claim to be understood in keeping with the shared norms, structures, and resources of linguistic-communicative grasp. One could make this point more simply by contrasting the predicament of Davidson's Mrs Malaprop with that of Empson's maiden aunts, obliged to 'maintain [their] defences and equilibrium' and 'live as well as [they] can' despite having to cope with all manner of conflicting pressures and demands. For in such cases—fairly typical, Empson thinks, of the human predicament at large—we can best come up with an adequate interpretation by first seeking to assign some 'sensible' (non-contradictory) import to their various motives, beliefs, and attitudes, and then, at the point where logico-semantic analysis can go no further, supposing them to be at any rate 'in possession of the right number of principles' and hence as owning a 'fair title to humanity' (*STA* 243). Thus the optimization-procedure, as Empson understands it, is one that on principle makes the greatest allowance *both* for their capacities as speakers and interpreters of language *and* for their resourcefulness in handling situations which may go well beyond the scope of what would normally count, for linguists or philosophers, as a theory of interpretation. This is why Empson firmly rejects any version of the discontinuity principle that would treat poetry—even the sorts of poetry that put up maximum resistance to logical analysis or plain-prose paraphrase—as belonging to a special, supra-rational or aesthetically privileged realm of 'paradox' where such standards simply don't apply.[12] On the contrary, he thinks: it is in just such cases that our interpretative 'machinery' is most fully engaged, whether by way of teasing out the various orders of implied contradiction, or again, by imputing conflictual motives and intentions whose complexity requires that we should treat them 'with all the tact at our disposal'. At any rate there is nothing to be gained—and much to be lost—if we jump to some variety of special-case doctrine which fixes a well-nigh insuperable gulf between utterer's meaning and linguistic meaning, 'passing' and 'prior' theories, or poetry (where paradox supposedly reigns supreme) and normal or everyday language.

II Extraordinary Language: Empson and Derrida

This is why Empson works on the opposite principle, one that assumes a strong continuity—or a large measure of common ground—in each of these instances. 'This seems an important point', he remarks, 'because I am treating the act of communication as something very extraordinary, so that the next step would be to lose faith in it altogether' (*STA* 280). What he is talking about here is not (or not only) the most 'advanced' forms of seventh-type ambiguity, that is to say, those instances where rational understanding is strained to the limit and beyond. As the context makes clear, his remark is intended to have a

[12] See n. 8 above; also Christopher Norris, *William Empson and the Philosophy of Literary Criticism* (London: Athlone Press, 1978).

much wider application, both to other (less complicated) cases of the sort and indeed to all kinds of communicative utterance in so far as the capacity for linguistic understanding must itself be regarded as something 'extraordinary', and not just a matter for routine acceptance.

This is where Empson parts company with at least one dominant strain in present-day philosophical thinking about language and interpretation. The closest parallel is with Derrida's reading of Austin, a reading notorious—at least among mainstream speech-act philosophers like John Searle—for its 'perverse' and 'wilful' seeking-out of problems in a text (Austin's *How to Do Things With Words*) that makes such regular appeal to the norms and conventions of everyday, ordinary usage.[13] But this is precisely Derrida's point: that the orthodox reading is premissed on a set of taken-for-granted distinctions—'ordinary' *versus* 'extraordinary' language, 'standard' *versus* 'deviant' usage, 'serious' *versus* 'non-serious' utterances, genuine (communicative) speech-acts *versus* those 'uttered in jest' or encountered in plays, poems, novels, etc.—whose effect is massively to narrow the range of admissible or bona fide cases. Moreover, it prevents a 'serious' exponent of speech-act theory such as Searle from reading Austin at anything like the level of refinement, subtlety, and (not least) conceptual rigour that his text properly demands.[14] For if there is more to that text than is dreamt of in Searle's philosophy this is not just a matter of those typically offhand yet pointedly relevant Austinian *jeux d'esprit* that happen to possess more appeal for a 'literary' reader like Derrida than for one trained up on the normative conventions of Anglo-American analytic philosophy. What Derrida, like Empson, wants us to appreciate is the difficulty of drawing any confident, categorical line between 'ordinary' and 'extraordinary' language. And this because even the most (apparently) straightforward instances of everyday communicative language may turn out to harbour complications—or problems for speech-act theory—which cannot be handled on the orthodox account. Moreover, there is evidence enough *in Austin's text*—for instance, in his use of knowingly

[13] See J. L. Austin, *How To Do Things With Words* (Oxford: Oxford University Press, 1963); also Jacques Derrida, 'Signature Event Context', *Glyph*, 1 (1975), 172–97; John R. Searle, 'Reiterating the Differences', ibid. 198–208; Derrida, 'Limited Inc abc', *Glyph*, 2 (1977), 75–176, and 'Afterword: Toward an Ethic of Conversation', in Gerald Graff (ed.), *Limited Inc* (Evanston, Ill.: Northwestern University Press, 1989), 111–54.

[14] Searle, 'Reiterating the Differences', and also *Speech Acts: An Essay in the Philosophy of Language* (Cambridge: Cambridge University Press, 1969).

'deviant' or offbeat examples, his short way with typecast distinctions (his own very often among them), and his express desire to 'play old Harry' with philosophical fetishes like the fact/value dichotomy—that Austin was indeed very much aware of those problems that Derrida raises.[15] In other words, we shall do justice neither to Austin nor to 'ordinary language' if we adopt the Searlean-orthodox line which keeps such difficulties firmly out of view for the sake of maintaining a clear-cut sense of what properly, rightfully, or normally counts as an instance of genuine communicative language.[16]

Any comparison between Derrida and Empson had better make allowance for their real and, on Empson's side, emphatically stated differences of view. In fact Empson read only one essay by Derrida—at my request—and responded, rather like Searle, with an outburst of sheer exasperation which scarcely augured well for that proposal.[17] I should therefore not wish to suggest that they were converging on a shared set of ideas with regard to the relation between truth, language, and logic, or the issue as to what makes the grade as an adequate interpretation theory as applied to instances of 'deviant' or 'extraordinary' language use. Still the case is worth pressing a bit further since there are, I think, strong grounds for maintaining that Empson's approach to seventh-type ambiguities—and, beyond that, his development of a theory of Complex Words—can serve as a corrective to current misconceptions surrounding these issues. Most important here is their shared belief that what goes on in instances of everyday ('ordinary') language and communication is a great deal more complex and thus more akin to other—'extraordinary'—cases than we tend to suppose on a straightforward (whether 'common-sense' or orthodox speech-act) account of linguistic-communicative competence. And conversely, those 'extraordinary' cases must always at some point come within reach of our normal interpretative 'machinery' if we are to make any sense of their otherwise extravagant and incomprehensible claims. After all, as Empson puts it in *Complex Words*, 'I am trying to write linguistics and not psychology; something *quite* unconscious and unintentional, even if the hearer catches it like an infection, is not a part of the act of communication' (31).

[15] Austin, *How To Do Things With Words*. [16] See nn. 13 and 14 above.

[17] For Empson on Derrida, see *A* 52–3. See also my discussion of this piquant episode in Norris and Nigel Mapp (eds.), *William Empson: The Critical Achievement* (Cambridge: Cambridge University Press, 1993), 40–2.

This had been already his main worry about the more extreme instances of seventh-type ambiguity: that they might force the interpreter back onto talk of depth-psychological conflicts and neuroses, or maybe (at the limit) psychotic states of mind quite beyond reach of any adequate, i.e. rationally answerable, mode of analysis. There is one chapter in *Complex Words* where Empson is driven to something very like this despairing conclusion. It is the essay '"All" in *Paradise Lost*', a brief and rather baffled discussion which discovers such a range of highly charged emotive and associative meanings in the word that there seems no way to articulate its 'grammar' of logico-semantic implication (*SCW* 101–4). Thus Milton is an absolutist, an 'all-or-nothing' man whose poem is about 'all time, all space, all men, all angels, and the justification of the Almighty' (101). Moreover, he is constantly raising the stakes to a point where there seems no choice—even for a commentator like Empson—except to impute some deeply paradoxical sense to his use of the word. 'All else is unimportant beside one thing . . . he delights in the harshness of a theme which makes all human history turn on an absolutely trivial action' (101). And there is another, more suggestively secular-humanist but just as paradoxical set of implications: 'the generosity of the proud man also requires the word; when he gives he gives all. It is as suited to absolute love and self-sacrifice as to insane self-assertion' (101). We are here very close to the kinds of extreme case—such as Herbert's poem 'The Sacrifice' and Hopkins's 'The Windhover'—which provided Empson with his crowning (most 'spectacular') examples of seventh-type ambiguity. However, they present much more of a difficulty for his approach in *Complex Words* since that approach is premissed on the normative assumption—ethical as well as logico-semantic—that analysis *need not and should not* stop short or give up its quest for rational comprehension at the point of acknowledging some 'deep' paradoxical import beyond the furthest powers of unaided human intellect.

'If this case is a fair sample', Empson concedes, then 'it looks as if the real contrast is between the different depths of unconsciousness that are being tapped.' Perhaps all the same 'one could draw up equations for the effect of *all* in Milton, relating not so much senses of the word as whole contexts in which it has become habitual' (104). Yet this would defeat the very purpose of Empson's argument, amounting as it does to a vote of no confidence in the capacity of speakers and interpreters (or poets and readers) to stretch their minds around even the most complex, paradoxical, or deep-rooted conflicts of motive and intent. Such equations 'would no longer be tracing a clear-cut, if sub-conscious, mental operation, like those which let us talk straight ahead and get the grammar in order; they would be concerned with something more like a Freudian symbol' (104). So this was one case where the method appeared to come up against its limit, obliging Empson to retreat from the business of detailed verbal analysis to a broader sense of what the poem implied about Milton's embattled psychology and his hard-put attempt to make humanly tolerable sense of the Christian doctrine of atonement. 'That his feelings were crying out against his appalling theology in favour of freedom, happiness and the pursuit of truth was I think not obvious to him, and it is this part of the dramatic complex which is thrust upon us by the repeated *all*' (104). Such was the approach that Empson took up in his next book, *Milton's God*, where there is still a good deal of close-focused textual commentary, but where the emphasis falls more squarely on issues of doctrinal, motivational, and depth-psychological import.

So there is a sense in which the chapter on Milton in *Complex Words* constitutes a limit-case or even, in some ways, an outright defeat for Empson's method. Even so, he suggests, 'the critic would still be dealing with verbal effects to which a "purely emotive" linguistic theory could not be applied' (104). For to take this line would be to give up altogether on the attempt to understand Milton—to interpret his heroic struggles of mind and conscience—in adequate, i.e. humanly and ethically intelligible terms. All the same, 'I do not mean to deny that a reader can best absorb them by accepting and trusting his own emotions as he reads' (104). And this is quite a large concession, despite Empson's ready acknowledgement elsewhere that talk of 'emotions' may well be justified—indeed indispensable—so long as we can think of them as somehow being 'absorbed into the equations', or as not putting up any ultimate resistance to logico-semantic analysis. For in Milton's case the resistance goes so deep, or so far back into the twilight realm of 'sub-conscious' authorial psychology, that in the end 'you get an obviously important word for which an Emotive theory seems about all that you can hold' (*SCW* 101). At which point, Empson suggests, 'we can only connect the different uses in [a] vague and distant way', since 'there is no variety of senses in the word' and it thus functions merely as a 'logical connective', a kind of all-purpose receptacle for feelings that Milton was unable (or unwilling) to get more clearly into focus. This is about the closest that Empson ever comes to a Davidsonian (minimalist-semantic) view of what goes on in the process of linguistic understanding. Still it is a highly untypical case, one that—by his own and (I think) any reasonable standard—stands way beyond the usual range of communicative utterance and could therefore be taken, 'charitably' perhaps, as an exception that proves the rule. Even so, Empson is very far from adopting Davidson's line of least resistance, that is, his idea that in such cases we should give up the anyway futile endeavour to explicate meanings or expressive intentions in truth-based propositional, logico-semantic, or other such theoretical terms and instead make use of sheer 'wit, luck and wisdom' plus whatever serendipitous 'passing theory' happens to suit our purpose.[18] On the contrary, Empson maintains: it is only at the point where analysis encounters its limits—where the logico-semantic 'machinery' reveals some deep-laid nexus of emotive or conflictual meanings—that we can fairly claim to have achieved some grasp of what Milton was himself up against in the effort to make humanly tolerable sense of his 'appalling' theological theme.

Nothing could more clearly illustrate the difference between 'complex words' and 'minimalist semantics' as alternative routes to a generalized theory (or non-theory) of linguistic interpretation. In neither case—Empson or Davidson—is the approach confined to exceptional instances, whether poets (like Herbert, Milton, and Wordsworth) who press beyond the limits of rational-discursive understanding, or speakers (like Mrs Malaprop) whose language exhibits a sublime disregard for the rules and conventions of everyday communicative utterance. That is to say, both thinkers are committed to a version of the continuity principle which denies any ultimate difference between problematic cases of this sort and the way that speakers and interpreters generally manage to figure out each other's meanings and intentions. However, this resemblance has sharp limits when it comes to explaining just what is involved, for Empson and Davidson, in the process of communicative uptake. On Empson's account, the lesson to be learned from such 'extraordinary' cases—seventh-type ambiguities or (as we shall see) 'Type IV' equations—is that these occupy one end of a scale which also extends to our other, more everyday dealings with language where the process may likewise involve great complexities of tacit or 'preconscious' interpretative grasp. Thus he—like Derrida—takes the view that there is more going on in (so-called) 'ordinary language' than is allowed by systematizing speech-act theorists or by those who use it, in the standard Wittgensteinian fashion, as a shorthand appeal to common-sense values, to shared 'language-games' or 'forms of life'

[18] Davidson, 'A Nice Derangement of Epitaphs', 173.

outside of which nothing can properly count as an instance of meaningful utterance.[19]

This is why Empson remarks in *Seven Types* that the 'act of communication' is itself something 'very extraordinary'. His comment is clearly intended to apply not only to a poem such as Herbert's 'The Sacrifice'—where the poet is dealing, 'on the scale and by the methods necessary to it, with the most complicated and deep-rooted notion of the human mind'—but also, in some degree at least, to our everyday competence as speakers and interpreters of language (*STA* 233). Davidson would likewise seek to persuade us that there is no difference—or less than we commonly suppose—between straightforward instances of shared linguistic grasp and those other cases (metaphors, malapropisms, Freudian slips, *hapax legomenai*, and the like) where we have to adopt some passing theory in the absence of any such resources. However the conclusion he draws from this is exactly the opposite of Empson's. On Davidson's view what is chiefly instructive about these latter types of case is their suggestion that we *always* get along for the most part in this ad hoc, intuitive, context-specific way; that the very idea of 'sharing a language' may have no useful (interpretive or explanatory) work to do; and hence that there may be rather *less* going on—at any rate less in the way of complex mental or logico-semantic operations—than linguists and philosophers of language normally suppose. In so far as there is anything 'complex' here it is the sort of complexity that figures obscurely in our day-to-day hunches about other people's meanings, motives, acts, and intentions, and not the sort that could ever—in principle—be captured by a theory of language or interpretation.

III Complex Words and the Grammar of Assent

We can best get a sense of just how much more is involved in Empson's approach to these issues by examining his cardinal distinction between 'head meaning' and 'chief meaning', which I think Davidson most likely had in mind when formulating his own ideas about prior and passing theories. For Empson, the 'head meaning' of a complex word is that which 'holds a more or less permanent position as the first one in its structure' (*SCW* 38). There may,

[19] See especially Ludwig Wittgenstein, *Philosophical Investigations*, trans. G. E. M. Anscombe (Oxford: Blackwell, 1951).

he allows, be various criteria for deciding on this, such as its 'being the most frequent in use or the one supported by derivation'. Moreover—and crucially for Empson's later chapters of applied literary analysis—'a word may change from having one meaning as the head to having another, or a writer may impose a head meaning of his own' (38). All the same, as with Davidson's 'prior theory', we are here in the region of a relatively generalized (high-level) order of semantic grasp where communicative uptake depends much more on the interpreter's being 'at home' in the language than on his or her picking up local indications that the word has undergone some semantic shift in response to peculiarities of context or of speaker's/author's intent. Perhaps, Empson concedes, 'the term is merely a convenience which needs subdividing'; still 'it never refers only to the example of a use of the word which is being considered at the moment' (38). It thus remains distinct from what Empson designates the 'chief meaning' in any given case: that which 'the user feels to be the first one in play at the moment', or which 'the speaker if challenged would normally pick out . . . as "what he really meant" ' (38). And again, by way of helpful analogy: 'if the "chief meaning" is allowed a suggestion of local or tribal chieftains I think it can easily be remembered as applying only to a local occasion'.

Thus there are, on his reckoning, 'five ways in which a word can carry a doctrine'. The first has to do with existence-assertions—symbolized by Russell's ∃—whose truth-conditions may well be obscure, or whose analysis may lead rather quickly into regions where there seems little choice but to accept, like Davidson, that 'truth' must be relativized to speaker's belief or the attitude of holding-true. At the limit, Empson thinks, 'the complexity of the word is simply that of the topic', so that (for instance) 'most newspaper headlines . . . must be supposed to make assertions of this sort' (*SCW* 40). Such cases are therefore not of much interest for his own purpose, except in so far as 'the feeling [they give] of simplicity and irreducibility is often borrowed by the other types, to make themselves stronger, so that they are easily confused with it' (40). But the prospects for understanding improve very markedly—so Empson maintains—when attention shifts to the logical 'grammar' (or the structures of logico-semantic implication) whose range is roughly covered by the other four ways in which doctrines are carried by words. For these are less open to the kinds of rhetorical imposition—by false analogy, suppressed premisses, affirming the consequent, and so forth—which can easily work their effects where the whole weight of argument is borne by some strong if obscure use of the existence-assertion.

I had better now explain Empson's logico-semantic 'machinery' in a bit more detail so as to convey just how far short of it Davidson falls by retreating to a 'minimalist' position where there seems little point in maintaining the distinction between head and chief senses, 'prior' and 'passing' theories, or matters of generalized linguistic competence and matters of localized or once-off interpretative grasp. First Empson's chart (*SCW* 54) of the five equations according to the implied order of priority between subject and predicate:

The major sense of the word is the . . .	Subject	Predicate
The sense demanded by the most immediate context is the . . . Subject	II	I
. . . Predicate	III	V
The order of the two senses is indifferent:	IV	

Type IV would seem to cover existence-assertions of the vaguer, more inclusive or logically unsupported kind, as well as 'deep' paradoxical truth-claims or instances like Wordsworth's keyword 'sense' where 'the middle term is cut out' and where 'the whole poetical and philosophical effect comes from the violent junction of sense-data to the divine imagination given by love' (*SCW* 296). However, we can get more idea of how the method works from Empson's description of the various sorts of equation—or orders of logico-semantic entailment—that are carried by complex words. For it then becomes clear that such 'deviant' (Type IV) cases can best be understood against the normative background provided by Types I to III and V. This applies even to those deeply recalcitrant examples where it seems that the whole weight of argument is borne by some paradox or false analogy which must either be taken on its own rhetorical terms (as carrying an obscure but powerful existence-assertion) or else treated as merely 'emotive' and hence beyond reach of rational understanding. In so far as we are able to interpret them at all—rather than consign them to some utterly private dimension of associative whimsy, chronic malapropism, linguistic psychopathology, or the like—then they cannot be entirely discontinuous with our 'normal waking habits' of logico-semantic grasp.

This is simply to acknowledge the great variety of ways in which a single word can 'carry a doctrine' or be felt to communicate some item of purportedly veridical belief. Of course such assertions may be false or misleading, a point to which Empson repeatedly returns when discussing the more dubious sorts of Type IV equation. Still one can best begin by trying to assign a rational (or at any rate humanly intelligible) meaning or motive as most likely present in the speaker's mind whenever an utterance seems to carry some kind of assertoric force. This brings Empson out pretty much in agreement with Davidson's 'principle of charity', that is, the idea that speakers will normally mean what they say, that their meanings or intentions must be construed on a basis of imputed (presumptively true) beliefs, and therefore that we must count them 'right on most matters' if they (and we) are to have any chance of achieving communicative uptake.[20] The same rule applies—as both Davidson and Empson suggest—to cases where the belief in question may strike the listener/reader as either plain false or in need of some further, perhaps more 'charitable' interpretation. Thus, in Empson's words, there is often the sense of an obscure truth-claim 'when really the mental goings-on are more confused'. Even so, 'a "verbal fiction" may need a great deal of looking into, and the full analysis of it may be very complex, but so far as the speaker is wholly deceived by it I think we must accept his own view that he is simply using it for an existence assertion' (*SCW* 40). For otherwise—and up to this point he agrees with Davidson—we cannot make a start in understanding what they say on the basis of belief-ascriptions which may diverge widely from our own ideas of rational, justified, or warranted belief but which none the less enable us to figure out their intended meaning by a process of more or less complex rational reconstruction.

In short, we need to count them 'right on most matters'—or wrong only with regard to certain specific items of belief—if we are to see how some localized instance of mistaken reasoning or false analogy has got in the way of our construing their words at face (truth-preserving) value. So it is that we are able to interpret even the more irrational (Type IV) equations as the upshot of obscure yet intelligible processes of thought which can still provide a basis for communicative uptake despite all the deep-laid obstacles involved. However, there is a crucial difference between Davidson's and Empson's way of applying this generalized principle of charity. In Empson's case it requires a recognition that some beliefs are indeed false, and that to interpret them properly—i.e. against the background of warranted or justified belief—is to see just how far, and in what precise ways, they deviate from the kinds of

[20] Davidson, 'On the Very Idea of a Conceptual Scheme', 197.

logico-semantic structure that characterize our 'normal or waking habits of thought'. In Davidson, conversely, the principle assumes such an all-purpose 'charitable' guise that it leaves no room for elementary distinctions between truth and the attitude of holding-true, or veridical belief and whatever lays claim to that title on the say-so of this or that (maybe confused, mistaken, or ignorant) collocutor. This is why Empson is so careful to distinguish between, on the one hand, the idea that we should interpret speakers as most likely having reasons (or intelligible motives) for saying and believing what they do and, on the other, the equally important principle that those beliefs may on occasion be wrong—products of false analogy and the like—and therefore interpretable only by way of a more complex critical-evaluative treatment.

This may give some idea of just how much has dropped out in the process of translation from Empson's highly elaborated theory to Davidson's minimalist-semantic approach. According to Davidson, linguists and philosophers are way off the mark when they presume that we can best do justice to speakers and interpreters by supposing them to go through some complicated process of thought like that which Empson describes, at whatever tacit or preconscious level. Rather, if there is any credit to be had, it is for their knack of managing perfectly well—exceptional cases aside—without this requirement of 'sharing' or 'possessing' a language, and indeed without any reference to 'language' as philosophers normally construe it, i.e. in terms of some 'prior theory' that purports to explain how communication comes about. Moreover, those exceptional cases again prove the rule, though here in a minimalist-semantic sense which completely reverses the gist of Empson's argument. For what they demonstrate, in Davidson's view, is the fact that neither speakers, interpreters, nor (indeed) theorists of language and interpretation have any need to resort to such complicated theories in order to account for so everyday a thing as the act of linguistic communication. Quite simply, we *just do* make sense—at any rate most of the time—of those various utterances that come our way, whether through a normal degree of convergence between utterer's meaning, linguistic meaning, and various context-related cues and clues, or else (as with Mrs Malaprop) through a readiness to cut out linguistic meaning and go straight for the 'charitable', good-sense-maximizing option. In this latter sort of case the gist of their utterance *just is* whatever creates least problems in accomplishing the passage from context or circumstantial warrant to speaker's intention, suitably (i.e. charitably) construed. On Davidson's account we can save ourselves a lot of trouble by extending this approach to other, more normal or everyday types of linguistic occurrence. For here also there is not much use for the idea of 'knowing a language' if we can simply get the hang of utterer's meaning with the odd bit of help—where needed—from this or that feature of the relevant context.

Attentive readers of Derrida on Austin will already have picked up the warning signs in this downright appeal to intentions and context as somehow pre-given—there to be relied on—in all (or even most) speech-situations.[21] Sufficient to say that it raises quite a number of difficulties, not only—as Searle would argue—from a wilfully trouble-making 'deconstructionist' standpoint but also for anyone prepared to entertain the range of cases that actually come up in the business of everyday (whether 'normal' or 'deviant') linguistic communication. On the one hand there is the well-known problem of specifying what should count as an adequate criterion for speaker's intent, given the lack of any direct—linguistically unmediated—access to his or her present state of mind in the act of utterance. For it then becomes impossible to draw any firm, categorical distinction between 'sincere' (authentic, genuine, or felicitous) speech-acts and those that in some way fail the sincerity test, as for instance through being spoken merely in jest, with ironic or deceptive intent, or perhaps by just reciting the relevant form of words in a routine, mindless, or uncommitted manner. On the other hand there is no great help to be had from Austin's suggested alternative appeal to *context* as a means of deciding when and where—i.e. under what appropriate circumstances—such speech-acts may be taken as properly, authentically, or genuinely binding. In cases like this, he maintains, there is still an obligation to abide by one's words quite apart from any private reservations, any weasel clause or get-out provision that happened to be going through the speaker's mind at the time of utterance. Austin takes various examples like this as a clear indication that context is enough—especially when coupled with factors of a social, cultural, legal, or suchlike institutional nature—to avoid the otherwise problematic appeal to sincerity conditions (or utterer's intent) as the sole criterion for speech-act felicity. Yet Derrida is able to show—taking a leaf from Austin's book—that cases can arise (and not only in the realm of far-fetched thought-experiment) where there is *just no deciding* what should count as a normal, legitimate context of utterance. In short, this argument necessarily fails to the extent that there

[21] See n. 13 above.

exists no closed or well-defined class of appropriate speech-acts in context, or no adequate decision procedure by which to discriminate genuine (or binding) from non-genuine (or inconsequential) examples of the kind.

It is well to be clear—since Derrida's opponents (Searle especially) have misunderstood him on this point—that there is no question of his simply rejecting the criteria of speech-act sincerity or of context as a relevant consideration in cases like this. Nor would he for one moment deny that there might very often be a crucial difference—in ethical if not in legal or contractual terms—between meaning and not meaning what one says. After all, if Derrida were really such a thoroughgoing sceptic in this regard as he is sometimes made out to be then my comparison here could scarcely stand up, given Empson's long and impassioned campaign against what he called the 'Wimsatt Law', or the orthodox New Critical veto on talk of authorial meaning or intention.[22] Rather, it is Derrida's aim to draw attention to the various problems, anomalies, and borderline cases that must be seen to complicate any overly typecast or methodical approach as soon as one reflects on the sheer open-ended variety of possible speech-act instances and contexts. It seems to me that this approach has much in common with Empson's attempt to put the case for an intentionalist approach to literary criticism—or to linguistic understanding in general—while none the less acknowledging how much this may involve in the way of complex, at times quite 'extraordinary' logico-semantic grasp. Indeed, it is through the various postulated orders of implicit verbal equation that he seeks to reconcile the sorts of extreme ideational or (very often) psycho-biographical complexity brought to light in the later chapters of *Seven Types* with his growing conviction that poetry had better make sense by our normal standards of rational-communicative grasp.

That is to say, *Complex Words* can be seen as a key to what many readers have found so problematical about the relationship between 'early' and 'late' Empson, the one (so it is said) a brilliantly inventive close reader with no strict regard for authorial intent and the other a critic who insists absolutely on the prime obligation to discover and respect what the author originally meant.[23] The crucial point here, he suggests, is that we not think of intentions as belonging to some ultimately private mental realm shut off from the wider contexts of human social and linguistic interaction but rather as manifest in

[22] See Empson's various attacks on this doctrine in *A* 67–189.
[23] See especially Empson, *A*. See also *UB* and *FC*.

and through those logico-semantic structures. This in turn goes along with Empson's distaste for emotivist theories of meaning and value—or for vague appeals to 'feeling' by anti-cognitivists in various fields of debate—which likewise make it a mystery how we could ever get on communicative terms with anyone outside our own heads. Thus: 'much of what appears to us as a "feeling"... will in fact be quite an elaborate structure of related meanings' (*SCW* 56–7). And again: although 'Emotions and Moods may well be important in calling out and directing the interaction', still 'it seems clear that the first thing to examine is the result, what may be called the logic of these unnoticed propositions' (*SCW* 39). For the trouble with emotivist doctrines, whether in literary criticism or ethics, is their readiness on the one hand to accept the claims of logical positivism at face value, and on the other to discount the truth-content of any language—everyday or poetic—that doesn't measure up to those same (in any case largely unworkable) standards.[24] All of which offers some grounds for supposing that 'the emotions in the words will normally evoke senses that correspond to them (except in swear-words, intensifiers, and for that matter raving), and the structure to be examined is that of the resultant senses' (55). Otherwise—on the emotivist view—there would seem no limit to what 'language can get away with' by imposing false or irrational beliefs, like the paradoxes of Orwellian doublethink, which exploit the presumed incapacity of human thought to muster any defence against them.

Of course it is still open for the sceptic to argue—like Schiffer—that this all presupposes what has yet to be proved, that is, the validity of an intention-based and propositionally structured semantics that would make good its claim to reunite the various components that analysis had put asunder.[25] Yet Empson already had the outline of an answer in the closing chapter of *Seven Types of Ambiguity* where he countered the likely and (as it turned out) the soon forthcoming objection of 'appreciative' critics, those who felt that poetry—or their own enjoyment of it—was somehow threatened by any such hard-pressed 'analytical' approach.[26] To adopt this defensive posture, he

[24] See especially, *SCW* 1–38, where he takes issue with I. A. Richards's emotivist theory of poetic meaning, itself adopted very largely in response to the logical positivist claim that the only meaningful (truth-apt) modes of utterance were the strictly tautologous propositions of logic and the empirically verifiable (or falsifiable) statements of the natural sciences. See also his Appendices I and II on 'Theories of Value' (414–34) for Empson's case against emotivist approaches to ethics or moral philosophy.

[25] Schiffer, *Remnants of Meaning*.

[26] See n. 10 above.

thought, was to underrate both the resilience of poetry—the likelihood of its emerging unharmed, even enhanced, after the rigours of verbal exegesis—and the reader's capacity likewise to benefit through a better, more conscious (even self-conscious) understanding of his or her intuitive responses. No doubt it may be said—and with some justification—that 'the business of analysis is to progress from poetical to prosaic, from intuitive to intellectual, knowledge', in which case the objectors can plausibly maintain some version of the stock ('intuitive' *versus* 'analytical') dichotomy. From this point of view '[a] poetical word is a thing conceived in itself and contains all its meanings; a prosaic word is flat and useful and might have been used differently' (*STA* 290). However, as Empson shows in *Complex Words*, there is a lot more going on in such 'flat', 'useful', and 'prosaic' sorts of language than is likely to be grasped by any reader who espouses the anti-analytic line. And by the same token—Empson maintains—there is less difference than might be supposed between the kinds of complexity that characterize poetic language and those that enter into our normal, everyday-communicative uses of language.

This is also to say that we shall get much closer to an author's intentions if we allow for the extent to which *all* communication involves both 'intuitive' and 'analytic' modes of understanding. For the alternative, as Empson sees it, is to introduce a false and harmful dichotomy, one that places poetry in a realm apart—accessible solely by grace of 'intuition', or maybe through privileged poetical tropes such as paradox, irony, etc.—while ignoring the sorts of complexity and richness that analysis can uncover in our everyday 'prosaic' uses of language. Besides there are other strong grounds, in literary criticism as elsewhere, for preferring an approach that has the courage of its rational convictions or analytic bearings, and which therefore doesn't have to rely too much on the warrant of unaided intuition. After all, 'it often happens that, for historical reasons or what not, one can no longer appreciate a thing directly by poetical knowledge, and yet can rediscover it in a more controlled form by prosaic knowledge' (*ST* 290). Such is indeed the chief claim for Empson's method in *Complex Words*: that however 'prosaic' the terms of analysis (or the logico-semantic 'bits of machinery'), still they provide a useful apparatus or range of working hypotheses whereby the critic may be helped to interpret meanings of the utmost range, subtlety, and expressive power. Of course one may also need a good dictionary to hand—preferably one organized 'on historical principles', like the *OED*—in cases where the word has undergone some shift in its normal or acceptable range of usage. But of course Empson is not proposing anything like a Quinean experiment in 'radical translation', or a theory of scratch interpretation artificially divorced from all the usual contexts of natural-language communicative grasp.[27] Rather he is attempting to show just how much 'analysis' may be required in order for speakers and interpreters (or poets and critics) to achieve the sort of intuitive feel for language that allows them to communicate across and despite any shifts of historical-semantic perspective.

This applies just as much to everyday speech-situations of the type envisaged by Davidson, situations (that is) where the interpreter is confronted with some anomalous, deviant, or otherwise puzzling expression that cannot be construed straightforwardly in accordance with his or her 'prior theory' as given by a knowledge of the language concerned.[28] For here also what must be in play—if interpretation is to succeed—is a sense of the various possibilities that exist (from metaphor, paradox, and irony to malapropism and downright falsehood) whereby to explain why the utterance took that form and also what (if any) meaningful or sensible construction to place upon it. This range of options undergoes a drastic narrowing with the switch from Empson's theoretically refined yet highly flexible and context-sensitive treatment of 'head meaning' vis-à-vis 'chief meaning' to Davidson's starkly dichotomous conception of 'prior' *versus* 'passing' theories. Indeed, the closest analogies in *Complex Words* are those—like Milton's 'all'—that pretty much elude any logical analysis (or means of rational comprehension) and those involving Type IV equations such as Wordsworth's 'sense', where the word's meanings are pushed to opposite extremes ('sense-data' and 'the divine imagination given by love') and where its middle-range senses are effectively elided or suppressed. In such cases the reader may be justified in complaining that 'what is jumped over is "good sense"; when Wordsworth has got his singing robes on he will not allow any mediating process to have occurred' (*SCW* 304). And again, more pointedly: '[i]t does not seem unfair to say that he induced people to believe he had expounded a consistent philosophy through the firmness and assurance with which he used equations of Type IV; equations whose claim was false, because they did not really erect a third concept as they pretended to' (305).

[27] W. V. Quine, *Word and Object* (Cambridge, Mass.: MIT Press, 1960), and *Ontological Relativity and Other Essays* (New York: Columbia University Press, 1969).

[28] Davidson, 'A Nice Derangement', 168–73.

Even so, as Empson rather oddly concedes, 'the result makes very good poetry, and probably suggests important truths' (305). That is to say, analysis in the logico-semantic mode can perfectly well go along with a high degree of enjoyment or appreciation, even when the analysis is pressed fairly hard and comes up with reasons for supposing that enjoyment to derive from some dubious (rhetorically powerful but logically flawed) sources. Here again, what makes this possible—what enables the poetry to achieve its effect and Empson to concede its expressive power despite his philosophical misgivings—is the background assurance that rational understanding can take us quite a long way, and that where it comes up against limits or obstacles still the effort pays off since we are then better placed to see just why they have arisen. On Davidson's account, conversely, all that remains is the flat choice between a generalized notion of linguistic-interpretative competence incapable of handling any novel expression—any utterance that departs even slightly from the norm—and a passing 'theory' whose field of application is 'vanishingly small' since it works only (so far as we are entitled to presume) for just one speech-act in just one context of usage. Nothing could be further removed from the approach that Empson develops to a high point of theoretical refinement in the opening chapters of *Complex Words* and then puts to the test through a range of case studies, some of which succeed to striking effect while others are instructive precisely in so far as they turn out to resist such treatment. What is lacking from Davidson's account is this idea of language as a constantly negotiable interplay between the multiple senses of words, their structures of logico-semantic implication, and—above all—their capacity to articulate the subtlest nuances of speaker's intent through the differing degrees of prominence attached to those various senses. All in all it strikes me that philosophers of language have a good deal to learn from Empson, not least with regard to the still fairly hopeful prospects (*pace* Davidson and Schiffer) for an intention-based, logically accountable, and context-sensitive theory of communicative discourse.

12

Monogamy and the Next Step? Empson and the Future of Love in Einstein's Universe

Katy Price

Empson left 'Letter IV' out of his *Poems* (1935) because, as he later explained, 'the basic feelings seemed to have nothing to do with the moral, arrived at by allegorizing Eddington; it seemed sententious.'[1] Characteristically, this raises more puzzles than it resolves: the basic feelings, the moral, and the allegory from Eddington are far from straightforward. Empson probably never performed the poem in public, describing it years later as 'very much about a neurotic condition, and not I think suitable for a poetry-reading' (*CP* 273). Still less than satisfied when preparing his *Collected Poems* (1949, 1955) he published no further clues. Surrounded by more evidently successful and inviting pieces in that collection, the fourth Letter has drawn scant critical patience. Philip and Averil Gardner, in their valiant reading of it, suspected Empson of being 'basically undecided about what he wanted his letter to convey', expressing their regret that 'the "therefore" of stanza 4, while making the reader see stars, does not enable him to understand the "stars less monogamously deified" which he sees'.[2] This 'obscure and problematic' poem, they observed, 'moves

[1] Empson's note to 'Letter IV' for *Collected Poems* (1955), in *CP* 273.

[2] Philip and Averil Gardner, *The God Approached: A Commentary on the Poems of William Empson* (London: Chatto & Windus, 1978), 142.

stiffly, its archaic manner ill-suited to its modern scientific analogies and hampering their clear expression and argumentative effect'.[3]

John Haffenden's work on the poems, the life, and the letters offers material for a fresh attempt on 'Letter IV'. The poem is as frustrating as it is ambitious but I want to show that its apparent failure brings to a head the profound humanistic enquiry into contemporary scientific knowledge that runs through Empson's 'undergraduate' verses. A partial exegesis of 'Letter IV', this essay will explore some contexts for Empson's engagement with Eddington's expository writing. Reading the poem alongside its spaced out companions in the Letter series, especially 'Letter I' and 'Doctrinal Point' (embedded between Letters IV and V in the *Collected Poems*), focuses the challenge posed by the poem's central conceit, which proposes a shift from unsatisfactory romantic models of rising (a hatching cicada, evaporating water, an airship) to a more socially viable arrangement based on rotation with respect to the stellar universe. In manuscript notes to 'Doctrinal Point' Empson registered a lack of metaphysical nerve in his recent work: 'My last two poems have been failures for lack of political or economic convictions.'[4] Reminding himself that Marvell with his Coy Mistress 'didn't believe in tearing pleasures with rough strife', Empson noted that 'a great appearance of decision, of knowing one's own mind, is part of the (dynamic end of) metaphysical poetry. If only as a means of riding the storm of this universal doubt.' 'Letter IV' does not appear to know its own mind and this represents a turning-point in Empson's metaphysical endeavour; subsequent poems shift away from attempts to follow the example of Donne using the new cosmology of Einstein and Eddington. This shift also marks Empson's precipitate physical departure from the academic and social contexts that framed his uses of astronomy.

Those Cambridge contexts, emerging from the pages of *Experiment* magazine (where Letters I and III were initially published) and from other Cambridge undergraduate publications, yield a set of overlapping stories with a characteristic savour of the 1920s about them, connoting themes around intimacy that range from gymnosophy to companionate marriage to impotence. In its obscurities and dislocutions, 'Letter IV' draws the exigencies of cosmology and sexuality into a mutually questioning relationship, each putting the other under pressure in the search for workable new forms of intimacy for, and

[3] Ibid. 136–7.

[4] Unpublished typescript, Empson Papers, Houghton Library, Harvard University, bMS ENG 1044.

with, the contemporary universe; 'If only as a means of riding the storm of this universal doubt.' Retrieved from amongst insect larvae, Atlantic icebergs, exploding airships, and music of the spheres, its compromised allegory resonates with two larger, related questions: what does a poem know; and what kind of scientific knowledge is amenable to human existence? I will give a brief account of the poem's content before discussing two contexts that framed Empson's approach to these questions.

Provisionally titled 'Monogamy and the Next Step', the poem was renamed to form part of the occasional series of Letter poems written out of unrequited passion for Empson's Cambridge contemporary Desmond Lee.[5] The fourth Letter elaborates models of rising across the first three stanzas: a cicada larva hatches and tunnels to the surface; part of an iceberg evaporates; airships are filled with Helium or Hydrogen. Searching for a fitting analogy to celebrate the uplifting influence of his beloved, the speaker finds each model casting doubt over the healthy advancement of this affair. In stanzas four and five he turns to an alternative model of rotation drawn from the larger scale of the stellar universe. Refining his use of this model between the poem's first publication in a pamphlet in 1929 and its appearance in the *Collected Poems*, Empson also refined the basis of his engagement with contemporary science.

The adventure begins cheerfully enough:

Hatched in a rasping darkness of dry sand
 The child cicada some brave root discovers:
Sucks with dumb mouth while his long climb is planned
 That high must tunnel through the dust that smothers:
 Parturient with urine from this lover
Coheres from chaos, only to evade,
An ordered Nature his own waste has made,
And builds his mortared Babel from the incumbent shade.

(*CP* 57)

The cicada larva sucks sap from a nearby root and replenishes its supply of liquid, spraying the surrounding earth or sand and turning it into a paste

[5] On Empson and Lee, see John Haffenden's introduction to the Letter poems in *CP* 212 and *WE1* 232–9, 253–5, and 351. Desmond Lee studied Classics at Corpus Christi College, gaining a first class with proficiency in Greek and Latin verse composition in Part I of the Tripos (1928) and a first class with special merit in his specialist area of philosophy and in the rest of the examination in Part II (1930).

that can be formed into the sides of a tunnel.[6] If the beloved is the source of sap, the cicada-lover's conversion of this helpful juice into a waste product of his own might signal an unhappy solipsism in festering passion, but the poem characteristically resists such straightforward anthropomorphization as it moves out on to the surface.[7] The 'ordered Nature' formed from waste is 'evaded'; yet the bathetic 'mortared Babel', dwarfed by the 'incumbent shade', brings fresh doubt about a genuine exchange between partners. In unpublished notes to the poem Empson stressed the ambiguity of 'from', as 'to get away from' and 'using as his material', and John Haffenden has noted the oppressive resonance of 'incumbent' from works by Edward Young and Milton.[8] 'Letter IV' is trying to find a way out of the condition fallen into in Letters I and II, where a collapsing star, a cave, and the darkness of interstellar spaces all worked to defy communication or intimacy (*CP* 31–2).[9]

Perhaps taking a cue from the more promising deployment of solar rays in 'Letter III', the speaker turns to a model of evaporation:

> On my unpointed Atlantic where bergs float
>   In endless cold: its scream of gulls: the claw,
> A Roman feather at the back of the throat,
>   Wave-shutter, hanging, flapping, nape and jaw;
>   You lay your sunbeam and a part can soar
> As tear-clouds, safe beneath their maker, move
> In air-ships' gross security, rove and prove
> The virgin's fertile lands, Spain-stolen, treasure-trove.

Free in contrast to a 'mortared Babel', the 'unpointed' Atlantic is, nevertheless, a much nastier environment than the 'pointless places' where 'Letter I' began its ill-fated interstellar romp; the self-induced, over-glutted nausea of a 'Roman feather' gives way to impressionistic dismemberment on the waves. The liberating ray enables at least a part, if not a reassembled subject, to escape and move across the Atlantic and reach a warmer, more fertile climate:

[6] John Haffenden supplies an account of the cicada 'enigma' from J. H. Fabre, *Social Life in the Insect World* (trans. 1912), *CP* 273–4.

[7] See, for example, Empson's review of Maurice Maeterlinck's *Life of the White Ant*, cited in John Haffenden's notes to 'The Ants', *CP* 156.

[8] The quotation is from notes that Empson supplied to Edward Wilson (also a contributor to *Experiment*) in Dec. 1929, cited in *CP* 274.

[9] For a reading of 'Letter I', see Katy Price, 'Flame Far Too Hot: William Empson's Non-Euclidean Predicament', *Interdisciplinary Science Reviews*, 30: 4 (Dec. 2005), 312–22.

the 'tear-cloud' full of rain was likened by Empson to an airship 'full of expensive people which it is taking to America' (*CP* 275). Their destination may be a wealthy and fertile place but allusions to colonial history—Spanish acquisition of the Virgin Islands and subsequent British raids on Spanish gold under the virgin Queen Elizabeth—cast unease over the conclusion, much as the Babel reference undermined the first stanza's evasion of waste-fuelled order. Still, a colonizing adventure sounds healthier than anything offered by the poem so far; the discrepancy of scale between sunshine beloved and raincloud lover is less oppressive than a larval existence beneath 'incumbent shade', while the trip to America forms an encouraging association with Donne and his lady.[10]

Before arrival, however, the airship interjects a disaster-bound argument over the relative merits of Helium and Hydrogen for lifting:

> The highest in his bowels (God had come)
> Israel, determined to digest, had striven;
> 'I will not let thee go,' told Helium,
> The unvalenced self-enclosing air of Heaven.
> These risings have more earth-born gas as leaven,
> Cheaper, less 'bitter in the belly,' free
> If rain to make but little in the sea
> Or if on fire to make too fierce an empyry.

Jacob's struggle to 'digest' a higher power was successful; Empson represents the angel in the night as Helium, a noble gas (named after the sun-god) that does not combine readily with other elements. Hydrogen is cheaper but also more disappointing or dangerous because it will form compounds easily—as H_20, perhaps, making a small splash in the ocean; or burning up in an explosion. In the 1929 pamphlet version of 'Letter IV' stanza three ended with: 'Bursting, to make but little in the sea, | And by its closing, scatter us from our empyry.'[11] A cloud bursts into tears; passengers tumble from punctured luxury. By the time 'Letter IV' appeared in Empson's *Collected Poems* a succession of hydrogen airship tragedies warranted a more disastrous conclusion to this third stanza, its fire making 'too fierce an empyry' and recalling the 'Flame far too hot' with which 'Letter I' had concluded.

[10] On the liberating association of America with space travel in Empson's reading of Donne, see John Haffenden's introduction to *ERL1*.

[11] William Empson, *Letter IV* (Cambridge: W. Heffer & Sons, 1929).

Sylvia Townsend Warner's helpful—if understandably hazy—recollection of an explanation given her by Empson over dinner provides a key to the shift in the argument between the third and fourth stanzas:

> Then he explained his R. 101 to me: helium, the ur, the unassimilable gas, first used for lifting airships, afterwards nitrogen [hydrogen], more common, and explosive, being a mixer—so when we use love to lift the soul, it is a mixer gas, and we must be careful accordingly, love better for getting on with our fellows. He told me that gravity was framed by the influence of *all* the stars.[12]

Lifted by 5 million cubic feet of hydrogen, the R101 crashed in France during a storm on its maiden voyage to India in October 1930. In retrospect, airships offer the ultimate modernist symbol of technology in the service of national and imperial interests. War had made control of the skies vital to control of land; in peacetime airships promised rapid and luxurious travel to far-flung territories. The British airship programme culminated in a race for the skies between the privately funded (or 'capitalist') R100 and the Labour government's ('socialist') R101.[13] Both schemes were abandoned following the R101 tragedy but airship development continued in Germany and America.[14] Inert helium, the preferred lifing gas, was considerably more expensive than hydrogen and was unobtainable outside the United States.[15] Hydrogen was therefore the only option when Germany launched the *Hindenburg* in 1936. The airship was engulfed by flames during a voyage in May 1937 and passenger hydrogen dirigibles were subsequently abandoned. In symbolic terms, these enormous dirigibles offered a perfect metaphor, as it turned out, for bursting imperial interests.

Empson connects the hubris of Babel to the colonial airship's 'gross security', turning away from these doomed models to propose a metaphysical star turn:

> Therefore, my dear, though you can have it all
> As giving goes, the car more safe would ride
> Slung on star-netting of a larger ball

[12] Sylvia Townsend Warner, diary entry for 11 Apr. 1930, quoted in *CP* 273. Nitrogen, like helium, is inert but could not be used to lift airships as it is heavier than air.

[13] Douglas Botting, *Dr Eckener's Dream Machine: The Historic Saga of the Round-the-World Zeppelin* (London: HarperCollins, 2001), 233.

[14] Peter W. Brooks, *Zeppelin: Rigid Airships 1893–1940* (London: Putnam Aeronautical, 1992), 161.

[15] Ibid. 190.

Putting its eggs in wicker-work skywide:
Stars less monogamously deified:
Who not by light, merely by being far,
Make real Rotational Phenomena,
Prove that I satellite and you true centre are.

Here is the poem's moral: humans, like hydrogen, have an explosive tendency to interact physically; this prompts a shift away from exclusive romantic pairings to a new arrangement whereby 'we . . . love better for getting on with our fellows': a larger, cosmological view in which the rotation of one body round another is framed by the motion of the rest of the universe. Attributed in Empson's note to Eddington, the scheme is elaborated in a fifth and final stanza:

Who, being fixed and far, calm and surprise:
Being no further, shutter and enclose
A rounded universe: who name the size,
Imply the creature that can count their rows.
Your sun alone yielding its beauty glows
In growth upon the planet. They are song
Or call the tune to make the dancing throng
Free only as they aloof compose it and are strong.

Before investigating the cosmological allegory I want to explore two contexts for Empson's moral: Elsie Phare's contributions to *Experiment* magazine and Norman Glaister's address to the Heretics. Both of these are centred on May 1929, the date given to 'Letter IV' on its first publication six months later in the 'Songs for Sixpence' series of pamphlets edited by *Experiment* contributors Jacob Bronowski and James Reeves. During the intervening period Empson was banished from Cambridge.

I

Elsie Elizabeth Phare (1908–2003) arrived in Cambridge on a scholarship from Devon in 1926; a brilliant scholar, she baffled academic authorities during the inter-war years with her ability to write promising 'masculine' poetry and by a request for remission from teaching when pregnant.[16] Described in a recent account of the *Experiment* group as 'the most academically successful of them all',

[16] Anon., 'Elsie Duncan-Jones', *Daily Telegraph*, 21 Apr. 2003.

she was also, I would suggest, the closest in critical temperament to Empson.[17] Their discussion in letters of her early work on Hopkins indicates a shared spirit of earnest playfulness with which they enlivened critical tools received from I. A. Richards.[18] Phare's essay on 'Valéry and Gerard Hopkins' appeared in the first number of *Experiment*, along with Empson's first Letter poem, his 'Part of Mandevil's Travels', and 'Disillusion with Metaphysics'.[19] Here she elaborated the contrasting forms of logic through which Valéry and Hopkins were able to order experience in new ways, the former rearranging language to achieve a perfectly balanced equilibrium, the latter dislocating it to create a cinematographic 'essential fluidity'.[20] Hopkins's dynamism emerges as more dangerous and compelling than Valéry's static approach; he is 'so thoroughly at ease in the storm that he quite unnecessarily prolongs the turmoil . . . he deliberately eschews relief'.[21] Empson's sympathy with Hopkins's style is indicated in his manuscript notes to 'Doctrinal Point' with their reference to 'riding the storm of this universal doubt'. *Experiment* number three, featuring Empson's 'Letter III' and his reading of 'The Sacrifice', carried a review essay by Phare on Hemingway's recent fiction.[22] Here she discussed the impotence of Jake in *Fiesta*, a condition depicted by Hemingway as 'certainly no warrant for suicide, scarcely an adequate reason for eccentric behaviour and possibly, the involuntary nature of the deprivation apart, not a misfortune at all'.[23] She noted that 'Jake achieves a wider diffusion of interests, has larger eggs in more baskets than anyone else in the book', concluding that the

> quantitative solution is in fact shewn as working so successfully that at the times when Jake is most conscious of the pathos of his situation—he is constantly in the

[17] Jason Harding, '*Experiment* in Cambridge: A Manifesto of Young England', *Cambridge Quarterly*, 27 (1998), 287–309 (p. 290). Elsie Phare was awarded the 'title' only to her first-class degree with distinction.

[18] On Phare's involvement with the *Experiment* group see *WE1* 159–60; on Empson's engagement with her writing on Hopkins in formulating his own work on ambiguity, see 208–10 and *SL*.

[19] E. E. Phare, 'Valéry and Gerard Hopkins', *Experiment*, 1 (Nov. 1928), 19–23; Empson, 'Letter', 4, 'Part of Mandevil's Travels', 38–9, and 'Disillusion with Metaphysics' (subsequently published as 'Dissatisfaction with Metaphysics'), 48.

[20] Phare, 'Valéry and Gerard Hopkins', 21. [21] Ibid. 22.

[22] E. E. Phare, 'Ernest Hemingway', *Experiment*, 3 (May 1929), 13–16. She discussed the short story collections, *In Our Time* (1925) and *Men Without Women* (1927), and the novel *Fiesta* (1927), the British edition of *The Sun Also Rises* (1926).

[23] Phare, 'Ernest Hemingway', 15–16. This summary of Phare's argument is taken from my own discussion of *Experiment* magazine: 'Finite but Unbounded: *Experiment* Magazine, Cambridge, England, 1928–31', *Jacket*, 20 (Dec. 2002), <http://jacketmagazine.com/20/price-expe.html#fnB6>, accessed 4 Jan. 2006.

company of the woman whom he loves—there is always a hint that he is only making an attempt to see himself as other people do, to adjust his ideas of his situation to a set of values less fluid than his own.[24]

As a philosophical response to physical conditions, the 'quantitative solution' leads to a more flexible disposition, rather than a restriction of Jake's perspective. In the context of Phare's essay this aligned Jake with Hemingway's characters displaying 'the refinements of civilization'. Emphasizing that Hemingway's men of few words are by no means symptomatic of 'the return to the primitive', she discussed the 'necessary detachment' of both the author and his key characters from their circumstances. She saw such an attitude engendering coherence, in narrative as in life, where 'belief in the quantitative solution tends ultimately to make people manage their lives with extreme care and delicacy'.

The 'quantitative solution' to intimacy under post-war conditions is seen working not in some avant-garde ménage but in a man whose impotence has fuelled a more creative—or more clinical—approach to attachment. By May 1929, when *Experiment* number three appeared, Empson may have felt that his unreciprocated affections for Desmond Lee had produced a 'neurotic condition' not unlike the situation faced by Hemingway's Jake. He had by now established a relationship with Elizabeth Wiskemann but clearly retained a strong affection for Lee.[25] The purpose of his Letter poems, typed and sent to Lee but never acknowledged, turned away from a traditional metaphysical argument persuading the beloved into bed and towards the realization of 'necessary detachment' through which these various affections might be managed. The parameters offered by Elsie Phare's criticism are instructive here. In practical terms for the living of life there may not be much to distinguish between inhabiting turmoil in the manner of Hopkins and the more 'civilized' refinement in Hemingway's detachment but the two poses are temperamentally quite different. In his 1955 note to 'Letter IV' Empson said that he had 'tinkered with it a bit . . . perhaps making it tidier rather than better' (*CP* 273). This tinkering shifted the poem's conclusion away from a temperamental alignment with Hemingway's Jake and towards the prolonging of turmoil associated with Hopkins. By inhabiting turmoil the poem produced knowledge of human circumstances in tension with messages about the future of science found in talks given at the Heretics and in contemporary science writing.

[24] Phare, 'Ernest Hemingway', 16.

[25] See *WE1* 241, 233.

II

The aim of enlisting science in a cheerful 'quantitative solution', with 'eggs in wicker-work skywide', signals an inclination away from modernist performance of decaying civilization (exemplified in *The Waste Land*) and towards the type of futurology performed at meetings of the Heretics, the forum for 'discussing morality without religion' founded by C. K. Ogden in 1909.[26] Several talks delivered to the Heretics were published in Kegan Paul's expansive series of octavo books inaugurated with J. B. S. Haldane's *Daedalus: or, Science and the Future* (1923).[27] These included Normain Haire's address to the Heretics, on 'Happiness and Marriage', published as *Hymen; or, the Future of Marriage* (1928). Other To-day and To-morrow titles not given as talks at the Heretics but of particular relevance to the themes of 'Letter IV' include Vera Brittain's *Halcyon, or, the Future of Monogamy* and J. D. Bernal's *The World, the Flesh and the Devil*, both published in 1929.

Empson was president of the Heretics during the academic year 1928 to 1929, and on 5 May 1929 delivered his talk on 'Ambiguity'; the following week Dr Norman Glaister was billed to speak on 'Monogamy and the Next Step'.[28] Glaister's introductory remarks may be gathered from an undated typescript among his papers headed 'Monogamy—and the next step'.[29] Introducing himself as 'a medical psychologist by profession', Glaister spoke of his commitment to the Order of Woodcraft Chivalry, a 'small body with a queer name' which he found afforded 'opportunities for experimental research in education and in sociology more freely than any other organisation that I have been able to find'. He then outlined what he saw as the 'ultimate subject-matter for study', the relationship between human minds and their environment: 'when the conscious mind of man is the unit under consideration or, still more, if we are on the right track in looking for a more complex and potentially more competent

[26] On Empson's involvement with the Heretics, see *WE1* 107–10. The quotation is from a retrospective of the Heretics by P. Sargant Florence, 'The Cambridge Heretics (1909–1932)', cited in *WE1* 108. On the To-day and To-morrow series as modernist futurology, see Tim Armstrong, *Modernism* (Cambridge: Polity Press, 2005), 11.

[27] I am grateful to Liana Ashenden for sharing her research on the 'Today and Tomorrow' series.

[28] *Cambridge Gownsman*, 4 May 1929, 2.

[29] Uncatalogued manuscript held at Braziers Park. I am very grateful to Hilda Salter and Veronica Wallace for locating this typescript and for supplying further information on Glaister's work.

group-mind based upon the co-ordinated activities of many human brains, the environment which we try to bring into our calculations is nothing less than the whole universe.'[30] In 1929 recent scientific work appeared to support such a project; as Glaister noted, 'the most advanced of the pioneers—physicists, astronomers, mathematicians—who are exploring the nature of the universe have recently presented their findings to us in terms which make it at least as acceptable as an environment for living minds as for living bodies'.

At that time the most prominent of these 'pioneers' was of course Eddington, whose Gifford Lectures on *The Nature of the Physical World* had been published in 1928, fuelling debate around the new physics in philosophical, literary, and theological circles. While Eddington was careful to stress that physical law operated within its own self-contained system of meaning, isolated from spiritual or moral significance, he gave special importance to the human mind as our primary means of contact with the physical world. The 'alchemist Mind', as he invitingly expressed it, transmutes the shadowy physical symbols into a world of sensory experience, a world that admits 'beauty and purpose—and, alas, suffering and evil'.[31] In his notes for the Heretics talk Glaister expressed regret that 'the whole-time biologist and even the psychologist has usually been unable to find time to revise the nineteenth-century materialism upon which his science has been based'; consequently he found his own 'spiritual affinities in the scientific world especially among the philosopher-physicists'.[32] He then ventured, 'if I were not too near to the shadow of Professor Eddington I might pretend to have tinkered with cosmos-building'.

The shadow of 'Professor Eddington' lay across Empson's metaphysical endeavour as he sought to analogize affairs of the heart in terms of the latest cosmological ideas, while maintaining an essential humanistic distinction between the laws governing the natural world and the dilemmas facing human subjects. This was most explicitly addressed in 'Doctrinal Point', which teases Eddington's subjectivist account of physical law. Magnolias, the poem

[30] The 'group-mind' was Glaister's key concept, which he continued to develop after the OWC had disbanded; his legacy continues today at Braziers Park, an educational community in Oxfordshire.

[31] Arthur Eddington, *The Nature of the Physical World* (Cambridge: Cambridge University Press, 1928), p. xvii. On the literary implications of Eddington's insistence on the priority of mind, see Gillian Beer, 'Eddington and the Idiom of Modernism', in J. E. McGuire and Trevor Melia (eds.), *Science, Reason and Rhetoric* (Pittsburgh: University of Pittsburgh Press, 1995), 295–315.

[32] Glaister had initially written 'philosopher-psychologists', a slip that underlines his reading of Eddington's popular exposition as primarily concerned with the human mind.

argues, simply follow instructions in their sap; 'they know no act that will not make them fair':

> Professor Eddington with the same insolence
> Called all physics one tautology;
> If you describe things with the right tensors
> All law becomes the fact that they can be described with them;
> This is the Assumption of the description.
> The duality of choice becomes the singularity of existence;
> The effort of virtue the unconsciousness of foreknowledge.
>
> That over-all that Solomon should wear
> Gives these no cope who cannot know of care.
> They have no gap to spare that they should share
> The rare calyx we stare at in despair.
> They have no other that they should compare.
>
> (*CP* 59)

Solomon's resolution of dilemmas is as irrelevant to plant life as it is to Eddington's shadowy world of self-referential symbols. Empson departed from the astronomer's argument at precisely the point where Glaister waded in: where the human mind invests the uncaring physical world with wider significance. The poet's engagement with figures such as Eddington or Glaister enabled him to clarify his own position; with their doubting procedure and argumentative turns his poems enact the form of gentlemanly debate through which he learned to learn at Winchester and which continued in his engagement with contemporaries at Cambridge.[33] This form was also an explicit feature of the To-day and To-morrow series: 'Written from various points of view, one book frequently opposing the argument of another, they provide the reader with a survey of numerous aspects of modern thought.'[34] The key point of difference Empson found in Eddington, Glaister, and other writers on questions of scientific progress was a too ready application of findings from the natural or physical world to human affairs.

This turn of argument is nuanced by the fact that Empson shared with his scientific and literary contemporaries an intense preoccupation with

[33] On the culture of education at Winchester, see *WE1* 92–6; for similar contexts at Cambridge, including the Heretics as a forum for debate, see 100, 106, 108.

[34] Advertisement for the To-day and To-morrow series included in volumes, with a listing of available titles.

epistemological unity, whereby connections between the arts and sciences might reveal a broader framework for human experience.[35] The primitivism of modernist writings—in literature and in the sciences—often worked to idealize the epistemological and social unity of tribal experience, either mourning its loss or locating itself on the threshold of a dawning age of new-found coherence. Empson's metaphysical love poems seek out such coherence only to register its impossibility all the more sharply; 'Letter I', in particular, proffers the totemic common life-blood or *physis* of Francis Cornford's classical studies only to discover its extreme opposite in the isolating effects of intense space-time curvature under relativity theory. Glaister's own application of tribal religion and Eddington to the moral health of modern individuals is thematically so close to Empson's early poetry that it throws the poet's troubled stance into relief, highlighting the distinctive character of his modernism.

Glaister's recommendation for the 'next step' after monogamy is not included in the typescript carrying this title, which only outlines his introductory remarks. But the nature of his 'experimental research in education and in society' can be established from his involvement with that 'small body with a queer name', the Order of Woodcraft Chivalry. The OWC was founded in 1916 by Ernest Westlake (1855–1922) and family, drawing together Quaker interests, recapitulation theory, and the principles of Ernest Thompson Seton's Woodcraft Indians (the American inspiration for Baden-Powell's Boy Scouts). Taking up recapitulation theory from the work of G. Stanley Hall, Westlake emphasized the need to 'recognise with the poets that barbarism is essential to human life, and ... to show how to avoid it in adult life by taking a dose of it at the proper season'.[36] The work of Jane Harrison and her Cambridge colleagues (including Francis Cornford, who taught Desmond Lee) offered ancient models such as the cult of Dionysos; Westlake described the 'religious side' of the Order as 'an application of Miss Harrison's work, which might, indeed, have been written for us. As a sympathetic analysis of primitive religion, it contains just what we want.'[37] Lodges for co-educational

[35] This was discussed by Michael Whitworth in his paper on Empson and Michael Roberts at the Versions of Empson conference, 2003. See also his *Einstein's Wake: Relativity, Metaphor, and Modernist Literature* (Oxford: Oxford University Press, 2001).

[36] Derek Edgell, *The Order of Woodcraft Chivalry, 1916–1949, as a New Age Alternative to the Boy Scouts*, 2 vols. (Lewiston, NY: E. Mellen Press, 1992), i. 57.

[37] Ibid. 186.

camping were established in the years following the war, with plans for a wilderness school near Fordingbridge in Hampshire.[38] During the 1920s the OWC extended its focus from educational camping for children to address the needs of adults who had missed the 'proper season' for expression of their savage instincts, yet the means for such expression remained a matter for strenuous debate between the more pagan elements of the OWC and their Christian counterparts. During the 1920s the unity of the OWC was severely undermined by debates on questions of sex; Dr J. Norman Glaister (1883–1961), a psychiatrist at Finsbury Park mental hospital who joined the organization in 1924, saw the OWC as an opportunity to put into practice his views on the social organism, using the division between conservative and radical viewpoints, as an opportunity to expound his own theories about the group mind.[39]

In an essay on 'The Order as a Social Organism', published in the OWC journal *Pine Cone* in October 1925, Glaister stressed that the 'resistive attitude' (looking to the past) and the 'sensitive attitude' (looking to the future) each had a role to play. He employed a biological analogy to illustrate: '[t]he human mind confronted by this ethical dilemma is in a position strictly comparable to that of an amoeba . . . in contact with a granule of unfamiliar material.'[40] The amoeba may, he explained, 'harden its skin and hold itself aloof', or alternatively 'soften its cell-wall, flow around the interesting tit-bit and engulf it in its substance, and in so doing secure an accession to its own size and strength, in the event of the strange body proving good for food'. The move from analogy to identity was, for Glaister, entirely unproblematic: 'This conflict within the amoeba is evidently of the same nature as that fundamental conflict of human life with which we are dealing.' In his vision for the future Glaister hoped that individual minds would 'learn to specialise decisively in either the sensitive or the resistive capacity and to co-operate consciously with each other'. But 'in the meantime', he explained, 'the individual mind of each man or woman has to deal as best it can with the problems which confront it'. Four years later in his address to the Heretics Glaister enlisted Eddington in the search for 'a more complex and potentially more competent group-mind based upon the co-ordinated activities of many human brains'.

[38] The Forest School opened in Sept. 1929; ibid. ii. 398. Members of the Nicholson family attended, including two of Nancy Nicholson's children by Robert Graves; ibid. ii. 406.

[39] Ibid. i. 258–61.

[40] J. Norman Glaister, 'The Order as a Social Organism', *Pine Cone*, 3: 10 (Oct. 1925), 24–31.

Glaister's own liberal views on adult sexuality were mild compared to H. D. Jennings White's promotion of sex training for children or the activities of Harry Byngham, an advocate of gymnosophy who heralded the OWC as 'the erect Penis of the social organism'.[41] In 1930 Glaister married Dorothy Revel, also a member of the Order and a Quaker, at a 'woodcraft wedding'.[42] While the ceremony raised protest from conservative members who resented this usurpation of Church authority, their 'troth-plighting' was mild in comparison to Byngham's gymnosophy on the Sussex Down in the presence of invited representatives from the press in the autumn of 1925.[43] Byngham was suspended from his Chieftainship following this episode, but even this behaviour hardly breached the bounds of monogamy as we would conceive of it today, his co-gymnosophist being his fiancée. More interested in minds than bodies, Glaister is likely to have offered the Heretics a quantitative solution to the monogamy question along similar lines to that represented by Hemingway's Jake: the cool integration of intimate relations between partners in a broader social context.

Debates around monogamy between the wars tended to focus on revised, more sustainable forms of commitment between exclusive partners rather than the advocacy of multiple sexual adventures. A title such as 'Monogamy—and the next step' would, like Vera Brittain's book in the Kegan Paul series, *Halcyon, or, the Future of Monogamy*, have indicated hopes for the ascendancy of rational thought over physical desire. Glaister was not alone in associating such hopes with the interconnection of minds and with a division of humanity into progressive and regressive types. J. D. Bernal's contribution to the To-day and To-morrow series is a more prominent and influential example: *The World, The Flesh and the Devil: An Enquiry into the Future of the Three Enemies of the Rational Soul* proposed a vision of mechanically adapted beings capable of joining by 'intimate intercommunication of minds'. These beings, Bernal speculated, would adapt to their radically changed physiological existence by sublimating the sexual impulses into scientific research and aesthetic creation; a division between progressive and conservative types might lead to a 'di-morphism in humanity in which the conflict between the humanizers and the mechanizers will be solved not by the victory of one or the other but by the splitting of the human race'.[44] Inhabiting the 'cold emptiness of space' these beings would

[41] Edgell, *Order*, i. 274–5, 278–9. [42] Ibid. ii. 436–8. [43] Ibid. i. 212–13.
[44] J. D. Bernal, *The World, The Flesh and The Devil* (London: Kegan Paul, 1929), 78–9, 71–2.

be better off 'containing no organic material at all', while mechanized sense organs would enable them to extend their perception across much broader reaches of time and space.[45]

Modernists poets of diverse temperaments countered the tendency of science writers and their audiences to transfer the cold rationality of physical science to human affairs or—more frequently, as with popular enthusiasm for Eddington—transfer the warmth of human experience to the shadowy world of mathematical symbols. Where Eliot deplored the popular trend of ethical or religious enthusiasm derived from expositions of the new physics, and Auden mocked the 'Universal-Complex sensibility', Empson allowed his sympathy with this pervasive frame of thinking to run its course before diverting away from it, undertaking a 'more desperate effort of the imagination' which he felt was required in response to contemporary science writing.[46] The difficulties inherent in trying to work a new balance between mathematics and affective life can be read into the dramatic temperature fluctuations in 'Letter IV'. To begin with the cicada emerges from a dark tunnel to 'incumbent shade'; 'endless cold' is then mitigated by 'a sunbeam' but culminates in 'too fierce an emypry'; finally the fixed stars provide a reference frame without shining any direct light on the local system, while only the local sun 'glows | In growth' on its satellite.[47] This last arrangement is introduced by 'Therefore, my dear', signalling the poem's 'argufying' turn and Empson's intention that this ought not to be received by the reader as a merely mental experience but rather as a 'bang on the nose' (*A* 170). There's a poignancy in the use of 'Therefore' in an address between lovers with regard to the future form of their intimacy; rather than selfishly rejecting outmoded or inconvenient romantic forms the speaker has an air of turning to face something inevitable and practical: 'the car more safe would ride.' This poignant tone was enhanced when Empson revised the poem's last four lines. Inspecting the adaptation of his allegory more closely also points to the distinctive modernist futurology of his analogizing approach, where cosmology and sexuality are brought together only to underscore disparity between them. 'Letter IV' may have

[45] Ibid. 74–5.

[46] T. S. Eliot, 'Religion and Science: A Phantom Dilemma', *Listener* (23 Mar. 1932), 428–9; W. H. Auden, 'Letter to Lord Byron', *Letters from Iceland* (London: Faber, 1937), 103. Empson's phrase is drawn from his review of Maeterlinck, cited in n. 7 above.

[47] I am grateful to Helen Small for her observations on the theme of temperature in discussion following this paper at the Versions of Empson conference.

failed in its intended allegory but this failure may in itself be read as a broader allegory for the relations between poetic and scientific knowledge. Such a possibility emerges through Empson's characteristic teasing of Eddington's epistemological commitments.

III

The cosmological allegory in stanza four may be glossed as follows: distant stars do not shed any direct light on the affair but they help to make sense of it simply by providing a frame of reference; this is less monogamous not in terms of inviting others to participate on intimate terms but simply in ceasing to operate as an idealized romantic world apart; the 'less monogamously deified' stars, not forming part of this binary system, nevertheless constitute the reality of that system's motion. This role for the fixed stars invokes the critique of Newtonian mechanics associated with Ernst Mach (1838–1916), an association that comes out more strongly in the explanation recalled by Sylvia Townsend Warner, '[h]e told me that gravity was framed by the influence of *all* the stars' (*CP* 273), and in a manuscript note where Empson elaborated on the conceit of stanza four: 'fixed-stars, not apparently giving much light, but in (special) theory of relativity (actually *owing* to their distance) = the reality of diurnal rotation, the difference between earth round sun (-woman) and sun round earth anthropo- (pre-humanist) hence self-centred. Their fixity, the imaginative relief of their presence.'[48] The earth's daily rotation on its axis may be mistaken for the sun and stars revolving around the planet but observation reveals the sun to be 'true centre' of this system; as Eddington explained, '[t]he belief that the earth rotates on its axis was suggested by the diurnal motions of the heavenly bodies'.[49] This change of perspective is analogized by Empson into a progressive shift from self-centred romantic love to a form of devotion capable of taking other bodies into account, a more 'real' and 'true' picture of things.

The 'reality' obtained in the Machian view comes at the cost of absolute knowledge. Where Newton had argued for absolute space, time, and motion,

[48] Cited in *CP* 276. The reference to special relativity here is misleading; see n. 51 below.

[49] Arthur Eddington, *Space, Time and Gravitation* (Cambridge: Cambridge University Press, 1920), 152.

Mach claimed that such things were 'pure things of thought, pure mental constructs, that cannot be produced in experience'.[50] He believed that the closest we could get to absolute space was the reference frame represented by the fixed stars (by virtue of their great distance and combined mass) and he held that Newton's laws implicitly referred all motions to this inertial frame.[51] Einstein was much influenced by Mach's general philosophical outlook and, while his special theory of relativity did not make use of the fixed stars as such it was, like Newtonian mechanics, limited to inertial frames of reference.[52] This was a limitation that Einstein sought to overcome by extending his theory to deal with accelerating frames, thereby bringing gravitation into the picture. Empson's poem follows this further development by referring to debates over the cosmological implications of Einstein's law of gravitation in the fifth stanza. Read alongside Eddington's take on these debates in 1920, the conclusion to 'Letter IV' emerges as more than simply a poetic testing of Einstein's universe as an environment fit for human lovers; it is looking forward to an epistemology that will somehow be more habitable than those currently offered by science writers and their critics.

In his discussion of absolute rotation in *Space, Time and Gravitation* Eddington declared his divergence from 'the continental relativists', maintaining that '[i]n this book the tradition of Faraday and Maxwell still rules our outlook'.[53] Eddington's allegiance to British traditions within physics entailed prioritizing fields of force over matter; this was inflected through his own conviction that matter was epiphenomenal to observation.[54] Eddington objected to the

[50] Ernst Mach, *The Science of Mechanics: A Critical and Historical Account of its Development* (1893), trans. Thomas J. McCormack, 6th edn. (LaSalle, Ill.: Open Court, 1960), 280. I am grateful to William Vanderburgh for alerting me to the Machian view in Empson's poem and manuscript note.

[51] Robert DiSalle, 'Space and Time: Inertial Frames', *The Stanford Encyclopedia of Philosophy (Summer 2002 Edition)*, ed. Edward N. Zalta, URL = <http://plato.stanford.edu/archives/sum2002/entries/spacetime-iframes/>.

[52] Empson's manuscript reference to '(special) theory of relativity' is misleading because the fifth stanza of his poem is concerned with gravitation and therefore with analogizing *general* relativity. He was well aware of the difference between Einstein's 1905 and 1915 work on relativity and this insistence on the special theory in his note suggests that the poem was intended to perform its own, analogous movement from restricted to more general circumstances across the last two stanzas.

[53] Eddington, *Space, Time and Gravitation*, 156, 163–4.

[54] I am grateful to Matthew Stanley for reading a draft of this paper and helping me to contextualize Eddington's views. These contexts are further explored in *Stanley's Practical Mystic: Religion, Science, and A. S. Eddington* (Chicago: University of Chicago Press, 2007). On Eddington's pedagogical role at Cambridge in relation to the Maxwellian tradition, see Andrew Warwick, *Masters of Theory: Cambridge and the Rise of Mathematical Physics* (Chicago: University of Chicago Press, 2003).

positivist view associated with Mach, that 'only those things are to be regarded as being in causal connection which are capable of being actually observed'; such a view encouraged, as Eddington put it, the placing of 'matter on a plane above geodesic structure in regard to the formulation of physical laws, though it is not easy to see in what sense a distribution of matter can be regarded as more observable than the field of influence in surrounding space which makes us aware of its existence'.[55] Discussing Einstein's cylindrical model of space-time, Eddington protested that this necessitated 'the existence of vast quantities of matter . . . far in excess of what has been revealed by our telescopes'. It is typical of Eddington's expository style that he should elaborate this model only to bring out what he considered to be its latent absurdity. His account provides the terms for Empson's final stanza:

> We can see that, the constant in the law of gravitation being fixed, there may be some upper limit to the amount of matter possible; as more and more matter is added in the distant parts, space curves round and ultimately closes; . . . The more matter there is, the more space is created to contain it, and if there were no matter the world would shrink to a point.[56]

Finding this prospect 'rather bewildering', Eddington noted that it was nevertheless 'welcomed by those philosophers who follow the lead of Mach'.[57] This mistrust of the Machian view and of associated cosmological models is what Empson seized upon for his allegory in 'Letter IV', using his unhappy love affair to tease Professor Eddington in a way that was made more explicit in 'Doctrinal Point'. In his poem Empson has the fixed stars 'shutter and enclose | A rounded universe' (the poem's fixed stars are 'no further' because this universe is finite). Yet there is a turn back towards the astronomer's idealism in the 'creature' that can count the rows of stars, a line that recalls the closing paragraph of *Space, Time and Gravitation*: 'We have found a strange foot-print on the shores of the unknown. We have devised profound theories, one after another, to account for its origin. At last, we have succeeded in reconstructing the creature that made the foot-print. And Lo! it is our own.'[58] Caught between philosophical outlooks, 'Letter IV' is content with neither mind nor matter as the dominant trope in its analogizing of intimacy.

This restlessness informs the poem's concluding message about distance between lovers, yielding an ambiguity which Empson intensified as he revised

[55] Eddington, *Space, Time and Gravitation*, 156.
[56] Ibid. 163–4. [57] Ibid. 163. [58] Ibid. 201.

the ending. Contrasted to the sun which alone casts life-giving light upon its satellite planet, 'They' evokes the distant stars which shape the affair by virtue of their great distance and number (they are 'strong'). Yet the third-person plural may also refer to the binary couple, able to make the world revolve around them only by remaining impossibly aloof and strong in the face of the rest of society. The poem's moral points to the former reading but there is perhaps a nostalgia here for the separate planet of Donne and his lady, however lonely their separation might ultimately prove. The earlier version had proposed a more straightforward arrangement:

> And as your sun, by yielding beauty, glows
> And moves upon the planet, they, as strong,
> Resound, by being held aloof, their song,
> Compose earth's nature, are his laws, consist his throng.
>
> (*CP* 276)

In revising this ending Empson produced less mechanical lines that exploit the persuasive strength of the stanza form, running over line endings to attain their rhymes. The revised lines are driven by a heightened ambiguity, blurring the moral distinction between warming rays of traditional, unworkable amorous devotion and the equally problematic cool detachment of the ultra-civilized modern lover.[59] The ambivalence is already present in the poem's turning-point.

While a simple biographical reading in terms of the poet's affection for Desmond Lee does not fit the poem's argument (an argument persuading the beloved to depart from monogamy is hardly necessary in a case of unrequited love), its wranglings are not entirely removed from the poet's own romantic situation during his time at Cambridge. Empson's note about 'sun (-woman)' suggests a female lover and a process of maturation in the young male who moves from adolescent, self-centred fantasies to find himself in orbit around her 'true centre'—a roving satellite, whose wanderings are grounded by her presence and whose relationship with her only works because he is free to interact with others. Empson would surely have thought such a reading in

[59] The relationship between 'Civilised refinement cutting one off from other people and the scientific discovery making the world strange, was explored by Empson in 'Earth Has Shrunk in the Wash'; see *CP* 235 and Muriel Bradbrook, 'Sir William Empson (1906–1984)', *The Collected Papers of Muriel Bradbrook*, iv. *Shakespeare in his Context: The Constellated Globe* (Hemel Hempstead: Harvester Wheatsheaf, 1989), 191.

bad taste, and while the poem is not finally committed to that proposal, its presence may have contributed to his lack of enthusiasm for performing or publishing 'Letter IV'. Empson's gendering of the poem in this note, in contrast to the use of distinctly un-gendered pronouns throughout the Letter poems, does suggest a deployment of the cosmological analogy to register a transition from homosexual/homosocial affections to a universe which includes women as sexual partners and friends. The two forms of affection are not mutually exclusive but young men have to work at finding ways to have them both without disaster. Empson was interested in trying out such arrangements, or at least in fantasizing about them, during his Cambridge years—even before he had arrived at the point of simultaneous affection for Desmond Lee and Elizabeth Wiskemann. His literary experimentation beyond conventional monogamy in 'Letter IV' may owe as much to his reading of Joyce as to the example of Donne.[60]

The cold emptiness of space is pertinent here. In 'Donne the space man' Empson imagined Donne, at the time he took Anglican Orders, 'thankful to get back from the interplanetary spaces, which are inherently lonely and ill-provided'; revising his own youthful reading of the 'Valediction: of weeping' Empson stressed the 'great . . . isolation of these starry habitations' which leaves the lovers 'pathetically vulnerable' (*ERL1* 84, 107). Arguing, years later, for the triangle proposal in *Ulysses*, Empson found Joyce attempting to work a more 'progressive' relationship through Bloom and Stephen:

> Budgen reported Joyce as saying they become like stars, eternal and remote, and plainly that is the effect: but does it imply that Stephen will not return? Stars usually drift apart, but sometimes collide, causing turmoil; and for the author to turn on a chill by technique does not even pretend to alter the characters. The process of bargaining is often felt as a chill. (*UB* 226)

Caught between the chill of bargaining beyond conventional monogamy and the cold loneliness of traditional romance, 'Letter IV' stands, in its apparent failure, as a futurological demand for some further alternative. But what kind of knowledge has the poem produced in arriving at this point?

Analogizing sexuality through contemporary cosmology, Empson's metaphysical love poems explore the drawbacks of different forms of intimacy:

[60] Haffenden proposes the connection between Empson's undergraduate interest in multiple affections and his reading of *Ulysses* (*WE1* 117).

the coldness, the isolation, and in extreme cases (such as the gravitational collapse in 'Letter I') complete loss of any basis for communication. As such they use science to generalize and dramatize personal experience. But what, if anything, does sexuality do for science in these poems? By inhabiting different cosmological features Empson's lovers have a tendency to locate epistemological pressure points, intensifying the contribution made by beliefs about what science is for and how it may or may not operate. Attempting to do with Einstein what he saw John Donne doing with Copernicus, Empson's poems discovered greater extremes of isolation for lovers in space as a result of the new theory's greater generalization and removal from human scales of experience. In direct tension with the warming up of the new physics in popular exposition at the time, the failure of 'Letter IV' may be read as an opening of speculation about the possibility of a scientific epistemology that really does engage with affective life. Introducing his Empson lectures of 2003, Michael Wood suggested that hesitation with regard to knowledge in literature may be better described not as 'indecision or undecidability but patience'.[61] In this essay I have tried to show that the hesitations of 'Letter IV' are bound up not only with Cambridge contexts of knowing (and with their loss) but also with Empson's own peculiar version of modernist futurology, of the demand for new worlds or for new ways of living in this one.

[61] Michael Wood, *Literature and the Taste of Knowledge* (Cambridge: Cambridge University Press, 2005), 12.

13

Empson's Pregnancy

Susan J. Wolfson

'I am going on steadily with Intraverbal Structure but keep running into puzzles, in fact I am only inventing the theory after tidying up the literary evidence for it, so I don't know how long I shall still take,' confessed William Empson to his Cambridge friend Ian Parsons (*SL* 153). In the book gestating, *The Structure of Complex Words*, he kept faith with the genetic priority of literary evidence: 'I find it hard to choose between theories at all in this field,' he admitted (or boasted), 'except by coming across examples in which one theory works better than another' (*SCW* 368). For Empson, literary evidence is the proof of theory, not the other way around. 'Pregnancy', a chapter-title in *Structure of Complex Words*, concerns one model for how words play across structures, setting various possibilities vibrating as the syntax labors to deliver:

> as we listen to a sentence, we often cannot fix the required shade of meaning on the words near the beginning till we have heard the end; we are regularly exercised in the partial process, therefore, even when the final meaning appears single and definite, and this is why the alternative meanings are often less fully cut out at the end than we think. (*SCW* 325)

No less interesting than this analysis is the spectacle of Empson's writing at work, and I'd venture to suggest that in his generous exercise of this consensual 'we', Empson insinuated his own initials, WE, as midwife in the delivery of meanings from pregnancy. Listening to Empson's sentence, I wondered how much 'Empson' himself might be read into such an exercise, more particularly, read by arresting the gender term, pregnancy, he summons for this production of meaning. Empson was working this out in 1951, a few decades before the critical profession would scrutinize gender tropes, and Empson himself was no gender theorist. Even so, with an interest in refining words in social and historical contexts, the question comes into play for Empson; and because Empson is the player, the effects are vibrant, and ultimately self-reflexive.

This vibration usually happens within a structure that Empson has marked for other business. In the midst of an argument about ambiguity or complexity, he will bump into a bit of gender that wasn't on his agenda, but which petitions for and is granted a hearing. Take his discussion of Keats's *Ode on Melancholy* (chapter 7 of *Seven Types of Ambiguity*). As if in meta-summation, this chapter addresses the 'most ambiguous' type of ambiguity, 'when the two meanings of the word, the two values of the ambiguity, are the two opposite meanings defined by the context, so that the total effect is to show a fundamental division in the writer's mind' (*STA* 225). *Ode on Melancholy* is no cool mapping of division, but a structure of words that 'pounds together the sensations of joy and sorrow till they combine into sexuality' (249). This is adolescent male sexuality, and the ode itself issues from a male perspective: 'a parody, by contradiction, of the wise advice of uncles'—here, an education on the pleasure-in-pain principle. Amidst his admitted 'pleasure' in voicing the extravagant lesson, Empson is caught by an ambiguity: the sly shift of *She* from female beauty as a rich object of male gazing into an aesthetic dominatrix of the male poetics of melancholy. This double-play occurs in the relay from stanza two to stanza three. Stanza two was advising policy 'when the melancholy fit shall fall':

Then glut thy sorrow on a morning rose,
  Or on the rainbow of the salt sand-wave,
    Or on the wealth of globed peonies;
Or if thy mistress some rich anger shows,
  Emprison her soft hand, and let her rave,
    And feed deep, deep upon her peerless eyes.

3

She dwells with Beauty—Beauty that must die;
  And Joy, whose hand is ever at his lips
Bidding adieu; and aching Pleasure nigh,
  Turning to poison while the bee-mouth sips:
Ay, in the very temple of Delight
  Veil'd Melancholy has her sovran shrine

Empson is interested in the transformation of She in the melancholy fit: '*She* is at first *thy mistress*'; then with the turn, 'She dwells with Beauty' she 'becomes *Veiled Melancholy* itself' (251). Keats's structure of words doesn't just report this turn; its grammar embodies it. How apt that Empson recalls this as 'Ode *to* Melancholy' (239, 249)—a petition-preposition more anxiously laden than the coolly ironized thesis implied by Keats's on.

What isn't ambiguous to Empson is the gender strife in Keats's aesthetic syntax. It is the structure that sustains everything else. Stanza two ends with advice to the young man to imprison his mistress's hand, even as the poet's hand writes languorously about the richness of her anger. Then She prevails, not even as a recovered mistress, but as the 'sovran' deity of his aesthetic initiation: 'His soul shall taste the sadness of her might | And be among her cloudy trophies hung', is how Keats terminates his structure of words. About this sentence, no longer avuncular advice but a stern invoice, Empson remarks: 'in the swoon of this achievement, he has lost life, independence, and even distinction from her' (252). Swooned Keats himself to Fanny Brawne: 'I should be affraid to separate myself far from you'; 'I have no limit now to my love'; 'I could die for you'; 'You have ravish'd me away by a Power I cannot resist; and yet I could resist till I saw you.'[1]

Empson's marking of the gender structure in these complex words is so casual, however, so incidental, that it seems plainly assumed: '*She* has become *joy, melancholy,* and the beautiful but occasionally raving *mistress*; the grandeur of the [last] line is unquestioned because everybody takes this for granted' (252). That this everybody is male is also taken for granted. Empson's pedagogy often assumes this circuit, especially if the lesson involves a knowing wink about that fundamental opposite, 'woman'. Here is W. W. Robson, for one, on the wit of Empson's breezy paraphrases in *Milton's God:* 'We must all enjoy these; I particularly enjoyed the epitome of God's genial speech to Adam [*Paradise Lost*, 8. 399–411]: "What d'you want a woman for, hey? *I* don't want a woman" ' (*MG* 184).[2] These pronouns can be only male in this enjoyment.

But even as Empson assumes this male clubbiness, it is the character of his criticism to catch what is taken for granted. A little earlier on

[1] John Keats, *The Letters of John Keats*, ed. Hyder E. Rollins, 2 vols. (Cambridge: Harvard University Press, 1958), ii. 223–4.

[2] W. W. Robson, 'More Empson than Milton?', review of *Milton's God* (rev. edn.), *Oxford Review*, 1 (1966), in John Constable (ed.), *Critical Essays on William Empson* (Aldershot: Scolar Press, 1993), 431–40 (p. 436).

in chapter 7 of *Seven Types*, he had been considering how effects subversive to rhetorical intention can be issued 'by some disorder in the action of the negative; as by its being easily passed over or too much insisted upon' (239). His very first example is the *in medias res* launch of *Ode on Melancholy*, and here he admits the masculine specificity of Keats's aesthetic initiation:

Thus in the Keats *Ode to Melancholy*

No, no; go not to Lethe; neither twist[3]

tells you that somebody, or some force in the poet's mind, must have wanted to go to Lethe very much if it took four negatives in the first line to stop them. The desire to swoon back into pure sensation, abandonment of the difficulties of life, femininity (from the masculine point of view), or death from consumption is taken for granted in the reader. (239–40)

What 'is taken for granted in the reader' is the structure of a masculine point of view. Empson's reading of the rhetorical psychology is sharpened by a reflection on gender in no small part because gender difference has the same structure as the seventh type of ambiguity: 'two opposite meanings defined by the context' and related to 'a fundamental division'. Empson's transcription of 'Imprison' (Keats's spelling) as 'Emprison' may even register an unconscious embarrassment at reading the letters of his own name into the masculine poetics that he now concedes.[4] This is an Empsonian moment: 'He loves a misprint; it is intelligent and illuminating because it suggests buried meanings,' said Stanley Edgar Hyman of Empson's own acts of attention.[5]

[3] True to his argument for emerging meaning, Empson advises us that across this chapter, 'the whole poem is quoted gradually' (250 n. 6); he gives the whole stanza on 249–50.

[4] Vexed by Empson's breezy carelessness, Newell Ford triumphantly exposed 22 errata in Empson's quotations of *Ode on Melancholy,* sniping that even pedantry-averse New Critics 'must admit that meaning—and therefore ambiguities, ambivalences, ironies, their cardinal values—are distorted... when a mistress's soft hand is *imprisoned* rather than *emprisoned*', or 'when an "Ode *on* Melancholy" becomes an "Ode *to* Melancholy"', 'Empson and Ransom's Mutilations of Texts', in Constable (ed.), *Critical Essays*, 218–20 (pp. 219–20). It's tempting to think Empson's ghost was dictating editor Constable's unwitting distortion of the title of Ford's essay as 'Empson's... Mutilations of Tests' (220)—though erroneous, a fine perception of Empson's quarrel with such examinations.

[5] Stanley Edgar Hyman, 'William Empson and Categorical Criticism', in *The Armed Vision: A Study in the Methods of Modern Literary Criticism* (1948; rev. edn. New York: Vintage, 1955), 237–77 (p. 243).

Empson's willingness to see 'the masculine point of view' in 1930—well before there was a recognizable female presence in critical or academic establishment, and well before gender was in wide critical discussion—is a close-reading practice that, in Michael Wood's view, is not only 'meant to complement historical knowledge' but is a version of such knowledge, 'since the behaviour of words is an aspect of social life'.[6] Empson's candor about 'masculine' is continuous with the principles Terry Eagleton admired in him: the premise of language—even in its poetic compressions, shifts, and ellipses—as fundamentally 'ordinary', susceptible of rational paraphrase, 'a type of utterance in continuity with our usual ways of speaking and acting'.[7] Although I'd pause over Eagleton's tagging of this ethic as typically 'English' (i.e. 'not American') and as antithetical to New Criticism (as Eagleton reports it: simultaneously hieratic in technique and pandering to low desires for coherence and closed unity),[8] I am interested in his gender-marking of Empsonian ambiguities: 'points where the poem's language falters, trails off or gestures beyond itself, pregnantly suggestive.'

Eagleton's adverb gestures to that 'Pregnancy' chapter in *Complex Words*—the name for potentials related to, but not stated in, the obvious sense. Demonstrating his point with the word itself, Empson involves the familiar denotation of 'pregnancy', gestation, with two punning etymologies: one, from *preindre*, meaning to press into consciousness; the other, from *praegnus*, indicating conceptual generativity (inventive, suggestive, meaningful). The 'extra sense of the word is most naturally described as "the pregnant sense" even if it appears alone' (*SCW* 321). Yet in so far as pregnancy, in common sense, relates to a female body, it's a loaded purchase. To say 'most naturally', as Paul Fry has commented, is to naturalize an obviously unnatural vehicle in male rhetoric.[9] And yet not only does Empson not pause over this extravagant appropriation, he turns for explication to a decidedly masculine agon:

The stock example of a pregnant use in its full form is given by Hamlet when speaking about his father:

[6] Michael Wood, 'William Empson', in *The Cambridge History of Literary Criticism*, vii. *Modernism and the New Criticism*, ed. A. Walton Litz, Luke Menand, and Lawrence Rainey (Cambridge: Cambridge University Press, 2000), 219–34 (p. 219).

[7] Terry Eagleton, *Literary Theory: An Introduction* (Minneapolis: University of Minnesota Press, 1983), 52.

[8] Ibid.

[9] Paul H. Fry, *William Empson: Prophet Against Sacrifice* (London: Routledge, 1991), 50.

HOR.: *I saw him once; he was a goodly king.*
HAM.: *He was a man, take him for all in all,*
I shall not look upon his like again.

(*SCW* 321)

Hamlet's rejoinder, Empson proposes, appeals 'to some general background of ideas about what men ought to be', makes 'some reference to men in general', in order to narrow 'the pregnant use of *man*' to 'those truly manly, in this case to King Hamlet alone'. The 'business of a pregnant use' is 'to shift from an idea to an ideal': 'some virtue which most men do not have but *ought* to have' (321–3). This categorical *ought* issues from the unmarked gendered culture in which *man* is the measure, refined with implied negatives:

No doubt there could be an occasion when a woman or boy was suggested to do some important bit of work, and the reply was 'no it needs a man'. The virtues required on that occasion might now come forward to fill the gap. But it seems clear that a listener could follow this use of *man* without remembering any such occasion even in his subconscious mind. A good deal of sociology would be needed to fill out this gap which seems so obvious to everyone. I imagine it really depends on the custom of telling a boy to be a little man (indeed, to be like father, which would fit the Hamlet situation very closely); this is at once part of every man's background and so remote from any context he is likely to recall that the disposition to understand the pregnant use seems to exist on its own. (323)

What d'you want a woman for? This is a structural definition of man: man versus boy and woman ('passion's slave' is soon added (325)), those marginals in the power-grid of man's world and its lexical currents—part of every man's background.

There is a good deal of sociology to fill out this pregnant use and its customary (not natural) cultural syntax. Across this refinement of *man*, the trope of pregnancy has a way of reminding us how marginal women are in the system of values that organizes the world of *Hamlet*. What's a stock example for woman? 'The same trick', proposes Empson, 'can be used for depreciative pregnancy—"a very woman" is [such an] example', where the 'suasive' force of the statement is to say 'that this is how you had best regard a woman, even if the woman in view has not yet shown herself "typical"' (323). There may be seven types of ambiguity, but there seems to be only one type of woman—a unified text for the male *you* who is sorting out the pregnant senses (are these 'typifying', adding the normative to the specific use? or are these 'qualifying' subtractions or depreciations of the normative?). So little does an embodied woman (whether *a* or *the*) matter, that Empson is happy enough to dismiss a 'qualifying pregnancy' as 'not really a pregnancy at all' (329).

I mean no bill of indictment in reading the gender-text of Empson. What's winning about Empson is his capacity for self-reflection, or self-impregnating, so that questions begged manage to poke forward (as he puts it) for a rehearing, usually on another occasion. 'There is a strong idea of "manly" in *honest*, and an irony on that gives its opposite' (he says parenthetically in another chapter) about Iago's pregnant slurs on Cassio (*SCW* 222). This manly idea (with the oppositional irony) is pregnant in his reading of Hamlet's 'he was a man'—a typifying that has 'to exclude someone'. Empson means this someone to stand for lesser or collateral rivals, but that the other exclusion, woman, is on his mind, is clear when he is teasing a phrase of which H. G. Wells was rather fond, 'Man will reach out to the stars':

> It is true that in general *manly* and the pregnant *man* are 'virile'; whereas the pregnant *humanity* and *human*, not having sex to consider, are 'humane'; but it is not clear that any virtues are excluded from the man who reaches out to the stars. Indeed, women are probably meant too, though the word concentrates on the male . . . so as to leave them very much in the background. (*SCW* 327)

What is pregnant about this anatomy is that even though women are left in the background in the pregnancy of Wells's *Man*, they abide 'in' the back of Empson's thinking, and emerge in his reflection on his critical scheme.[10]

Empson as critic talked to women as well as men; among his interlocutors were the formidably strong minds of Rosemund Tuve, Muriel Bradbrook, and Helen Gardner, and he quite admired tough-minded women: 'it seems certain that women writers *don't* get good effects *only* by making themselves womanly', he advised an aspiring female poet in Japan, with praise for the aberrant sorority:

> Emily Bronte was as 'unwomanly' as George Sand though in a different way. Jane Austen accepted the limitations of her life as a basis for art, but she depended on a

[10] Michael Wood's shrewd observation of Empson's affection for 'a whole series of images for oblique or reclusive locations in the mind—"the back of your mind", "the back of his mind", "wandering about in your mind", "lying about in his mind"' ('William Empson', 220)- is nicely transferable to the serial texts of Empson's own critical mind.

strong 'catty' side that you could hardly call 'womanly'. I wouldn't worry about that if I were you.

If anything I should say your art was too womanly rather than not enough. (*SL* 76)

For all the calm certainty, it turns out that Empson himself worried the question, especially on that 'catty' side. Here's a teacherly moment, with that word in play, in *Milton's God.* Empson is explicating the type of slavish mind that God's Heaven breeds in loyal angels:

When I was a little boy, about eight I think, I read a story in my sister's *Girls' Own Paper* about a catty girl who accused another girl of tightlacing, whereas the truth was, the story explained, that all these girls, including the catty one, were ill and in pain because they had to tightlace. I crept away sweating with horror, but feeling I had learned an important truth about the way people behave. (*MG* 111)

The voyeuristic trespassing surprises Empson with a sweat-squeezing sympathy, felt on his pulses, with the constraints of female experience. True, Empson's subject is not female social constraint; it's self-abjecting power plays in a world of no exits. Yet the vehicle of explication does its work by putting a man into a girl's place. And it's a vehicle that Empson frequently rides. Eagleton is on this track when he remarks, in *Literary Theory,* that Empson's critical principles have a generosity toward the reader that 'solicits his or her active participation' in the production of meaning, or solicits a him capable of inhabiting a her. If the value of Empson's method is a devotion to 'the general contexts in which words are socially used' (Eagleton proposes), it is no special pleading to say general includes gender—a social sense of the factitiousness of making oneself womanly (or manly).[11] Eagleton's welcoming of feminist criticism for raising questions central to 'literature and other sorts of discourse' is in key, though it paradoxically treats feminist criticism as a project for female critics only.[12] Empson's sense of reading as an activity that brings to bear 'whole social contexts of discourse, tacit assumptions of sense-making which the text may challenge but with which it is also in continuity' proves the deep genetic logic on which his pregnant gender criticism delivers.[13]

The ethical kinship of Empsonian reading and gender criticism emerges more visibly when Empson takes examples from works that not only involve a good deal of sociology in meaning, but also stage this for critical scrutiny.

[11] Eagleton, *Literary Theory*, 52. [12] Ibid. 209. [13] Ibid. 52.

That brief notation of a masculine point of view in *Seven Types* comes just a few pages after a discussion of a linguistic complexity in Shakespeare fraught with the political structures of gender and sexuality. Empson has been busy teasing out the way a set of words, a single syntax, can convey 'two opposed impulses': 'towards control' and 'towards yielding, whether yielding to fear so as not to act or to suggestion so as to act' (*STA* 235). We can see how Melancholy aesthetics will come into play, but the immediate interest is an early scene in *Measure for Measure* that shows how 'complete opposites are a normal property of the language of faint and distant innuendo' (236). It is literally a pregnant moment. Claudio has been condemned for the unsubtle crime of fornication ('our mutual entertainment | With character too gross is writ on Juliet'),[14] and he wants his rhetorically talented sister to petition Angelo for mercy. On the very day that Isabella has decided to leave the pathology of Vienna for the pathology of the votarists of St Clare, imprisoned Claudio is banking on something like a sublimated sexual power in her chaste theatrical figure. He deputizes his friend Lucio to 'Acquaint her with the danger of my state; | Implore her, in my voice, that she make friends | To the strict deputy; bid herself assay him. | I have great hope in that; for' (here Empson picks up the text)

> in her youth
> There is a prone and speechlesse dialect
> Such as move men.
>
> (I. ii. 183–8)

Isabella moves Angelo to intentions that Claudio hadn't anticipated, and she recoils from the tyranny that demands her body in return for sparing her brother's body. Empson is more sensitive to the assault than, say, Hazlitt, who, using the reviewer plural that implies assent, declares 'we' are not 'greatly enamoured of Isabella's rigid chastity' (though he concedes 'she could not act otherwise than she did').[15] And he doesn't spare Claudio, in whom he hears the knowingness of a man who has just turned a woman's body into a public text. If Claudio convinces himself that Isabella won't be compromised, Empson reads against the grain, to find his words playing double. Here is Empson's

[14] William Shakespeare, *Measure for Measure*, ed. E. S. Nagarajan (New York: Signet, 1988), I. ii. 157–8.

[15] William Hazlitt, *Characters of Shakespear's Plays* (1817; London: Taylor and Hessey, 1818), 320.

pregnant sarcasm about that 'prone and speechlesse dialect'—'the stainless Isabel, being spoken of by her respectful brother':

> *Prone* means either 'inactive and lying flat' (in retirement or with a lover) or 'active,' 'tending to,' whether as *moving men*, by her subtlety or by her purity, or as moving in herself, for pleasure or to do good. *Speechlesse* will not give away whether she is shy or sly, and *dialect* has abandoned the effort to distinguish between them. [*Such as may move men*] makes its point calmly, with an air of knowing about such cases (*STA* 236)

Shakespeare's syntax lets meanings that seem opposite translate into each other. Refusing Hazlitt's consensual *we*, Empson confesses his own hesitation with a confessional *I*—an arresting figure here, because *Seven Types* tends to prefer a representative *we*). This shift to *I* is, in effect, a qualifying pregnancy in Empson's masculine clubbiness, and he continues the sentence above with a labor to set Claudio's policy initiative, desperate as its material circumstances may be, in the perspective of his own ethical discomfort:

> with an air of knowing about such cases, and indeed, I feel very indelicate in explaining Claudio's meaning. It is difficult to put the workings of the mind into a daylight which alters their proportions without an air either of accusation or of ribaldry; he is making no moral judgment of his sister's character, only thinking that as a weapon against Angelo she is well worth being given a try. (236–7)

The heightened indelicacy that Empson indicates, without exactly explaining, is a structure of gender that appears Empsonically: that 'disorder in the action of the negative'. Here, it is a reluctance to be seen indulging in accusation or ribaldry, but putting these suggestions in play anyway, the words are aired for his reader along a self-exculpating syntax of reluctance.

Empson returns to this situation in 1938 (an essay later set in *The Structure of Complex Words*) with a brilliant tracking of *sense* that faces the true issue of Claudio's pregnant surmise. The occasion is Angelo's first aside, as Isabella's entreaty for Claudio's life hits (inadvertently or with deft aim, it is not clear) a nerve in asking Angelo to ask his 'heart what it doth know | That's like my brother's fault' (II. ii. 137–8). The heart does know, so intimately, that its sense beats out both sensation and logic. Empson homes in on this aside:

> *She speaks and 'tis*
> *Such sense, that my Sense breeds with it, Fare you well.*
>
> (II. ii. 142–3)

Noting Pope's emendation of *breeds with it* to *bleeds with it*, Empson suggests that the reduction to 'pity only' shows only 'how obscure the Shakespearean structure of meaning in the word had become to the Augustans'. What interests him is how the tenor of *sensuality* (not lost on Lucio) shifts across this sentence, yet still compounds (rather than first one, then another): 'Angelo's first use of the word is "wise or reasonable meaning" and then the meaning "sensuality" ... pokes itself forward and is gratified by the second use of the word as pun' (*SCW* 274). Instead of settling *sense* in one direction, the pun catches the conflicts of life in a repressive regime. 'I am not sure that "sensuality" can be called the chief meaning of the word; the suggestion of *breeds* ("my Sense breeds with it") is rather that both the "meanings in his mind" and his "sense-data" have sensuality growing inside them.'

Empson's sensitivity to likely psychological conflict—to a generous-minded view of Shakespeare's characters not as rhetorical constructs, but as personalities that appeal to one's social experience—is what puts this reading, implicitly, into a critical text. 'In real life', he says (with cheerful unembarrassment about how some might theorize all three words),

> it seems rather unlikely that this pun would occur to Angelo. It occurred to Shakespeare ... but to Angelo the combination of meanings in the word can only appear as a hideous accident. The only touching side of Angelo is that he is genuinely astonished by his desires. (*SCW* 274)

The verbal action is the effect of social repression, so that 'the real irony' (the critical contradiction that this complex word focuses) is that Isabella's 'coldness, even her rationality, is what has excited' Angelo: 'the two things are patently connected as in the word, though not in his system of ideas' (274–5). Empson finds the unconscious, both individual and cultural, speaking through language, equivocating reason with repressed erotic intent: 'if you take his character as capable of struggle and development you need to suppose that his language carries the marks of it' (277).

Empson often finds a clarifying foil in his own capable struggle—or better, irritation—by another reader. This is different from the sympathy with the common reader that Eagleton admires; it's more like sparring. About the end of *Measure for Measure*, it is G. Wilson Knight's meliorative reading (in *The Wheel of Fire*, published in 1930, the same year as *Seven Types*) that hones Empson's edge. Knight's too 'highminded and warmhearted generosity' to the Duke—he represents 'a psychologically sound and enlightened ethic', says Knight[16] —provokes Empson to declare what he finds 'really offensive' about him: the way he 'treat[s] his subjects as puppets for the fun of making them twitch' (*SCW* 283). Where Knight sees a 'kindly father' performing an 'experiment' of 'ethical philosophy' on his 'children' with an aura of 'mysterious dignity', Empson sees a malicious, self-righteous manipulator.[17] That Empson's view is not a substitution for Knight's, but a critical complication of its operations, reflects the perverse operation of the play as a whole: of power corrupted not when it means to corrupt, but when it pursues best intentions—or a play that looks like a 'romantic comedy' but plays out by 'keeping the audience's teeth slightly but increasingly on edge' (*SCW* 284).[18]

Yet if Empson sharpens his teeth on Knight's Duke, he also has a Hazlitt-like distaste for Isabella—a lass not coldly chaste, just cold. He decides 'we' (now it's *we*) can forgive the Duke at least for deceiving her about Claudio's death 'because Isabella turns out not to care a rap about Claudio, and we wanted to know whether she would' (*SCW* 283–4)—a distaste similar to Knight's revulsion at 'Isabella's ice-cold sanctity'. 'Now we know our Isabel', Knight assures us with that sense of full possession that licenses judgement: 'Is her fall any less than Angelo's? Deeper, I think . . . Her sex inhibitions have been horribly shown . . . she has to find a new wisdom . . . the duke is watching her keenly, to see if she has learnt her lesson.'[19] Her reward for this lessoning (and lessening) is a command marriage to the Duke, from whom (Knight says in a fantasy beyond the ending) 'she will learn . . . wisdom, human tenderness, and love'.[20] Empson doesn't go off this deep end, but he does sentence Isabella to her silence at the play's end (after she has pleaded for mercy for Angelo): 'it seems hard to guess what she could have said that would greatly alter our impression of her' (285).

One thing she did do was preserve her chastity, or, in Renaissance-speak, her honesty. In the fascinating census Empson takes of *Honest* in another

[16] G. Wilson Knight, '*Measure for Measure* and the Gospels', in *The Wheel of Fire: Interpretations of Shakespearean Tragedy* (1930; New York: Meridan, 1957), 73–96 (p. 74). 'There is a pervading atmosphere of orthodoxy and ethical criticism, in which is centred the mysterious human insight and Christian ethic of the protagonist, the Duke of Vienna' (76).

[17] Ibid. 79, 82.

[18] In the back of Empson's mind is his same similar shiver ('setting a reader's teeth on edge') in *Milton's God* (John Milton, *Paradise Lost*, ed. Alastair Fowler (Harlow: Longman, 1971), III. 198–200; *MG* 120). *Paradise Lost* will be abbreviated to *PL* in the remainder of this chapter.

[19] Knight, '*Measure for Measure* and the Gospels', 92–3. [20] Ibid. 96.

chapter of *Complex Words* ('Honest Numbers'), of almost four dozen shades of meaning, 'women' get only one purchase: 'Of women: chaste.' A few other senses, moreover, are explicitly manned: 'having manly vigour'; 'likely to act for himself'; 'always recognisable as a gentleman'; 'a reliable member of our set' (204–5). *Honest* is set as a man's word, and operates in man's world. Even when it refers to female chastity, you could say that this is a man's word and world, too, woman's chief praise in his system. Isabella surely knows this; it is the context of her opposition to sexual harassment. If we allow this 'scheme' of *honest* to shade the final scene of *Measure for Measure,* Isabella's honesty—in the senses both of her ethical character and her uncertain fate in the Duke's erotic designs—is unreadable. In that notoriously edgy ending, she has no agency. Empson keeps his question about Isabella restricted to character, refraining from reading its formation by a regime no less prone to punish sexuality than to license the sexual manipulation of women by powerful men, putting them to tests and experiments in which whatever they do, they are not honest. Would it be fairer to say that Isabella takes the rap, rather than doesn't give one? Eagleton's admiration for Empson's 'profoundly sociable theory of language', of meanings 'inscribed in practical social life', of the involvement of the literary instance with 'terms which crystallize whole social grammars or practical logics of sense', saturates Empson's attention to *sense* in *Measure for Measure,* but without a measure of the gender grammar.[21]

But under another name, the taming not of Isabella, but of the Shrew, Empson revisits the question by reading the resistant, or unreadable woman in the structure of complex social worlds. This structure is, in effect, the word writ large, prone to competing logics of understanding and terms of value. In *The Taming of the Shrew,* the ambiguous site is Kate's final sermonizing of the wives: is this capitulation, or an ironic performance of capitulation, or an illusion of ironic freedom that gilds the chain? Empson finds a focus for these questions in the contradiction in the play's title. The tamer 'wants to marry a woman of spirit. Even so, if his method of training is to break her spirit, how can she continue to give this kind of satisfaction?' (*SSS* 28). In this local ideological conflict, Empson understands the social grammar of male tyranny and female resistance. His essay, 'The Strengths of the Shrew', becomes a kind of debate in his mind between the fun of taming and a disturbance about

[21] Terry Eagleton, 'The Critic as Clown', in *Against the Grain* (London: Verso, 1986), 149–65 (p. 153).

what it might mean as social prescription, social endorsement. 'She goes to church to marry Petruchio, willingly we must suppose', says Empson (28). Yet here, the consensus-building *we* reflects a certain unwillingness in having to suppose by prescription; nor is Empson any more confident about Petruchio's pride in 'how to tame a shrew' (v. i. 197): 'This boast to the audience is I think sincere and confident in the claim to be doing the shrew a kindness', says Empson (28); but his syntax is structured to invite his own audience to query the argument, and to indicate, by his own thinking, that he would be inclined to resist it.

It is not long before Empson is thinking about female resistance, transvaluing the structure of Isabella's supposed coldness or indifference to men who would use her body one way or another:

> The obedience owed by daughters to fathers was always short of the absolute at one point: a woman might refuse to marry—indeed, the reason why she says Yes in the Marriage Service is that even at the altar she is entitled to say No. She may not marry against her father's wishes, but she may choose to be an old maid, sometimes a nun. (29)

[S]ometimes a nun is the choice Isabella makes as the best course for an honest woman in her world. Substitute tyrannical deputy for insistent father, official chambers for institutional altar, and licensed rape for compelled Marriage Service, and the system of consent evaporates into *Measure for Measure*. And the subject of enquiry shifts, accordingly, from 'what's horrible about Isabella?' to 'what's horrible about Vienna?' That Empson has this syntax in mind in measuring the strengths of Shakespeare's Shrew is clear in his next sentence, when he comments that woman's choice to opt out of the heterosexual economy (he's thinking of the resistance movement in *Lysistrata*) 'has always been a basic weapon of Women's Rights, so that the demanding heroines of Jane Austen are more political than she would realize' (29). Whether or not Austen deserves credit here, what is certain is that Empson has made women's rights and writing the pivot of the essay.

From here on, he contests the male club that cheers Petruchio. His earlier hesitations of 'I think' and 'we must suppose' prove pregnant, seeming even to have been seeded for this emergence: 'He beats the priest at the wedding for dropping the prayer book . . . and is always beating his servants in her presence. A pretence is kept up that this is done to honour her, but with such transparent untruth' that one feels that the project is really terrorism, to coerce Kate 'out of fright' (30). An older argument is that this is all farce, and in farce convention bodies feel no pain. But in a play so sharply tuned to the politics of genre conventions (whose interests are served and whose aren't by accepted practices), it is not irrelevant to put Empsonic pressure on this line of excuse.

What Empson's pressure sorts out (as it had begun to do with the aesthetic pedagogy of Keats's School of Melancholy) is gender-differentiated reception: 'Thus the male part of the audience may decently rejoice, not at seeing a woman beaten down by the superior strength of a man, but at seeing the offensive strength familiar in their wives overwhelmed by a man who can nag back' (30). *[O]ffensive* has a nice Empsonic layering of gender reference—to the offense men may take; to the offense women may advance. With a shrewd historical sense, Empson reads gender strife on the theatrical stage where, he shows, it is not quite verisimilar, but rather disconcerting in sharpening its own political point:

> Indeed, come to think of it, a man rather than a boy would presumably take the part of the shrew; thus the joke is not so much that women are weak as that this character is unnaturally strong for the part of a woman. I grant that Katherina speaks of her weakness in her final sermon, but I think that this would raise a laugh. (31)

Kate has an effect on stage because she both is and is not woman. Having earlier tamed Kate as concept—'she is not a man-hater, like one type of masculine woman'—Empson finds himself a bit of a man-hater, at least of one type of masculine man, and is rather glad to see him put down by a woman who, underneath it all, is all man.

This hunch helps Empson negotiate that critical mare's nest: where to locate, or even by what measure to locate, the ironic structure of Kate's complex words in her sermon to the wives, not only on stage but beyond. He allows the sheer irony of her not believing a word of what she preaches; but his preference is to recall that seventh type of ambiguity, the one that occurs when 'the two values of the ambiguity, are the two opposite meanings defined by the context, so that the total effect is to show a fundamental division in the writer's mind' (*STA* 225)—or, in the generous productivity that Empson sees in ambiguity, a division in the social mind:

> The author and the audience may be expected to believe it all, and the great natural energy of the shrew will always give an appearance of believing what she says; but a

frank admission that she is just repeating her lesson, while she upbraids the other two wives, would seem a natural thing to admit into her tone and voice. (*SSS* 31)

Empson sees some social determinants in this natural thing: an Elizabethan attitude toward women that 'comes more naturally to us than the Victorian' (33), this transmission by force of two world wars creating emergencies in which 'ladies had to be let out of the drawing-room because there was so much they were needed to do'. Once they were doing it, a regime of taming and control seemed unnatural. The woman 'is bullied', proposes Empson, 'not because she is weak but because she is strong'.[22]

Which brings me, naturally, to Milton's God and his treatment of Milton's Eve. More than any other literary character about whom he wrote, Milton's Eve encouraged Empson to think through a woman's perspective on oppressive and dogmatic authority. He saw in Milton's Eve a proto-critical intelligence of a special kind. A major precursor in this critique is Wollstonecraft's *Vindication of the Rights of Woman* (1792), which is revelatory not only for its anticipations of Empson's argument but also for its differences. An oppositional reader of official creeds and a philosopher in the temper of dissident rationalism, Wollstonecraft is an agile critic of the continuity of literary texts with the social text.[23] Writing about the modeling of Eve, she is also writing about the claim of divine authority for that social creation called 'Woman'.

[22] A barometer of Empson's ambivalence about female strength, parodic female strength (a man in drag), and male control is the unsettling effect his paraphrase has on Paul Fry. In the unpublished essay on the play, Empson comments that 'Spenser, especially in Book V of the *Faerie Queene*, has much more theoretical belief that women ought to be under the control of men, but regards their strength as obvious' (*SSS* 33). In an essay published the next year (1962) in the *New Statesman*, the specter of the man-hating masculine woman appears as 'lesbian', and Empson ironizes the question of heterosexual strife in view of the male cast on Shakespeare's stage. To the extent that Kate recalls Britomart, Petruchio's policies have 'nothing to do with contempt for women'; they are a Spenserian perception of female strength: 'Spenser thought it urgent for men to keep women under control, because women are so like horses; this is not at all a bad view, but it is very unlike Shakespeare's feeling for women everywhere else' (*SSS* 36). To Fry, the simile seems a 'quite uncharacteristic bit of men's club talk' (*Prophet Against Sacrifice*, 50); but the context suggests that Empson is ironizing this tone even as he may indulge it.

[23] So Christopher Norris introduces Empson's critical temper, *William Empson and the Philosophy of Literary Criticism* (London: Athlone Press, 1978), 1. Empson's refusal 'to impose *a priori* notions of poetic structure which accommodate only a limited play of the reader's rational intelligence' is continuous with his respect for the reader's role in the production of meaning (46) within a 'human context of a rich and diverse experience' (54–5).

Eve has 'all the "submissive charms" ', she remarks, citing *Paradise Lost*, IV. 498, and leaning on both words: born to be submissive, potentiated only in seductive charm.[24] Tracing out the way Milton delineates Eve's innocence in a syntax of compliance, sexual attractiveness, and subordination to Adam, she reads his verses against the grain:

> For contemplation he and valor formed,
> For softness she and sweet attractive grace;
> He for God only, she for God in him.
>
> (IV. 297–9)

It matters mightily that this design of 'attractive graces' appears first in *Paradise Lost* in the attributes of Sin, who wins the affections of the rebel angels and enamors her father Satan thus (II. 760–5). In such syntax, grace recoils only as sin scarcely disguised. Would 'grace' be called 'sweet attractive' in male embodiment? This is a good case for Empson's receptivity to 'any verbal nuance, however slight, which gives room for alternative reactions to the same piece of language' (the opening paragraph of *Seven Types* (19)). Empson himself finds the openness of Milton's language to alternative actions no small part of what makes the formation of Eve a rather sinister joke on God's part: 'by supplying the temptress he is machining the Fall' (*MG* 184). Empson means to defend Adam; Wollstonecraft means to indict the supplier's ways to woman: 'Thus Milton describes our first frail mother.'[25] This *our* is pointed at everyone, taking a commonplace and using it to unsettle complacency. Empson puts this point bluntly, freer than Wollstonecraft was to impugn divine planning: one of the things 'absolute foreknowledge' knows is that 'he has created' mankind 'badly'. And this amounts to a botched formation for which woman will take the heat: 'The irritation of an artist against a bad piece of his own workmanship is a sympathetic thing, and would be one of the few decent feelings ever allowed to God by Milton, even though farcically unjust' (*MG* 175).

In refusing the divine wisdom in this arrangement, and contending for women's independent development of virtue through the trials of knowledge that always test men, Wollstonecraft in effect joins the devil's party, which she

[24] Mary Wollstonecraft, *Vindication of the Rights of Woman* (1792), in *The Vindications*, ed. D. L. Macdonald and Kathleen Sherf (Peterborough, Ontario: Broadview Press, 1997), 143.
[25] Ibid. 126.

reforms as the party of rational faith, with Milton's qualifications (ironically) found wanting:

> when he tells us that women are formed for softness and sweet attractive grace, I cannot comprehend his meaning, unless... he meant to deprive us of souls, and insinuate that we were beings only designed[,] by sweet attractive grace, and docile blind obedience, to gratify the senses of man when he can no longer soar on the wing of contemplation.
>
> How grossly do they insult us who thus advise us only to render ourselves gentle, domestic brutes![26]

To expose a formation for a partial interest that amounts to a gross insult Wollstonecraft uses *we* and *us* in no general sense. It is gender specific. 'Milton could not have brought a child into *Paradise Lost*, because one sensible remark would have destroyed the whole crazy piece of engineering', surmised Sir Walter Raleigh—a comment Empson really liked (*MG* 168). Empson likes a pastoral child such as Alice in Wonderland, to alienate and bewilder what is taken for granted. Such a child, as Eagleton remarks, is 'a type of the critic': incessantly questioning, an outsider who 'can see both more and less than the insiders', set in a 'social marginality [that] is the source at once of its blindness and insight'.[27] The stand-in for the child in *Paradise Lost*, proposes Empson, is 'Woman'.[28]

This is in fact how Wollstonecraft reads Milton's Woman, subjected to 'exactly the arguments that I have used to children; but I have added, your reason is now gaining strength' and preparing you 'to *think*'.[29] Wollstonecraft as thinking Woman shows how a being formed for subordination may be provoked into insubordinate, rational opposition. This is the force of her proto-Empsonian critique of the keyword *innocent*: 'Children, I grant, should be innocent; but when the epithet is applied to men, or women, it is but a civil term for weakness.'[30] Had she been writing *The Structure of Complex Words*, she would have put *innocent* through its paces, along with the sorority of faint praises, such as *delicate* and *obedient*. As for *delicate*, Empson's own glosses on its shades of *spoilt*, *sickly*, and *fastidious*—especially in their fall on a feminine structure (see his chapter, 'Statements in Words')—could have been hers: 'women ... act contrary to their real interest ... when they cherish

[26] Ibid. [27] Eagleton, 'Critic as Clown', 150.
[28] In *Some Versions of Pastoral*, Empson gave Dr Bentley the 'important role' of applying 'one touch of common sense' (126).

or affect weakness under the name of delicacy.'[31] If, as Geoffrey Hartman wrote of Empson, the power of *Seven Types* is to show 'how precious the unity of form was, or how rebellious language was',[32] both Wollstonecraft and Empson rupture the unity of form by teasing keywords into rebellion against automatic suggestions.

Wollstonecraft pushes past Empsonian ambiguity, which still respects a logic in contradictions of the seventh type. In *Paradise Lost*, this type takes shape as 'moral paradox', especially in the face of 'temptations . . . meant to be pitched staggeringly high' (*MG* 228). Wollstonecraft won't let the Woman question sit as paradox, but uncovers a contradiction that would have to wait almost two hundred years for professional feminist theorizing—or a little before, for Empson's sarcasm. Like Empson, she finds a division in Milton's mind that amounts to a foundational fissure in the structure of his high argument. Against the verse in Book IV that arrays Eve's subordination to Adam (634–8), Wollstonecraft calls up that passage that amuses Empson and Robson—Adam complaining of his loneliness in Paradise:

in the following lines Milton seems to coincide with me; when he makes Adam thus expostulate with his Maker.

'Hast thou not made me here thy substitute,
And these inferior far beneath me set?
Among *unequals* what society
Can sort, what harmony or true delight?
Which must be mutual, in proportion due
Giv'n and receiv'd; but in *disparity*
The one intense, the other still remiss
Cannot well suit with either, but soon prove
Tedious alike: of *fellowship* I speak
Such as I seek, fit to participate
All rational delight—'

(*PL* VIII. 381–92)[33]

Her italics on *unequals, disparity, fellowship* make the same point as Empson's proposal of a sinister trickster: wanting no unequal, Adam gets one, made

[29] Wollstonecraft, *Rights of Woman*, 128. [30] Ibid. 127. [31] Ibid. 160.

[32] Geoffrey H. Hartman, *Beyond Formalism: Literary Essays 1958–1970* (New Haven: Yale University Press, 1970), 365.

[33] Wollstonecraft, *Rights of Woman*, 128.

on a 'line of subordination in the mental powers'—as Wollstonecraft puts it.[34] This is not a marriage made in heaven: 'Only "absolute in loveliness", the portion of rationality granted to woman, is, indeed very scanty', she remarks; 'denying her genius and judgment, it is scarcely possible to divine what remains to characterize intellect' (referring to VIII. 547).[35] She parses this rueful oxymoron and its afterlife of faint praise: 'As a philosopher, I read with indignation the plausible epithets which men use to soften their insults; and, as a moralist, I ask what is meant by such heterogeneous associations, as fair defects, amiable weaknesses, & c.?'[36]

Throughout *Rights of Woman,* she hits the oxymoron 'fair defect' not just in the Empson-spirit of sounding a division of mind but with an aim at a damning contradiction in cultural inheritance. For women to 'submit to be a *fair defect* in creation' (Adam's post-lapsarian term for Eve's original state: *PL* X. 891–2) is to puzzle the subtlest efforts 'to justify the ways of Providence' to women.[37] The policy of 'cramping a woman's mind . . . in order to keep it fair' leaves woman as damned as Satan: 'would it not be a refinement on cruelty only to open her mind to make the darkness and misery of her fate *visible?*' asks Wollstonecraft.[38] No light, but rather darkness visible is what hell-flames show Satan (*PL* I. 63)—or any woman who, not realizing her cultural doom, might think of her mind as her salvation.[39] One legacy of the Fall, at least to minds prone to discern wickedness in female intellectual ambition, is an inability 'to distinguish innocence from imbecility'.

This last remark isn't Wollstonecraft's sarcasm. It's Empson's, biting on the Tillyard line that reads into Eve's anxiety and aspirations a fall before the Fall (*MG* 147–8). Empson comes at Wollstonecraft's protest against disparity from another angle, or rather angel. He is reading the sentence that produces her figure, 'fair defect | Of nature': Adam's lament that God didn't take the

[34] Wollstonecraft had already quoted Adam on equality in *Vindication of the Rights of Men* (1790), gendering *manly* as a term of republican liberty: 'Among unequals there can be no society;—giving a manly meaning to the term', in *The Vindications*, 92. For a subtle reading of the shapes and consequences of Milton's webs of contradiction, see Ronald Levao's essay, ' "Among Unequals What Society": *Paradise Lost* and the Forms of Intimacy', *Reading for form*, ed. Susan J. Wolfson and Marshall Brown (Seattle: University of Washington Press, 2006), 99–128 (esp. 117 and 26n).

[35] Wollstonecraft, *Rights of Woman*, 166. [36] Ibid. 144. [37] Ibid. 158. [38] Ibid. 211.

[39] See also her reference to this Satanic purview in *Mary*, ch. 19, as Mary describes her hopelessness, *Mary, A Fiction* (1788), ed. Gary Kelley (Oxford: Oxford University Press, 1976), 44, and in *Rights of Men,* to image the Protestant effect on Roman Catholicism: 'this faint dawn of liberty only made the subsiding darkness more visible' (41–2).

pattern of Heaven, 'peopled . . . | With spirits masculine', all 'angels without feminine' (*PL* X. 889–93). Where Wollstonecraft locates the seeds of cultural misogyny, Empson sees a counter-motion (entertained and displaced into Adam's petulance):

> As to the idea that Milton betrays homosexuality by letting angels love each other, which Robert Graves used as an accusation, and C. S. Lewis felt to need earnest rebuttal, I think that a sensitive man who took Milton's attitude to women, especially a classical scholar, would be bound to toy in fancy at least with the happiness of having an understanding partner who need not be continually snubbed. There is not much evidence that Milton felt so, but if he did it is to his credit. We know from the Divorce Pamphlets that he considered an understanding partner as the basic requirement for the ennobling of a physical act of love. (*MG* 106)

Also involved in Empson's surmise, I imagine, is the woman to whom he dedicated *Milton's God*, Hetta Empson (*MG* 6).

It is from a sense of this latent Milton that Empson develops a pregnant sympathy with Eve's perplexity. He starts out with some old saws about 'woman': 'I do not have to deny that she is confronted at the crisis with a variety of arguments, some of them less worthy than others. She is typically a woman in that her decision is intuitive' (*MG* 159). But then he catches himself, and satirizes the critical reflex:

> at least, Milton would have said so, because it was angels who were intuitive, meaning that their minds worked too fast to need the discursive reason . . . but Eve is intuitive in the modern sense that she lumps the arguments together and cannot afterwards pick out the one that decided her. Nowadays a critic is expected to pick it out, thus defining his position; but Milton would have said that she did not know, any more than all we critics do. (159)

Empson no sooner presents, and absents himself from, a figure of typical woman, than he finds himself in a qualifying type of ambiguity. If a critic proves *he* is not *she*, defined in the archetype of Eve, it is Milton's Eve, paradoxically, that gives the original form of critical intuition, 'what all we critics do'. Hence this typical critic:

> our judgment is often misled by our emotions, and there seems to be nothing in the feeling itself, at any rate before we give it attention (perhaps at the expense of something else which also needs attention) to show whether it is Emotive or Cognitive, whether we have adequate reasons for it in the background or not. This

is the basis in experience of the question, and it is then developed into philosophical or psychological issues about what an adequate reason would be, or about what an emotion is.

This is Empson in the opening paragraph of *The Structure of Complex Words* (*SCW* 1).

This humane critic might as well have been channeling Eve's psychology, as Milton represents it and Empson reads it out, shifting from that axiom about woman into generic critical complications. Eve hears the rules only from Adam, and is otherwise an outsider to male conversation. No wonder she falls for the first creature, besides Adam, who addresses her without condescension, and who does so, moreover, with Wollstonecrafty logic:

will God incense his ire
For such a petty trespass, and not praise
Rather your dauntless virtue, whom the pain
Of Death denounc't, whatever thing Death be,
Deterred not from achieving what might lead
To happier life, knowledge of Good and Evil?

(*PL* IX. 692–7)

As if this were another of those 'stages of advancing logical disorder' (the anatomy of *Seven Types of Ambiguity* (69)), Empson speaks as friend of the court, paraphrasing this 'argument of the serpent': 'That is, she feels the answer to this elaborate puzzle must be that God wants her to eat the apple, since what he is really testing is not her obedience but her courage, also whether her desire to get to Heaven is real enough to call all her courage out' (*MG* 159). God has written the type of text that always fascinates critical minds, 'a difficult puzzle about his intentions' (159–60). Eve is a student with an appetite not so much for apples as for puzzling applications.

She may not yet be the mother of 'the Intentional Fallacy': W. K. Wimsatt's argument 'that the design or intention of the author is neither available nor desirable as a standard for judging'.[40] But Empson (for all his oft expressed antipathy to 'the Wimsatt Law'[41]) sees Eve in the territory, and God's prohibition

[40] W. K. Wimsatt, *The Verbal Icon: Studies in the Meaning of Poetry* (Lexington, Ky.: University Kentucky Press, 1954), 3.

[41] The phrase from a late Valentine's day letter, 14 Feb. 1977, to Christopher Ricks (*SL* 685) shows Empson consistently taking exception to this theoretical and interpretive principle. In Empson's eyes (which had scanned *The Verbal Icon* by the time he was writing *Milton's God*), Wimsatt was one of those who preferred 'moral truth' to 'moral problems' (*MG* 261).

as a kind of poem 'detached from the author at birth' (to quote Wimsatt's play with a post-pregnancy trope) 'and go[ing] about the world beyond his power to intend about it or control it'.[42] Pregnancy of text, though fostered by silence and slow time, is born into the talk of its readers: 'The poem' (says Wimsatt) 'is embodied in language, the peculiar possession of the public . . . an object of public knowledge.'[43] This is very close to how Empson describes God's 'intentions' in Eve's apprehension: she 'recognizes them as a puzzle', and her puzzling mind embodies the original public possession of an object of knowledge. This is also Empson's text, put on the page for his public:

> *In plain then, what forbids he but to know,*
> *Forbids us good, forbids us to be wise?*
> *Such prohibitions bind not.*

This means that you ought not to obey a God if your conscience tells you that his orders are wrong; and that, if your God then sends you to Hell for disobeying him, you were still right to have obeyed your conscience (*MG* 160; *PL* IX. 758–60).

Empson continues this lesson with the humanity of his own professional devotions, to other readers and to the social obligations of teaching:

> As so often in human affairs, her problem is one of Inverse Probability. Thus a candidate in an Intelligence Test often has to think 'Which answer is the tester likely to have thought the intelligent one?', and this tends to make him [or *her*, obviously] irritated with the whole test. In this case, if God is good, that is, if he is the kind of teacher who wants to produce an independent-minded student, then he will love her for eating the apple . . . But if he didn't mean that, then he has behaved rather queerly, and it doesn't appear that he deserves to be obeyed. (*MG* 160)

Robson, though a fan of *Milton's God*, thought Empson just guessing, his 'kind heart prompting his ingenious head', he said in *Oxford Review*.[44] He wished a better argument: 'when Empson brings out the dignity and pathos of Eve', he proposes, 'we feel that he is admitting that Milton's feelings were crying out against his appalling theology.'[45] Whether by *admitting* Robson means *allowing*

[42] Wimsatt, *Verbal Icon*, 5. [43] Ibid. [44] Robson, 'More Empson than Milton?', 437.

[45] Ibid. 433. In *The Structure of Complex Words*, Empson writes of Milton: 'That his feelings were crying out against his appalling theology in favour of freedom, happiness and the pursuit of truth was I think not obvious to him, and it is this part of the dramatic complex which is thrust upon us' by key repetitions (104). Ricks, for one, prefers this formulation to the argument that Milton '*consciously* doubted that God was just', Christopher Ricks, 'The Ways of God', *New Statesman* (27 Aug. 1965), 292–3 (p. 293).

or *confessing* he doesn't say. The ambiguity enriches the courageous but patent fantasy of Empson's projection of a paradoxical God—the tester who wants to see his instructions courageously refused.[46]

Taking Robson to heart, Empson realized he had been so focused on refuting 'orthodox readers' with no interest in Eve's psychology except as the playground of a Satanic design, that he had neglected 'textual evidence'. I'm quoting these phrases from a letter to the editor of the *Oxford Review* in which Empson returns to the text, beginning with the proposal that Milton shows Eve with an independent desire (perhaps Satan-encouraged but not Satan-spawned) for knowledge. It is knowledge of a particular kind, '*ethical* knowledge', and what 'is clearly present in her mind' is the idea 'that a risk *ought* to be taken for so great a purpose'.[47] Empson takes up one of the verses mentioned by Robson as offering 'no support' for the argument, and reveals a profound support.[48] It is Milton's imagination of Eve addressing the forbidden tree (just prior to the 'conscience' versus 'obedience' reflection, above):

> Thy praise he also who forbids thy use
> Conceals not from us, naming thee the tree
> Of Knowledge, Knowledge both of Good and Evil;
> Forbids us then to taste, but his forbidding
> Commends thee more, while it infers the good
> By thee communicated, and our want.
>
> (*PL* IX. 750–5)

In *Milton's God*, Empson had welcomed Tillyard's efforts (in *Milton*, 1930—also the same year as *Seven Types*) to address the apparent condemnation of Eve's rebellion against irrational authority in relation to Milton's politics of rebellion: 'if Milton had been in the Garden of Eden, he would have eaten the apple at once and then written a pamphlet to prove that it was his duty to do so.' 'This has always seemed to me very profound', Empson cheered, and he was sorry that Tillyard repented of it in later years, in *Studies in Milton* (*MG* 172).

A woman assessing the cultural system that was firmly in place in 1792, whatever the French Revolution, Wollstonecraft articulated what she saw as outside Milton's understanding, and read Milton oppositionally. Empson sees

[46] Robson, 'More Empson than Milton?', 436 (referring to *MG* 163, 180).
[47] Empson, 'Correspondence: *Milton's God*', *Oxford Review*, 3 (1966), in Constable (ed.), *Critical Essays*, 441–3 (pp. 441–2); *SL* 417–19.
[48] Robson, 'More Empson than Milton?', 436.

opposition pregnant in Milton: *Paradise Lost* contains the counter-statement within the structure of its apparently single-minded theology, and so becomes a type of Ambiguity. If 'the central function of imaginative literature is to make you realize that other people act on moral convictions different from your own', then 'it makes an important difference to one's reading of Milton if he can be found good at such acts of imagination' (*MG* 261). So Empson responds to Robson with a reading lesson, defending Tillyard's original hunch by surmising how a rational God might view a woman's ambitions for moral self-improvement:

She does not say that God wants her to eat, I grant, . . . but Eve here explicitly means *ethical* knowledge, and there is considerable difficulty in maintaining that it is better not to know good from evil. The idea is a paradox, and Eve recognizes that, so definitely that it ends her speech because she decides to eat at once. . . . If she admittedly does not yet know good from evil, she cannot justly be blamed for any action, let alone one admittedly designed to teach her how to tell good from evil . . . I cannot guess what Robson takes her words to mean, or how he can assert that they refute my argument. Now that he has made me look at them again, I find it even harder to understand how Milton could have brought himself to argue that they put her in the wrong.[49]

Not only do Empson's reflexive second looks reinforce a critical sympathy for Eve's teasing out of ambiguity but so, too, does the large ethical structure of his defense: 'Empson is paying Milton the highest compliment he can', proposes Robson, 'when he tries to make Milton seem as clever as himself.'[50] Empson pays him an even more wicked compliment, I think, when he reads his conception of Eve into the company of clever and paradoxical readers—makes her, in effect, the original type, the Great Mother of Empson's way of reading.[51]

[49] Empson, 'Correspondence', 442–3; *SL* 419–20.

[50] Robson, 'More Empson than Milton?', 436.

[51] For calling this essay into being, I am grateful to Matthew Bevis and the lively conference he organized on Versions of Empson at the University of Sheffield in 2003. For stimulating attention to this essay, I am grateful to Ronald Levao, Christopher Ricks, Garrett Stewart, and Michael Wood. It first appeared, in somewhat different form, in *Literary Imagination* 2004, and I am grateful to the editor's kind permission to use the material here.

14

An Interview with William Empson

Christopher Norris and David B. Wilson
Introduced by David B. Wilson, with Annotations by John Haffenden

In the autumn of 1970 I was temporarily over from Finland. I had been commissioned by my publishers to produce a language course for Finnish schools based on authentic recordings of English teenagers. For this purpose I had been provided with a state-of-the-art portable tape recorder. It was also my intention, whilst in London, to collect material for a study of William Empson as a poet-critic. At that time I was rather pleased with myself as I had just had accepted for publication a piece on John Donne[1] which began, with Empsonian insouciance, 'Anyone who has read John Donne's "The Flea" in a French translation will have noticed . . . ' It went on to argue, quite wrong-headedly, that Donne's poem was a nexus of occluded French puns (*puce, pucelle, pucelage, dépuceler*, and the subjunctive *puisse*), clearly derived from the poems collected as *La Puce de Mme Desroches* (1583). I had originally entitled the article 'Donne the *Puce* Man', but for some reason the editor wouldn't allow this. I didn't go quite so far as to suggest that Donne had been secretly and bigamously married to Mme Desroches's beautiful daughter, Catherine, between whose breasts a flea had been seen rapturously *parquée*. But that was

[1] David B. Wilson, '"La Puce de Madame Desroches" and John Donne's "The Flea"', *Neuphilologische Mitteilungen*, 72 (1971), 297–301.

only because Empson had not yet shown the way with the example of his Marvell essays in *Using Biography*. (I later learned that my piece had been accepted for publication, not because of its Empsonian cleverness, but because it was thought to be the work of a certain elderly and respected Ronsard scholar who had to be humoured and happened to have the same name as myself.)

I thought that whilst I was in London Empson and I should have a meeting of minds. But how to effect it? One day, whilst trying to locate some early Empson book reviews in the stacks at the Senate House library, I found that I kept bumping into another young man who was obviously looking for the same material. We got talking. I told him what I was doing in London, and he (Christopher Norris) explained that he had just started work on a Ph.D. on Empson's literary criticism. Somewhat later we discussed the special issue of *the Review* (June 1963) which had been devoted to Empson's poetry and which contained an interview of Empson by Christopher Ricks. I suggested that, since I had the recording equipment, it might be worth approaching Empson to see if he would consent to give a similar interview to us, but one which (unlike Ricks's) would also consider his critical writings. Chris Norris had already met the great man and had obviously been approved of; he thought Empson might be amenable, so I sent off a polite letter.

Empson's reply was typically gruff: 'I realise that I ought to be grateful at having young men interested in my work, but really I am only interested in the work I am trying to do now.' But he agreed to see us some six weeks hence, which was the earliest his commitments permitted—'Better get it over.' Rather too much was drunk on the day that Empson handsomely entertained us at his Hampstead home, and memory can play strange tricks. Also, I was too worried about the coming interview to pay too much attention to things happening around me. But I do have one very clear memory. At some point early on Empson explained that the house had recently been refurbished and then, apropos of nothing, suddenly declared: 'I can honestly say that I have experienced sexual pleasure in every room, do you see?' I remember politely looking around me for signs of this, having interpreted Empson's 'do you see?' with a Finnish literalness. Pondering this *obiter dictum* later, I wondered if perhaps Empson had meant that the house had been redecorated *because of* his peripatetic pleasures. An ambiguity of the sixth type?

The day also had two memorable framing incidents. On arrival at the Empson house an urchin was waiting for us on the doorstep with the information that 'Bill's down the boozer.' In the pub Empson immediately inveigled us into playing shove-halfpenny, a game at which he displayed considerable dexterity and cunning, and played with childlike enthusiasm. After the interview, evening opening time having arrived, we again repaired to the pub. There I was severely scolded by Empson for giving half a crown to some carol singers collecting for Shelter, or one of the other charities for the homeless. 'Don't you realise what those people are?' he hissed at me with quite unexpected venom. I was miffed and told him that he sometimes carried his anti-Christian offensive too far, but he obviously thought I was beyond the pale and studiously ignored me for the rest of the evening. Clearly Empson looked at the world with different eyes from the rest of us: what I saw merely as a harmless group of carol singers collecting money for a good cause, he saw as a roving and predatory gang of torture-worshippers.

Of course, we met William Empson towards the end of his career when, to many, he appeared a Quixotic or (to use John Haffenden's inspired epithet) a 'pixilated' figure, tilting at neo-Christian windmills. It might be better to say that he had an excess of what Lorca called *duende* (a word of somewhat similar etymology to 'pixilated' in that it originally denoted an imp or goblin). I doubt if the English matador Henry Higgins [*sic*] had Empson in mind when, in 1972, he provided the following gloss, but it is remarkably apt: 'to have "*duende*" meant that one played, sang, lived, or fought bulls "with feeling". There was a sense of irony that surrounded those that had it. Their performance tended to be either wonderful or awful, and more often the latter. What was important was that these men and women seemed to represent the whole range of human experience and possibilities. People who had *duende* were splendidly imperfect.' Looking back, I realize that it was exceptionally kind of William Empson to agree to be interviewed by us, that it was clearly an ordeal for him, and one which I suspect he later regretted. He was a shy man who gave interviews very rarely, and he had an awful lot on his plate then. Apart from his heavy duties at Sheffield, which kept him there most of the time, he had a lot of ongoing writing and deadlines to meet. Also, 'Laura Riding is on my tail again.' And he mentioned in passing that he had recently had a long spell in hospital. Those who knew Empson well say that he sounded tired on the tape, though the sardonic and somewhat querulous patrician voice and the mischievous indiscretions and distortions are unmistakably there. I sent him a transcript of the interview for his emendations. He apologized for being too busy to look at it immediately and then there was a postal strike and nothing more was heard. Soon after that I returned to Finland, where 'it is this deep blankness is the real thing strange'. Writing textbooks took up too much time and my essay on Empson never got written. And the interview was largely forgotten until Haffenden advertised in the *TLS* for Empsoniana.

You said to Christopher Ricks that you might consider writing some more poems when you left Sheffield.[2]

Yes, I've always been saying that, but it becomes silly if you go on saying it. I have to get myself disentangled first. I think it's important to avoid getting out of harness with the inflation going on. I thought I was going to be able to sit back when I retired, but it's becoming very unlikely now. So a more brisk and externalized attitude to the world will have to be maintained as long as my health lasts. The old men are all trying to get into the entertainment business now, you know. It's rather different from writing poems, as a matter of fact.

On the whole, do you think your criticism a more important achievement?

Well, it's what I know I have on my plate. I don't have to decide that kind of thing you're asking.

When did you last write a poem?

Well, I'm trying to think. I wrote several in Peking under the communists, but I don't think I've printed any.[3] I decided they were all bad. They were getting too sort of tight, you know—too worked-up and so on. It was about then, I think, I decided I wouldn't try. I'd leave it till I was out of the wood more.

You haven't been writing any at Sheffield?

No, no. I've not even been trying or succeeding in preventing myself or anything of that kind. A long way away. But, as I say, I don't feel I'm cut off from it. I might hope to get back.

What do you think it was that made the poems become over-complicated?

[2] 'I hope that when I'm made to retire, I'll be able to start writing again' ('William Empson in conversation with Christopher Ricks', *the Review*, June 1963); in *CP* 115.

[3] The only poems known to have been written by Empson during his second period in Peking (1947–52) are 'The ages change, and they impose their rules' (*CP* 102) and 'Chinese Ballad' (103); also a longer work, 'The Wife is Praised' (*WE2* 666–71).

Oh no, when they're good I don't think they're over-complicated. I think they're complicated in the way that life really is. But if it becomes a habit it becomes dead, of course.

This opens into the question of exactly what you see as the role of conflict in poetry. In an early review of George Barker's poems you said that his idea of conflict, or the poem as the working out of a neurosis, a clinical object as you later called it, was a very doubtful view. Perhaps it relied on a concept of poetry as a very isolated art, assuming too readily that the public wouldn't lend a sympathetic ear. Whereas later you talk of your own poetry as being a poetry of conflict.[4]

Yes, certainly. Well, I did feel isolated, you see. I don't think that Chaucer felt like this at all. He regarded it very much as a novelist regards prose, anyway a successful novelist. But in recent years, poets have got to feel the possibilities of what you can do with language briefly are so great, and then if you're going to try to do this you become self-enclosed. It became a thing which people who were feeling isolated were using as their art. But this development is quite recent, isn't it? It's not a hundred years old—I mean this idea that poetry is used by people almost going mad to prevent themselves from going mad. But, even so, poetry written like that is still an externalizing process. I mean the man is trying to retain his sanity by writing something which is intelligible to his outside self, if nothing else. And he is still trying to externalize it when he is doing that. That's why there are some very good bad poems, of course.

How much were you influenced by Robert Graves? You've said that you were influenced by his kind of verbal analysis. But in his early books, for example *Poetic Unreason* and *On English Poetry*, he seems to anticipate some of your ideas—the conflict theory of poetry and also when he talks about poetry of the Jekyll and Hyde variety, which

[4] 'If sincerity in poetry is to write only when you must the thing becomes in a sense clinical, and once it has done its work of healing neurosis the poet will stop out of mere honesty. However hard to shake off in feeling this is clearly a misleading aesthetic even within its own limits; due partly to taking poetry too seriously and partly to feeling too sure it has no public' ('The Use of Poetry', *New Statesman and Nation*, 18 May 1935); repr. in *A* 413–14 (p. 414). Empson consistently referred to his own verses as seeking to follow the example of the metaphysical tradition of John Donne; in the draft of a BBC broadcast, *The Poems of William Empson* (15 Dec. 1952), he wrote: 'Some theories of poetry maintain that poetry ought first to state a conflict and then resolve it, but this kind of poetry seems to thrive on *un*-resolved and direct conflict, which is only resolved if at all by giving this sense of the strangeness of the world.'

seems to anticipate your seventh type of ambiguity, poetry where the latent content and the manifest content represent opposite sides of a conflict.[5]

Of course, everybody was talking about Freud and things like that. I might have got it from many other people who are now forgotten, as well as Graves. But I bet I had read more of Graves than I remember now, and I certainly was keen on this stuff and wanted to imitate it. But it didn't seem very out of the way. It was the idea that you wanted to use Freudian theory on literary criticism. This was the thing Graves picked up a generation before me. We all had it knocking about.

Are you prepared to endorse anything which has been written about you, either as a critic or as a poet?

I'm afraid I haven't read much of it. Anyway, I don't think it would matter what my opinion was. But no, nothing leaps to mind. People have often been very kind to me. I'm not meaning to say that I've been wronged. I've been extravagantly praised. I don't feel I need to worry about that.

Roger Sale wrote very well about *Some Versions of Pastoral* in the *Hudson Review*, but you wrote a letter back, rather a cross letter, I think.[6]

Well, it was merely particular points that I felt I had been misunderstood about. But often people think they're praising me when they say things that I was brought up to believe were very wrong. Like I remember Josh[7] saying to me when we'd been in the country—he's a sailor, you know, and sailors are always afraid of cows—and he said to me: 'You really aren't afraid of cows, are you? I've been watching.' Well, I was brought up to believe that the good man simply could not be afraid of cows. It was unthinkable, as they liked to say. And I gaped at him with astonishment: 'How could you suppose I would be in fear of cows?' And I feel this when

[5] Empson always acknowledged the influence upon *Seven Types of Ambiguity* (1930) of *A Survey of Modernist Poetry* (1927), by Laura Riding and Robert Graves; but he had also read at an early stage the two separate works by Robert Graves: *Poetic Unreason* (1925) and *On English Poetry* (1922). On Graves, see *WE1* 176–229.

[6] See Roger Sale, 'The Achievement of William Empson', *Hudson Review*, 19: 3 (Autumn 1966), 369–90. Empson's reply is in *Hudson Review*, 20: 4 (Winter 1967–8), 534–8.

[7] For 'Josh' (Michael Avery), familiar of Francis Bacon, John Minton, John Deakin, and William and Hetta Empson, see a fictionalized biography by Nigel Richardson, *Dog Days in Soho: One Man's Adventures in Fifties Bohemia* (London: Victor Gollancz, 2000). See also *WE2*, esp. 423–31.

I see people writing down what I meant in poems. I feel that again and again. How could you have supposed I was wrestling with a fear of cows? Still, mind you, I feel it's very sensible to be afraid of the sund'ring herds. As a matter of fact they can trample you into the mud perfectly well. But the way to handle cows is to refuse to let them know you're afraid of them. That much I know at any rate. I don't know if this seems off the point.

You've said that you are not very happy with your influence as a poet.

Oh, I think that's long over. I shouldn't think I've influenced a poet for twenty years, thank God for it.

How do you view your influence as a critic?

Well, it isn't my fault. I do think that this method is often used frightfully badly now, but it isn't my fault, I'm sure. I have got rid of that fear. For that matter it isn't the fault of Baudelaire or Mallarmé or Verlaine or any of them. They weren't doing a scandal-mongering cats' tea party, which is what it has been turned into—a process of doing what Leavis calls 'moral judgement'. I seem to read so much American literary criticism, and I do think that the Americans have carried this process further. Apart from a few devoted Leavisites the English critics are quite a varied body, aren't they? And not all in a tail in the way that I do think the American ones have been becoming. In Sheffield, you know, we get a lot of northerners and, especially the girls rather than the boys, they've been brought up to scold just as much whether it's a Roman Catholic school or a Methodist school. They say they'd have hanged the Ancient Mariner from the yard-arm with their own hands. There was a nice one about the civil war in which the knights of the Round Table are destroyed, and the girl wrote down: 'Well, of course, it's rather sad that they're all dead, but you do feel that justice has been done.' And I told them that they were very wicked, do you see? What they were taught at their wicked schools has made their opinion simply very wicked, and they glare at me and I glare at them. But a conflict between what they're taught at school and what they're taught at college is beginning to develop, I think. So, when I talk in this quarrelsome way about literary critics, I'm really meaning the school teachers at these girls' schools. But it also applies to a great many people writing in the American magazines. But it doesn't apply to most of the English colleagues that I actually meet. But there it is. Of course, I don't habitually meet Leavis and I suppose he does talk like that, most of the time. I think it's a very bad thing. Completely morally wrong, and also completely destructive of any taste for literature, do you see?

In fact, yours is a moral criticism, but people have criticized you for the semantic preoccupation, for being unconcerned with moral issues.[8]

That's right. I've been scolded for not being but, now that I've seen what other people are doing, I think I was moral all the time. When Leavis told me I wasn't moral, I thought I probably wasn't, but now I think I am.

So would you still endorse what you said in 'My Credo: The Verbal Analysis' a long time ago in the *Kenyon Review* that you merely wanted to explicate the machinery of poetry to give a basis for evaluative judgements?[9]

Oh no. I don't feel that now because I've had my nose rubbed in the immoral morals so much, do you see? I feel I ought to rebut immoral morals. But that is merely the result of being exposed to so much of them. I feel I ought to do something about it. But it isn't because my opinions have changed. It's like a kitten putting out its paw to interfere with the wool-winding. It's an impulse to join in the process.

In fact, you put a great stress on consciousness and moral self-awareness and also on character analysis, especially with Shakespeare and the Elizabethan dramatists.

Well, of course, yes. I don't see how you can help doing that.

[8] In a review of *The Structure of Complex Words*, C. W. M. Johnson summed up this adverse trend with the pronouncement: 'if Empson could bring himself to focus upon some larger critical issue and produce a book less narrowly concerned with pushing to extremes a minor obsession with semantics, he would do much to efface his reputation as an eccentric. Perhaps he likes that reputation, but in the best parts of *Complex Words* there is a rationality, a maturity of critical judgment, that ought to be given freer play' ('Complex Work', *Accent* (Autumn 1951), 236).

[9] 'There is room for a great deal of exposition, in which the business of the critic is simply to show how the machine is meant to work, and therefore to show all its working parts in turn. This is the kind of criticism I am interested in, and I think it is really often needed . . . Going back to the question of Valuation: I do not mean to say, what would be a very foolish thing to say, that criticism has nothing to do with valuation. It has to do with it all the time, because you cannot even say just how some element works without suggesting how well it works. But to assess the value of the poem as a whole is not the primary purpose of this kind of criticism, or at any rate ought only to emerge from the analysis as a whole' ('The Verbal Analysis', *Kenyon Review*, 12 (Autumn 1950); *A* 106).

How do you feel about all these negative laws the American critics have erected—the Intentional Fallacy and the Affective Fallacy?[10] It seems to be a point of responsibility in your criticism to talk about intentions and psychological effects on the reader.

Yes, indeed. I was very pleased going through some work of reference looking up something else to find that 'K' in W. K. Wimsatt stands for 'Kurtz'. And nobody called 'Kurtz' has ever understood an English poem. They've been trying to do it for two hundred years. So you needn't say there's a law of nature that Kurtz can't understand the intention of an English writer. I think it's a peculiarly absurd law. But, of course, you're on very treacherous ground when you say your own intuitions are right—they're often wrong, but they're all you've got to go on. You must try and correct them and develop them, but you must not simply indulge them. But to say that you aren't allowed to have any such thing is merely to destroy the whole subject altogether, I think.

You do often tend to react to prevailing schools of critics. Many of your best reviews grew out of a definite quarrel with a critic.

Yes, I think so. More than that, I think in all this theoretical stuff I was trying to do, it's only when I see where a theory is going wrong that I feel I understand the theory. Or, for that matter, if I see the theory is going right I feel that this is OK. You must see the theory in operation before you can feel anything about it. That is really the matter, I do think, with Chomsky and modern linguistics and all that. I agree with I. A. Richards that there is no point where it ever wants to be useful in the way we want a theory to be useful, do you see? And our much simpler and more homely kind of linguistics was always intended to be used for something. And the grand Chomsky stuff is not, I think. It, therefore, doesn't provide any help in avoiding the obvious faults of so much literary criticism. I'm talking all the time about academic criticism of older literature, you know. I'm afraid I'm just very backward on what goes on about recent literature.

You mentioned Richards. A lot has been said about Richards's influence on you. How do you view your influence on Richards, which

[10] See the essays by W. K. Wimsatt and Monroe C. Beardsley, 'The Intentional Fallacy' (1946) and 'The Affective Fallacy' (1949), in Wimsatt, *The Verbal Icon: Studies in the Meaning of Poetry* (Lexington, Ky.: University of Kentucky Press, 1954), 3–39.

comes out very strongly in some of his poems, for example 'The Screens'?[11]

I don't know about that, I'm afraid. He's a lot older, you know. He was my teacher. I don't think I've influenced him much really. The processes of the world no doubt have influenced him. I mean what has been happening in our subject would influence him, of course.

Was he interested in the principles of Basic English when he taught you?[12] Because it seems to me that your prose paraphrases, separating out different meanings of ambiguity, were rather similar to the paraphrases in the article on Wordsworth and Basic—separating off the meanings into simple statements.

You mean I wrote a thing in Basic English about Wordsworth?[13]

That's right.

Oh no, that was long after, do you see. That was done when I was trying to earn money in Boston after I'd been robbed in Chicago to pay to go back to England in 1939. It was just a piece of hack work, though I enjoyed doing it. Where did you read it?

It was a WRUL radio talk originally and printed in the *Kenyon Review*, I think. How long were you involved with Basic English? Are you still involved?

No, I'm no use about it. But I still think it's the right way to do the first years of English. But, of course, Richards has been spending years in altering the original thing at various points. I'm not quite sure what his position is now. But he's frightfully good at it. What you really need is some foreign government, some foreign Ministry of Education, to take it seriously. Until you get it being used on a large scale, you can't test out what the remoter consequences are. I do think that Ogden made a great mistake, and Churchill made a great mistake, by describing it as an international language. That only frightens people. It annoys the French and horrifies the English. If you say it's the right way to do

[11] See 'The Screens' (from *The Screens and Other Poems*, 1960), in I. A. Richards, *Internal Colloquies: Poems and Plays of I. A. Richards* (London: Routledge & Kegan Paul, 1972), 157–61.

[12] See Rodney Koeneke, *Empires of the Mind: I. A. Richards and Basic English in China, 1929–1979* (Stanford, Calif.: Stanford University Press, 2004).

[13] Empson undertook in the autumn of 1939 to write several radio scripts in Basic English for short-wave broadcast by Station WRUL in Boston, Mass.; these included 'Basic English and Wordsworth' (published in *Kenyon Review* (Autumn 1940)); reprinted in *A* 232–8.

the first years for a foreigner learning English, it really is very much better than bad teaching of English. But the rival schemes have absorbed so much of what Ogden had to tell them that, while shouting at the tops of their voices that they wouldn't touch it with a barge pole, they've stolen it. So, to a great extent, the battle has been won. But to have a consistent scheme, so that if you knew what a foreigner who knew a moderate amount of English knew—I mean, if there was an agreed wordlist of what everybody should learn first of English—it would be very much simpler. You would know what the other man knows, which, if you are at all conscientious of these matters, is completely baffling when talking to foreigners. Half the time they only know the hard words.[14]

Did you experiment with Basic English when you were teaching in China and Japan?

I don't know about experimenting. I tried to support it. I once lectured for an hour, writing in Basic English on the blackboard all the time. I call that being sufficiently sunk in being a Basic English man, don't you think?

I wonder if I could fill in some gaps in your life. What did you do between leaving Cambridge and going to Japan?

Well, there was hardly any time. Richards fixed it up almost at once. There wasn't a year, I don't think.

I gather you left Cambridge in 1929?

And went to Japan in '30, I think. It was very rapid. Oh yes, I had settled into Bloomsbury, it's quite true. I went to Spain with John Marks,[15] and then I had just settled into Bloomsbury. So I remember that I did go to Japan from

[14] On Basic English, a simplified form of the English language, with a rudimentary grammar and a vocabulary of only 850 words, devised by the polymath C. K. Ogden (1889–1957) and promoted by I. A. Richards, see *C. K. Ogden: A Collective Memoir*, ed. P. Sargent Florence and J. R. L. Anderson (London: Elek, 1977); the essays by Empson collected as 'I. A. Richards and Basic English', in *A* 193–238; and two further pieces by Empson, 'Basic and Communication' and 'Basic English and the Modern World', in *SSS* 161–75. 'The kiss of death was the support of Sir Winston Churchill,' Empson would recall years later. In a speech at Harvard University on 6 Sept. 1943, Churchill praised the Basic English method as 'a very carefully wrought plan for an international language'; and he went on to envision a chilling version of imperialism: 'The empires of the future are the empires of the mind' (quoted in 'A Joint Staff in Peace: Mr Churchill on Allied Unity', *The Times*, 7 Sept. 1943, 3; see Churchill, *His Complete Speeches, 1897–1963*, vii. *1943–1949*, ed. Robert Rhodes James (New York: Chelsea House Publishers, 1994), 6826). See also Empson's later comment in 'The Hammer's Ring' (1973), in *A* 223.

[15] J. H. E. P. Marks (1909–67) was a fervent hispanophile. He went to Spain with Empson in the summer of 1929. After graduating from Magdalene College, where he had edited *Granta*, Marks

Bloomsbury. And I do remember telephoning Carter Paterson [a removals firm] and saying: 'Everything you find on the floor, would you pack and send off to me.' This was all the packing I did and it turned up perfectly all right. Nobody could pack like that now. Isn't that splendid to be able to do that? Of course, it was just one packing case with a lot of books really. But I didn't realize how hard packing would seem on every later occasion. So I remember that I did go to Japan from Bloomsbury. But you see the broad answer is: my father had left me two hundred a year and this seemed to me perfectly sufficient. I didn't, as I do now, regard myself as in difficulties unless I've been earning money. I didn't feel I needed to earn anything at all. I was learning to write books, talking to my friends. And coming back from Japan it never crossed my mind that I needed employment. I needed to get some books out. The two hundred a year then was quite enough. And now, of course, it's nothing.

Did you spend this year working on *Seven Types*?

Most of the book was written after leaving Cambridge. It had to be worked on very hard. I remember now, I did do a lot of typing in Marchmont Street.

The myth is that the book was written very quickly—within six weeks.

Nonsense. It took a great deal of writing.

What happened between coming back from Japan and going to China? Were you working on *Some Versions* then? This would be 1934.

I'd done nearly all of it in Japan, but I finished it up back in Marchmont Street. I remember having a great struggle boiling it down, getting it sufficiently short to be tolerable to read. That I considered very hard.

You were involved in Mass Observation in the middle thirties.

I really forget when that fitted in. But, you see, from late '34 to '37—only three years in London—I really don't know what I was doing. I was busy and contented.

I suppose Mass Observation might tie in with certain of the interests of *Some Versions*?

spent some time in Spain. After initial wartime work at the Ministry of Information, he was seconded to the BBC where he made broadcasts to Spain. He served for ten years from 1943 as correspondent of *The Times* in Madrid.

Yes, but really I didn't do very much of that. I went once to Bolton and very entertaining and fascinating it was, but hardly more than a weekend. I can't pretend to have been at all deep in it.[16]

Did you know George Orwell very well?

He was Indian editor at the BBC when I was Chinese editor. We saw a lot of each other there. I admired him very much. I think very highly of him. But I don't think we influenced each other a bit.[17]

When did you first meet Eliot?

He came to Cambridge when I was an undergraduate and did the something lectures.[18] He was willing to be spoken to every Friday over coffee at eleven in the morning or something like that, and I went to several of those. I rather think that was the first time I saw him. He had kind of offered to sacrifice himself by talking to students, and I took advantage of this. And then I saw him occasionally in London. He was very public-spirited in a way. There was the poetry society of Harold Monro.[19] He would turn up once a week. And they had an upstairs room at a pub and a kind of discussion went on—very like what George Fraser did after the war in London, I should say.[20] I used to go

[16] On Empson's limited but lively involvement with Mass Observation, see *WE1* 422–9 and *May the Twelfth: Mass-Observation Day-Survey*, ed. Humphrey Jennings and Charles Madge (London: Faber & Faber, 1937).

[17] See Empson, 'Orwell at the BBC' (1971) in *A* 495–501; and John Morris, 'That Curiously Crucified Expression' (originally 'Some Are More Equal Than Others', 1950), in Audrey Coppard and Bernard Crick (eds.), *Orwell Remembered* (London: British Broadcasting Corporation, 1984).

[18] T. S. Eliot delivered the Clark Lectures at Trinity College, Cambridge, in 1926: see *The Varieties of Metaphysical Poetry*, ed. Ronald Schuchard (London: Faber & Faber, 1993). See also Empson's entertaining memoir, 'The Style of the Master' (1948), in *A* 361–3. Empson was reintroduced to Eliot in a letter from I. A. Richards in Sept. 1926: see *Selected Letters of I. A. Richards*, ed. John Constable (Oxford: Clarendon Press, 1990), 52–3. It was in consequence of Richards's tip-offs that Eliot wrote to Julian Bell on 2 Jan. 1930 that he was keeping an eye on Empson, Jacob Bronowski, and T. H. White (Julian Bell Papers 2/15, Modern Archive Centre, King's College, Cambridge).

[19] Harold Monro ran the Poetry Bookshop from 38 Great Russell Street (opposite the British Museum). Empson wrote of Monro in a Japanese periodical: 'He stood for the old Bohemian tradition, still strong, they say, in the nineties, by which all sorts of literary people would meet each other as a matter of course . . . he had the good humour, and power of enjoyment, and power of scorn, which can keep such a thing going . . . He carried with him in his last years an air of rich emotional life, which he had enough range of talk to sustain in all companies' ('Harold Monro', *The Rising Generation*, 67 (1 June 1932), 151).

[20] George Fraser (1915–80), poet and critic; after the war, he was British cultural adviser in Tokyo, in succession to Edmund Blunden. For some years he lived in London as a freelance writer, earning his living as a reviewer for the *TLS* and other periodicals—and (as Empson indicates)

and listen to the great man, but it doesn't mean that we were on close terms. I listened to him with great curiosity, of course. A wonderful chap.

Some of the later remarks that Eliot let drop, some of the uncollected comments, showed a complete change of heart in him. Can you remember any?

Yes, I wish somebody would collect them. I do remember his voice so clearly. Somebody was asking him about some scolding of other critics he had been doing in earlier years and he said: 'I was very sick in soul when I wrote that passage. I now think it wholly wrong, probably harmful. I wish that I had time to clear up many mistakes I made in my prose, but I suppose I never will now.' And there the matter dropped, but I thought it was very majestic. No doubt it was literally true when he said he couldn't bear to read his own prose. He found it too disagreeable. Most of it he wrote in a very polemical frame of mind—intended for a particular situation which was clear in his mind. He was always very much conscious of the immediate purpose of a piece of writing, and when that was dead it was merely disagreeable to think of it again. And so he actually never did read it over. When he was confronted with a question about it he sometimes answered like this.

Was there any question of him modifying his Christian views towards the end of his life?

Oh no, I don't think so. He thought he was being more Christian. He thought he was becoming charitable at last and that earlier, when he thought that he was being very Christian, he was merely actuated by the purposes of the Devil, which he was always skilful in finding out. But he certainly considered that his loathing of sex—I feel that's wrongly phrased—but this queer way he had been accustomed to talk about sex—he now entirely abandoned. He was now converted to married love and anything he had said before had been written when he was very sick in soul.[21]

cultivating emerging writers—before taking up an academic appointment at Leicester University, 1958–79, where he ultimately became Reader. Empson and Fraser were to become good friends after the end of the war.

[21] Empson was to recall of Eliot, in a review of *The Waste Land: A Facsimile and Transcript of the Original Drafts*, ed. Valerie Eliot (1971): 'I was much impressed by the chalk-white face with the swollen purple lips, and felt confident that he had been brooding over the Crucifixion all night, or some other holy terror. But I never spoke to him about his religion, and might be asked now whether I have any evidence for this interpretation of his appearance. Well, it all seemed consistent. Literary

Were your Cambridge poems much influenced by his quatrain poetry? The Sweeney poems and 'Whispers of Immortality', which you discussed in *Seven Types*—the witty ironies, the juxtaposition of ideas?

I never have understood about influences. We all admired him and quoted him and so on, of course.

Do you feel yourself as being, in a sense, in the same critical tradition—a poet-critic working from your creative interests to your critical preoccupations? Johnson, Coleridge, Eliot—do you see any continuous line there?

Well, it isn't the kind of thing I'd think about, you know. I should have thought most good critics have been poets too and have had a consistent kind of interest which comes out in both. It doesn't seem to me surprising. You wouldn't need to be in a line, would you?

You'd agree with Eliot then in saying that the critic who doesn't write poetry is probably channelling the wrong interests into his criticism—a kind of suppressed creative wish? I suppose it might be said of Leavis perhaps—his emotion and enthusiasms are rather getting the better of his critical judgement—well, with Lawrence at least. You might feel Leavis was living vicariously through Lawrence, through the moral interests he discovers.

I don't know. I don't think you feel that Leavis wished he had written poems somehow, do you? I think it's very hard to tell about that. But I think Leavis often simply didn't understand what the modern poets—I mean my generation—were up to. But that's a rather different thing. I don't think if he'd written poems he'd have understood it any better. So I don't think one can make much of that.

It's almost a critical truism that Empson's poetry is a working out of Empson's critical principles. How do you react when you see this? Do you feel it's being very unfair to your poetry?

I was irritated when a very worthy man who writes all those detective stories—J. I. M. Stewart—said that Empson was like T. E. Hulme, who had

gatherings talk a good deal about the sexual lives of other writers, and Eliot always welcomed any report of a crackup in these affairs, as a mercy in disguise; I thought at first it was a kind of joke, but it came out firmly and steadily. "The greater torment | Of love satisfied" was a quite practical doctrine to him' ('My God, man, there's bears on it', *Essays in Criticism*, 22: 4 (Oct. 1972), repr. in *UB* 199).

written a few poems just to show that he could, to illustrate his line of talk, and after that gave it over.[22] This, I thought, was a typical Oxford common room crack. I thought it quite wrong. But that is the only point when I have to confess it got under my skin slightly.

Were you inspired to write *Seven Types of Ambiguity*, a very close analysis and rigorous type of criticism, by people like Hulme who adopted a very unintellectual approach?

I didn't think it very illuminating what he says about poetry—all about fitting the curve exactly. It's a draughtsman's point of view, isn't it? I'd never have fitted the curve exactly out of those horrible things you buy in sets. The kind of mathematical curve I was dealing with would never fit any of those sets at all. I never quite understood what experience Hulme was writing from in this description of how you can be perfectly accurate in poetry by pushing round the piece of plastic till the curve was just right.

You rebuked the critics for criticizing your own poems in linguistic terms and yet they are full of a kind of imagery—geometric imagery and dynamic imagery. I'm thinking of poems like 'Legal Fiction' and 'The World's End'.

Oh yes, it's only when they say that imagery is a substitute for the thinking, the line of thought, that I think it's harmful, do you see? I'm afraid I have sometimes talked as if you shouldn't pay imagery any attention at all. But of course it's very traditional—it goes right back to all the words we've borrowed from Latin and Greek. But you find it quite early—eighteenth-century critics seldom talk in detail about images, but then they talk like people do now. You see, I've had to read so many examination papers—the children now, if they don't know how to go on, just gasp out 'image' like so many fish, do you see? Hardly a line without the word 'image' coming in. Whenever they're confronted with a poem, when they don't know what to say, they use this blanket escape word.

What about muscular imagery?

[22] T. E. Hulme (1883–1917), philosopher and poet, was killed in the First World War. His writings were published in *Speculations: Essays on Humanism and the Philosophy of Art*, ed. Herbert Read (London: Kegan Paul, 1924); 'The Complete Poetical Works of T. E. Hulme' (just five poems) was included in an appendix.

Well, it's a very good thing. It's much more important in the poem than visual is, I should have thought. But then I'm not a visualizer. It is, in a way, part of the argument. The process of arguing is so much a process of activity, and that is what you need in a poem—a great deal more than sitting back and looking at the picture.[23]

You have put a much greater stress on consciousness and self-awareness. You seem to have moved away from any Buddhistic notions you might have entertained earlier. I remember a review of Koestler's book *The Lotus and the Robot* in which you praised him for having, in a salutary way, removed any illusions people might have as to the effectiveness of transcendental thought.[24] You seem once to have entertained these ideas more readily.

I'm glad the young people have been having so much California Buddhism, you know. I think it is a good thing. It's astonishing how much it's come in. And they all know a few decisive Buddhist words now, which I consider is a very good thing. I'm not against Buddhism. I think it's a tremendous cleaning agent.[25] But I don't think that it clears up the literary scene very much though, do you? I hardly think of it in those terms.

I notice that when you discussed Marvell's 'The Garden' more recently in the lecture you gave to the Aesthetics Association you discussed it

[23] 'In literary criticism, where people are always talking about images, they have to be assumed to mean visual images; whereas the scientific use of the term includes muscular images . . . It has been known for at least a century that many people don't have visual images, and think without them, but the literary critics have stubbornly refused to pay any attention' ('Rhythm and Imagery in English Poetry', *British Journal of Aesthetics* (1962), repr. in *A* 157–8). In a later review Empson would reiterate his dislike for what he called 'the prattle about "imagery" now standard in academic criticism'; see 'Yeats and the Spirits' (1973) in *A* 352–3.

[24] 'The spirituality of the East and the materialism of the West, one should readily agree, have become harmful clichés which deserve attack; indeed the book would be justified if the chapter on Yoga Research induced even one young Indian on the verge of those practices to believe that their promise of magical power is false' (Empson, 'A Full-Blown Lily', *New Statesman* (6 Jan. 1961), repr. in *A* 605).

[25] Empson had written to Kathleen Raine on 26 Mar. 1948: 'my picture of the Buddha is that he made a superb attempt to clean up Indian mysticism by carrying it to extremes . . . I have felt at times that Buddhism was true, but the hardening of Aldous Huxley into disapproval of everybody who isn't an arahat does now rather unreasonably make me feel that it isn't' (British Library: Deposit 10318 Raine).

in much more down-to-earth terms than you did originally in *Some Versions.*[26]

I do think it was quite sensible to say what I did. But if you think about how people come to look at these things, it's sensible to compare an entirely different civilization which thought the same kind of thoughts. I was immediately told that I thought Marvell had copied them out from some Buddhist. Of course he hadn't. The whole interest of it is that these two civilizations were growing almost independently, like two great trees in a park. And if you compare the way Marvell is thinking with the way the Buddhists think about it, you'll see that it is, in a way, a permanent thing, which the human mind is likely to do, precisely because it was not influenced, because it is an independent thing.[27]

This would be part of your anti-neo-Christian offensive—the responsibility to allow your own conscience to think things out and not to acquiesce in some paradox?

Yes, I think that is so. But I wouldn't want to acquiesce in a Buddhist paradox either. But I think we need a more definite case before I can see what you are looking for. I don't feel that I have changed my mind about that. I've stopped talking about it because it was in the minds of the young people already.

I remember in *Some Versions* you said that, in a sense, 'The Garden' gave a vicarious employment for the mind, and the problem of employment was anyway such a pressing problem that any solution, however irrational it might seem, was in a sense a valuable concept. But in the later lecture you said that meditation was no answer, and that if one of your sons came back and said that he didn't want to hold

[26] Empson, 'Rhythm and Imagery in English Poetry', in *A* 147–64.

[27] When Frank Kermode asserted, in 'The Argument of Marvell's "Garden"' (*Essays in Criticism*, 2 (July 1952), 226–7), 'that "The Garden" must not be read as autobiography . . . The pseudo-biographical critic . . . diverts attention from the genre just as certainly as . . . Mr Empson [does] when he invites us to reflect upon the Buddhist enlightenment [*SVP* 99–100]', Empson responded: 'a probably useful article by Mr Kermode shows that the notions Marvell was playing with were then extremely familiar to the educated public. So I would have presumed, and surely I was not thought to be saying that he must have learned them from a Buddhist. We have only two or three independent civilizations to compare, developing in parallel through thousands of years, and it has a steadying effect to compare them. Marvell was playing with deeply rooted ideas, so native to human life that any full civilization would arrive at them; that is what he was claiming himself, so that he would only be mildly interested to hear that the East agreed with him; but I think I was right to point it out' ('Answers to Comments', *Essays in Criticism*, 3 (1953), 114–20).

down a pay packet and would simply sit in the garden meditating all day, you'd take rather a dim view of it.[28] It seemed rather a different emphasis.

It wouldn't have suited either of my sons, of course. Some people it might suit. Maybe it was rather a mistake to print 'The Fire Sermon' before the poems. It hadn't occurred to me that everybody would think I was professing myself to be a Buddhist. So I had to answer that with some violence.[29] But I haven't changed my mind about the subject, at any rate not consciously.

Well, actually you said in *Some Versions of Pastoral* that unemployment in any life was a serious prospect and that even an imaginative satisfaction, an imaginative employment of the faculties, was in a sense a valuable fulfilment.[30]

Very odd. Well, I don't know how I came to say that. I'm not accustomed to the problem of unemployment, so my advice on the subject is useless. I don't know how I came to say that. It sounds rather silly to me.

Do you still find *Some Versions of Pastoral* a satisfying book? I do feel it's quite the best you've written.

I wish people would pay more attention to *Complex Words*, if only to tell me where it's wrong. It seems to have dropped into a silence. The modern linguists are not interested in that kind of thing. Apart from C. S. Lewis who said that parts of it were wrong, quite probably rightly I should think, nobody has discussed it at all really. And I feel that its claims should be answered.[31] So that is where I would like to be talked about. But I've no wish to grumble. In general I think I've been amply recognized. But it is just that the interests of linguistics have moved away from that kind of thing, as they have from Richards's kind of thing.

[28] 'If one of my sons said he needn't hold down a pay packet because he could get as much experience by sitting in Appleton House garden as by learning a skill, I would think it a bit much' (Empson, 'Rhythm and Imagery in English Poetry', in *A* 159).

[29] See 'Mr Empson and the Fire Sermon', *Essays in Criticism*, 6: 4 (Oct. 1956), and 'Everything, Beggars, Is On Fire', *Arrows* (University of Sheffield), New Year edition, 1957, in *A* 599–600.

[30] See *SVP* 102–3.

[31] C. S. Lewis took Empson gently to task on the meanings of the word 'wit'; see his *Studies in Words* (Cambridge: Cambridge University Press, 1960), 93–6. Empson was equally gracious when he came to review Lewis's book, albeit under the shelter of anonymity, in the *TLS*; see 'Professor Lewis on Linguistics', *Times Literary Supplement* (30 Sept. 1960), 627.

Has there been any interest in your proposals for dictionaries, a new classification?[32]

No, never a bite. One Chinese was quite interested but I don't think anything was done. They are, of course, strong on that. But I don't know whether anything has happened about it since.

Do you think that the theory and the practical criticism in *The Structure of Complex Words* tend to separate out?

They were very largely written separately. I mean the theory was fitted on to the material, but I think it really did fit the material. There was a rather failed chapter on 'all' in *Paradise Lost* which I added. I was at an American summer school and they were talking about this material and saying 'these examples are all selected to fit your theory', which they weren't really. They were the kind of examples I was interested in. But they said: 'Take some very general word which recurs, but on the face of it doesn't seem to carry a complexity of meaning.' And 'all' in *Paradise Lost* did fulfil that very much. That was the only time I took a case for a theoretical reason—because I was challenged to. But otherwise I think that the kind of example I'd been puzzling about and the theory I was making up in general, not surprisingly, fitted each other almost too neatly, but it wasn't because they were planned to.

I think very few people could have read the appendices you wrote there on moral values and value judgements. I hardly think people could accuse you of being irresponsible and morally unaware.

I don't know that they were very original or important. They were needed as support for the theoretical position.

How do you account for the fact that you've been much better received in the States than over here?

They're very energetic, aren't they? Besides I don't think that's quite true. One gets leading schools here who make the noise, but actually I should say the broad opinion has accepted me generously. I couldn't feel shut out. I'm always being asked around to talk to other universities and so on. The actual turnover of thought in the profession is very unlike what you'd gather from reading the trade papers, as a matter of fact. Don't you think that? There is

[32] See the closing chapter of *The Structure of Complex Words*, where Empson turns his attention not only to lexicography but also to metalexicography (the study of how words are treated in dictionaries).

such a variety of opinion knocking about in almost any English Department you visit.

How do you feel about Leavis's cries of persecution? Do you think he's exaggerating?

Well, in that position when he was young there were a lot of other people like him. Someone I knew well, who was my age, the present Professor of Spanish, was hanging about for years getting about three hundred a year tutoring and so on. I think he had a time in London University and then he returned as a professor and it was all worth while.[33] But it was much the same if you were a lawyer, do you see? The whole idea was that if you were going in for the learned professions you had parents who were backing you and you would spend a lot of time very ill-paid until the prizes arrived later in life. But if you were throwing it open to people who hadn't got parents who were prepared to back them all the time, they regarded this as a very shocking affair. I don't think Leavis was treated worse than a number of other people. He was in the middle of a process of social change and I think he was right to complain about it. But the idea that he was being treated worse than a number of other people was merely erroneous.

Do you think he's rather exaggerating this issue of the Two Cultures with C. P. Snow?[34]

I think dear old Snow, if you went into it, understands a lot of English poetry which Leavis never has done. I don't know which cultures they're talking about. I do think Snow is a dull novelist, but that's a thing many a cultured man would be.

You didn't take any part in the debate. Why not?

I think it's too absurd. Good gracious!

[33] Edward Meryon Wilson was Professor of Spanish at Cambridge University and a Fellow of Emmanuel College. Empson urged him to translate *Soledades* by Don Luis de Góngora, and published in *Experiment* the first fragments of Wilson's verse translation. Wilson wrote on 2 June 1930—when T. S. Eliot had accepted an extract for the *Criterion*—'If the whole is published may I dedicate it in part to you? You first suggested the work, and I think your poems have had their influence on my method of versifying, with Milton & Dryden' (Houghton). Twenty-five years later, Wilson was as good as his word: he named Empson as one of two dedicatees of *The Solitudes of Don Luis de Góngora* (Cambridge: Cambridge University Press, 1965), and noted in his Preface: 'William Empson's poems represent a different kind of influence on my work' (p. x).

[34] For a full discussion of the Two Cultures rumpus, see Ian MacKillop, *F. R. Leavis: A Life in Criticism* (London: Allen Lane, 1995), 314–25.

Leavis brands Snow a 'Wellsian', doesn't he? I think you've professed an admiration for Wells and associated him with Donne.[35]

Oh yes, a wonderful chap, a most imaginative man.

A lot of critics have pointed out that the cultures at Cambridge were very well unified while you were there. One thinks of people like Kathleen Raine, Charles Madge, Bronowski . . .

Yes, I suppose so. But I think they usually are. But you see, L. C. Knights, much more than Leavis I suppose, was concerned with saying that the good use of English—having a good English style—was essential to understanding the world. Unless you had a good style you couldn't understand anything in morals or science or anything else. And coming back from China—the first time I'd taught in England was when I arrived in Sheffield, which Knights had just left—I couldn't help feeling that the language was fairly well known in these parts. The contrast was so great. I couldn't go on telling the scientists that they were no good unless they'd studied Shakespeare first. Knights has never wavered from this tremendous claim for English literature study.[36]

You've said that you don't like much of modern poetry.[37] Why is this? Is it the irrational element in it?

I don't know. It's merely a failure of taste. It's a very usual thing with old men, you know. The power to receive and appreciate a new line is one of the earliest things to go, I should have said. So whenever you see an old buffer giving a prize you must remember that, worthy though the old buffer may be in other ways, someone else has had to tell him who to give the prize to, otherwise he would be giving it to the wrong person.

Have you read much modern poetry?

[35] See 'Literary Criticism and the Christian Revival' (1966), where Empson insisted that John Donne, as a professional theologian, would have known all about developments in the science of cosmology, in *A* 634.

[36] L. C. Knights (1906–97) was Empson's predecessor as Professor of English Literature at Sheffield, 1947–52. Thereafter he became Winterstoke Professor of English at Bristol, 1953–64, and King Edward VII Professor of English Literature, Cambridge, 1965–73. Empson and Knights met while teaching at the Kenyon School of Letters at Bloomington, Ind., in 1950.

[37] 'Well, honestly, I don't like much of it. But it's largely because I'm an older buffer' ('William Empson in conversation with Christopher Ricks', *CP* 121).

I give a prize every year in Sheffield for poetry. I have to take advice. I follow my rules scrupulously.[38] But I certainly see a fair amount of it. I had a long period in hospital, the latter part with eye trouble, so I was happy to listen to the mercifully piped radio, and I found that I liked pop music very much. I've been a great admirer of the Beatles ever since. 'Hello, Goodbye' is the only modern poem I admire since Philip Larkin. I think there's a great deal more to be said for them than for the chaps without the guitar who just recite against a background.

How do you reconcile your dislike for the irrational in art with your admiration for Dylan Thomas?[39]

I don't think he's irrational a bit. Once you've got the point of it, it's perfectly clearly argued. He isn't irrational, but he's very elliptic. He's very self-indulgent, too. A lot of it, I'm afraid, I can't make out. When I can't make it out I don't like it. But the parts I like seem to me tightly and fiercely argued.

You once said that parodies are appreciative criticisms. Thomas, of course, wrote a parody of you. Have you read any of the other parodies, for example Richard Kell's or Hobsbaum's?[40]

They all seem to be as dull as mutton, the truth is. But I thought that Dylan's one, though a bit rough, was fairly funny. I thought that was all right, but the other ones I've seen I didn't think were very funny—they weren't sufficiently pointed. But I haven't made any study of it, I'm afraid. I agree in general that parody is a very important mode of criticism, and when Leavis denies it that is only because Leavis cannot afford to be parodied, of course.

Could you explain the dedication of *The Gathering Storm*? It's dedicated 'In memory of Phyllis Chroustchoff'.

She was my landlady. I was staying with her in Marchmont Street and she killed herself not long before it came out. I felt a large part of my life in which I'd been . . . Now had I been writing these things in her house? No, as a

[38] In the 1960s and 1970s, Empson took a real interest in the poetry of Geoff Hill and Nick Malone, both students at Sheffield; he wrote an introduction for Malone's long poem *The Burial of Crispin Pike* (London: Workshop Press, 1974).

[39] See Empson's essays and reviews on Dylan Thomas collected in *A* 382–412.

[40] See Dylan Thomas's parody of Empson, 'Request to Leda: Homage to William Empson', first published in *Horizon*, 6 (July 1942), and incorporated in *The Death of the King's Canary*. Richard Kell's 'Empsonium' appeared in *London Magazine*, 6: 10 (Oct. 1959), 55–6; Philip Hobsbaum's 'Lines for an Assistant Lecturer: Imitated from William Empson', *Essays in Criticism*, 10: 4 (Oct. 1960), 436.

matter of fact not. She'd left some time before. It was before I went to Japan I was in her house, but I was still friends with her and saw her friends. She was an Englishwoman who had married a white Russian, descended from the noble family who owned the lands on which the slave [Nikita] Khrushchev was born, I understand. And so a real connection with the statesman of this remote kind.[41]

And who was Miss Hatakeyama? Was she a pupil of yours?

No, she was just a schoolteacher somewhere in the north of Japan who wrote asking to have the rough English of her poems polished up. I thought they were very good. I did see her once. She turned up in Tokyo after she'd sent me all these poems and I'd sent them back, and I was very keen to keep up the connection. But she was very sort of shrinking. I never saw her again and she didn't leave an address. But there was no quarrel—she was just shrinking.[42]

Why did you publish her poems in *The Gathering Storm*?

I thought they were good poems. I mean it's the same way I published 'The Fire Sermon', with no idea of saying I'd made it up. After all, it's a very small text, isn't it? I thought any good poetry which came my way I'd much better print. But it's quite true I didn't make it up.

Why did you publish 'The Birth of Steel', the masque [for the Queen's visit to Sheffield in 1954], at the end of *Collected Poems*?

I think it's good, you know. I know it's awfully out of fashion. But, of course, it's intended to be set to music in the very elaborate way it was. I thought it went off like anything. But I quite see it's deliberately annoying people to a certain extent because it does read so very flat. It certainly wasn't intended to be satirical at all. The lady [i.e. the Queen] was a little suspicious. She wanted to make quite clear that she knew it was funny. Once this was made clear it was all jolly fun. I had to talk to the Queen. She said she had been wondering why nobody laughed at the performance, but she had decided that it must have been because they'd seen the rehearsals so often. 'Yes, ma'am,' I said, lying. I realized the necessary way to talk to royalty. Actually they hadn't

[41] On Phyllis Chroustchoff, see *WE1* 415–21.

[42] On Empson and Chiyoko Hatakeyama, see *WE1* 331–45; Peter Robinson, 'Very Shrinking Behaviour', *Times Literary Supplement* (18 July 2003), 13–15, and a follow-up letter from Robinson, 'Ice cream with Empson', *Times Literary Supplement* (24 Oct. 2003), 19.

laughed because they were so bloody frightened. But if you like to pretend they were all thoroughly bored with the show, I'm quite willing to agree to that. I had to present the goddess to the Queen. I said: 'The Queen, the goddess. The goddess, the Queen.' They were identical. I felt very groggy. I didn't know which of these women was real at all. However, the Queen was at once completely at ease. She wasn't at all sure if I was making fun at her great office, but being sweet to a young girl she knew exactly how to do it. So I had only to bow and retire. No, I thought it was a splendid affair and great luck for me because I'd just been fished up out of communist China. They weren't at all sure whether I was OK. After this display of loyalty there was no more trouble from that quarter. There again, I did it because I was told to. The Vice Chancellor sent for me and said: 'Empson, the Queen will be visiting Sheffield next term and I wish you to write a few lines receiving her as the first Elizabeth would have been received.' And I said: 'Well, there's a practical difficulty about that. It was blasphemy. They told her she was God.' 'Tell her she's God again,' he said. And so I did. I thought this was magnificent Yorkshire behaviour. Worked like a charm, too. Everybody liked it. They were a little frightened.[43]

There's a great deal of difference between *Poems* (1935) and *The Gathering Storm* (1940), both in subject-matter and in tone. Was there a conscious effort to break out of your earlier style or was it a more natural development arising out of your involvement in Japan?

The title does simply mean the feeling that the Second World War is bound to come. It is all political really, isn't it? It's a change of subject.

But you said that towards the end of *Poems* you felt you were beginning to parody yourself.

Well, it was becoming dead. It wasn't as if it was anything so lively as becoming a parody. It was using the same forms without their being lively. But writing about the approach of war hadn't been much of a change, only turning to another subject.

One feels that the two volumes were written for completely different audiences. Were you conscious of this at the time?

[43] For *The Birth of Steel: A Light Masque*, see *CP* 104–10, 403–5, and Empson's memoir of meeting and managing the Queen, 'The Queen and I', in *SSS* 220–31.

I don't think that I had an audience really. Except for the joke about Auden which was for a funny magazine.[44] I felt that I was concerned with something that was visibly happening under our eyes, and that was naturally what you wanted to write about. However, I think I'm agreeing with you. One would feel more of an audience with that.

The poems in *The Gathering Storm* seem less neat than those in the previous collection. The feeling seems to be impressing itself much more on the form, sometimes breaking the form down. I'm thinking about 'The Teasers' and 'Ignorance of Death', where it becomes prose.

Yes, certainly.

How did you arrive at these forms you used? I'm thinking especially of the villanelle, which I think you were the first person to use since Austin Dobson and writers of that period.

Oh, no. My generation used it because Joyce had in the *Portrait of the Artist*, and he no doubt was copying the nineties' versifiers who used it because they thought it was musical, whereas my lot all thought you had to make it mean something different every time you repeated the line. So we made it much more taut. You wipe the eye of Joyce and do it with more bang.

Were you very conscious of using a certain form for a certain poem or did the poem dictate the form as you wrote it?

Oh, I think so. You try out lines and rhymes till you feel what shape the poem needs to be. It's very hard to say what comes first. But, as a rule, you would find yourself committed to a verse form from fairly early.

How did you write 'Missing Dates'? At what stage did you realize you were writing a villanelle?

It was quite rapid. I did notice that. I did it fairly straight off—about four hours or so, which is much shorter than usual. I went out and had a beer—they had opened before I'd finished—and I felt: 'Now then, I mustn't get out of the mood.' I came back and fitted in the last bit. I then got the final bang. So I remember this—the only one I do remember writing, because I thought that was remarkably quick. And it needed no altering afterwards—often I have to do an awful lot of mucking about. I think of Byron writing his 'So we'll go

[44] Empson, 'Just a Smack at Auden', *CP* 81–2.

no more a-roving'—a wonderful poem, I think—as part of a letter, almost straight down.[45]

Which of your poems are you proudest of? Do you like the anthology pieces? Do you feel you are fairly represented by them?

'Missing Dates' I like. I'm inclined to think 'Bacchus' is my best poem. It is difficult, of course. You can't expect the public to like it.

Do you think you may like 'Bacchus' partly because it bears out some of your critical theories? It does seem particularly a case study of ambiguities—the play on 'cope', for instance.

Oh, I don't think that. I don't know which they'd be.

Do you find 'the singing line' in 'Bacchus'?

The missing line?

'The singing line'. It's a very difficult poem to read without reference to the notes.

I'm afraid that was done very much as separate lines. I wrote it in Japan feeling . . . We hadn't many friends really. I would go to an upstairs room and eat Chinese food, writing this stuff, drinking saki in the evening, very comfortable and relaxed. But you couldn't be more isolated from any . . . I mean that it was written while drinking, which very little of my poetry was. But it does make it a very self-enclosed process, especially if you're fitting the lines together in that way afterwards. I think it is too self-enclosed, but it doesn't make it bad.

Did the ambiguities develop naturally out of the context?

Oh, yes. I wouldn't go through picking them up. I think that would be depressing, of course.

A lot of critics look at your early verse and take the despair as being most typical. They talk about 'despairing wit' and 'desperate sophistication'. In fact, especially in your later criticism, you've become very optimistic.

I'm not despairing on theory, but optimistic in practice? I think it would be rather a libel to say so. I should have thought our prospects are desperately bad.

[45] See Empson's early essay on Byron's 'So, We'll Go No More A-Roving', in *A* 325–7.

You seem to react against people like Hugh Kenner who take a very glum view of the world.[46] There's a correspondence with Wren-Lewis, too, I remember, entitled 'Resurrection' in the *Critical Quarterly*, where you said the world was 'wonderful beyond all telling.'[47] It seemed very typical of your stand in your later criticism.

Wren-Lewis, yes. Isn't that queer? I see he's quite a distinguished modern Christian. I don't know whether he's altered his views at all, but it did seem a very odd affair. As to being optimistic, Wren-Lewis is, isn't he? He thinks that the scientists can do everything for us, and I was being reactionary and saying you ought to admire the world and not say that everything good in it was invented in test tubes in the last century.

Yes, but all his positives were extra-terrestrial, weren't they? He had to posit some kind of resurrection before he could find anything of value in life.

No, I think your kind intentions are rather losing themselves there. I might be called reactionary in saying I couldn't stand the views of Wren-Lewis. You wouldn't say I was being optimistic there.

But you tend to find happy endings, to put it rather crudely. *Ulysses*, particularly, when you wrote to combat Kenner's view. And in *Lear*, too, you made it a very constructive ending, by comparison with Maynard Mack.[48]

I'm delighted to hear you say that. It was one of the points at which we really exploded after my long attempt to improve the mind of Hobsbaum. He said it wouldn't be worth his while reading *Lear* if he took an entirely nihilistic view of it, like Empson. And he believed it all meant we're going to heaven. I thought it great impudence of Hobsbaum, who didn't believe in anything of the kind. Why should *King Lear* not be good enough for Hobsbaum unless it told him he was going to heaven? I refused to teach Hobsbaum any more after that.[49]

[46] See Empson on Hugh Kenner's *Dublin's Joyce*: 'Humanism and Mr Bloom' (1956), in *A* 475–8.

[47] See Empson, 'Resurrection' (1964), in *A* 614–17.

[48] See Empson's review of *'King Lear' in Our Time*, by Maynard Mack: 'Next Time, A Wheel of Fire' (1967), in *SSS* 56–62.

[49] Philip Hobsbaum wrote to David Wilson on 28 Oct. 2002, after seeing a transcript of this interview: 'it cannot be true that he refused to teach me, since he remained my very active research supervisor until my PhD was conferred. That was in 1968, at an examiners' meeting over which he presided . . . [H]e caricatures my view regarding the demise of King Lear. That may be found

What do you think of Wilson Knight? You several times express great respect for him, although his Christian and Symbolist views must be repugnant to you.

Well, there I have been influenced. I admired it very much when I read it.[50] I still think it's very good, but I'm very much out of sympathy with it now. I feel that you need to get back to taking an interest in character and regard the overall effects of the poetry as a background thing. I think he's awfully good about saying what the background effect is. And, of course, he is a practical amateur actor and producer. He knows a lot about the theatre. But I do think you've got to take it in more theatrical terms. I don't think you can get away from that. But, of course, a lot of what he said was quite true. I think he's a wonderful old chap.

Will you write anything more about Jonson? Your approach is a very new one. Unlike Eliot, who said that the characters of humours are flat, you say they should be analysed with some degree of complexity, especially in the case of *Volpone*.[51]

It was always a very odd theory, wasn't it? But I do think you would find it was usually said. Coleridge said it quite as strongly as Eliot. I don't think Coleridge had much feeling for the theatre. So few of the people who write about plays really like them, I think. You do need to accept what goes over big and seems decisive, and also how the audience is going to decide. It doesn't matter what the sermons are saying—the author tends to be on the side of the runaway lovers and against the arranged marriage, do you see? And to say that everybody would have told you that this was very wicked is off the point. For that matter they'd have told you that the whole theatre was very wicked. The idea that you went there to see imitations of the Morality Plays would have been laughed at by any

in a chapter entitled "Survival Values" in my book *A Theory of Communication* (London: Macmillan, 1970). The chapter in question is identical with that of the same title found in my PhD thesis. In that chapter I dissented from any simply Christian interpretation of the play's denouement, such as Empson mischievously ascribes to me.' See also Hobsbaum, 'Empson as Teacher: The Sheffield Years', in Christopher Norris and Nigel Mapp (eds.), *William Empson: The Critical Achievement* (Cambridge: Cambridge University Press, 1993), 294–307.

[50] See Empson's review of G. Wilson Knight's *Principles of Shakespearean Production*: 'Playing Shakespeare' (1936), in *SSS* 78–9.

[51] See Empson's essays on *Volpone* and *The Alchemist*, along with a further piece entitled 'Volpone again', in *ERL2*.

don of the period. And a don of this period, if he'd been asked about the subject, would have been told that he was all wrong from beginning to end, wouldn't he?

What do you see as being the useful place of critical theory as an abstract study in the way René Wellek would approach it, without very much reference to specific texts?

Well, I always have worked from texts. Though if I'd been told to work up a set of theory articles—if it had been policy in some way—I don't think I'd have said no. But I never thought it was likely to do them any good—the students themselves, I mean. It's like the view of Wittgenstein that you should try and teach them not to be philosophers—that is, you should try to solve the problems ad hoc as they arise. But I think that you do find people holding general theories who have to be coaxed by examples to see that they don't always work. I do a practical criticism class where I am continually warning them against the wrong beliefs which have been instilled into their minds. But I don't feel that I'm then going to advocate a specific doctrine—only trying to make them able to see the particular poem which we have mimeographed.

Do you think that Wimsatt and the New Critics have raised too many do's and don't's, restricted their field too much?

I've accepted a whole lot of American stuff, I'm quite sure. I always have been very bad at giving credits, I'm afraid, but not I think out of grudgingness. It's merely that it only seems worth while saying where you have a point of disagreement which is worth following up. Saying where you got something from is self-regarding in a way, rather than doing justice. I don't feel the need to hand round sugar buns to every child. I know I ought to do it much more than I do, and if I did I would realize how much I am using other people's work all the time. We're all using each other all the time, you know. If you tried to give the credits on an adequate scale you would be cluttering everything up very much.

Which American critics do you like? What about Kenneth Burke?

Yes, it's been getting into a wedge somehow, hasn't it? Getting into a crevice. I did read a lot of it. I probably have been influenced by it, but I wouldn't want to read much now. And he really does like sacrifice, do you see? He believes that the literature about sacrifice is splendid, as indeed it often is, but the idea that this would actually happen, and that he is recommending a barbaric and very disagreeable thing, simply cannot enter his mind. It's very remote from anything he would really like to happen.[52]

Have you given much assent to any of the classical texts—Longinus or Aristotle? Can you remember reading them through and thinking: 'Yes, that hits the nail on the head'?

Not really. I'm afraid I can't say that. It seems very odd, I always think, the *hamartia* business, the tragic flaw. That even Ben Jonson, who undoubtedly had read *The Poetics*, probably in Latin, never mentions it, nor does anyone else. He illustrates it as much as Shakespeare does. They always show a popular hero who has one thing the matter with him, a man the audience can admire, though you can see why the tragedy is going to come. But I don't think it's the kind of thing you would nod your head at, as at a wise remark of Polonius. You don't need to be told that to write a play. It's a thing which any good playwright knows before he starts. So very many of the wise remarks of the classics, though well worth making and quite true, I don't believe affected the Elizabethans very much. What they were very prone to say was: 'Well, there was an old lady in Norwich and she'd committed a murder thirty years before. They made her go to the theatre and she upped and confessed, and that proves it does you good.' This childlike prattle was the reason for the play within a play in *Hamlet*, for that matter. I don't think that any theoretical argument from the Greeks would have affected their minds at all. And now I think you want the light on and some tea, don't you?

Recorded at Studio House, Hampstead Hill Gardens, London, 20 December 1970

[52] Kenneth Burke remarked about *Milton's God*: 'by his stress upon "torture" rather than the sacrificial principle in general, [Empson] picturesquely deflects attention from the central relationship between religion and the social order' ('Invective Against the Father', *The Nation* (16 June 1962), 541). The adverb 'picturesquely' is a sarcastic euphemism; Burke also called Empson 'rabid', as did other critics who considered him 'vitriolic' in his fixation on the horrid meaning of what Burke termed 'the sacrificial principle in general'—a sentimental locution if ever there was one. Burke and Empson had become good jousting friends at the Kenyon School of English, Gambier, Oh., in the summer of 1950.

SELECT BIBLIOGRAPHY

Works By Empson

EMPSON, WILLIAM, *Poems* (London: Chatto & Windus, 1935).

—— *Some Versions of Pastoral* (1935; repr. London: Penguin, 1995).

—— *Seven Types of Ambiguity*, 3rd edn. (1953; repr. London: Penguin, 1995).

—— *William Empson Reading Selected Poems* (Hull: Marvell Press: *Listen* LPV 3, 1961).

—— and PIRIE, DAVID B. (eds.), *Coleridge's Verse: A Selection* (London: Faber and Faber, 1972).

—— *The Structure of Complex Words*, 3rd edn. (1977; repr. London: Penguin, 1995).

—— 'Postscript', in Christopher Norris, *William Empson and the Philosophy of Literary Criticism* (London: Athlone, 1978).

—— *Milton's God*, rev. edn. (Cambridge: Cambridge University Press, 1981).

—— 'Empson on Tennyson', *Tennyson Research Bulletin*, 4 (1984), 107–9.

—— *Using Biography* (London: Chatto & Windus, 1984).

—— *Essays on Shakespeare*, ed. David B. Pirie (Cambridge: Cambridge University Press, 1986).

—— *The Royal Beasts and Other Works*, ed. John Haffenden (London: Chatto & Windus, 1986).

—— *Argufying: Essays on Literature and Culture*, ed. John Haffenden (London: Chatto & Windus, 1987).

—— *Faustus and the Censor: The English Faust-book and Marlowe's 'Doctor Faustus'*, ed. John Henry Jones (Oxford: Blackwell, 1987).

—— *Empson in Granta* (Tunbridge Wells: Foundling Press, 1993).

—— *Essays on Renaissance Literature*, i. *Donne and the New Philosophy*, ed. John Haffenden (Cambridge: Cambridge University Press, 1993).

—— *Essays on Renaissance Literature*, ii. *The Drama*, ed. John Haffenden (Cambridge: Cambridge University Press, 1994).

—— *The Strengths of Shakespeare's Shrew: Essays, Memoirs and Reviews*, ed. John Haffenden (Sheffield: Sheffield Academic Press, 1996).

—— *Complete Poems of William Empson*, ed. John Haffenden (London: Allen Lane, 2000).

—— *Selected Letters of William Empson*, ed. John Haffenden (Oxford: Oxford University Press, 2006).

All Other Works

ADAMS, ROBERT MARTIN, 'Empson and Bentley: Something about Milton Too', *Partisan Review*, 21 (Mar.–Apr. 1954), 178–89.

—— 'Hero of the Word', *New York Review of Books*, 32: 6 (11 Apr. 1986), 32–5.

ADORNO, THEODOR, 'On the Dialectic of Tact', in *Minima Moralia* (1951), trans. E. F. N. Jephcott (London: Verso, 2005).

ALPERS, PAUL, 'Empson on Pastoral', *New Literary History*, 10: 1 (1978), 101–23.

—— *What is Pastoral?* (Chicago: University of Chicago Press, 1996).

ALVAREZ, A., 'A Style from a Despair: William Empson', *The Twentieth Century*, 161 (1957), 344–53.

ARMSTRONG, TIM, *Modernism* (Cambridge: Polity Press, 2005).

ARNOLD, MATTHEW, 'On Translating Homer: Last Words', in *On the Classical Tradition*, ed. R. H. Super (Ann Arbor: University of Michigan, 1960).

—— 'The Study of Poetry', in *English Literature and Irish Politics*, ed. R. H. Super (Ann Arbor: University of Michigan, 1973).

ASHTON, LEIGH (ed.), *Chinese Art* (London: Kegan Paul, 1935).

ATHANASIUS, *De incarnatione verbi dei*, ed. and trans. 'a religious of C.S.M.V.' (1944; rev. edn. New York: St Vladimir's Seminary Press, 1996).

AUDEN, W. H., 'Letter to Lord Byron', *Letters from Iceland* (London: Faber, 1937).

—— and ISHERWOOD, CHRISTOPHER, *Journey to a War* (London: Faber, 1939).

AUSTIN, J. L., *How To Do Things With Words* (Oxford: Oxford University Press, 1963).

BEER, GILLIAN, 'Eddington and the Idiom of Modernism', in J. E. McGuire and Trevor Melia (eds.), *Science, Reason and Rhetoric* (Pittsburgh: University of Pittsburgh Press, 1995), 295–315.

BENTLEY, RICHARD, *Dr Bentley's emendations on the twelve books of Milton's Paradise Lost* (London, 1732).

BERLIN, ISAIAH, *Against the Current: Essays in the History of Ideas*, ed. Henry Hardy (London: Hogarth Press, 1980).

—— *The Roots of Romanticism*, ed. Henry Hardy (London: Chatto & Windus, 1999).

BERNAL, J. D., *The World, The Flesh and The Devil* (London: Kegan Paul, 1929).

BLOOM, HAROLD, *The Anxiety of Influence: A Theory of Poetry*, 2nd edn. (New York: Oxford University Press, 1997).

BOAL, BARBARA M., *Human Sacrifice and Religious Change: The Khonds* (New Delhi: Inter-India Publications, 1997).

BOTTING, DOUGLAS, *Dr Eckener's Dream Machine: The Historic Saga of the Round-the-World Zeppelin* (London: HarperCollins, 2001).

BRADBROOK, MURIEL, 'Sir William Empson (1906–1984)', *The Collected Papers of Muriel Bradbrook*, iv. *Shakespeare in his Context: The Constellated Globe* (Hemel Hempstead: Harvester Wheatsheaf, 1989).

BROOKS, CLEANTH, *The Well Wrought Urn: Studies in the Structure of Poetry* (New York: Harcourt Bruce, 1947).

BROOKS, PETER W., *Zeppelin: Rigid Airships 1893–1940* (London: Putnam Aeronautical, 1992).

BUDGEN, FRANK, *James Joyce and the Making of 'Ulysses' and Other Writings*, introd. Clive Hart (Oxford: Oxford University Press, 1972).

BURKE, KENNETH, 'Exceptional Improvisation', *Poetry*, 49: 6 (Mar. 1937), 347–50.

CARROLL, LEWIS, *Alice's Adventures in Wonderland and Through the Looking-Glass*, ed. Hugh Haughton (London: Penguin, 1998).

CARTER, PHILIP, *Men and the Emergence of Polite Society* (Edinburgh: Pearson, 2001).

CAVALLI, LUIGI LUCA (ed.), *African Pygmies* (Orlando, Fla.: Academic Press, 1986).

CHURCHILL, WINSTON S., *The Second World War*, 6 vols. (London: Cassell, 1948–54).

—— *His Complete Speeches, 1897–1963*, vii. *1943–1949*, ed. Robert Rhodes James (New York: Chelsea House Publishers, 1994).

CLENDINNEN, INGA, *Aztecs: An Interpretation* (Cambridge: Cambridge University Press, 1991).

COLERIDGE, S. T., *Collected Letters of Samuel Taylor Coleridge*, ed. Earl Leslie Griggs, 6 vols. (Oxford: Oxford University Press, 1956–71).

—— *The Notebooks of Samuel Taylor Coleridge*, ed. Kathleen Coburn *et al.*, 5 vols. (Princeton: Princeton University Press, 1957–2001).

—— *Lectures 1795 on Politics and Religion*, ed. Lewis Patton and Peter Mann (Princeton: Princeton University Press, 1970).

—— *Biographia Literaria*, ed. James Engell and Walter Jackson Bate, 2 vols. (Princeton: Princeton University Press, 1983).

—— *Table Talk*, ed. Carl Woodring, 2 vols. (Princeton: Princeton University Press, 1990).

—— *Poems*, ed. John Beer (1963; rev. edn. London: Everyman, 1999).

COLLINI, STEFAN, 'Smack Up: Argufying and Illumination in the Letters of William Empson', *Times Literary Supplement* (7 July 2006), 3–5.

CONSTABLE, JOHN (ed.), *Critical Essays on William Empson* (Aldershot: Scolar Press, 1993).

COPPARD, AUDREY, and CRICK, BERNARD (eds.), *Orwell Remembered* (London: British Broadcasting Corporation, 1984).

CRANE, R. S., *The Idea of the Humanities and Other Essays Critical and Historical*, 2 vols. (Chicago: University of Chicago Press, 1967).

DAVIDSON, DONALD, *Inquiries into Truth and Interpretation* (Oxford: Oxford University Press, 1984).

—— 'A Nice Derangement of Epitaphs', in R. Grandy and R. Warner (eds.), *Philosophical Grounds of Rationality: Intentions, Categories, Ends* (Oxford: Oxford University Press, 1986), 157–74.

DAVIES, NIGEL, *Human Sacrifice in History and Today* (London: Macmillan, 1981).

DE LAS CASAS, BARTOLOMÉ, OP, *A Short Account of the Destruction of the Indies* (1552), ed. and trans. Nigel Griffin (London: Penguin Books, 1992).

DE MAN, PAUL, *Blindness and Insight: Essays in the Logic of Contemporary Criticism*, 2nd edn. (Minneapolis: University of Minnesota Press, 1983).

DERRIDA, JACQUES, 'Signature Event Context', *Glyph*, 1 (1975), 172–97.

—— 'Limited Inc abc', *Glyph*, 2 (1977), 75–176.

—— 'Afterword: Toward an Ethic of Conversation', in Gerald Graff (ed.), *Limited Inc* (Evanston, Ill.: Northwestern University Press, 1989), 111–54.

DISALLE, ROBERT, 'Space and Time: Inertial Frames', *The Stanford Encyclopedia of Philosophy (Summer 2002 Edition)*, ed. Edward N. Zalta, URL =<http://plato.stanford.edu/archives/sum2002/entries/spacetime-iframes/>.

DOBRÉE, BONAMY, 'Poetic Pitfalls', *Spectator*, 145 (29 Nov. 1930), 850–1.

DONOGHUE, DENIS, 'Some Versions of Empson', *Times Literary Supplement* (7 June 1974), 597–8.

DOOLITTLE, HILDA [H.D.], *Collected Poems 1912–1941*, ed. Louis L. Martz (Manchester: Carcanet, 1984).

DOUGLAS, MARY, *Implicit Meanings: Essays in Anthropology* (London: Routledge & Kegan Paul, 1975).

—— *Risk and Blame: Essays in Cultural Theory* (London: Routledge, 1992).

EAGLETON, TERRY, *Literary Theory: An Introduction* (Minneapolis: University of Minnesota Press, 1983).

—— *Against the Grain: Essays 1975–1985* (London: Verso, 1986).

EDDINGTON, ARTHUR, *Space, Time and Gravitation* (Cambridge: Cambridge University Press, 1920).

—— *The Nature of the Physical World* (Cambridge: Cambridge University Press, 1928).

—— *The Expanding Universe* (London: Harmondsworth, 1940).

EDGELL, DEREK, *The Order of Woodcraft Chivalry, 1916–1949, as a New Age Alternative to the Boy Scouts*, 2 vols. (Lewiston, NY: E. Mellen Press, 1992).

ELIAS, NORBERT, *The Civilising Process* (1978–82), trans. Edmund Jephcott (Oxford: Blackwell, 1994).

ELIOT, CHARLES, *Hinduism and Buddhism: An Historical Sketch*, 3 vols. (London: Edward Arnold, 1921).

ELIOT, T. S., *Homage to John Dryden: Three Essays on Poetry of the Seventeenth Century* (London: Hogarth Press, 1924).

—— 'Religion and Science: A Phantom Dilemma', *Listener* (23 Mar. 1932), 428–9.

—— *Selected Essays 1917–1932* (New York: Harcourt, 1932).

ELIOT, T. S., *The Complete Poems and Plays of T. S. Eliot* (London: Faber, 1969).

—— *The Waste Land: A Facsimile and Transcript of the Original Drafts Including the Annotations of Ezra Pound*, ed. Valerie Eliot (London: Faber and Faber, 1971).

—— *The Varieties of Metaphysical Poetry*, ed. Ronald Schuchard (London: Faber and Faber, 1993).

EVERETT, BARBARA, 'Reviews', *The Modern Language Review*, 57: 3 (July 1962), 415–17.

FLORENCE, P. SARGENT, and ANDERSON, J. R. L. (eds.), *C. K. Ogden: A Collective Memoir* (London: Elek, 1977).

FORSTER, E. M., *Goldsworthy Lowes Dickinson* (1934; London: Arnold, 1973).

FOUCHER, ALFRED, *The Beginnings of Buddhist Art* (London: Humphrey Milford, 1917).

FRASER, G. S., *A Stranger and Afraid: The Autobiography of an Intellectual* (Manchester: Carcanet New Press, 1983).

FRY, PAUL H., *William Empson: Prophet Against Sacrifice* (London: Routledge, 1991).

FULLER, DAVID, 'William Empson: From Verbal Analysis to Cultural Criticism', in Patricia Waugh (ed.), *Literary Theory and Criticism: An Oxford Guide* (Oxford: Oxford University Press, 2006), 152–65.

GADAMER, HANS-GEORG, *Truth and Method*, trans. Garrett Burden and John Cumming (New York: Crossroad, 1982), 263.

GARDNER, PHILIP, and GARDNER, AVERIL, *The God Approached: A Commentary on the Poems of William Empson* (London: Chatto & Windus, 1978).

GATES, HENRY LOUIS, *The Signifying Monkey: A Theory of Afro-American Literary Criticism* (New York: Oxford University Press, 1988).

GEERTZ, CLIFFORD, *Available Light: Anthropological Reflections on Philosophical Subjects* (Princeton: Princeton University Press, 2000).

GILL, ROMA (ed.), *William Empson: The Man and His Work* (London: Routledge & Kegan Paul, 1974).

GIRARD, RENÉ, *Violence and the Sacred* (1972; English trans., Baltimore: Johns Hopkins University Press, 1977).

—— *Things Hidden since the Foundation of the World* (1978; English trans., London: Athlone Press, 1987).

GLAISTER, J. NORMAN, 'The Order as a Social Organism', *Pine Cone*, 3: 10 (Oct. 1925), 24–31.

GRANDY, RICHARD, 'Reference, Meaning, and Belief', *Journal of Philosophy*, 70 (1973), 439–52.

GRAVES, ROBERT, *The Complete Poems*, ed. Beryl Graves and Dunstan Ward (London: Penguin, 2003).

GREEN, A. R. W., *The Role of Human Sacrifice in the Ancient Near East* (Missoula, Mont.: Scholars Press, 1975).

GRIFFITHS, ERIC, *The Printed Voice of Victorian Poetry* (Oxford: Oxford University Press, 1989).

GROSS, JOHN, *A Double Thread: Growing Up English and Jewish in London* (Chicago: Ivan Dee, 2002).

HACKING, IAN, *Mad Travellers: Reflections on the Reality of Transient Mental Illnesses* (London: Free Association Books, 1999).

HAFFENDEN, JOHN, *William Empson*, i. *Among the Mandarins* (Oxford: Oxford: University Press, 2005).

—— *William Empson*, ii. *Against the Christians* (Oxford: Oxford University Press, 2006).

HALDANE, J. B. S., *Possible Worlds and Other Essays* (London: Chatto & Windus, 1927).

—— and EMPSON, WILLIAM, *The Outlook of Science* (London: Kegan Paul, Trench, Trubner & Co., 1935).

—— and —— *Science and Well-Baing* (London: Kegan Paul, Trench, Trubner and Co., 1935).

HALE, J. K., *Thomas Bentley to Dr Pearce: New Light on Richard Bentley's Edition of Paradise Lost* (Wellington: Turnbull Library Record, 1981).

HAMERTON-KELLY, ROBERT G. (ed.), *Violent Origins: Walter Burkert, René Girard and Jonathan K. Smith on Ritual Killing and Cultural Formation* (Stanford, Calif.: Stanford University Press, 1987).

HAMILTON, IAN (ed.), *The Modern Poet: Essays from The Review* (London: MacDonald, 1968).

HARDING, JASON, '*Experiment* in Cambridge: A Manifesto of Young England', *Cambridge Quarterly*, 27 (1998), 287–309.

HARDY, BARBARA, 'William Empson and Seven Types of Ambiguity', *Sewanee Review*, 90 (1982), 438–9.

HARRIS, ROY, *Rethinking Writing* (London: Athlone, 2000).

HARTMAN, GEOFFREY H., *Beyond Formalism: Literary Essays 1958–1970* (New Haven: Yale University Press, 1970).

HARTZELL, RICHARD W., *Harmony in Conflict* (Taipei: Caves, 1988).

HATAKEYAMA, CHIYOKO, *Sekishu e no Banka* (*Elegy to my Left Hand*) (Tokyo: Shupansha, 2005).

HAUGHTON, HUGH, 'Journeys to War: Auden, Isherwood and Empson in China', in Douglas Kerr and Julia Kuehn (eds.), *Travellers in China* (Hong Kong: University of Hong Kong Press, 2007).

HAZLITT, WILLIAM, *Characters of Shakespear's Plays* (1817; London: Taylor and Hessey, 1818).

HENGEL, MARTIN, *The Atonement: The Origins of the Doctrine in the New Testament* (1980), trans. John Bowden (London: SCM Press, 1981).

HILL, GEOFFREY, 'The Dream of Reason', *Essays in Criticism*, 14 (1964), 91–101.

HIRSCH, E. D., *The Aims of Interpretation* (Chicago: University of Chicago Press, 1976).

HOBSBAUM, PHILIP, 'Lines for an Assistant Lecturer: Imitated from William Empson', *Essays in Criticism*, 10: 4 (Oct. 1960), 436.

HODGSON, RALPH, *Collected Poems* (London: Macmillan, 1961).

HOLLINGTON, MICHAEL, 'Richards and Empson in China: The Recollections of Professor C. P. ("Possum") Fitzgerald', *AUMLA* (1996), 90–1.

HOLT, MACK P., *The French Wars of Religion, 1562–1629*, 2nd edn. (Cambridge: Cambridge University Press, 2005).

HOPKINS, KEITH, and BEARD, MARY, *The Colosseum* (London: Profile Books, 2005).

HULME, T. E., *Speculations: Essays on Humanism and the Philosophy of Art*, ed. Herbert Read (London: Kegan Paul, 1924).

HYMAN, STANLEY EDGAR, *The Armed Vision: A Study in the Methods of Modern Literary Criticism* (1948; rev. edn. New York: Vintage, 1955).

HYNES, SAMUEL, *The Auden Generation: Literature and Politics in England in the 1930s* (London: Bodley Head, 1976).

JENNINGS, HUMPHREY, and MADGE, CHARLES (eds.), *May the Twelfth: Mass-Observation Day-Survey* (London: Faber and Faber, 1937).

JOHNSON, SAMUEL, *Lives of the English Poets*, 2 vols. (London: Oxford University Press, 1906).

JONES, JOHN HENRY, 'Empson Soup: A Personal Memory of William Empson', *The CEA Forum*, 18: 2–4 (1988), 7.

JOYCE, JAMES, *Ulysses*, ed. Hans Walter Gabler (London: Bodley Head, 2002).

KEATS, JOHN, *The Letters of John Keats*, ed. Hyder E. Rollins, 2 vols. (Cambridge: Harvard University Press, 1958).

KELL, RICHARD, 'Empsonium', *London Magazine*, 6: 10 (Oct. 1959), 55–6.

KENNER, HUGH, 'Alice in Empsonland', *Hudson Review*, 5 (Spring 1952), 137–44.

KERMODE, FRANK, *An Appetite for Poetry* (London: Fontana, 1990).

KLEIN, LAWRENCE, *Shaftesbury and the Culture of Politeness* (Cambridge: Cambridge University Press, 1994).

KNIGHT, G. WILSON, *The Wheel of Fire: Interpretations of Shakespearean Tragedy* (1930; New York: Meridan, 1957).

KOENEKE, RODNEY, *Empires of the Mind: I. A. Richards and Basic English in China, 1929–1979* (Stanford, Calif.: Stanford University Press, 2004).

LEAVIS, F. R., 'Intelligence and Sensibility', *Cambridge Review*, 52 (16 Jan. 1931), 186–7.

—— *How To Teach Reading: A Primer for Ezra Pound* (Cambridge: Minority Press, 1932).

LEVAO, RONALD, '"Among Unequals What Society": *Paradise Lost* and the Forms of Intimacy', *Modern Language Quarterly*, 61: 1 (2000), 79–108.

LEWIS, C. S., *Studies in Words* (Cambridge: Cambridge University Press, 1960).

LINTOTT, A. W., *Violence in Republican Rome* (Oxford: Oxford University Press, 1968).

LOVEJOY, A. O., *The Great Chain of Being: A Study of the History of an Idea* (1936; repr. Cambridge, Mass.: Harvard University Press, 1961).

LUCAS, F. L., *The Decline and Fall of the Romantic Ideal* (Cambridge; Cambridge University Press, 1936).

LUI, JAMES J. Y., *The Art of Chinese Poetry* (London: Routledge, 1962).

MACH, ERNST, *The Science of Mechanics: A Critical and Historical Account of its Development* (1893), trans. Thomas J. McCormack, 6th edn. (LaSalle, Ill: Open Court, 1960).

MACKILLOP, IAN, *F. R. Leavis: A Life in Criticism* (London: Allen Lane, 1995).

—— 'Revisiting Empson: Successive Fireworks of Contradiction', *CCUE News*, 18 (Winter 2004), 13–15.

McLaverty, James, *Pope, Print and Meaning* (Oxford: Oxford University Press, 2001).

Malone, Nick, *The Burial of Crispin Pike* (London: Workshop Press, 1974).

Martial, *Martial: Epigrams*, ed. D. R. Shackleton Bailey, 2 vols. (Cambridge, Mass.: Harvard University Press, 1993).

Mitchell, W. J. T. (ed.), *Against Theory: Literary Studies and the New Pragmatism* (Chicago: University of Chicago Press, 1985).

Milton, John, *Paradise Lost*, ed. Alastair Fowler (Harlow: Longman, 1971).

—— *The Works of John Milton*, ed. F. A. Patterson, 18 vols. (New York: Columbia University Press, 1931–8).

Morgan, Marjorie, *Manners, Morals and Class in England, 1774–1858* (Basingstoke: Macmillan, 1994).

Neusner, Jacob, *Judaism when Christianity Began: A Survey of Belief and Practice* (Louisville, Ky.: Westminster John Knox Press, 2002).

Norris, Christopher, *William Empson and the Philosophy of Literary Criticism* (London: Athlone Press, 1978).

—— 'Some Versions of Rhetoric: Empson and de Man', *Genre*, 17: 1–2 (Spring and Summer 1984), 191–214.

—— and Mapp, Nigel (eds.), *William Empson: The Critical Achievement* (Cambridge: Cambridge University Press, 1993).

—— *Resources of Realism: Prospects for 'Post-Analytic' Philosophy* (London: Macmillan, 1997).

Orwell, George, *Orwell: The War Broadcasts*, ed. W. J. West (London: Duckworth, 1985).

Pagden, Anthony, *The Fall of Natural Man: The American Indian and the Origins of Comparative Ethnology* (Cambridge: Cambridge University Press, 1982).

—— *Lords of all the World: Ideologies of Empire in Spain, Britain and France c. 1500–1800* (New Haven: Yale University Press, 1995).

Page, Norman, (ed.), *Tennyson: Interviews and Recollections* (London: Macmillan, 1983).

Pearce, Zachary, *A review of the text of Milton's Paradise lost: in which the chief of Dr Bentley's emendations are considered* (London, 1733).

Phare, E. E., 'Valéry and Gerard Hopkins', *Experiment*, 1 (Nov. 1928), 19–23.

—— 'Ernest Hemingway', *Experiment*, 3 (May 1929), 13–16.

Phillips, Adam, 'No Reason For Not Asking', *LRB* (3 Aug. 2006), 26–7.

Piaget, Jean, *Langage et la pensée chez l'enfant*, trans. Marjorie Warden as *The Language and Thought of the Child* (London: Kegan Paul, 1926).

—— *Judgement and Reasoning in the Child* (London: Routledge & Kegan Paul, 1929).

—— *The Child's Conception of the World* (1929; London: Paladin, 1973).

—— *The Child's Conception of Physical Causality* (London: Routledge & Kegan Paul, 1930).

Pickering, Mary, *Auguste Comte: An Intellectual Biography* (Cambridge: Cambridge University Press, 1993).

POLLOTT, RICHARD, 'The Poet's Repose: William Empson and the Faces of the Buddha', *PN Review*, 32: 3 (Jan.–Feb. 2006), 54–6.

PRICE, KATY, 'Finite but Unbounded: *Experiment* Magazine, Cambridge, England, 1928–31', *Jacket*, 20 (Dec. 2002), <http://jacketmagazine.com/20/price-expe.html #fnB6>

—— 'Flame Far Too Hot: William Empson's Non-Euclidean Predicament', *Interdisciplinary Science Reviews*, 30: 4 (Dec. 2005), 312–22.

PROUST, MARCEL, 'Contre l'obscurité', in *Contre Sainte-Beuve*, ed. Pierre Clarac and Yves Sandre (Paris: Gallimard, 1971), 390–5.

—— *À la recherche du temps perdu*, ed. Jean-Yves Tadié, 4 vols. (Paris: Gallimard, 1987).

—— *Against Sainte-Beuve and Other Essays*, trans. John Sturrock (Harmondsworth: Penguin, 1988), 135–9.

QUINE, W. V., *Word and Object* (Cambridge, Mass.: MIT Press, 1960).

—— *Ontological Relativity and Other Essays* (New York: Columbia University Press, 1969).

RANSOM, JOHN CROWE, 'Mr. Empson's Muddles', *Southern Review*, 4: 2 (July–Apr. 1938–9), 322–39.

RICHARDS, I. A., *Practical Criticism* (1929; London: Routledge, 1964).

—— *Coleridge on Imagination* (London: Kegan Paul, 1934).

—— *Principles of Literary Criticism*, 2nd edn. (London: Kegan Paul, 1934).

—— *Poetries and Sciences: A Reissue of* Science and Poetry *(1926, 1935) with Commentary* (London: Routledge, 1970).

—— *Internal Colloquies: Poems and Plays of I. A. Richards* (London: Routledge & Kegan Paul, 1972).

—— *Selected Letters of I. A. Richards*, ed. John Constable (Oxford: Clarendon Press, 1990).

RICHARDSON, NIGEL, *Dog Days in Soho: One Man's Adventures in Fifties Bohemia* (London: Victor Gollancz, 2000).

RICKS, CHRISTOPHER, 'The Ways of God', *New Statesman* (27 Aug. 1965), 292–3.

—— *The Force of Poetry* (Oxford: Oxford University Press, 1984).

—— 'William Empson', *The Proceedings of the British Academy*, 71 (1985), 539–54.

—— *Essays in Appreciation* (Oxford: Oxford University Press, 1998).

—— *Allusion to the Poets* (Oxford: Oxford University Press, 2002).

ROBINSON, PETER, 'Very Shrinking Behaviour', *Times Literary Supplement* (18 July 2003), 13–15.

—— 'C. Hatakeyama [trans. W.E.]', *PN Review*, 31: 2 (Nov.–Dec. 2004), 55–60.

RODENSKY, LISA, 'Empson's Seven Types of Ambiguity', *Essays in Criticism*, 53: 1 (2003), 54–67.

RYLANDS, GEORGE H., *Words and Poetry*, introd. Lytton Strachey (London: Hogarth Press, 1928).

SALE, ROGER, 'The Achievement of William Empson', *Hudson Review*, 19: 3 (Autumn 1966), 369–90.

ST GEORGE, ANDREW, *The Descent of Manners: Etiquette, Rules and the Victorians* (London: Chatto & Windus, 1993).

SCHIFFER, STEPHEN, *Meaning* (Oxford: Clarendon Press, 1972).

—— *Remnants of Meaning* (Cambridge, Mass.: MIT Press, 1987).

SCHLEIERMACHER, FRIEDRICH, *Hermeneutics and Criticism and Other Writings* (1838), ed. Andrew Bowie (Cambridge: Cambridge University Press, 1998).

SEARLE, JOHN R., *Speech Acts: An Essay in the Philosophy of Language* (Cambridge: Cambridge University Press, 1969).

—— 'Reiterating the Differences', *Glyph*, 1 (1975), 172–97.

SHAKESPEARE, WILLIAM, *The Riverside Shakespeare*, ed. G. Blakemore Evans *et al.* (Boston: Houghton Mifflin, 1974).

—— *Shakespeare's Sonnets*, ed. Katherine Duncan-Jones (London: Arden, 1997).

SHELLEY, PERCY BYSSHE, *Poetical Works*, ed. Thomas Hutchinson, corrected by G. M. Matthews (Oxford: Oxford University Press, 1970).

SMITH, JAMES, *Shakespearian and Other Essays* (Cambridge: Cambridge University Press, 1974).

SMITH, JONATHAN, Z. *To Take Place: Toward Theory in Ritual* (Chicago: University of Chicago Press, 1987).

—— *Drudgery Divine: On the Comparison of Early Christianities and the Religions of Late Antiquity* (London: RoutledgeCurzon, 1990).

SNYDER, GRAYDON F., *Ante Pacem: Archaeological Evidence of Church Life before Constantine* (Macon, Ga.: Mercer University Press, 1985).

STALLWORTHY, JOHN, *Louis MacNeice* (London: Faber and Faber, 1995).

STAPLEDON, OLAF, *Star Maker* (1937; London: Victor Gollancz, 1999).

—— 'Escapism in Literature', *Scrutiny*, 8: 3 (Dec. 1939), 298–308.

STONIER, G. W., 'Complexity', *New Statesman and Nation*, 10: 243 (19 Oct. 1935), 568–70.

STRIER, RICHARD, *Resistant Structures: Particularity, Radicalism, and Renaissance Texts* (Berkeley: University of California Press, 1995).

SWINBURNE, CHARLES, *Swinburne: Poems and Ballads*, ed. Morse Peckham (Indianapolis: Bobbs-Merrill, 1970).

TENNYSON, ALFRED, *The Poems of Tennyson*, ed. Christopher Ricks, 2nd edn., 3 vols. (London: Longman, 1987).

THOMAS, DYLAN, 'Request to Leda: Homage to William Empson', *Horizon*, 6 (July 1942).

THOMPSON, MARK, 'Versions of Pluralism: William Empson, Isaiah Berlin, and the Cold War', *Literary Imagination*, 8: 1 (Winter 2006), 65–87.

TRUSSLER, SIMON (ed.), *Burlesque Plays of the Eighteenth Century* (Oxford: Oxford University Press, 1969).

TURNBULL, COLIN M., *The Mbuti Pygmies: Change and Adaptation* (New York: Holt, Rinehart and Winston, 1983).

TUVE, ROSEMUND, 'On Herbert's "Sacrifice" ', *Kenyon Review*, 12 (1950), 52–75.

WALEY, ARTHUR, 'Mencius on the Mind', *Times Literary Supplement* (15 Sept. 1932), 634.

—— *Chinese Poems* (London: Unwin, 1961).

WARNER, SYLVIA TOWNSEND, *Mr Fortune's Maggot* (1927; repr. London: Virago, 1978).

WARWICH, ANDREW, *Masters of Theory: Cambridge and the Rise of Mathematical Physics* (Chicago: University of Chicago Press, 2003).

WATSON, GEORGE, *Never Ones for Theory? England and the War of Ideas* (Cambridge: Lutterworth, 2000).

WHITWORTH, MICHAEL, *Einstein's Wake: Relativity, Metaphor, and Modernist Literature* (Oxford: Oxford University Press, 2001).

WILEY, BASIL, *The Eighteenth Century Background: Studies on the Idea of Nature in the Thought of the Period* (London: Chatto & Windus, 1949).

WILLIS, J. H., *William Empson* (New York: Columbia University Press, 1969).

WILSON, DAVID. B., ' "La Puce de Madame Desroches" and John Donne's "The Flea" ', *Neuphilologische Mitteilungen*, 72 (1971), 297–301.

WILSON, EDWARD MERYON, *The Solitudes of Don Luis de Góngora* (Cambridge: Cambridge University Press, 1965).

WIMSATT, W. K., *The Verbal Icon: Studies in the Meaning of Poetry* (Lexington, Ky.: University of Kentucky Press, 1954).

WITTGENSTEIN, LUDWIG, *Philosophical Investigations*, trans. G. E. M. Anscombe (Oxford: Blackwell, 1951).

—— *On Certainty*, ed. G. E. M. Anscombe and G. H. von Wright, trans. Denis Paul and G. E. M. Anscombe (Oxford: Basil Blackwell, 1974).

—— *Remarks on Frazer's 'Golden Bough'*, ed. Rush Rhees (Retford: Brynmill Press, 1979).

WOLLSTONECRAFT, MARY, *Mary, A Fiction* (1788), ed. Gary Kelley (Oxford: Oxford University Press, 1976).

—— *Vindication of the Rights of Woman* (1792), in *The Vindications*, ed. D. L. Macdonald and Kathleen Sherf (Peterborough, Ontario: Broadview Press, 1997).

WOOD, MICHAEL, 'William Empson', in *The Cambridge History of Literary Criticism*, vii. *Modernism and the New Criticism*, ed. A Walton Litz, Louis Menand, and Lawrence Rainey (Cambridge: Cambridge University Press, 2000), 219–34.

—— *Literature and the Taste of Knowledge* (Cambridge: Cambridge University Press, 2005).

WORDSWORTH, WILLIAM, *The Prelude: 1799, 1805, 1850*, ed. Jonathan Wordsworth *et al.* (New York: Norton, 1979).

—— *Selected Poems*, ed. Damian Walford Davies (London: J. M. Dent, 1994).

WRIGHT, ARTHUR F., *Buddhism in Chinese History* (Stanford, Calif.: Stanford University Press, 1959).

YEATS, W. B. (ed.), *Oxford Book of Modern Verse* (Oxford: Oxford University Press, 1936).

ZUOLIANG, WANG, 'William Empson in Kunming', *Foreign Literatures*, 1 (1980), 2–3.

INDEX